Berthold M. Kuhn
with Dimitrios L. Margellos

Global Perspectives on Megatrends
The Future as Seen by Analysts and Researchers from Different World Regions

Berthold M. Kuhn
with Dimitrios L. Margellos

GLOBAL PERSPECTIVES ON MEGATRENDS

The Future as Seen by Analysts and Researchers from Different World Regions

Bibliografische Information der Deutschen Nationalbibliothek

Die Deutsche Nationalbibliothek verzeichnet diese Publikation in der Deutschen Nationalbibliografie; detaillierte bibliografische Daten sind im Internet über http://dnb.d-nb.de abrufbar.

Bibliographic information published by the Deutsche Nationalbibliothek

Die Deutsche Nationalbibliothek lists this publication in the Deutsche Nationalbibliografie; detailed bibliographic data are available in the Internet at http://dnb.d-nb.de.

ISBN-13: 978-3-8382-1563-1
© *ibidem*-Verlag, Stuttgart 2022
Alle Rechte vorbehalten

Das Werk einschließlich aller seiner Teile ist urheberrechtlich geschützt. Jede Verwertung außerhalb der engen Grenzen des Urheberrechtsgesetzes ist ohne Zustimmung des Verlages unzulässig und strafbar. Dies gilt insbesondere für Vervielfältigungen, Übersetzungen, Mikroverfilmungen und elektronische Speicherformen sowie die Einspeicherung und Verarbeitung in elektronischen Systemen.

All rights reserved. No part of this publication may be reproduced, stored in or introduced into a retrieval system, or transmitted, in any form, or by any means (electronic, mechanical, photocopying, recording or otherwise) without the prior written permission of the publisher. Any person who does any unauthorized act in relation to this publication may be liable to criminal prosecution and civil claims for damages.

Printed in the EU

Table of Contents

Table of Interviews 9

Table of Figures 13

Introduction 17

Chapter 1: How to Identify Global Megatrends? 21
    1.1 Previous Studies on Megatrends 21
    1.2 The Pentagon Model 26
    1.3 Visions, Risks, and Trends 29
    1.4 Global-local Nexus 31

Chapter 2: Who Shapes the Future? 33
    2.1 Shapers 35
    2.2 Think Tanks 40
    2.3 Consulting Firms 44
    2.4 International Cooperation and Global Governance 46

Chapter 3: Climate Action and Sustainability 51
    3.1 The Extent of the Risk 53
    3.2 Global Agendas for Sustainability Policies and Climate Action 56
    3.3 What Kind of Action is Needed? 61
    3.4 Growing Engagement of International Organizations, Research, and Advocacy Groups 65
    3.5 Climate Actions at the Level of Cities 74
    3.6 The Future of Climate Action and Sustainability Transformations 77
    3.7 Sustainable Tourism 88

Chapter 4: Digitalization 93
4.1 Dimensions of Digital Growth: New Business Opportunities 94
4.2 Artificial Intelligence 107
4.3 Data Protection and Cybersecurity 108
4.4 Governance of Cyberspace and Anti-trust Legislation 114
4.5 Digitalization and Sustainability 118

Chapter 5: Inequality 121
5.1 Dimensions of Inequality 122
5.2 Measuring Inequality 124
5.3 Drivers of Inequality 126
5.4 Tackling Inequality 149

Chapter 6: Demography 159
6.1 Diversity of Demography Trends 162
6.2 Aging Societies 169
6.3 Demography and Other Megatrends 172

Chapter 7: Urbanization and Smart Cities 175
7.1 Drivers of Urbanization 177
7.2 Smart Cities 180
7.3 Urbanization and Other Megatrends 184
7.4 The Greening of the Construction Sector 188

Chapter 8: Health and Nutrition 193
8.1 The Globalization of Health 194
8.2 The Impact of the COVID-19 Pandemic 202
8.3 The Future of Health Systems 207
8.4 The Future of Food and Eating 209

Chapter 9: Green Economy 219
    9.1   Green Economy and Green Growth 221
    9.2   Green Growth versus Degrowth 227
    9.3   International Cooperation in Support of the Green Economy 231

Chapter 10: Sustainable Finance 235
    10.1 From Ethical Investment to Sustainable Finance 239
    10.2 Mainstreaming of Sustainable Finance 241
    10.3 Greenwashing of Investment Strategies 248

Chapter 11: Democracy and Governance Innovations 251
    11.1 Concepts, Discourses, and Political Trends 253
    11.2 Empirical Democracy Research and Proliferation of Index Projects 260
    11.3 Practices of Participatory and Consultative Democracy 267

Chapter 12: Multipolar World Order and the Future of Multilateralism 273
    12.1 Hegemonic Shift? 275
    12.2 The Rise of China: How Long Will it Last? 281
    12.3 Old and New Western Alliances 287
    12.4 The Geopolitical Impact of the COVID-19 Pandemic .. 291
    12.5 The Future of Multilateralism 296

Chapter 13: Civilizational Developments: Diversity, Individualization and Loneliness, Gender Shift, and Identity Politics 309
    13.1 Diversity Trends 310
    13.2 Individualization and Loneliness 317
    13.3 Gender Shift 321
    13.4 Identity Politics 327

Chapter 14: Migration **331**
    14.1 Rising Numbers of Migrants 333
    14.2 Migration as Subject of Political Controversies 335
    14.3 The Future of Migration and Migration
         Management 336

Chapter 15: Visions for the World in 2030 and Beyond **351**
    15.1 Outlook on Megatrends 352
    15.2 Vision Talk: Three Experts Share their Future
         Perspectives 357

Table of Interviews

Chapter 3: Climate Action and Sustainability

Swithin Lui and Sofia Gonzales-Zuñiga,
    New Climate Institute; Germany; Hong Kong, and Peru   69
Line Niedeggen and Asuka Kähler,
    Activists, Fridays for Future, Germany; Germany and
    Germany/Japan   72
Janos Pasztor,
    Executive Director, C2G2 (Carnegie); Switzerland;
    Hungary   78
Thomas Scheutzlich,
    NDCP coordinator and Consultant, Chile; Germany   85
Nirmal Shah,
    Chief Executive, Nature Seychelles; Seychelles   89

Chapter 4: Digitalization

Sachin Gaur,
    MixORG and Chief Executive EU-India digitalization
    project; India   97
Jillian York,
    The Electronic Frontier Foundation, Germany; U.S.   111
Heiko Vainsalu,
    Programme Director of Technology, e-Governance
    Academy (eGA); Estonia   116

Chapter 5: Inequality

Badiul Alam Majumdar,
    The Hunger Project/Professor at Dhaka University;
    Bangladesh   131
Christian Joel González Cuatianquis,
    Professor at Universidad Autónoma de Coahuila;
    Mexico   135
Sarah Anderson,
    Co-Editor, Inequality.Org; Professor and director at the
    Institute for Policy Studies; U.S.   138

Chapter 6: Demography

Catherina Hinz,
   Director at Berlin Institute for Population and
   Development; Germany 166

Chapter 7: Urbanization and Smart Cities

Xanin García,
   Professor at Instituto Municipal de Planeación de
   Saltillo (IMPLAN), Saltillo City; Mexico 182
Thomas Fritsche,
   Founder and Chief Executive, TF Architects Shanghai;
   China; Germany 190

Chapter 8: Health and Nutrition

Sonu Bhaskar,
   Director of Global Health Neurology and Translational
   Neuroscience Lab, Australia; India 195
Abinet Tasew,
   Programme Manager, CARE USA; Ethiopia 211
Myriam Preiss,
   (former) Senior Researcher FU Berlin; Germany 215

Chapter 9: Green Economy

Emily Benson,
   Director for Engagement for the Green Economy
   Coalition, IIED; United Kingdom 223

Chapter 10: Sustainable Finance

Bjarne Steffen and Florian Egli,
   Senior Researchers at ETH Zurich; Switzerland 245

Chapter 11: Democracy and Governance Innovations

Thamy Pogrebinschi,
   Senior Researcher at the WZB Berlin Social Science
   Center; Germany; Brazil 265

Marie Jünemann,
    Federal Executive Board Spokeswoman at Mehr
    Demokratie e.V.; Germany   269

Chapter 12: Multipolar World Order and the Future of Multilateralism

Wang Huiyao,
    Chief Executive, Center for China and Globalization
    (CCG); China   293
Shada Islam,
    Professor at College of Europe/Ex-CEO Friends of Europe;
    Belgium; Pakistan   278
Parag Khanna,
    Founder of FutureMap, bestselling author; former foreign
    policy advisor to Barack Obama; Singapore, U.S./India   299
Peter Makari,
    Executive at Global Ministries of the Christian Church
    and United Church of Christ; U.S.; U.S./Egypt   304

Chapter 13: Civilizational Developments

Peter Mousaferiadis and Máximo Plo Seco,
    Founder of Cultural Infusion/Diversity Atlas; Australia;
    Greece and Director of Operations for Europe of Cultural
    Infusion; Spain   314
Lena Papasabbas,
    Zukunftsinstitut (The Future Institute); Germany   324

Chapter 14: Migration

Anna Triandafyllidou,
    Professor, Canada Excellence Research Chair on Migration
    and Integration at Ryerson University; Canada; Greece   339
Anna Knoll,
    Head of the Migration Program European Centre for
    Development Policy Management (ECPDM);
    Netherlands; Germany   342

Mehari Taddele Maru,
    Part-time Professor at the School of Transnational Governance and Migration Policy Centre at the European University Institute and Coordinator of the Young African Leaders Program; Italy; Ethiopia   346

Chapter 15: Visions for the World in 2030 and Beyond

Rosa Alegria,
    Futurista; Brazil   357
Umar Sheraz,
    Senior Researcher at nextgenforesight.org; Pakistan   357
Andreas Rickert,
    Co-Founder/CEO of PHINEO, former McKinsey consultant; Germany   357

Table of Figures

Chapter 1: How to Identify Global Megatrends

Figure 1.1:	Pentagon Model of Megatrends	27

Chapter 2: Who Shapes the Future?

Figure 2.1:	SITRA's Megatrends	43
Figure 2.2:	The Roland Berger Trend Compendium	45

Chapter 3: Climate Action and Sustainability

Figure 3.1:	The United Nations Sustainable Development Goals	59
Figure 3.2:	Total Primary Energy Demand in China in the Announced Pledges Scenario (APS), 1980–2060	66
Figure 3.3:	Categories of the Climate Change Performance Index (CCPI)	68

Chapter 4: Digitalization

Figure 4.1:	Volume of Data/Information Created, Captured, Copied, and Consumed Worldwide from 2010 to 2025 (in Zettabytes)	95
Figure 4.2:	Mobile Payment User Share 2021, % of Smartphone Users (2021)	101
Figure 4.3:	Market Share of Mobile vs. Non-Mobile Payments in China (2018)	102

Chapter 5: Inequality

Figure 5.1:	The Elephant Curve: Average Annual Wealth Growth Rate, 1995–2021	126
Figure 5.2:	Inequality of Market/Disposable Income in Relation to the Gini Coefficient	143
Figure 5.3:	Mean Top Rates of Income and Inheritance Taxes in 20 countries and Trade Union Density in Ten Countries, 1890–2010 (percent)	144

Figure 5.4:	Bottom 50 Percent, Middle 40 Percent and Top 10 Percent Income Shares Across the World in 2022	145
Figure 5.5:	Top 10 Percent of Income/Gini Coefficient-Share Unionized	150
Figure 5.6:	Development of Wage Inequality in Germany	155

Chapter 6: Demography

Figure 6.1:	Countries with more than 150 million people by 2030	165
Figure 6.2:	Europe's Total Population	166
Figure 6.3:	Countries or Areas with the Largest Percentage Point Increase in the Share of Older Persons Aged 65 Years or Over Between 2019 and 2050	169

Chapter 7: Urbanization and Smart Cities

Figure 7.1:	Urbanization over the Past 500 Years, 1500 to 2016	176

Chapter 8: Health and Nutrition

Figure 8.1:	Confirmed COVID-19 Infections by Region	202

Chapter 9: Green Economy

Figure 9.1:	Green Growth Index Framework	232

Chapter 10: Sustainable Finance

Figure 10.1:	Green Finance Publications and Annual Absolute Growth of Green Finance Publications, 1990–2020.	235
Figure 10.2:	U.S. Dollar Value of Social, Sustainability and Green Bond Issuances 2015–2020.	242

Chapter 11: Democracy and Governance Innovations

Figure 11.1:	Democracies and Autocracies	262

Chapter 12: Multipolar World Order and the Future of Multilateralism

Figure 12.1: Percentage of Global GDP 1820–2012   282

Chapter 13: Civilizational Developments

Figure 13.1: Number of Marriages in Each Year per 1,000 People in the Population   318
Figure 13.2: Gender Equality Index 2021   323

Chapter 14: Migration

Figure 14.1: Total Number of International Migrants at Mid-Year 2020   334
Figure 14.2: Origins and Destinations of International Migrants in 2019 (in percent)   334

Introduction

This book presents an analysis of megatrends and emerging issues that will strongly influence different spheres of life in many countries and at different levels, covering political, economic, natural environmental, social, and cultural dimensions.

To identify megatrends, we used the Pentagon Model, a framework developed by Berthold Kuhn in the context of his research and teaching activities at Freie Universität Berlin. It focuses on five criteria to prioritize big trends: (1) level of coverage by research activities, (2) level of political attention, (3) level of interest to global investors and business communities, (4) level of media coverage, and (5) attention paid by social movements.

The analyses of the twelve prioritized megatrends that we identified are based on a comprehensive review of reports on economic, technological, socio-cultural, and political developments, on various exchanges with think tanks and international organizations, and on a series of interviews with analysts and researchers from different countries and world regions with various disciplinary and professional backgrounds, and a mix of age groups and genders.

This book aims to analyze the relevance and the potential impact of twelve megatrends, but it also presents a critical reflection on different aspects of these trends. We make due reference to the work of international organizations, especially the United Nations, leading think tanks, research networks, and experts. The motivation to write this book stemmed from our passion to understand the challenges and opportunities that humanity faces in the next decade, and to learn about new research, business models, and initiatives trying to make the world a better place. Translating this passion into easily digestible and well-communicated writing to inform those interested in the future is at the heart of this book.

Berthold Kuhn's engagement with trends has provided him a rich variety of beneficial insights across a range of issues. His proven record in forecasting key developments and emerging issues related to climate action and sustainable finance, among other trends, and his extensive contacts with leading researchers and analysts from different world regions motivated him to write this book. He works at Freie Universität (FU) Berlin and as an adviser to international cooperation agencies and think tanks. He is a father of three children and currently lives with his family in Berlin, but has worked and lived in many cities on different continents. The book benefited from many vivid discussions with co-author Dimitrios Margellos, who produced the summaries of the expert interviews and made some substantial contributions to the chapters on Inequality, Digitalization, and Health. Furthermore, the book benefited from exchanges with colleagues and students at FU Berlin and FU Berlin's partner universities.

The COVID-19 pandemic and its global economic and social consequences have triggered a new wave of interest in future risks and trends. COVID-19 has made it clear to many of us that crisis situations can accelerate change. Millions of lives have been lost. Family life and work have been disrupted. The lockdowns have caused financial disasters, companies and nations have faced innumerable challenges, and the lives of many people have been decimated. However, the restrictions have also sparked innovations and raised the importance and acceptance of research and researchers in public opinion.

The Russian invasion of Ukraine shocked people in Europe and across the world during the time the co-authors completed the manuscript of this book. The massive economic sanctions launched by the United States (U.S.), the European Union (EU) and many countries, will heavily impact on trade, economic and political cooperation. They were meant to halt Putin's expansionist military operations, but will have serious repercussions on Europe and other parts of the world, too. The co-authors have predicted more geopolitical assertions in the context of an increasingly multi-polar world order (chapter 12). While the analysis remains valid, the war in Ukraine goes against conventional wisdom and poses more questions than anybody has answers for.

The Russian economy was relatively disconnected from many important megatrends which may have added to Russia's

Introduction

geopolitical assertion by military means. Under the current regime this trend will not be reversed, and Russia and its closest allies will bear dire consequences of its decoupling with many powerful economies.

This book will also pay due attention to the rise of China, which has challenged Western societies, economic policies, and political systems in many ways. China's growing influence is subject to a significant number of expert analyses. Graham Allison coined the term "the Thucydides Trap" which refers to the likelihood of violent encounters between a rising power and an incumbent hegemon. The former German Foreign Minister Joschka Fischer is one of many authors who refer to the analysis of Thucydides, one of the greatest historians, on the rise of a rival power.

The rise of China has indeed surprised most political scientists. China has been underestimated for a long time, especially by political scientists in the United States and Europe. For decades now, China has been increasing its influence all over the world and in international relations, but it is now faced with growing attempts to curtail its influence in the context of systemic rivalry declared by the United States and the European Union. However, we refrain from overestimating China and neglecting development in other parts of the world. We have interviewed experts from many different countries and world regions to present diverse perspectives on megatrends. Global governance will be more multipolar than in the form of world order we have experienced in recent decades. This book is meant to provide a framework for reflection and analysis of trends that will shape the future of humanity.

Chapter 1

How to Identify Global Megatrends?

Megatrend has become a kind of buzzword mostly used by futurists or consulting firms trying to sell their analyses of emerging business opportunities. However, a growing number of research institutions, international organizations, and think tanks are reflecting on megatrends with the purpose of engaging in dialogue and influence policymaking. For many of them, megatrends are defined more broadly and in line with the short definition provided in the Introduction to this book.

Global megatrends are trends that strongly influence different spheres of life in many countries and at different levels, covering political, economic, natural environmental, social, and cultural dimensions.

This book is based on our own research as well as on expertise and insights from analysts and researchers from different professional backgrounds and world regions. We aim to present a state-of-the-art analysis of trends and topics of global relevance which will shape the future of both our generation and those that follow.

1.1 Previous Studies on Megatrends

This is not the first book which aims to identify megatrends that will shape future global development. John Naisbitt was a pioneer of future studies. His book *Megatrends: Ten New Directions Transforming Our Lives* was first published in 1982. It focused mainly on the United States but also attempted to present a global outlook. Naisbitt accurately predicted the change from industrialized to information societies. He did not exactly forecast the rise of social media but anticipated the growing importance of social interactions in the context of technological development. He also predicted the trend toward globalization which shaped the decades after the publication of the book. He was not able to forecast important world

Global Perspectives on Megatrends

historical events such as the collapse of the Soviet Union or the rise of China and was wrong about the potential of some sub-trends, like online shopping.[1] His co-author, Patricia Aburdene, later published her own books on future trends. One of them is called *Megatrends 2010: The Rise of Conscious Capitalism*.[2] It received significant attention in the business community and helped to promote the trend of Corporate Social Responsibility (CSR) which had taken off around the year 2000 when the Global Compact of the United Nations was launched.

Richard Watson, who advises organizations in the field of scenario planning and strategic foresight, published his book *Future Files* in 2008. In his book he elaborates on five trends that will shape the next 50 years: aging; the power shift eastwards; global connectivity; GRIN technologies, referring to Genetics, Robotics, Internet, and Nanotechnology; and the environment. His focus is predominantly on the U.S. and the Anglo-Saxon world, though he is also conscious of developments in Asia and the Middle East. The environment is somewhat half-heartedly addressed.

The European Environmental Agency defines global megatrends as follows: "Global megatrends are global, long-term trends that are slow to form but have a major impact once in place. They are the great forces that are likely to affect the future in all areas throughout the world over the next 10 to 15 years. Furthermore, they are often strongly interconnected."[3]

Today it is easier for pundits to learn, analyze, and forecast developments in other parts of the world. We live in a much more globalized world with better access to data and information. This explains why we are witnessing a strong growth of think tanks and/organizations engaged in future studies and strategic foresight. Most of the leading think tanks are situated in the United States and Europe but other parts of the world are catching up, including China and India. Think tanks typically conduct research, engage in policy dialogue activities, and provide advice to policymakers.

The larger think tanks, including the Bertelsmann Foundation (based in Gütersloh, Germany), Brookings (Washington D.C.),

How to Identify Global Megatrends?

Bruegel (Brussels), Carnegie (Washington D.C.), Chatham House, (London), the Center for China and Globalization (Beijing), and many others, have global outreach. Since the 1990s, we have seen a growing number of reports and academic publications dealing with future analysis and megatrends. There are now many smaller and medium-sized institutes and associations that explicitly deal with forecasts, future research, and megatrends. The Association of Professional Futurists (APF) was founded in 2002 and has more than 500 members. It emerged as a network of practicing futurists who act as analysts, consultants, and speakers.

The Economist Intelligence Unit, a global frontrunner of business intelligence, has established a Global Forecasting Unit, currently headed by Agathe Demarais. In Germany, the Zukunftsinstitut (The Future Institute), is one of the leading names for future research. Matthias Horx has presented a number of well-referenced analyses and well-visualized maps for understanding future trends and how they are interconnected. In Switzerland, Swissfuture, an association of researchers focusing on future trends, contributes to the systematic and method-based examination of the future. The U.S.-based Future Today Institute pays special attention to technology trends. Some of the business-oriented organizations tend to pursue a technology-oriented method and, thus, engage in a rather narrow approach to megatrends.

International organizations and government policy initiatives make significant contributions to future-oriented analysis, too. The Asian Development Bank (ADB) has implemented a technical assistance project on "Demonstrating Future Thinking and Foresight in Developing Member Countries" and/organized futures and foresight workshops with government experts.[4] The World Bank is well known for engaging in forward-looking economic analysis with many countries. One of its publications on the open knowledge platform focuses on "Outlook 2050" and strategies to support countries on their way to decarbonization. We have seen a number of "Vision 2020," "Vision 2025," and economic foresight studies from various countries and institutions outlining scenarios and strategies to cope with future challenges. Although none of the reports predicted the COVID-19 pandemic, they are far from irrelevant. Such reports and programs give us an idea of the agenda of political leaders and decision-makers in influential institutions and multinational companies. Their agenda matters and shapes trends. Examples include Made in China 2025, India's Vision 2020, Saudi Vision 2030, and Project Ireland 2040, which are all underpinned by big investment decisions and ambitious work plans.

It is useful to glance through policy reform and economic planning documents at the country level. However, in the context of this book we have focused more on independent and in-depth analyses of future trends published by think tanks and eminent researchers. Chapter 2 will focus on who is shaping and researching megatrends and will pay special attention to the work of think tanks. Consulting companies specializing in strategic advice on future challenges are also trend-setters. Most of them focus on new technologies. However, many of them have adopted more global and broader views and have elaborated on trends such as sustainability transformation, climate change, smart cities, and inequality.

The Bertelsmann Foundation is a major think tank in Germany which has launched a series of megatrend reports. One of its flagship reports identifies three global trends: globalization, demographic change, and digitalization.[5] Climate change, sustainability issues, and inequality are missing from this list even though the foundation engages in these issues in various contexts.

PwC prioritizes five trends: rapid urbanization, climate change and resource scarcity, the shift in global economic power, demographic and social change, and technological breakthroughs.[6]

The European Environmental Agency (EEA) has also worked on megatrends and identified clusters of drivers of change:

- Cluster 1: Growing, urbanizing, and migrating global population;
- Cluster 2: Climate change and environmental degradation worldwide;
- Cluster 3: Increasing scarcity of and global competition for resources;

How to Identify Global Megatrends?

- Cluster 4: Accelerating technological change and convergence;
- Cluster 5: Power shifts in the global economy and geopolitical landscape;
- Cluster 6: Diversifying values, lifestyles, and governance approaches.[7]

Though not explicitly related to trends, one of the most important global reference frameworks is the United Nations 2030 Agenda for Sustainable Development and the 17 Sustainable Development Goals which cover aspects of economic, social, and environmental development and stress partnerships at different levels (SDG 17). The 17 Goals were adopted by all member states of the United Nations in 2015, as part of the 2030 Agenda for Sustainable Development which set out a 15-year plan to achieve the Goals.[8] The German Agency for International Cooperation, die Deutsche Gesellschaft für Internationale Zusammenarbeit (GIZ), explicitly states that "Global megatrends provide the backdrop for the 2030 Agenda for Sustainable Development."[9] China and many other countries across all continents produced reports on the SDGs highlighting their commitment and strategy for implementation. The SDGs have spread to a growing number of institutions across the world, the business and finance community, and civil society organizations. Civil society organizations were pioneers in working on issues of sustainable development cutting across sectoral policy-making goals. The concept of sustainable development has been promoted by many activists across the world. One of the leading proponents has been Anil Kumar Agarwal, the founder-director of the Centre for Science and Environment, one of India's leading environmental NGOs. The 2030 Agenda and the Sustainable Development Goals will receive special attention in this book as they indeed constitute a powerful reference framework for action, not only at the level of states but also for the private sector, the financial industry, and civil society initiatives.

1.2 The Pentagon Model

We propose a relatively simple framework to identify and prioritize megatrends. We call it the *Pentagon Model*. It focuses on five criteria relating to the relevance of trends.

The five key criteria, the pentagon factors, that make up a megatrend are the following:

1. Research and, particularly, research coverage of the trend by researchers and analysts from different disciplinary background in different countries and regions.
2. Level of political attention for the trend in a significant number of countries and regions.
3. Significant interest from global investors. This acknowledges that investments have great potential to promote trends.
4. Media coverage of the trend. This refers to traditional media and social media.
5. Strength of social movements and advocacy actions related to the trend.

These factors represent different spheres of societies: scientific and research, state, and government institutions; financial and business sectors; media; and civil society. When we introduce certain megatrends, we shall quickly see that the aforementioned factors are all met.

We emphasize these five different factors because we see many business consulting firms using the term *megatrend*. In our understanding, megatrends affect not only the business world but also societies as a whole.

How to Identify Global Megatrends?

Figure 1.1: Pentagon Model of Megatrends

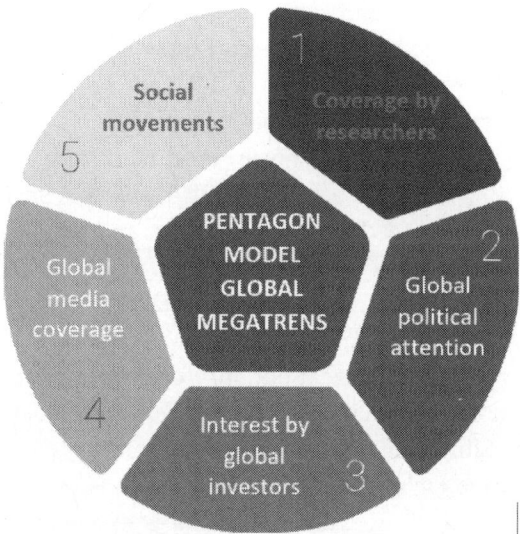

Source: Berthold M. Kuhn

In constructing and subsequently putting to use this model, we have thus come up with the following twelve global trends, which will shape the future in the next 10–15 years.

Global Megatrends:

- Climate Action and Sustainability;
- Digitalization;
- Inequality;
- Demography;
- Urbanization and Smart Cities;
- Health and Nutrition;
- Green Economy;
- Sustainable Finance;
- Multipolar World Order and the Future of Multilateralism;
- Democracy and Governance Innovations;
- Civilizational Developments: Diversity, Individualization and Loneliness, Gender Shift, and Identity Politics;

- Migration.

The trends of climate action and sustainability, digitalization, and inequality will be presented first. We regard these as the most universal trends, though we do not propose a detailed ranking of trends because many of them are closely interconnected.

Climate change is already affecting our lives and our very existence on Earth and will continue to do so in such a way that sustainability transformations are needed across countries and sectors, including in energy production, mobility, and housing. New business models and the financial sector will play critical roles in supporting sustainability transformations.

Climate change receives major attention from researchers from different disciplines. We are also witnessing a proliferation of government policies tackling climate change, while climate protection has become a decisive factor for investment decisions, which also drives new business models. Climate change is extensively covered by the media and is addressed by a large number of civil society organizations. It is at the very origin of the emergence of new social movements, such as the teenage movement Fridays for Future, and Extinction Rebellion.

While digitalization seems to primarily affect the business sector and the investment community, it is also promoted by government policies, including education policies, and extensively discussed by civil society and social movements—for example by trade unions in the context of "the future of work." It affects almost every aspect of our daily life, from online shopping and dating to education and digital health.

Inequality is the subject of many research projects and remains a chief concern for almost all governments in all countries. Globalization has exacerbated inequality in many ways and affects policymaking and investment decisions—for example, in the field of housing. The media cover inequality extensively and the issue is addressed by many different social and political movements.

1.3 Visions, Risks, and Trends

How do megatrends emerge? We can distinguish between push and pull factors that influence trends. Push factors refer to crisis situations and risks; pull factors to visions for a better future. Push factors could include a pollution crisis which is hazardous to our health; pull factors could be technological aspirations.

It is also worth thinking about intended and unintended consequences of human actions and how they relate to trends, either strengthening or weakening them. Intended consequences of research, business, or policy initiatives are meant to achieve set objectives. Unintended consequences are those which are not proactively pursued but hard to avoid.

In many situations, conditions are met so that both push and pull factors reinforce each other, support new developments, and set new trends. In all of the following trends we do indeed witness intended and unintended consequences.

Joseph A. Schumpeter, known for his theories on innovation and entrepreneurship, highlighted disruption as a driver for change through innovation. Schumpeter is regarded as one of the greatest economists of the first half of the twentieth century. He introduced the concept of "creative destruction," which he considered the driving force for innovation. Entrepreneurs perform the function of the change creator. He also emphasized the importance of a well-developed financial system that provides access to capital for investment.[10]

Disruptions are driven by efforts to master crisis situations, to address risks, and to overcome problems. In this regard, megatrends are collective efforts to cope with risks and challenges and to respond to crisis situations. This is evident for climate change and climate action. We need ambitious climate mitigation policies to reduce greenhouse gas emissions in order to avoid rising temperatures, rising sea levels, and extreme weather events. We also need ambitious climate adaptation policies to make our cities and our urban and rural livelihoods more resilient to the effects of climate change that already occur and will occur in the future, irrespective of our present-day action. Burning fossil-fuels produces irreversible damage as emissions stay in the atmosphere for a long time, since we have not scaled up carbon capture and storage technologies in a massive way — this is an unrealistic option given the efforts and costs involved at present.

COVID-19 is a prime example of how a crisis has accelerated an already existing trend, that of digitalization. Digitalization is a means to effectively respond to many logistical challenges, to ease global communication — for example, in times of lockdowns imposed by COVID-19 policies; and to manage, exchange, and analyze bigger data that could provide us with more accurate guidance and offer a range of automated services, including driving cars or organizing mobility services.

Inequality on the other hand is a trend that concerns the unintended consequences of change and development processes. Inequality is about variations of living standards across a given population or across the whole world. This is different from poverty. While poverty — defined mainly in terms of low-income levels, lack of well-being, and lack of access to facilities and services — has diminished massively in several countries and regions, the same cannot be said for inequality. Throughout human history, rising inequality has been perceived as a crisis situation and has led to the emergence of political and social movements driven by visions to curb inequality, sometimes using revolutionary means that have transformed political systems in fundamental ways.

In the world of finance, trends are closely associated with risks. Stock markets are very sensitive to risks by anticipating and setting trends and directing investment away from increasingly risky assets to sustainable business models. Tesla is a prime example. It's stock market value already exceeded the value of all other major car companies when Tesla still produced huge losses every day, while other companies delivered big profits.

We have consulted several global risk reports which are meant to stimulate thinking on strategies to cope with risks. The most prominent one is the "Global Risk Report" of the World Economic Forum (WEF). The 50th anniversary of the Forum in 2020 focused

How to Identify Global Megatrends?

on "Stakeholders for a Cohesive and Sustainable World." Climate change is regarded as a key challenge for sustainable development, whereas inequality is recognized as a major threat to social and political cohesion.

The Global Risk Reports of the WEF distinguish between different categories of risks:

- Economic;
- Environmental;
- Geopolitical;
- Societal;
- Technological.

WEF reports on the likelihood and impact of risks. This is a simple but powerful methodology to arrive at a ranking of risks and stimulate discussion on which actions are urgently needed to address risks and challenges.

Already in the year 2020, the World Economic Forum's top risks fall into the category of the environment, and they all rank very high in likelihood: extreme weather, climate action failure, natural disasters, biodiversity loss, and human-made environmental disasters.[11]

The 2021 Global Risk Report[12] and 2022 Global Risk Reports of the WEF distinguishes between three different risks horizon: 0–2 years (clear and present dangers), 2–5 years (knock-on effects), and 5–10 years (existential threats). In the 2022 report, extreme weather events rank top in the 0–2 years horizon and climate action failure ranks top in the 2–5 year and 5–10 year horizon.[13]

1.4 Global-local Nexus

Megatrends play out in different ways in different localities. Understanding trends is about understanding the context of the changing environment we are living in. This helps us to anticipate and to prepare for challenges in the future.

The slogan "think global, act local" is about how to harmonize contextual factors with one's own sphere of life. The original phrase has been attributed to the Scottish town planner and activist Patrick Geddes, who believed that we should consider and work with the environment rather than ignoring or working against it. Some environmental activists have modified the phrase "think global, act local" to "act globally, act locally," demonstrating their commitment to influencing political decisions, pushing for global, regional, and national agreements, and acting in different places at the same time to protect the biosphere and reduce greenhouse gas emissions.

Jeremy Rifkin, the author of more than 20 books about the impact of scientific and technological changes on the economy, the workforce, society, and the environment, makes notable points in his new book *The Green New Deal*.[14] He urges that "we move toward emphatic impulses to larger collectivities and worldviews" considering that information flows facilitate actions of solidarity and empathy in a globalized world.

Protecting the global commons, which include the Earth's shared natural resources—the high seas, the atmosphere, the Antarctic, and outer space—is everybody's concern, everywhere, though to different degrees. Many forms of pollution, in particular air pollution, cross borders. Overfishing in one place affects livelihoods and business in other places. The loss of biosphere, land degradation, and deforestation not only impacts the local environment but also affects the global climate in negative ways. For many people such consequences are too abstract to influence their daily lives, but there is ample scientific evidence that it is precisely the high level of ignorance of global contextual knowledge that could threaten the very existence of life on Earth, at least in its present forms in some places.

We begin by exploring climate action, but before we do so, it is vital to address the question of who is shaping these megatrends and the world at large in the first place. This question often conjures images of borderline conspiratorial nature, but it is our goal to show that this is evidently not the case. There are more than enough people, organizations, companies, and think tanks all contributing, to different extents, to shaping the future, and we will explore these dynamics in the next chapter.

Chapter 2

Who Shapes the Future?

This book covers twelve megatrends. We have conducted extensive research on all of these trends, but we do not claim that we have become leading experts in each of them. Instead, bearing in mind the limits of our knowledge, we approached many researchers and analysts from different academic disciplines, professional backgrounds, countries, world regions, age groups, and genders, to provide us with advice and the necessary information on salient issues shaping these trends. The experts (see Table of Interviews) are all well networked with different kinds of affiliations to think tanks and universities and other institutions from the public, private, and non-profit sectors. They have a deep understanding of the topics we discussed with them and provided us with analyses which often went well beyond the state of the art of mainstream research, analysis, and media reporting.

In addition to the experts whom we interviewed for the chapters on megatrends, we also approached experts in future studies to share their ideas with us. Experts in future studies, often called 'futurists' are experts who systematically explore predictions and possibilities about the future. Many of them publish books, offer advisory services, and engage in dialogue with policymakers. The World Future Studies Federation (WFSF) is a UNESCO and UN consultative partner and global NGO with members in over 60 countries.

Futurists claim to have a good overview of emerging trends and state-of-the-art expertise in strategic foresight. Only a few, however, have deeper knowledge of specific topics. Our methodology consisted of combining our own analysis with the analysis of researchers, analysts, and futurists. In this final chapter, "Visions for the World in 2030 and Beyond," two renowned futurists and a very well-networked manager, book editor, and author on issues and trends of future concern came together for an interview with us. Their views are meant to complement our analysis based on megatrend research and the interviews with analysts and researchers on megatrends in the preceding chapters.

The interviews are a core part of this book. We wanted to write a book on megatrends which took into account different perspectives. Diversity was a key criterion when selecting our interview partners. We have identified analysts and researchers for expert advice and interviews in the process of diving deeper into emerging issues and megatrends. We found them through their publications, conference participation, and online research. Some were recommended to us; a few we knew personally from our involvement in international cooperation projects and our networking activities with think tanks. Berthold M. Kuhn has worked on sustainability transformation for many years, in his capacity as a university researcher at Freie Universität Berlin, Leiden University, Tsinghua University, and Xiamen University; as a consultant to the European Commission, international organizations, and think tanks; and as an expert on ethical investments. Dimitrios L. Margellos has also worked, lived, and traveled in many countries and has been engaged in academic and political work, especially on the issue of inequality.

As we have already mentioned, this is not the first book or publication on megatrends. We have witnessed a proliferation of institutes, experts, and publications focusing on megatrends. The motivation of some megatrend institutes, consulting firms, and experts is to provide well-paid advisory services to business groups and investors. Few make reference to other firms, institutes, or think tanks. We wanted to adopt a slightly different and more comprehensive approach. We make due reference to the many valuable contributions of others in the field of megatrend research by quoting their work and conducting interviews with them and we aim to present a thorough and critical analysis of recent research, analysis, and political debates.

Who Shapes the Future?

2.1 Shapers

In a sense, we all make contributions to shaping the future through the ways we act, think, contribute to discourses and analysis, and engage in relationships with others. There are, however, some distinct professions such as "strategists" and "futurists" which have been emerging in recent decades and which focus on foresight analysis and advice for companies and political leaders on trends. It would go beyond the scope of this chapter to present an exhaustive list of institutes and experts dealing with strategic foresight, future research, and megatrends. In this chapter and in the book, we shall focus on some key terms and institutes, especially think tanks, which are particularly engaged in future research, and we make due reference to international cooperation initiatives.

The World Economic Forum (WEF) is a leading organization engaged in the analysis of risks and future developments; many others are referenced in the following sub-chapter on think tanks and in the megatrend chapters. We highlight the WEF — which has recently come under attack by some conspiracy theorists — because it is indeed an influential think tank and because it coined the term "shapers." The WEF has more than 13,000 members in 150 countries and supports the Global Shapers Community, a network of young people under the age of 30 working together to address local, regional, and global challenges. It convenes the Davos Forum and publishes the widely referenced *Global Risks Report*[1], which we cited in the first chapter. We also worked with diverse smaller and medium-size organizations and with researchers and analysts not affiliated to the think tank or consulting industries. However, we recognize the power of leading think tanks in shaping discourses, influencing policymaking, and setting global agendas.

For us, shapers are researchers and experts, international and professional organizations, and especially think tanks, that work on future trends and contribute to agenda-setting and action in relation to trends. Contrary to what conspiracy theories might tell us, our future is not shaped by a few powerful individuals, or even just a small network of influential leaders who may be very present in the news. Undoubtedly, some political leaders, business tycoons, religious leaders, media moguls, and VIP social media influencers attract a lot of attention, but we should not fall prey to such simplistic narratives and all too elegant explanations of the world (which also often carry a lot of antisemitic ideas). The *HuffPost*, formerly *Huffington Post*, has published an article on conspiracy theories around Bill Gates and his foundation which may be of interest for some readers.[2]

Lists and rankings of powerful and influential people are entertaining to read, but they can perpetuate a worldview of concealed governance structures piloted by a handful of powerful individuals or simply exaggerate the actual influence on decision-making and agenda-setting of such people.

Time magazine, for example, lists pioneers, artists, leaders, titans, and icons. The listing includes people from politics as well as the entertainment industry. It is fun reading but not based on sophisticated criteria or empirical evidence.

Throughout history, great technological developments and philosophical ideas are often attributed to only a small number of people. Visionary people who engage in research, development, and marketing of new products and business models are still necessary. Elon Musk, the founder of Tesla, PayPal, and SpaceX, is one example. However, the modern world has become more complex, and it is worth noting that SpaceX has indeed received massive financial backing from the U.S. government. It is mainly institutions and interactions across disciplinary boundaries and between researchers and practitioners that influence megatrends.

In an effort to present the most accurate analysis of megatrends, we directed our attention to analysts and researchers who have made well-documented contributions to trends affecting the future of humanity. Innovations and processes of change are often engineered by people who research new technologies, publish widely referenced books, educate others, or are involved in strategic foresight and consulting to multinational companies, international organizations, governments, and leading non-profit organizations. The number of people involved in researching new

Who Shapes the Future?

technologies, founding innovative companies, and working on strategic foresight and future scenarios has been growing in recent years.

The start-up universe is particularly interesting to study. It perfectly illustrates the enormous drive for innovation. According to Startup Genome (2021), more than 80 ecosystems globally have produced a billion-dollar start-up, the so-called unicorns. When the term was popularized in 2013, only four ecosystems had produced unicorns or billion-dollar exits.[3]

Each megatrend presented in this book has a different story of growing attention and relevance across countries and regions. The Pentagon Model which we introduced in the first chapter tells us that megatrends also have much in common. They are widely referenced by analysts and researchers and are debated among expert communities and activists. Investors have a keen interest in understanding and forecasting megatrends. Media reports on powerful trends and social movements, and activists are inspired by them.

We do not hold particular megatrends in higher regard than we do others, but we nevertheless concede that some will impact the world more than others, those being climate action, digitalization, and inequality. This begs the question of who the shapers of these megatrends might be.

We have seen an exponential growth of experts from different disciplines working on climate change and sustainability topics. On climate change, the main shaper of the debate has been the Intergovernmental Panel on Climate Change (IPCC). The IPCC was established in 1988 by the World Meteorological Organization (WMO) and the United Nations Environment Program (UNEP) and was later endorsed by the United Nations General Assembly. The IPCC gathers thousands of scientists and experts who contribute to writing and reviewing reports which have gradually gained the highest level of political attention. The IPCC published its Sixth Assessment Report, "Climate Change 2021: The Physical Science Basis," in August 2021. The report provides new estimates of the chances of crossing the global warming level of 1.5°C in the coming decades, and finds that unless there are immediate, rapid, and large-scale reductions in greenhouse gas emissions, limiting warming to close to 1.5°C or even 2°C will be beyond reach.[4]

A very large number of sustainability initiatives across the world have pointed to the need to protect biodiversity and to change patterns of land use, production, and consumption. The United Nations presented the 2030 Agenda for Sustainable Development and the 17 Sustainable Development Goals in 2015. Unfortunately, it took an exceedingly long time until decision-makers realized that humanity, including every individual, had to adjust lifestyles to become part of the solution. At the same time, unhelpful advice has plagued policymaking for a long time, either through systematic failure, as in the case of mainstream economists, or through lobbying efforts by the fossil fuel industry. Richard Tol, a professor at the University of Sussex, wrote a famous paper in 2009 in which he argued that global warming would cause economic *gains* for people living in temperate zones, and that these gains would outweigh the losses to people living in the tropics.[5]

Digitalization has become a megatrend and a disruptive force in business and communication. New technologies have opened up new opportunities, from voice and facial recognition to autonomous driving. The pace of new development and new regulations is breathtaking for analysts. Recently, China has stepped up efforts to regulate its technology sector, a move which has reduced the market capitalization of some of its leading companies, especially Ali Baba.

Theoretically, it is clear that people are behind the big trends and are responsible for pushing digitalization. However, many people focus on the consequences of digitalization rather than on the visions and ideas of the smart people who initiate, engineer, and advance the process of digitalization. Analysis and decision-making power will increasingly be based on algorithms. An algorithm is a series of instructions that are executed step-by-step through the processing of data to solve a problem or to complete a task. Almost everybody is confronted with algorithms and uses them on a daily basis. Algorithms are designed by people and reflect the thinking of people and the technology companies employing them. There are too few efforts underway to decode the logic of thinking behind algorithms to make them transparent and point out the opportunities and threats of digitalization. Our analysis of the megatrend of digitalization is meant to make this big trend more understandable and to offer some critical reflections. The more people who know about megatrends, the more progress humanity will make toward "democratizing" future developments.

Inequality has always persisted in one form or another and continues to be a hot subject of political debates, philosophical reflections, moral considerations, and ideological campaigns. It has gained significant attention by researchers. The World Inequality Database (WID) is a major source of reference.[6] The books of Thomas Piketty, including *Capital in the 21 Century* and *The Economics of Inequality*,[7] have received extraordinary attention from scholars and the wider public. Inequality is a major source of conflict in societies. Thus, it truly matters for the future of humanity and is considered a megatrend. Degrees of inequality can vary widely, and chapter five will provide some insights into how to measure inequality and whether, where, and to what extent it is likely to increase in the next decade. How we look at inequality, however, depends on those who reflect on it and shape discourses that in turn influence political decisions. Who will shape discourses and set the agenda on inequality? Which views will dominate political agendas? Some organizations would argue that clashes between people with different levels of income and living standards are unavoidable. Others advocate for a redistribution of wealth or are engaged in promoting social justice and mitigating inequality through political or philanthropic work.

In the process of analyzing climate action and sustainability transformation, digitalization, and inequality, as well as other megatrends, we looked at the work of numerous think tanks which are engaged in research and dialogue on the future of humanity and the planet.

2.2 Think Tanks

What is a think tank? Answers to this question may vary in different political and cultural contexts. In the United States, we may see a greater interest in and perhaps more familiarity with the term *think tank* because think tanks play a more influential role in shaping public discourse and public policy than in other countries. Think tanks like the RAND Corporation wield a strong influence on U.S. foreign and security policy. They may convey a special, rather problematic image in being perceived as elitist organizations shaping policymaking behind the scenes. While this holds true for some think tanks, we have seen a significant growth in think tanks in different parts of the world that exhibit great diversity.

The Center for China and Globalization, a leading think tank in China, describes the function of a think tank as follows: "Through research reports, seminars, forums and meetings, as well as symposiums and proposals, think tanks play a role in setting agendas and conducting policy interpretation and research in the public arena. They also reflect public opinion and provide policy recommendations to the relevant government agencies through national consultation and democratic mechanisms."[8]

The United Nations has published a report, "Thinking the Unthinkable: From Thought to Policy — The Role of Think Tanks in Shaping Government Strategy."[9] The report refers to the increasing complexity and technical nature of policy problems, which play in favor of think tanks aiming to become more important in influencing policymaking. The Think Tanks and Civil Society Program (TTCPS) of the University of Pennsylvania publishes a Global Go To Think Tank Index (GGTTI) Report which has been designed "to identify and recognize centers of excellence in all the major areas of public policy research and in every region of the world." The report provides the following definition:

"Think tanks are public-policy research analysis and engagement organizations that generate policy-oriented research, analysis and advice on domestic and international issues, thereby enabling policymakers and the public to make informed decisions about public policy."[10]

The GGTTI 2020 report carries the heading, "helping to bridge the gap between knowledge and policy." This is probably an adequate description of how think tanks perceive their role. The annual reports from the University of Pennsylvania group thousands of think tanks by categories, countries, and regions. According to the latest report, there are currently 2,058 think tanks in North America (Mexico, Canada, and the United States) of which 1,872 are in the United States. There are 2,219 think tanks in Europe, and many more in other parts of the world. The number of think tanks in the United States has more than doubled since 1980. Asia has experienced a dramatic growth in think tanks since the mid-2000s. In an effort to diversify their funding base, think tanks have targeted businesses and wealthy individuals to support their core operations and programs. The growth of think tanks is driven by digitalization, easier access to information, and the increasing complexity of policy problems. This growth trend, however, does not apply to all countries and regions. In fact, the political and regulatory environment has grown hostile to think tanks and NGOs in some authoritarian regimes and reduced the space for critical and independent analysis and advocacy work. Authoritarian states tend to fear independent analysis, diversity of opinions, and unsolicited policy recommendations. They sometimes even prohibit their work, especially if foreign funding is involved. The Carnegie Endowment for International Peace, a leading U.S. think tank, argues that "since the mid-2000s, civic space has come under attack in many countries around the world... closing civic space now appears to be just one part of a much broader pattern of democratic recession and authoritarian resurgence. The international response seems stuck."[11] In chapter eleven on democracy and governance, we refer to index projects that aim to measure the quality of democracy, governance, and freedom of association.

In European countries, according to our observations, the image of think tanks is gradually changing. At least the educated public perceives them less as closed-shop institutions run by old boys's networks and more as networks of well-informed experts who engage in dialogue on salient issues. The number of think tanks that focus on lobbying for the vested interests of business groups or the agendas of political parties is rather small. Legal and tax regulation constrain lobbying activities for organizations that enjoy public benefit status. Many think tanks are registered as foundations and enjoy such status. In Europe and even more in the U.S., the image of non-Western think tanks tends to be far more negative. Many of them are—not always with good justification—labeled as arms of authoritarian regimes. We have observed that their presumed proximity to political leadership and their actual political influence tend to be overrated.

Think tanks very often deal with future trends. Some explicitly focus on analyzing future trends, megatrends, and are promoting related dialogue. They are setting agendas and influencing decision-makers in an implicit rather than an explicit way. Their analysis and reports are usually widely available on the internet, with electronic copies often available free of charge. Here are two examples: SITRA's megatrend analysis aims to provide an interpretation of the direction of global change-related phenomena. SITRA is a think tank that does not disguise its proximity to the legislature of a country. It is the Finnish Innovation Fund which acts as an independent public foundation and operates directly under the supervision of the Finnish Parliament.[12]

Who Shapes the Future?

Figure 2.1: SITRA's Megatrends

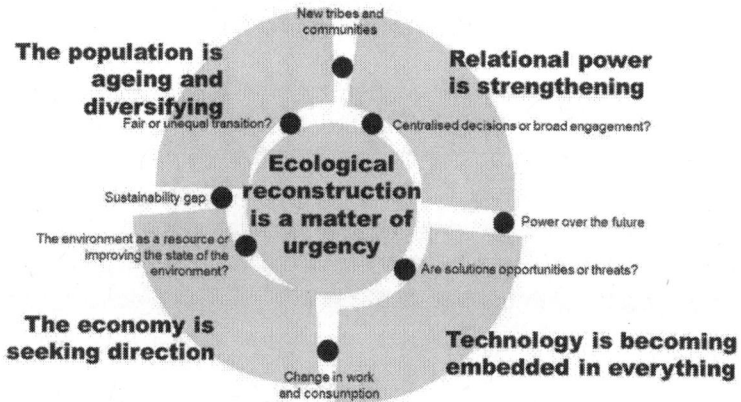

Source: SITRA (2020)[13]

Megatrends Watch describes itself as an independent, non-partisan private organization dedicated to advancing the study of megatrends and their potential impacts upon societies. It aims to strengthen the decision-making capacity of organizations by providing strategic intelligence designed to broaden the understanding of external opportunities and threats. It offers advisory services in foresight intelligence and future studies.[14]

What are (other) influential think tanks in the field of future research? There are many think tanks working on future trends and scenarios in specific fields of research and dialogue, for example, in the fields of technological, economic, and social development or geopolitics. Some think tanks carry "future" in their name.[15] They address different audiences. Some focus more on political leaders, others more on business communities; some are more research-oriented, others more consulting-oriented. Thus, it would be difficult to rank them according to their influence.

In Germany, the Zukunftsinstitut (The Future Institute) considers itself a leading think tank for future research and strategic foresight.[16] It is a rather small organization but has designed a widely referenced map on megatrends which presents a dozen interconnected future trends.

- 43 -

2.3 Consulting Firms

Consulting firms typically act as brokers for innovation and help companies and public institutions to optimize their business models. Information technology upgrades are often the focus of their consulting services. The major consulting firms also act as strategic consultants and present themselves as specialists for forecasting trends, change management, and process management.

Many consulting companies have produced reports on megatrends, mostly with the purpose of engaging with potential clients and providing advisory services related to strategic foresight and analysis of promising business trends.

McKinsey, a leading strategy consulting firm, has identified four global forces shaping all the trends. The first is the shifting locus of economic activity and dynamism to emerging markets like China and to cities within those markets. The second disruptive force is the acceleration in the scope, scale, and economic impact of technology. The third is the aging society. The human population is getting older. Fertility is falling, and the world's population is graying dramatically. While aging has been evident in developed economies for some time — Japan and Russia have seen their populations decline over the past few years — the demographic deficit is now spreading to China and will soon reach Latin America. The final disruptive force is the degree to which the world is much more connected through trade and through movements in capital, people, and information (data and communication).[17]

The big four accounting firms — PwC, Deloitte, EY, and KPMG — have all ventured into the analysis of megatrends. PwC, which operates in 157 countries, has produced a flagship report on megatrends. The company defines global megatrends as "macroeconomic and geostrategic forces that are shaping our world, and our collective futures in profound ways." Five megatrends are in the focus of the analysis of PwC are as follows:[18]

1. The shift in global economic power;
2. Demographic change;
3. Rapid urbanization;

Who Shapes the Future?

4. The rise of technology;
5. Climate change and resource scarcity.

Deloitte Consultants has also worked on five megatrends with a focus on financial services. The report identified clusters of innovation that are affecting business in the financial services industry: primary accounts, payments, capital markets, investment management, and insurance.[19]

The German consulting firm Roland Berger presented a comprehensive "Trend Compendium 2050" in 2021. It covers six megatrends spanning different economic and social dimensions, also including politics and governance.

Figure 2.2: The Roland Berger Trend Compendium

Source: Roland Berger (2021)[20]

Megatrends are important for marketing. Kantar Consulting, in cooperation with Prof. Peter Wippermann and Jens Krüger, has published a Value Index which focuses on consumers. The 2020 Value Index report is based on a comprehensive analysis of social media communication. The underlying assumption is that values drive trends. The ranking order is as follows: (1) Health, (2) Family, (3) Success, (4) Freedom, (5) Security, (6) Community, (7) Nature, (8) Acknowledgment, (9) Justice, and (10) Sustainability.

- 45 -

Kantar Consulting and the aforementioned experts also published a Chinese Consumer Value Index in 2019. For China, the highest ranked values are: (1) Success, (2) Security, (3) Health, (4) Simplicity, (5) Freedom, (6) Nature, (7) Family, (8) Community, (9) Recognition, and (10) Transparency.

2.4 International Cooperation and Global Governance

International cooperation is far more advanced, deeper, and broader than most people imagine or media coverage of political and economic tensions between powerful countries suggests. International organizations play a key role in promoting global exchanges. They shape debates on future trends in a significant way.

The state administrations of the world built a sophisticated global governance architecture in the decades after World War Two. The United Nations, its principal organs, and its specialized agencies, are important actors in international cooperation, though some of their budgets are relatively small and global consensus-building is an almost impossible task.

The former United Nations Secretary-General Kofi Annan was the chief architect of a new orientation for the United Nations. He decided that the UN should engage more with the business community. This new UN policy was announced at the World Economic Forum's summit on January 31, 1999. The UN Global Compact was launched soon after on July 26, 2000. The UN has gradually opened up and today involves many actors besides states. It has promoted a series of initiatives specifically targeted at the business and financial community to work on shared values and principles and to give a human face to the global market. The cooperation of the UN with civil society organizations and social movements has also intensified.

While the effectiveness of the work of many organizations of the UN has always been questioned, especially in the U.S., the broadening and deepening of its cooperation with non-state actors from 2000 onwards has rejuvenated the UN system in many ways.

Who Shapes the Future?

Today, the UN system leads the climate action and sustainability agenda with its conference series in the context of the UN Framework Convention on Climate Change (UNCCC) and the 2030 Agenda for Sustainable Development which has — to the surprise of some experts and media, including *The Economist* — developed into a powerful reference framework not only for international cooperation projects but also for policymakers in many countries to promote sustainability transitions at national and subnational levels, for city planning and development, and for asset management groups and investors.

The political analyst Ayad-Al Ani, professor at Stellenbosch University in South Africa and fellow of the Berlin-based Einstein-Zentrum Digitale Zukunft (Einstein Centre Digital Future), has pointed to the engagement of major global companies with the Sustainable Development Goals: He refers to Avanti Communications (satellite technology); 2030 Vision (a technology partnership that also includes SAP and Microsoft); Google; the software company Salesforce, whose CEO is also on the board of the WEF; and to the payment specialist Mastercard.

The climate crisis has provided the UN with an opportunity to start a number of significant new global initiatives and to structure and shape global policymaking on climate action. The UN is relatively decentralized and aims to reach out to countries and institutions in all parts of the world. The United Nations Development Program has a relatively strong presence in countries of the Global South. Bonn, a small city in the Rhine valley and the former capital of West Germany, hosts more than 20 United Nations institutions. The Secretariat of the United Nations Framework Conventions on Climate Change is one of them.

The Group of Seven (G7) and the Group of Twenty (G20) are informal governance clubs which hold annual summits of heads of state and governments to discuss issues of global importance. The G20, the group of the most economically powerful nations, is emerging as a key player in global politics. The G7 that gathers economically powerful countries of the Western hemisphere plus Japan, has lost influence in the context of the rise of China, India, and other countries of the Global South and is now focusing more on foreign policy and security.

The G20 focuses on economic development and finance but has extended its agenda to other areas, including those relevant to megatrends shaping modern economies. Several initiatives are associated with annual summit meetings, such as the Think Tank 20 group.

We have also witnessed the establishment of new institutions such as BRICS. Since 2009, the BRICS nations comprising Brazil, Russia, India, China, and South Africa have met annually at formal summits to advance the perspectives of emerging economies. China has also started other institutions and initiatives, such as the foreign policy and security-oriented Shanghai Cooperation Organization (SCO) and the Asian Infrastructure Investment Bank (AIIB), which is engaged in major infrastructure investments across Asia.

In the field of climate action, the South Korea-based Green Climate Fund (GCF), established within the framework of the United Nations Framework Convention on Climate Change (UNFCCC), is emerging as an important player in financing projects in the Global South. Alongside interstate institutions, we have witnessed an enormous growth in private sector associations, civil society organizations, and different kinds of social movements which shape debates on future trends and are involved in governance arrangements at different levels.

However, the governance of international affairs is still insufficient if we think about the magnitude of global challenges that humanity needs to tackle together. Political cooperation is lagging behind the dynamics of economic and social exchanges. We can see a growing interdependence of the world's economies, cultures, and populations driven by cross-border trade, technology, flows of investments, people, and information.

International organizations aim to catch up with new challenges for humanity. They have limited resources to work on their mandates but are still important agenda-setters. The UN works to promote peace and security, support development, and protect human rights. The organization has made a big effort to take a lead in the sustainable development and climate action agendas and has so far been successful.

Several world conferences led by the United Nations, especially those in Rio de Janeiro (1992 and 2012) and Johannesburg (2002), were instrumental in merging the development policy and the environmental policy agenda. These conferences have given birth to the global development goals, the 2030 Agenda for Sustainable Development and the 17 Sustainable Development Goals, which succeeded the first generation of global goals, the 8 Millennium Development Goals. Since 2000, when Kofi Annan was the Secretary-General of the UN, there has been a process of broadening engagement at the UN. Efforts have been made to reach out to the business community, to civil society organizations, to the financial industry, and to social movements such as Fridays for Future.

The United Nations 2030 Agenda for Sustainable Development has grown into a powerful reference framework for international cooperation. Unlike previous goals and programs, including the Millennium Development Goals, it is a truly one-world agenda because it requires efforts and policies of adjustment for all countries. Previous global goals, plans, and programs were based on the distinction between developed and developing countries. Rich countries were supposed to provide financial aid and technical support to poorer countries, but their own economic policies were not questioned. This changed with the environmental and climate crisis. It became more and more evident that the planet did not have the capacity to allow for models of unsustainable growth that accelerated environmental degradation, altering the climate through greenhouse gas emissions. The 2030 Agenda for Sustainable Development includes 17 development goals, 169 targets, and 232 indicators covering different social, economic, and environmental aspects. It was a complex undertaking involving a significant number of international organizations, nonprofits, and think tanks, to agree on the 17 goals that are supposed to represent a global consensus for development.

Today, the 2030 Agenda is a reference not only for international organizations and national governments but also for the private sector, including the finance industry. The UNDP has supported the development of a taxonomy for sustainable finance in China and India, which provides a classification of SDG-related finance and investment opportunities to banks and investors. Many asset management groups refer to the 2030 Agenda and the Paris Agreement in their effort to respect environmental, social, and governance criteria in their investment decisions. The chapter on sustainability transition will provide further insights into the sustainable finance trend which has witnessed a significant boom in recent years.

Chapter 3

Climate Action and Sustainability

This chapter analyzes why and how climate action and sustainability transformations will unlock their huge potential across the whole economy in the next decade and thereafter, at global, national, and local levels. A transformation toward a future vision for society of more sustainable production and consumption, and even a change of lifestyles, is increasingly called for as necessary and is already underway. Climate action is central to this vision because it affects every country on every continent. In its disruption of national economies, climate change is costing people, communities, and countries dearly today, and it will cost even more tomorrow.[1]

Which factors influence climate action across the globe? We propose a distinction between push and pull factors. So-called push factors refer to crisis situations which require governments at different levels to take urgent action, for example, severe pollution crises and natural disasters, at least partly attributed to global warming and rising sea levels. Pull factors refer to future opportunities and visions which are driving technological development and business innovation.

Climate action and sustainability transformations meet all the criteria for a megatrend as defined by the Pentagon Model. We are witnessing extensive research coverage by different disciplines, including those traditionally committed to researching climate change, such as the natural sciences, all the way to engineering and technology, agricultural science, social science, medicine, health science, and the humanities.[2] Many academic disciplines are already conducting research on climate change and sustainability issues and the *depth and breadth* of research coverage will further increase.

Political attention has reached the highest levels of international organizations. The United Nations Framework Convention on Climate Change (UNFCCC) has near-universal membership.

Global Perspectives on Megatrends

One hundred and thirty-seven countries have committed to carbon neutrality according to confirmed pledges to the Carbon Neutrality Coalition and recent policy statements by governments. More than 30,000 participants attended the 26th Conference of the Parties (COP) of the UNFCCC in Glasgow in November 2021. Numerous alliances to promote climate policies and action are emerging. The Carbon Neutral Cities Alliance (CNCA) unites leading global cities in their work to achieve carbon neutrality in the next 10–20 years.[3] Forests received prime attention at COP 26 and were discussed at the World Leaders Summit.

Climate action and sustainability are big investment and business opportunities. Investments in renewable energies are soaring and momentum is building. The Glasgow Finance Alliance for Net Zero, launched in April 2021, includes 450 leading financial institutions from 45 countries with total assets and assets under management of 130 trillion U.S. dollars. Hundreds of global financial institutions are exiting coal and shifting their investment to companies meeting higher standards of Environmental, Social and Governance (ESG) criteria. By 2019, 40 percent of the top 40 global banks and 20 globally significant insurers were already on board.[4] "Shifting the Trillions" is a report from Germany's Sustainable Finance Committee which sets out ambitious plans to promote sustainability transformations through policy initiatives targeting the financial sector.[5] Major asset management groups – not known to be among the usual suspects advocating resolute climate action – expect "a seismic shift in business models" in the context of the climate crisis.[6]

Media attention covers the drastic consequences of climate change and closely follows high-level climate action by international organizations and governments. Media coverage of climate change has consistently increased in recent years. Silvia Pianta and Matthew R. Sisco analyzed a comprehensive dataset representing more than 1.7 million online news articles covering climate change in 28 countries of the European Union in 22 different languages for the period 2014–2019. According to their study, the average daily number of climate change articles in 2019 is 4.8 times the average in 2014. Peaks of attention to climate change in the media usually occur in the months of November or December, corresponding to the Conferences of the Parties of the United Nations Framework Convention on Climate Change.[7]

Alongside the work of well-established environmental action groups on climate policies, we are seeing a proliferation of new social movements that advocate for more ambitious climate action. Many new movements focus on climate justice and inequality issues. The school strikes and mass mobilization of young people organized by the decentralized student movement Fridays for Future (FFF) made headlines in many countries.

3.1 The Extent of the Risk

Megatrends are connected to perceived risks, as we have learned in the introductory chapters. Climate action already receives significant attention today and the level of attention and action will only rise, as attested to by the World Economic Forum's (WEF) strong focus on it. Why has the need for climate action been ignored for many decades?

"Climate change is a notoriously elusive crisis," writes Diego Arguedas Ortiz, a science reporter working for the BBC and other media. "Drop some toxic chemicals in a river now and you will see dead fish within days, but what do you witness when you release carbon dioxide?"[8] Human activities contribute to climate change by causing changes in the Earth's atmosphere. The largest known contribution comes from the burning of fossil fuels, which releases carbon dioxide gas into the atmosphere.[9] According to the Annual Green House Gas Index (AGHGI), which measures the climate-warming influence of long-lived trace gases in the atmosphere, the concentrations of the most important long-lived greenhouse gases—carbon dioxide, methane, and nitrous oxides—are still steadily rising.[10]

For anyone up to date with scientific literature or who has traveled the world with open eyes, it is crystal clear that climate change is real. Climate change affects all regions around the world. It is most visible in the arctic regions but also in many coastal areas

Global Perspectives on Megatrends

and places affected by extreme weather events and rising sea levels. Jakarta is a prominent example. It is located in the Southern Hemisphere and is the most rapidly sinking city in the world, with some claiming that by 2050, 95 percent of the city will likely be submerged.[11]

The most widely referenced consequences of climate change in scientific literature are as follows:

- Rising temperatures in many regions of the world;
- Melting ice and rising sea levels;
- Increased frequency of extreme weather events, including hurricanes, droughts, and heavy rain;
- Risks to human health, for example, through heat waves, tsunamis, bush fires, and typhoons;
- Risks to wildlife and biodiversity with an impact on agricultural productivity.

The Intergovernmental Panel on Climate Change (IPCC) already pointed to the drastic consequences of climate change in its 2007 report regarding food (failing crop yields), water (decreases in water availability), ecosystems (damage to coral reefs, extinction of species), extreme weather events (storms, forest fires, droughts, flooding, and risks of large climatic shifts.

The impact of climate change varies across regions. While some regions experience more extreme heat waves and droughts, in other regions, extreme weather events and rainfall become more common. The melting of the glaciers and rising sea levels will produce different kinds of short-term, mid-term, and long-term effects. Some regions may benefit from new economic opportunities, while others will struggle to grow crops as they have done previously. Wine cultivation is shifting northwards in Europe; meanwhile, mudslides, changes in fruiting cycles, increases in pests and crop diseases, and shifting temperatures are threatening the livelihoods of Colombian coffee farmers.[12] Uncertainty about how the climate will develop means it is near impossible to prepare for such changes.

Climate Action and Sustainability

It is difficult to attribute each extreme weather event to climate change. However, the change in frequency is a clear indicator of climate change. More and more exact data are being collected on sea levels, surface temperature, the melting of glaciers, the extinction of species, and other changes to ecosystems.

The IPCC points to the risk of reaching tipping points. These are thresholds — perhaps even points of no return — that, when exceeded, can lead to unpredictable and fast changes in the state of the system. The IPCC states that the precise levels of climate change sufficient to trigger specific tipping points remain uncertain, but that the risk associated with crossing multiple tipping points increases with rising temperature. According to *Carbon Brief*, tipping points are "thresholds where a tiny change could push a system into a completely new state."

Tipping points include West Antarctic ice sheet disintegration, the dieback of the Amazon rainforest, West-African monsoon shift, Indian monsoon shift, Boreal forest shift, Atlantic meridional overturning circulation breakdown, permafrost loss, and Greenland ice sheet disintegration.[13]

In August 2021, the IPCC released its latest report, whose conclusions were terrifying in their affirmation of the scientific consensus.[14] What once were low-to-medium confidence predictions are now high-certainty estimates, while the message was clear: The best-case scenario, that is, momentarily crossing the 1.5°C boundary and only seeing reductions in the long term, requires net-zero emissions as soon as 2050.

Mark Carney, the United Nations special envoy on climate action and finance, estimates that human mortality related to climate change will be the equivalent of a coronavirus crisis every year from the middle of this century. The former governor of the Bank of England and head of the Bank of Canada points to the climate crisis and the urgently needed sustainability transition as an enormous investment opportunity.[15] There is little doubt that climate action and sustainability transformation constitute a major global trend, though there are still a few political leaders and think tanks that deny this.[16]

According to the Global Climate Risk Index (GCRI), in South Asia alone — where Bangladesh is one of the countries most affected — climate change is expected to force nearly 40 million people to migrate within their countries by 2050.[17] There are many other places, including the Maldives and the small island states (or "big ocean states") in the Pacific and Caribbean regions, as well as many coastal megacities that are already seriously affected by climate change. Climate change is intensifying the already high pressure on land and water resources in many densely populated areas. The ND Gain Climate Change Vulnerability Index is adding to the gloomy picture of the impact of climate change across different world regions.[18]

The dramatic loss of biodiversity is a key sustainability issue and is intricately connected to climate change. The European Commission acknowledges that "we cannot address biodiversity loss without tackling climate change, but it is equally impossible to tackle climate change without addressing biodiversity loss.[19] Protecting and restoring ecosystems can help to reduce the extent of climate change and cope with its impact. According to the International Union for Conservation of Nature (IUCN), more than 12,000 species are threatened with extinction. One-third of the world's coral reefs have died. It is an established fact that humans and human economic activities are currently driving climate change and represent the greatest threat to biodiversity.

3.2 Global Agendas for Sustainability Policies and Climate Action

The work of the IPCC, the United Nations body responsible for assessing the science related to climate change, has gained traction over the past decade. The IPCC's periodic reports focus on assessing the science related to climate change and reach a large audience. The organization gathers leading researchers from across the world who produce comprehensive assessment reports about the state of scientific, technical, and socio-economic knowledge on climate change, its impacts, and its risks, and about options for reducing the rate at which climate change is taking place.[20] The IPCC reports point to mounting evidence that the net costs of the damage caused by climate change are likely to be significant and to increase over time.

The latest IPCC report carried an even grimmer tone than the previous ones, but was overshadowed by the war in Ukraine, receiving little attention from the wide public. The report claims that half of the world's population is now "highly vulnerable", while "across sectors and regions the most vulnerable people and systems are observed to be disproportionately affected". Many ecosystems and species alike are also on the verge of collapse and extinction respectively. Reiterating previous established knowledge, the IPCC stresses that warming beyond 1.5°C degrees will cause irreversible damage to ecosystems and humans.[21]

The UNFCCC works closely with the IPCC. The Paris Agreement was concluded at the 21st Conference of the Parties (COP) of the UNFCCC in Le Bourget, near Paris, France, in December 2015 and was adopted by consensus by the 195 UNFCCC participating member states and the European Union. The Paris Agreement represents a milestone in the global governance of climate action and has triggered actions at all levels. It set the goal to limit global warming to well below 2°C, preferably to 1.5°C, compared to pre-industrial levels. States are obliged to submit so-called Nationally Determined Contributions (NDCs). NDCs have become mandatory for all parties, developing as well as developed countries. Emission reduction targets are not legally binding, but all countries need to submit NDCs and participate in the process of monitoring, reporting, and ambition-raising, supported by the UN and a number of international organizations and programs, such as the NDC Partnership. This is a significant step forward from the Kyoto Protocol adopted at the Earth Summit in Rio de Janeiro in 1992, which had a first period of commitment that only began in 2008. Developing countries — China fell within this category at the time — did not have any obligations in terms of setting their own targets for emission reductions.

The Paris Agreement is a landmark in the multilateral climate change process because, for the first time, a binding agreement brings all nations into a common cause to undertake ambitious efforts to combat climate change and adapt to its effects.[22] The agreement represents a dynamic process of more ambitious target-setting than the world has ever seen. However, the present targets and commitments are still not good enough to reach the goal of limiting global warming to well below 2°C, preferably to 1.5°C, compared to pre-industrial levels.

The Paris Agreement is not a stand-alone agreement. The Conferences of the Parties of the UNFCCC take place every year, unless the Parties decide otherwise, as they did in 2020 when COVID-19 struck and travel bans were imposed. The first COP took place in Berlin in 1995. The German city of Bonn, the former capital of Germany and a well-networked city, hosts the UNFCC Secretariat. The outcomes of the many COPs vary in significance. COP 15 in Copenhagen (2009) created a lot of frustration. The high-flying expectations of the Danish organizers were not met because climate diplomacy failed to overcome the stalemate between different groups, especially between Europe, Russia, China, and the United States. Six years later, France did somewhat better than Denmark, but the political circumstances were also different. China played a crucial role and made use of its bargaining power with countries of the Global South to mitigate the principle of common but differentiated responsibilities that stood in the way of a binding agreement in Denmark.

We have seen ups and downs in perceptions of the effectiveness of the negotiations. Most important, however, are the continuity of action and the broadening and deepening of debates on climate change. The annual COP summits on climate action have grown in size as well as impact. They host political leaders, high-level diplomats, and environmental policy administrators. In addition, they host a series of side events involving civil society organizations, representatives of cities, and networks from the business and finance communities.

Climate Action and Sustainability

The number and diversity of stakeholders to have expressed commitment to the Paris Agreement and emphasized their sustainability reporting are increasing. It is almost impossible for any major multinational company to ignore the agreement and continue with business as usual. Even a company like Vale, together with Rio Tinto Group and BHP one of the biggest mining companies of the world, and with a rather dubious record in environmental management, is trying to change course and makes reference to its commitment to the Paris Agreement alongside its goal to become carbon neutral by 2050.[23]

Next to the Paris Agreement and the subsequent COP conferences, the 2030 Agenda is today's major reference point and accountability framework for climate action and sustainability transformation. The 2030 Agenda covers 17 dimensions of sustainable development and is used by very diverse institutions, organizations, and companies, including the financial industry.

Figure 3.1: The United Nations Sustainable Development Goals

Source: United Nations[24]

The 2030 Agenda includes the Sustainable Development Goal 12 on consumption and production, which is probably the most innovative goal of the agenda. It makes clear that production is

- 59 -

coupled with consumption habits and vice-versa. Societies are required to produce, live, and consume in a different way.

Sustainable development is a comprehensive concept encompassing environmental, social, and economic aspects. It reflects growing awareness of the links between mounting environmental problems and socio-economic issues.[25] The World Conservation Strategy played a pivotal role in advancing the use of the concept at the global level.[26] The United Nations has worked on the promotion of the sustainable development concept for several decades. "Our Common Future," also known as the Brundtland Report, was published in 1987 and was years ahead of its time in its conception of development: "Development that meets the needs and aspirations of the present without compromising the ability of future generations to meet their own needs."[27]

The Sustainable Development Goals have been widely recognized by governments at all levels, companies of different sizes, professional associations, many advocacy-oriented nonprofits, and different faith communities. A letter from the Holy See of September 2016 regarding the 2030 Agenda for Sustainable Development has been published on the website of the UN General Assembly. The Pope analyzes the 2030 Agenda from the perspective of the Catholic Church and emphasizes the concept of human dignity. The German Ministry for Economic Cooperation and Development regularly engages with stakeholders from the private sector and civil society organizations as well as with the general public on the SDGs. It has also organized a conference on the engagement of different religions with the 2030 Agenda and the 17 SDGs, stressing that "the religions have long since acknowledged the one-world-reality, emphasized human dignity and ethical values across nations and borders and worked with poor and marginalized sections of society."[28] The International Partnership on Religion and Sustainable Development (PaRD) held its Annual Forum and General Assembly of Members in November 2021 in Stelle Stellenbosch, South Africa.

In Germany, the 2030 Agenda is a key reference framework for the work of Bread for the World, the globally active development and relief agency of the Protestant Churches in Germany which supports development cooperation projects in more than 90 countries. The same is true for Misereor, the German Catholic Bishops' Organization for Development Cooperation. The United Nations has also launched a task force on Engaging Faith-Based Actors for Sustainable Development. The Islamic Reporting Initiative (IRI) is among the key stakeholders. In 2015, the IRI was commended by the Organization of Islamic Cooperation (OIC), the second-largest intergovernmental organization after the United Nations, with a membership of 57 states across four continents. The organization won the 2018 Global Islamic Finance Award for the Sustainable Development Goals category.

3.3 What Kind of Action is Needed?

The debate on climate action and sustainability is very complex. Emissions of greenhouse gases, mainly carbon dioxide and methane, are related to production, transport, and consumption patterns in multiple sectors. They are also connected to deep-rooted economic, social, and cultural practices. Thus, climate action needs to be embedded into holistic approaches to change economic development pathways.

There are no quick fixes to halt climate change. The Japanese energy economist Yoichi Kaya has developed a mathematical representation of what drives carbon dioxide emissions, which are chiefly responsible for climate change. Simplified, it looks something like this:

Emissions = Population × GDP Per Capita × Energy Intensity × Carbon Intensity.[29]

Looking at the terms of this formula, it is inevitable that heated debates will arise as to which strategies are best suited to reducing carbon dioxide emissions. The focus of climate action is mostly on the latter two terms, energy intensity and carbon intensity, because the first two—population growth and GDP growth—are highly controversial to address. Energy intensity and carbon intensity could be reduced by technological innovations, especially the use of renewable energies.

Actions on climate change are typically grouped into several categories: climate mitigation, climate adaptation, carbon capture and storage, and geoengineering.

Climate mitigation focuses on reducing emissions, for example, by reducing fossil-fuel-based energy production through renewable energies, energy saving, and energy efficiency measures. Renewable energies have already become more competitive than most conventional energy sources and nuclear energy. The significant decline in the price of renewable energies has given the business community and governments confidence that green investments will pay off. This has happened much more quickly than many predicted. National energy structures, however, differ greatly depending on their reserves of natural resources like coal and gas. This explains why countries like Russia and Poland are reluctant to quickly shift to renewables.

Climate adaptation is about adjustment to climate change. Climate change has already happened and will worsen, at least in the near future, endangering livelihoods in many countries.

Other measures of climate actions have gained prominence more recently. Carbon capture and storage is about capturing carbon dioxide before it enters the atmosphere, transporting it, and storing it for centuries or millennia, for example in deep geological formations or in the form of mineral carbonates. The Orca, an installation built by Climeworks in Iceland, is able to capture 4,000 metric tons of carbon dioxide per year and could serve as a blueprint for similar technologies. In 2021, its costs were still high: 600–800 U.S. dollars per metric ton of carbon dioxide, far from the levels 100–150 U.S. dollars per ton that are necessary to turn a profit without the help of any government subsidies.[30] However, costs are expected to fall significantly in the next decade.

Geoengineering concerns deliberate, large-scale intervention in the Earth's natural systems to counteract climate change and refers as well to technologies like the installation of space reflectors, the injections of aerosols into the stratosphere, and albedo enhancement, which increases the reflectiveness of clouds or land surfaces so that more of the sun's heat is reflected back into space. The IPCC considers geoengineering part of the solution to successfully tackling climate change. Many activists, however, point to possible unforeseeable consequences for people and the environment, cite governance challenges, or consider geoengineering a very overrated technology in comparison to the potential of climate change mitigation efforts.

The strategies to combat climate change and promote sustainability transitions are diverse. The WEF has focused on technology development, citing examples of advanced sensor technologies to help create a healthier environment. Sensors can help farmers reduce the volume of chemicals in their fields, and "smart boats" can help fishermen manage their catch effectively, increasing profits and sustaining fish stocks in the sea.[31]

Many organizations recognize the great potential of nature-based solutions. Standing forests, healthy soils, mangroves, salt marshes, oceans, coral reefs, and other ecological systems all play a role in sequestering atmospheric carbon dioxide. One-third of the global challenge in reducing carbon dioxide emissions could be met by protecting healthy ecosystems and supporting reforestation alone. Another issue is the use of land. Climate protection can only succeed if the dramatic loss of biological diversity is halted and the global food system is made more sustainable.

This is a huge challenge and making international cooperation work in order to address climate change is a *must*. In addition to global summits aimed at raising climate policy ambitions, drafting regulations, monitoring, and reporting on NDCs, emissions trading is a widely discussed instrument. If well designed and implemented, it has great potential to curb emissions, especially if national-level and regional-level emissions trading schemes are harmonized and integrated into higher levels of governance mechanisms.

Emissions trading is a market-based approach to controlling pollution by providing economic incentives for reducing the emissions of pollutants in places where it is most cost effective.

"Countries and regions around the world are developing emissions trading systems as a means to place a price on greenhouse gas (GHG) emissions. Such programs are now in place in Europe, North America, China, and other parts of Asia — they are being considered in South America and several other regions."[32]

It is crucial to design these programs well, gradually connect emissions trading markets, and unify coverage of industries, ambitions, and standards across continents to set a level playing field for companies and thus make the incentive work. If the schemes are designed well, they include many economic sectors and gradually reduce the absolute number of allowed emissions in a significant way.

Emissions trading across countries and continents has long been criticized, including by climate activists. One of the arguments against global emissions trading is that one should not offer low-cost opportunities for polluters to offset emissions through projects in other parts of the world which are difficult to monitor.

Other strands of criticism focus on the frequently high caps for total emissions. This was a key problem of the European Emission Trading System (EETS), which has kept the price for carbon at a low level for a long time. This, however, has changed. There is now significant evidence that emissions trading provides strong incentives to reduce emissions and promote good practices and awareness in other parts of the world.

Patrick Beyer and Michaël Aklin even argue "that despite low prices, carbon markets can help reduce emissions." Using a statistical model and sectoral emissions data, they found that "the EU ETS, which initially regulated roughly 50 percent of EU carbon emissions from mainly energy production and large industrial polluters, saved more than 1 billion tons of CO_2 between 2008 and 2016."[33]

The approach must always be to avoid and reduce emissions and offset the emissions that cannot be avoided today through climate protection projects. How does emissions trading work in practice and how does it generate benefits?

Let us take, as an example, a family who lives in rural Africa and traditionally cooks with a three-stone stove. If this family receives an energy-efficient stove through a climate protection project, then not only does the carbon dioxide balance improve, but there are also other positive effects for the family: between 60 percent and 80 percent of firewood can be saved with an energy-efficient stove. This means enormous time savings for women and children who typically collect wood. In addition, the risk of burns and smoke development is significantly reduced.[34] At the same time, we should not forget that Africa as a continent emits the least carbon dioxide next to South America and climate action is primarily needed in countries with high per capita emissions.

Another important aspect of emissions trading is that it will lead to massive collection of pollution data on emissions in different industries and sectors. This is an indispensable step in curbing emissions in an effective, efficient, and transparent way and creates awareness in industries covered by cap-and-trade regimes.

With regard to climate justice, there are political and philosophical debates over who should take responsibility for reducing emissions. Oxford scholar Henry Shue has proposed a distinction between "subsistence emissions" and "luxury emissions." Subsistence emissions are those necessary for securing the basic right to subsistence, whereas luxury emissions are those that exceed a minimally adequate level of emissions. According to Shue, it is morally unacceptable to ask the poor to sacrifice subsistence emissions so that the affluent can maintain luxury emissions.[35]

3.4 Growing Engagement of International Organizations, Research, and Advocacy Groups

We are witnessing a growing engagement of international organizations, research, and advocacy groups in data collection and analysis, monitoring, and reporting on climate and sustainability policies. We argue that their work prepares the ground for more ambitious climate policies by many countries and companies. There are many specialized agencies and/organizations related to the United Nations that make substantial contributions to climate action and sustainability. Next to the UN organizations, there are also other international organizations that provide policy analysis and advice to governments.

China, by far the largest emitter of greenhouse gases, has shown openness to cooperation with organizations of the United Nations and other international and regional organizations. The International Energy Agency (IEA), a Paris-based autonomous intergovernmental organization established by the Organization for Economic Co-operation and Development (OECD), has drafted a carbon neutrality roadmap for China in response to the Chinese government's invitation to cooperate on long-term strategies to reach carbon neutrality in the energy sector. The IEA correctly affirms that there "is no plausible path to limiting the global temperature rise to 1.5 °C without China." It further points out that "the energy sector is the source of almost 90 percent of China's greenhouse gas emissions, so energy policies must drive the transition to carbon neutrality."

Figure 3.2: Total Primary Energy Demand in China in the Announced Pledges Scenario (APS), 1980–2060

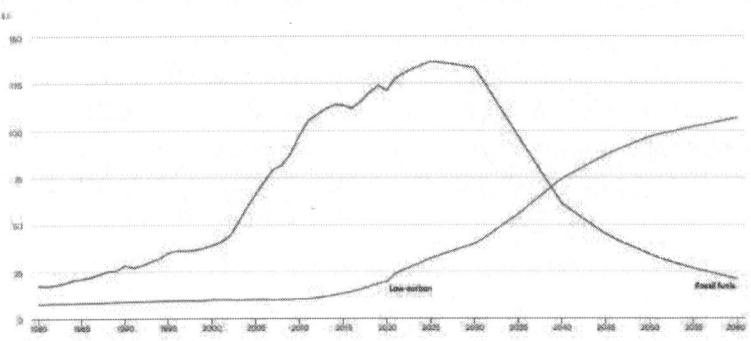

Source: IEA (2021)[36]

According to the IEA report "An Energy Sector Roadmap to Carbon Neutrality in China," solar energy will become the number one energy source for China by 2045. The IEA believes that China is capable of making the transition even faster.[37] The IEA's calculations demonstrate convincingly that energy transition is underway in China, even though structural adjustments are proving as painful as they are in many other countries.

The growing volume of climate action and sustainability data is providing political leadership in many countries and cities with the necessary information to act. The publishing house Elsevier has compiled a report on "The Power of Data to Advance the SDGs. Mapping research for the Sustainable Development Goals," which provides an idea of the broad range of academic disciplines engaged in sustainability research.[38] Scientific communities across disciplines tell us very clearly that the consequences of climate change will be disastrous for humanity if adequate response strategies are further delayed. Researchers point out that humanity's impact on the Earth is now so profound that a new geological epoch — the Anthropocene — needs to be declared to replace the current epoch, the 12,000-year-old Holocene, during which all human civilization developed, and which has been characterized by relatively stable climate since the last ice age.

The German nonprofit organization Germanwatch and the Climate Action Network (CAN) publish the Climate Change Performance Index (CCPI) in cooperation with more than 350 climate and energy experts. The report details specific challenges and policies in different countries and tracks countries' efforts to combat climate change. The CCPI is an independent monitoring tool that aims to enhance transparency in international climate politics and comparison of climate protection efforts and progress made by individual countries. The CCPI evaluates 60 countries and the European Union, which together generate over 90 percent of global greenhouse gas emissions. Using standardized criteria, the CCPI looks at four categories, with 14 indicators: Greenhouse Gas Emissions (40 percent of the overall score), Renewable Energy (20 percent), Energy Use (20 percent), and Climate Policy (20 percent).

Figure 3.3: Categories of the Climate Change Performance Index (CCPI)

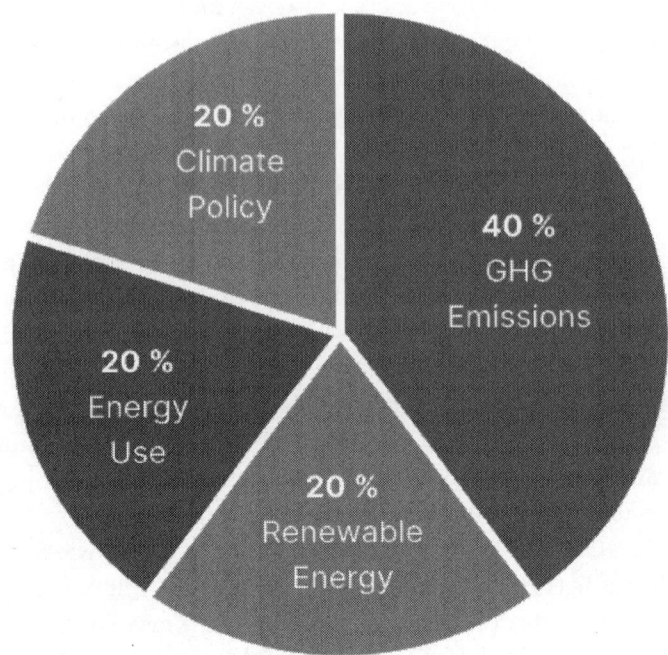

Source: CCPI (2021)[39]

No country performs well enough in all index categories to achieve an overall "very high" rating in the index. The top-runners in the 2022 CCPI are Denmark, Sweden, and Norway, followed by the United Kingdom, Morocco, and Chile.[40] India ranks relatively highly, in tenth, three places before Germany, which is often praised as a frontrunner in climate action. The main reason for this is that India still exhibits low per-capita emissions. Its emissions will probably never reach the level of the United States or most European countries, even though it has not yet abandoned its construction of new coal-fired plants.

India currently emits 1.77 tons of carbon dioxide per capita, compared to China's 7.41 tons per capita, Germany's 7.69 tons, and the United States's 14.24 tons. Nigeria, rich in oil, emits only 0.61 tons per capita.[41]

Climate Action and Sustainability

Jeremy Rifkin, in his book *The Green New Deal: Why the Fossil Fuel Civilization Will Collapse by 2028*, praises the European Union for its bold initiatives in the field of climate action and calls Germany "an undisputed world leader in addressing climate change." From a German perspective, his analysis comes as a surprise because the country is failing to meet its climate reduction targets, especially in the transport sector. Other countries also rank higher in index projects that compare climate policies, such as the aforementioned CCPI. However, policies in Germany and elsewhere in the EU are expected to change with the European Green Deal, announced by Ursula von der Leyen, president of the European Commission, in December 2019.The CCPI tries to balance different parameters of climate action and demonstrates that China-bashing or India-bashing is not quite appropriate, especially from the perspective of the United States, which ranks low in the index (55), just one place ahead of Russia (56).

The number of organizations joining the climate action movement is impressive. They accumulate expertise and knowledge, critically observe international conferences, policies, and regulations of countries, and are engaged in project work. The New Climate Institute (NCI) is one such organization and is involved in the CCPI. The NCI tracks, evaluates, and compares climate change mitigation actions from a wide range of national, subnational, corporate, and civil society actors and provides policy analysis and advice. We interviewed Swithin Lui and Sofia Gonzales-Zuñiga of the NCI to discuss the development of climate action strategies.

Interview with Sofia Gonzales-Zuñiga and Swithin Lui, NewClimate Institute

Q: How do you see global climate action developing? Which are the new priorities and strategies?
Sofia Gonzales-Zuñiga: Generally, in recent years, we have seen positive developments with regard to the implementation of the Paris Agreement, with countries making their targets and strategies more ambitious over time. In the five years since the Paris

Global Perspectives on Megatrends

Agreement, an increasing number of countries have also adopted net-zero targets and last year there was a "wave" of net-zero announcements from the major emitters. The transition to a zero emissions society has clearly begun but we are still missing action on the ground. In order to reach the ambition planned for mid-century, policy implementation needs to move faster.

Swithin Lui: On a national level, the difference in ambition over the past ten years for some countries cannot be overstated. Many influential companies, in particular in the U.S., have transitioned from greenwashing to action as they have begun matching and adapting to national carbon policies and long-term strategies toward net-zero. Even during the COVID-19 economic downturn, we have seen a continuing proliferation of climate targets from non-state actors. For example, in China, industry, corporations, and sub-sectors are already planning into the distant future to directly reflect government's high-level five-year and longer-term policy signals. In the upcoming decades, as the cheapest emissions reductions options are achieved and implemented worldwide, a greater focus of mitigation action will turn toward novel solutions in hard-to-abate sectors — such as heavy industry, aviation and shipping, agriculture, chemicals, freight transport, and construction — where full emissions reductions are not yet economically or technologically viable.

Q: What are some promising strategies to achieve carbon neutrality and how do the strategies of major economies differ? Do you think that China, the EU, and the U.S. will achieve their objectives?

Swithin Lui: There are numerous applicable strategies for all, which if designed and implemented in a smart and inclusive manner, can yield no-regret policies that also help achieve carbon neutrality while improving general quality of life. Phasing out fossil fuels in energy supply and replacing them with renewables, moving away from conventional polluting private transport modes, and scaling up building retrofits are some on a long list. Dependency on coal, the most carbon intensive source, varies globally and will remain a critical geopolitical topic for the next decade. The U.S. and the EU are currently moving toward phasing out coal in the next 20 years while in China, it is likely to remain a significant energy source for longer. Phasing out coal (and other fossil fuels) is a critical first step to ensure clean energy supply in the power sector, as promising solutions to reduce emissions in other economic activities such as transport and industry will require large-scale electrification and smart integration with the power sector. Thankfully, the economic case for renewable energy is already favorable compared to fossil fuels in most of the world today, and renewables will continue to get even cheaper with every year. A range of other promising novel energy solutions, such as the conversion of power to other fuels applicable in industry and transport, will receive large-scale R&D efforts in all major economies. Putting a price on carbon emissions is an essential step to incentivize clean technology; annual investment in clean technologies will need to double or triple annually to meet global climate targets in the next half century.

In the U.S. and the EU, much of climate action and technological incubation may be primarily driven by growing bottom-up pressure from international organizations, business communities, and civil society, while China continues to adopt a more top-down governance approach to climate policy. It is still expected that economies will stay on track with mitigation targets for the next decade, although it is clear that these targets are not ambitious enough. Achieving zero emission targets in the next 30–50 years for these economies is still uncertain and faces many unresolved challenges.

Sofia Gonzales-Zuñiga: The first step has been taken, there are commitments on the table, the pressure to take action is on and international relations between countries are playing a key role in maintaining the momentum for climate action. But the jury is still out as to whether countries can meet their commitments. Based on our analysis at the Climate Action Tracker, governments have yet to adopt sufficient policies to actually meet the targets they have set. There is little evidence pointing to a single promising strategy to achieve carbon neutrality, but a key element is the development of short- and medium-term plans and implementation roadmaps to define interim steps toward the mid-century goal.

Q: What will be the significance of carbon dioxide removal technologies in 2050?
Sofia Gonzales-Zuñiga: The Intergovernmental Panel on Climate Change refers to such technologies but also states that the deployment of carbon dioxide removal (CDR) measures entails clear risks. In general, through our assessment we often suggest that countries should avoid relying on forest sinks to achieve their climate targets as much as possible, given the high chance of carbon loss through deforestation or natural disturbance and eventual competition for land.

Another organization that has made even more headlines is the school-strike movement Fridays for Future (FFF), inspired by Greta Thunberg who sat outside the Swedish Parliament on every school day in summer 2018 to demand urgent action on the climate crisis.[42] She was soon joined by others, first in Sweden, later in Europe and in many other countries across the globe. In Germany, FFF activists, especially Luisa Neubauer and her cousin Carla Reemtsma, the FFF spokesperson, are regular guests on popular TV talk shows. FFF organized many online events during the COVID-19 restrictions and made big efforts to connect to media and the general public via digital means.

We talked to two FFF activists based in Germany and asked them about the future of the movement, as well as what they think should be done in terms of climate action.

Interview with Line Niedeggen and Asuka Kähler, Activists, Fridays for Future

Q: What are the best strategies to broaden and deepen consensus on ambitious climate policies at the global level?
Asuka Kähler: FFF like any other movement or organization must adapt to changing circumstances and contexts. School strikes are not really the way to go anymore, we need to change and adapt our strategies as an organization. During the pandemic, we organized digital events, email actions, and tried out other formats to keep

engaged with the public, the scientific, and also the policymaking community.

Q: Are we correct in the assumption that some or many in FFF advocate for system change, for overcoming capitalist structures to achieve the goals set by the Paris Agreement and achieving carbon neutrality as soon as possible? Do you see a trend in which FFF is developing?

Asuka Kähler: You are correct, as most, if not all current members would agree on this. There is of course the famous "system change, not climate change" slogan, so this is not really something that is being debated internally, nor is it controversial. There is a small minority within the organization, according to a latest internal poll in Germany, around one-quarter to be precise, that thinks we should still go on, but still, this does not mean that they don't believe in change of some form.

Line Niedeggen: I think I would also agree, if the word "capital" was not part of that sentence, as everyone agrees that the system is simply too slow to facilitate change as of this moment.

Q: Why do you have little confidence in the regulatory authorities of free market economies and in incentives for technology development to change course and implement far more ambitious objectives?

Asuka Kähler: The truth of the matter is that we are not moving quick and far enough with some adjustments in regulations and some incentives for technology development. Growth is simply not sustainable indefinitely and we need to prepare people slowly but surely for a stabilization and a reduction in the standard of living. Only then can we achieve global justice.

Line Niedeggen: To add to this, when people complain that they will lose too much, they account only for the rich people, not for the poor. Poor people will be more affected by climate change and the longer we wait, the more if will affect them.

Q: Did the COVID-19 pandemic raise your optimism or pessimism in the commitment of governments to fight climate change, in Germany and elsewhere?

Line Niedeggen: Yes and no. On the one hand, I think that more people see the need for systemic change as humans always try to learn from global crises and tend to be more open to changes in periods of crisis. The pandemic triggered a process of deeper reflections on issues of justice, including climate justice but also inequality issues. We have witnessed a strong surge of the Black Lives Matter movement, which shows the limits of tolerance toward inequality. This will also apply to burden sharing of the consequences of climate change. On the other hand, we have not seen sufficient green recovery packages. Many of the big spending packages of governments just aim to reset the old patters of production and consumption, or their initial green ambitions have been watered down.

The interviews with the New Climate Institute and Fridays for Future show that the climate action movement has made significant contributions to moving climate change to the top of many government agendas.

3.5 Climate Actions at the Level of Cities

Cities play a key role in promoting climate actions as many of them are very vulnerable to climate change. Many of the large agglomerations are near coastal areas and are affected by rising sea levels. Many cities suffer from heat concentrations; a heat wave infamously killed 15,000 people in France in 2003, most of them in Paris. Cities also contribute to accelerating anthropogenic climate change, as they consume two-thirds of the world's energy and create over 70 percent of global carbon dioxide emissions.

Cities are considered hubs of growth, research, and innovation. They often have a high concentration of visionary, educated, and cosmopolitan people and attract many business travelers and tourists. International organizations and the EU pay significant emphasis to promote climate action at the level of cities. The Circular Cities and Regions initiative is part of the European Commission's new circular economy action plan. It will implement circular solutions at local and regional scale and help deliver on the European Green Deal and the EU bioeconomy strategy.[43]

The C40 is one of the most powerful city networks and takes strong action on climate change and sustainability transformation. "Cities have the power to change the world" reads the C40 headline online. "For centuries, cities have been centers of commerce, culture and innovation, and the birthplace for some of humankind's greatest ideas. At this critical crossroads in time, we need the ideas that cities can create more than ever."[44]

Berthold Kuhn lived and worked for some years in the coastal city of Xiamen in the south of China. Xiamen is one of the most beautiful and innovative cities in China. Xiamen has carried the label of a low-carbon city since 2011 and is a global frontrunner in developing a "sponge city" approach. This term refers to all kinds of measures to protect urban areas from flooding and collecting and re-using rainwater in a smart way.

Many Chinese live in floodplain urban areas. The Chinese government has released a series of guidelines for building sponge cities. It wants 80 percent of its cities to collect and recycle 70 percent of rainwater by 2030. Zhengzhou, the capital of Henan province, announced as far back as 2018 that 90 percent of its core urban area would comply with sponge city standards.[45]

The city of Berlin, where the authors currently live, has also started to focus more on rainwater management and established a "rainwater agency" in 2018. The agency provides advisory services to construction companies and supports private initiatives, such as green roofs, with seed money. The city administrators are reluctant to call it a sponge city approach as the investment is much lower than in other places. Exposure to flooding is less dramatic than in most Chinese cities, but likely to increase in the context of climate change.

In the field of climate action, Berlin and many other German cities focus on decentralized and participatory policymaking and implementation. In 2000, the German Feed-in Tariff as part of the Energieeinspeisegesetz (EEG) — Germany's Renewable Energy Act that includes a permission for households to feed in electricity from solar panels into the public grid—came into force to promote the widespread production of renewable energy by giving people the chance to invest in renewable energy projects. Most renewable energy infrastructure in Germany is today owned by private individuals, cooperatives, and institutions. Freie Universität Berlin installed solar panels on its roofs and significantly lowered its long-term energy supply costs.

The Berlin city administration fosters partnerships and signs agreements with public utility companies, hospitals, and universities to improve energy efficiency. Berlin runs an Energy and Climate Protection Program 2030 (BEK 2030), which was adopted by the Berlin House of Representatives on January 25, 2018. This reflects the decision to make the city carbon-neutral by 2050. One of its most innovative features is the transparent digital monitoring systems, called diBEK which allow everybody to review the progress in implementation.[46] In addition, the system includes the monitoring of direct consequences of climate change in the state of Berlin. The diBEK is offered by the Senate Department for the Environment, Transport and Climate Protection. This is certainly a good practice, though some experts voiced doubts that the implementation and monitoring will meet expectations.

In Berlin, as in most other parts of Germany, the transport sector fails to achieve emissions reduction targets. The city of Berlin has enacted a new mobility law which came into being after a biking network initiated a public referendum in 2015, and a comprehensive follow-up process, called the "cycling law dialogue." The Mobility Act was relatively quickly adopted in June 2018.

The Berlin Mobility Act consists of several elements and takes account of diverse modes of transport. The individual elements will take shape over time. The incremental approach is an innovative feature of law-making. The law will ultimately ensure that walking, cycling, and public transport are prioritized. The expansion of bike lanes and the limitation of parking space for cars are underway. Citizens can even apply for subsidies to rent cargo bikes. However, the city government's plans met resistance from the local business community and others who deplore speed limits and the drastic reduction of parking space. In and around the creative area of Bergmannstraße in Kreuzberg, the sudden and drastic reduction of parking spaces was popular with young people and tourists. However, it was perhaps unhelpful to winning over the majority of people living or working in the area. Grassroots initiatives in Berlin tend to have a radical approach, focusing on banning private cars from the inner-city altogether or drastically restricting their use on the basis of vouchers. Der Volksentscheid Berlin Autofrei (Public Referendum Initiative on Car-free Berlin) collected more than 50,000 signatures in only three months in late 2021[47]. Fulfillment of the quorum requirement makes it mandatory for the Berlin city government, the Berlin Senate, to look into the matter.

3.6 The Future of Climate Action and Sustainability Transformations

The University of Cambridge Institute for Sustainability Leadership (CISL) measured the theoretical impact of three risk scenarios for combatting global warming.[48] The most positive scenario consists of a rapid shift from a fossil-fueled to a low-carbon world economy. This would require enormous investments in new infrastructure, especially renewable energy, as well as shifts in agricultural production, living, and consumption habits. The shift would be costly and produce a short period of high volatility and slow growth. Other scenarios of delayed action would be far more damaging, costly, and — importantly — reduce the predictability of climate change effects.

The sustainability transformation will happen, though we may not see linear progression toward more ambitious climate action. Eventually, however, climate and sustainability actions will affect almost all aspects of our lives. Climate skeptics — those ignoring mounting scientific evidence and questioning the impact of human economic activity on climate change — have contributed to challenging the trend. However, we believe that they will slowly become a tiny minority and steadily lose political influence. The electoral loss of President Trump, a climate change skeptic, is only one indicator. After he lost the presidential election in November 2020, the U.S. was able to re-engage in multilateral cooperation on climate action. Most of the U.S. business community and many city mayors had never stopped their climate action. Many had challenged the Trump administration throughout his presidential term. U.S. climate envoy John Kerry soon announced a freeze on new oil and gas leases on public lands and the doubling of energy produced by offshore wind farms by 2030.

Which climate action strategies and measures are promising, what kinds of reform and actions are needed, and which ones could realistically be implemented? How will proposed reforms and measures affect our lives?

As climate change worsens, there is a tendency to explore more options to tackle it. Different countries will prioritize different strategies when trying to balance climate-change–induced risks with economic, social, and political issues.

Carbon neutrality pathways is one subject, among others, related to future climate action, about which we spoke to Janos Pasztor, a seasoned career diplomat and climate expert who is now working as the executive director of the Carnegie Climate Governance Initiative (C2G) with offices in Geneva. He regularly speaks at international conferences and has much to share about how policy reforms and legislative proposals will develop.

Interview with Janos Pasztor, Director of the Carnegie Climate Governance Initiative

Q: How do carbon neutrality development paths differ between countries and regions? Which strategies are most promising and to what extent shall we see harmonization of strategies across major economies?

Janos Pasztor: Achieving climate neutrality by 2050 will require both rapid emissions reductions, and large-scale carbon dioxide removal approaches (to offset those emissions that prove difficult to cut).

How countries achieve this balance will vary depending on their politics, economies, and geography. Some will have more abundant natural resources, some stronger technology sectors, and some may be in a better position to pay others to do some of the work.

So the answer is paths will differ significantly. Rather than harmonizing approaches, the bottom line is that we need to agree on common definitions (such as what is "net-zero"), lay out our various responsibilities, and harmonize our methodologies for measurements so countries can work effectively together.

We should also keep in mind that we cannot simply be aiming toward net-zero. We will likely need to aim for net negative emissions if we seek to keep global warming below 1.5°C.

Achieving that can include many carbon dioxide removal approaches, both biological and technological. All of them create risks and challenges as well as benefits and opportunities, and need governance.

No one removal approach is likely to be enough. We should be cautious about overstating the potential for nature-based solutions, for example, as implementing them at large scale could create many challenges for the Sustainable Development Goals, including around land use and water. Permanence is also a challenge — forests are at risk of burning down; land may be converted to other uses.

Q: To what extent will we be able to extend carbon emissions trading schemes across countries and regions and build global carbon markets?

Janos Pasztor: I do not see it happening without a comprehensive global agreement, but countries and regions are indeed moving toward each other. We witness exchanges of ideas and practices between China and the EU, while the EU also talks to California and so on and so forth.

Many of the actors purchasing these credits are international corporations, which drive prices to similar levels, so we will see a gradual convergence of carbon price and harmonization of emissions trading across the globe.

Emissions trading, if well designed, sets strong incentives and also drives awareness-raising and, thus, is an important element of climate action.

However, we must also be careful to address common definitions and standards, so that international schemes genuinely achieve neutrality, and eventually net negative. There is scope for all sorts of accounting tricks in this area, which we must guard against. They may fool us, but they won't fool the atmosphere.

Q: How do you see global governance on climate action developing in the next decade? Will we see more global agreements? How can we balance ambition and inclusiveness, and will we see growing conflicts with countries in the Global South, for example, with reference to the principle of "common but differentiated responsibilities"?

Janos Pasztor: In short, yes, but first I want to make clear that when we talk about climate governance, we do not simply talk about government policies or regulation, but also about many different stakeholders (including CSOs, business, and so forth), in a broad process of learning, engaging in discussions, and participating in informed decision-making. This governance takes place at the local, national, and global levels, and different fora may be appropriate to tackle different issues.

Given this broader understanding of governance, I would say that ambition and inclusiveness are not at odds with each other. In fact, inclusive governance is essential to achieve the ambition we aspire to; without inclusion, we simply won't get there.

Of course, as you note, there are likely to be all sorts of areas of contention, which need to be resolved, but we cannot solve this problem if we don't resolve them.

With regards to my current area of interest, I see many gaps in carbon dioxide removal (CDR) governance that need to be addressed. This includes significant gaps in cooperation between international organizations which need to be addressed. As countries start working on the practicalities of achieving their 2050 net-zero commitments, they are coming to realize that they will not be able to achieve them without carbon dioxide removal, and that in practice this requires North-South cooperation.

For example, countries in the South may have a greater role than North in planting trees, and storing carbon, due to their geographic and economic situations. But how would that work?

Filling CDR governance gaps is therefore essential to achieve climate mitigation targets.

If we look ahead, we see other significant international governance gaps which will need to be addressed. This includes for solar radiation modification (SRM) — which is a set of approaches which would aim to reduce the global temperature by reflecting sunlight. But while these ideas could reduce climate impacts, they bring along many other challenges, which need to be addressed. And the simple truth is that no one knows how this will work.

We have to put these emerging CDR and SRM governance challenges on the table of global negotiations, for example in the context of G7 and G20 meetings.

Q: We are currently seeing a series of ambitious green deals and climate policy commitments. How many countries/regions will achieve carbon-neutrality in 2050?

Janos Pasztor: Nobody actually knows. While many countries have committed to climate neutrality, achieving it is much easier said than done. Most countries do not have clear measured and costed paths to achieve this, including how to achieve (or pay for) the large-scale carbon dioxide removal required to offset the most persistent emissions.

Some — perhaps many — countries will fail, while some will go beyond their initial targets. The bottom line is that achieving net-zero by 2050 is incredibly challenging even at a national level, let alone at the global level.

It is likely to require removing very large amounts of carbon dioxide from the air as well as using approaches which are not properly governed or ready for scale-up. And it's not just the technology that's a challenge — it's bringing societies and economies along, in what is really a short amount of time. My view is the world is quite unlikely to get there, but that must not stop us from doing everything in our power to make sure it does. We still have a chance, and we need to embrace it. The cost of not achieving this will be immeasurable.

Q: What will be the significance of carbon dioxide removal technologies in 2050?

Janos Pasztor: By the middle of the century there's every chance that carbon dioxide removal will be the main focus of climate policy, assuming most emissions have been reduced. Both biological and technological approaches will be playing a role.

Already we can see significant and growing interest from major companies and investors, and every indication is this will continue to rise. Some see this as the source of new billion-dollar — and perhaps trillion-dollar — businesses, although it is important to be wary of overclaiming what is actually feasible, given the many governance challenges that remain, and of playing to perverse incentives. As I said before, the technology is not enough: This is a society-wide challenge, and many important decisions needed to be made to remove gigatons of carbon dioxide in practice.

This includes addressing the potential sense in some quarters that carbon dioxide removal could be an alternative, rather than a supplement, to climate change mitigation efforts, which we must avoid.

In summary, climate policymakers will need to find ways of filling in the CDR governance gaps, to make sure CDR technology rolls out in an inclusive way in line with sustainable development goals, and keep up the pressure on removing all carbon dioxide emissions.

If we have not achieved climate neutrality by 2050, CDR will also need to be scaled up to a level that achieves net negative and removes sufficient carbon dioxide to ensure the world gets back to a safer temperature. This would likely be one of the biggest collective endeavors humankind has yet embarked upon.

The proposed policy reforms and new legislation will play out differently across countries and regions. In some countries, economic areas, and spheres of life, climate-policy–induced disruptions will be felt more than in others, especially by the lower-middle classes. Some lower income groups might have to give up their family cars, reduce international holiday travel, and cope with soaring utility costs, so their discontent at higher fuel prices, higher energy efficiency standards, and carbon taxes is understandable. In some countries, compensation schemes have been implemented, but people still feel are pushed to change their lives, which—for many—is already hard enough. Expert analysis, however, tells us that drastic changes are indeed needed and that they should be facilitated by smart compensation and phasing-out policies.

In areas where rapid change and disruptions will be needed, resistance to climate action is likely to be strong, especially among the middle-aged and older population who will have to change lifestyles and habits. The European Green Deal calls for a 90 percent reduction in greenhouse gas emissions from transport, in order for the EU to become a climate-neutral economy by 2050. Some issues are also emotionally charged. In Germany, resistance is strong in the field of mobility. Germany is a car-driving nation. It is global export champion of medium- and high-end vehicles. Driving a car was synonymous with freedom for past generations. Some highways still have no speed limits.

The shift toward electromobility experienced a slow start and met strong resistance in many countries, including Germany. Once the most technologically advanced, German carmakers became laggards in the field of electromobility. Eventually, electromobility began to take off slowly, as other global car markets, especially China, started heading toward electric vehicles. The German middle class, especially the younger generations, had also gotten used to cheap flights. The German railway operator, Deutsche Bahn, holds a monopoly on almost all routes. Trains are comfortable, though tickets are highly priced. Young people prefer buses which offer cheaper fares but pollute the environment more than trains. In many European cities, people are still used to parking their cars free of charge in front of their homes, even in big cities. While many want to delay any changes to the status quo, we can also see a growing number of people, especially younger people, campaigning for radical measures, for greener, car-free inner cities, and clear traffic priority for pedestrians, cyclists, and public transport, which are far more environmentally efficient and effective means of transport than individual cars. The new German political party, Klimaliste, stands for much more radical changes in climate action than does the Green Party, which for some has become part of the political establishment. It is challenging the slow pace of reforms by pointing to scientific facts and figures on climate change. Political conflicts are becoming more intense. The majority of people are still against radical change, though many educated people tend to agree with the need for change as long as it does not affect their personal lives. "Not in My Backyard" (NIMBY) is an attitude described by social scientists who research social resistance to technological change.

In electoral multi-party democracies, political parties need to muster support from large sections of the population if they want to win elections and rule the country. In countries with highly fragmented political landscapes, as is the case in almost all European countries, compromises are needed to form ruling coalitions. Disappointments usually set in quickly, coalitions fail, political alliances change, and government administrations often fail to meet their targets. This sounds like a gloomy outlook.

This is one reason why we are not advocating for the most radical political solutions to address climate change and biodiversity loss, like Extinction Rebellion and other activist groups, at least in the short run. We are aware of the complexity of policymaking and governance in modern societies and consider a determined but still balanced approach to be the most realistic way to achieve durable results.

What raises our optimism is the large number of researchers, experts, and activists from different background and disciplines who are analyzing the potential of climate actions and advising international and regional organizations, governments, cities, and corporations on how to overcome obstacles to implement effective climate action measures. We are also confident that new technological developments will make substantial contributions to emission reductions. The Royal Swedish Academy of Sciences awarded three scientists a Nobel prize in October 2019 for their work in developing lithium-ion batteries. Lithium batteries can be charged faster and more often than traditional batteries. As their weight and price continue to fall, they are playing an increasingly pivotal role in decarbonizing the transport sector by making electric vehicles cheaper.[49] We will further discuss the connection between technological development and sustainability issues in the following chapter on digitalization.

There are many institutions and experts involved in addressing climate mitigation and climate adaptation. Global attention usually focuses on the targets and strategies of bigger countries. Climate action, however, is a global movement. We should also listen to how it is conducted in smaller countries, and listen to what issues are at stake in the process of implementation. We spoke about this with Thomas Scheutzlich, who has been working in the Caribbean region for two decades and who provides advice to Caribbean regional organizations and national governments as well as international organizations. The Caribbean islands expect strong international support for adaptation measures, but they also want to demonstrate that they are supporting climate mitigation at their level best. However, structural issues and some vested interests stay in the way.

Interview with Thomas Scheutzlich, NDC Country Coordinator for Saint Lucia, Caribbean

Q: What are the key success factors for green energy shift policies from an international comparative perspective and what are typical stumbling blocks for such reforms?
Thomas Scheutzlich: There are many aspects to compare. Of course, energy infrastructure structures are different and pose different challenges to Caribbean countries. I would like to draw attention to some legal and regulatory issues which are sometimes overlooked. It is useful to compare the case of Germany and the Caribbean to illustrate my point. In the Caribbean, energy legislation is sometimes 10–20 years old and needs amendment, while

there is no obligation to formulate the regulations (rules on how to implement a law) within a time limit, unlike in Germany. In addition, most governments right now just do not have the capacity or the political will to actually implement the required legal amendments. In that sense, a lot of what I call "unfinished regulatory reforms" exist. One common factor in the Caribbean is the universal monopolies granted to electric utilities for the generation, transmission, distribution, and sale of electricity. These monopolies, which are also a result of small energy markets, are usually granted for many decades or are even unlimited in time. Centralized energy infrastructures make the islands more susceptible to a complete shutdown, should a hurricane or another natural disaster strike the centralized power infrastructure. On top of this, the energy usage (intensity) is also much higher compared for example to the EU.

Besides abundant renewable energy sources in Caribbean countries like solar power, wind power, and biomass — and in selected countries hydro and geothermal power — the region has a huge and largely untapped potential for energy savings that can be mobilized through the application of energy-efficient technologies in all sectors. However, the consequent application of energy-efficient technologies is still in "infant stage."

Q: How do you see the implementation of the Paris Agreement on climate action from the perspective of a consultant and advisor to international and regional organizations?

Thomas Scheutzlich: It is a comprehensive agreement that guides policies and investment decisions across the globe. Let me focus on the small island states in the Caribbean where I work a lot: For the Caribbean islands, the implementation of the Paris Agreement represents hope for global action, and is also an important opportunity to attract investments and build good and lasting development partnerships. Broadly speaking, there are two types of activities in the national NDCs: firstly, enabling activities, like the improvement of legal frameworks and increase of national capacities; and secondly, investment projects with quantifiable contributions to the avoidance of GHG emissions. Enabling activities are contained in most Caribbean NDCs and are a necessary precondition for the implementation of quantifiable investment projects. In other words, without increasing the national capacities and creating conducive legal frameworks, it will be difficult to attract national or foreign investments in mitigation and adaptation projects.

Q: How will climate change play out in the Caribbean region, one of the regions where you have worked for many years? How do you evaluate the prospects of protecting the island states through effective adaptation measures?

Thomas Scheutzlich: The Caribbean is a vulnerable region and climate change will only make the situation worse, with more and more dangerous hurricanes, floodings, troughs, earthquakes, and other extreme weather events threatening to strike the Caribbean territories. Volcanic eruptions have also been more common in the past decades, with St. Vincent recently having to evacuate an entire city. Centralized electricity generation facilities are outdated and must be decentralized in the interest of energy security. Emergency shelters like churches, schools, and public buildings need to be improved in terms of their climate resilience, civil structures, sanitary facilities, and emergency power supply to provide adequate protection of the public in the aftermath of natural disasters.

Other important critical infrastructure like secure water supply, sustainable public transport, and the protection of natural resources like forestry resources and agriculture also need to be developed and strengthened in order to increase the climate resilience of the Caribbean region.

Q: Will we see more migration in the future in the Caribbean region, relating to climate change?

Thomas Scheutzlich: Current trends suggest that this is not necessarily the case, as young people go to get their education abroad, in the U.S., Canada, or the EU for example, but return in their retirement, having achieved financial stability. Population numbers have been steady, so I do not see this being the case, even if sea levels rise, most islands apart from low-lying islands like the Bahamas, will be fine.

Q: How do you see the relationship between climate change and "between-country" and "within-country" inequalities?

Thomas Scheutzlich: In the Caribbean there is an existing culture, reinforced and fostered by the regional organizations CARICOM and OECS, of mutual help, mainly in times of disaster. When hurricanes Maria and Irma hit Dominica and other territories in 2017, the richer countries were there to help and this of course makes sense, as natural disasters do not discriminate and can hit any country at any time. One thing that is not developed at its best is the exchange of lessons learned and communication between the countries when it comes to setting and achieving their goals, and this is where I see climate change, not just as a threat, but as a fantastic opportunity for the Caribbean countries to work together and achieve much more.

3.7 Sustainable Tourism

We should not lose sight of tourism's place in the future of sustainability transformations. Mass tourism has provided many jobs and income opportunities but is also an alarming phenomenon that sees the gradual but systematic destruction of the most beautiful places in the world.[50] Tourism, especially international aviation, impacts carbon dioxide emissions heavily. The impacts of climate change are also of considerable magnitude for many regions in the long term. Some regions will become far less attractive if temperature continues to rise further and forest fires get out of control.

The UN 2030 Agenda for Sustainable Development, SDG target 8.9, explicitly refers to the promotion of sustainable tourism because it creates jobs and promotes local culture and products. The importance of sustainable tourism is also highlighted in SDG target 12.b.[51] Tourism, climate, and sustainability issues are closely interlinked.

International air travel and growth projections from the tourism sector are not compatible with the IEA's net-zero scenario. We need to ask whether and to what extent tourism will be able to cope with the massive challenges ahead.[52] What about the future of overseas travel destinations? How can different aspects of sustainability be balanced with climate action? Voices from the Global

South, especially places which could be seriously affected by both climate change and climate policies, are often overlooked. We talked with Nirmal Shah, a sustainable tourism expert from the Seychelles and chief executive of Nature Seychelles, the largest and oldest environment NGO in the Seychelles archipelago, where it is involved in environmental conservation and management. Nature Seychelles is a member of the World Conservation Union (IUCN). Nirmal Shah argues that we need to adopt a holistic approach to climate action and sustainability transitions and that we should not lose sight of the situation and interests of small states. His arguments help us understand why climate policies and sustainability actions need to take into account the needs and legitimate interests of places which have become tourism hot spots. Countries in the Global South will continue to ask for massive financial support to facilitate transitions and place great hope in new carbon neutral technologies.

Interview with Nirmal Shah, Chief Executive of Nature Seychelles

Q: Many countries and regions depend on income from tourists. It will not be desirable, and will be very difficult, if not impossible, to restrict tourism. What could the tourism sector contribute to the sustainability transformation and climate action?

Nirmal Shah: We must start from the beginning. A lot of people mistakenly believe that tourism is by itself unsustainable and engage especially in flight shaming, but what they do not understand is that small islands like Seychelles are the victims of climate change and so when people tell others not to visit them, we are in fact being doubly punished. Seychelles is the richest country in GDP per capita in Africa because of tourism and we are dependent on it to finance our developmental and environmental protection efforts, in line with the Sustainable Development Goals. Tourism is our bedrock for a sustainable society.

Q: The tourism sector has recommitted itself to be "climate neutral" by 2050 through its 2021 Glasgow Declaration: "A

Commitment to a Decade of Tourism Climate Action." How do you assess this commitment?
Nirmal Shah: I followed the COP26 closely and have taken part in the others in the past, but did not think that this one would yield the results I would like to see, so I did not go this time around. My question is: What does this mean? Most people focus on aviation and the accompanying carbon footprint, but tourism is tied to other sectors like agriculture and shipping which must also become sustainable and change their practices for tourism to be carbon neutral. Agriculture is responsible for 27 percent of greenhouse gas emissions and there is progress in aviation with zero-carbon fuels and electric planes, but if the other sectors do not follow, then the tourist sector cannot conceivably become zero carbon by itself.

Q: What are key strategies for a responsible recovery of the tourism sector from the COVID-19 crisis? What will be the key factors of success?
Nirmal Shah: The most urgent matter is that of vaccine equity. It is impossible for the tourist sector to rebound if people's uncertainty around travel is not addressed. You cannot have herd immunity in France and the U.K., while the countries that are the recipients of all these travelers are being deprived of vaccines.
The other aspect is that of non-pharmaceutical interventions, which a recent paper focusing on the case of Seychelles shows are incredibly effective at preventing spikes in cases. Everything from mask wearing to banning mass gatherings and controlling people at funerals, weddings, and so forth, can help.

Q: How will policy commitments and strategies on promoting sustainable tourism develop in the Seychelles?
Nirmal Shah: To understand this, one must also realize how important tourism is to Seychelles. Before the COVID-19 pandemic, tourism amounted to 60 percent of the country's GDP. As soon as the pandemic hit, the GDP fell at a rate of 19 percent, while it was growing at 5–6 percent beforehand. We are dependent on tourism as a country and are committed to transforming the sector into a sustainable one. Pre-Covid we had 300,000 tourists per year, a relatively low number. These are what we call high-value clients, who

> spend a lot of money in a short time span, while the money goes to local businesses, which are owned by Seychellois people. That holds true for everything from small- to medium-size hotels to taxis and car rental services.

Adaptation to climate change requires enormous resources. Many small islands depend on revenue from tourism. However, even rich islands will have difficulties to afford the growing amounts of investments needed to address the consequences of climate change. The island of Sylt in Germany bordering the Wadden Sea, a United Nations Scientific and Cultural Organization (UNESCO) world heritage site, host of the wind surf world cup, and celebrity getaway, is at the frontline of climate change. It is hit by weather extremes and sea level rise.[53] So far, the revenue from tourism has helped the island halt land loss, but the costs for adaptation measures could significantly increase in the next decades.

Climate action and sustainability transitions shape government policies, investment decisions, and industries across the world. This megatrend will affect the life of almost every person and will attract the attention of a still growing number of researchers and activists. We shall see new business alliances and new business models tackling climate change. Serious efforts are underway to develop scenarios, from global warming to the rise of renewable energy capacities, and the sales of electric vehicles. Climate change will take its toll; and political negotiations on loss and damages. Especially in the Global South, will take center-stage of global summits. We also predict that emission-trading will further expand across countries and sectors.

Chapter 4

Digitalization

Digitalization refers to the integration of digital technologies into everyday life. This chapter explores how digitalization impacts our professional and private lives; how it influences the future of our work and our social interactions; and how it leads to new business models, and the way we collect and process information. Digitalization will also impact our value systems, and on systems of societal governance and political rule.

How will digitalization play out in different sectors? We shall discuss "push" factors for digitalization and address salient questions covering important economic, political, and socio-cultural aspects of digitalization. The trend received a big push in the context of the COVID-19 pandemic. The Asian countries' recipe for early success was the strict implementation of three measures: "testing, tracking, and isolating". The use of digitized technologies to collect information about citizens' movement patterns is far less controversial in most Asian countries than in Europe. In this light, Jürgen Gerhards and Michael Zürn, two eminent German social scientists, pointed to some inconsistencies of data privacy regulations and practices in Europe and the U.S.: "In Western Europe and North America...there is a tendency to largely prohibit the state from digital invasion of privacy, but to allow large private digital companies to access personal data. This is the wrong way to go. Companies have to be strictly controlled; at the same time, the state must be enabled to fulfill central state tasks such as protecting the health of its citizens and fighting crime".[1]

Tech companies have increasingly begun facing ever more scrutiny for their handling of data and the way they are operating their platforms, as well as the content that their users are exposed to. When Facebook was accused by whistleblowers of knowingly hosting hate speech and illegal activity in autumn 2021, the decline of its image entered a new phase, eventually leading to a rebranding and name changing.

Part of the company's efforts to rebrand itself has also been the heavy investment into the Metaverse where virtual realities are blended with real-life experience Bill Gates predicts that most virtual meetings will move to the Metaverse, where 3D virtual avatars will replace Zoom's "black squares".

Companies immediately jumped on board, setting up virtual stores, while the cryptocurrency world saw it as a great advertising opportunity and is closely linked to the initial hype around the "new" technology. There are grave concerns in this initial stage, as such worlds have existed for decades now in video games, such as "Second Life" or "World of Warcraft", which were by no means defined by large corporations and advertising, and instead merely provided spaces where people could meet each other and or assume the life of someone else. The question of what this new world may look like hinges on the people who are shaping it behind the scenes and those who stand to gain the most from it.

4.1 Dimensions of Digital Growth: New Business Opportunities

Digitalization goes beyond the technical dimension of digitization. Digitization is about digitizing data, processes, and actions. Digitalization involves digitization but stands for new ways to live, to communicate, and to do business. It leads to a transformation of business models, of management processes, and to a change or adapting of behaviors.

We have witnessed a very strong growth of data volumes. Global data use amounted to 2 zettabytes in 2010, rose to 15,5 zettabytes in 2015, to around 60 zettabytes in 2020 and is projected to reach more than 150 zettabytes in 2025. Such enormous use of data is due to the tremendous growth both in industries and in personal use. The latter mainly applies to the use of social media, online tv streaming, online video streaming, e-commerce, and browsing for news.

Digitalization

Figure 4.1: Volume of Data/Information Created, Captured, Copied, and Consumed Worldwide from 2010 to 2025 (in Zettabytes)

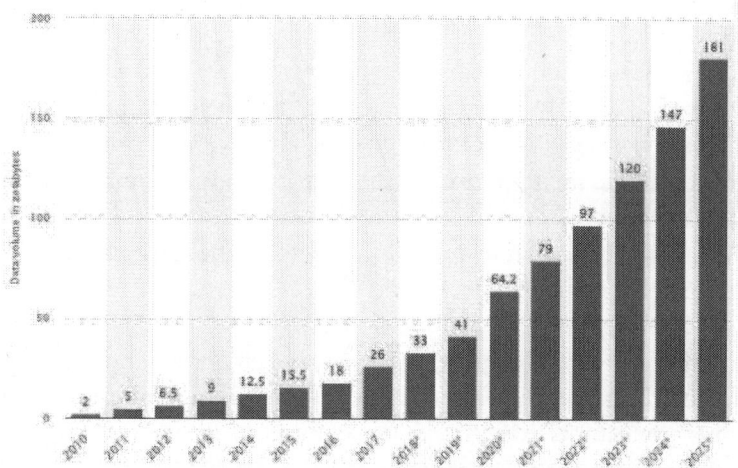

Source: Arne von See, Statista (2021).[2]

Some view digitalization as a trend that mainly affects people living in cities. The situation is rapidly changing in many countries, especially in China. Xiaowei Wang writes about the involvement of rural areas in the digital revolution: "The new socialist countryside will be filled with peasants starting e-commerce businesses, small-scale manufacturing, new data centers...rural revitalization envisions the use of blockchain and mobile payment to catalyze new businesses and will leverage big data for poverty relief and distribution of welfare benefits".[3]

Digitalization is driven by new technologies, new business models and new approaches to planning and management. In most places of the world, larger and smaller private companies, especially e-commerce businesses, start-ups and consulting companies, drive digitalization. The public sector, however, is also a big player in the sector. Smart city concepts give a big push to digitalization and such developments affect almost all citizens. It is evident that digitalization provides a series of advantages for all of us in terms of convenience and efficiency—think about electronic access to public services, traffic management, and participation in community development, but it also infringes on our privacy if sharing of personal data becomes mandatory to access essential services.

The COVID-19 crisis has pushed many governments to accelerate digitalization. Japan has long been considered a laggard in this race. COVID-19 exposed Japan's "half-baked digitalization" writes *The Economist*.[4] Subsidies took much longer time to reach households in Japan than in South Korea. A new agency was set up and Prime Minister Suga Yoshihide made a strong commitment to accelerate digitalization and introduce many more digital services for his fellow citizens.

Big data enables businesses, insurance companies, and government agencies to make more precise analyses and better-informed decisions, improve customized services and marketing and apply algorithms based on data analysis to improve production processes. Big data is used for many innovations in industrial production. Such innovations include cloud computing, augmented reality, the internet of things, autonomous robots, additive manufacturing, digital payments through blockchain technology, and cybersecurity.

Big data is used to make planning and operations smarter, meaning more interconnected and more intelligent. The term *smart* is used to describe systems that rely on processing big data to improve production, and services: smart mobility, smart grid, smart logistics, smart homes, and smart buildings. We also use the term in connection to cities; see chapter 7 on urbanization and smart cities.

In China and elsewhere, we also witness a boom in applying *Artificial Intelligence* (AI) in land management and agriculture. Smart farming technology is relatively advanced in parts of China. Around 19,000 drones are sold in China every year for agriculture alone, for uses such as spraying and spreading aids for cultivating large fields.[5]

We have talked to Sachin Gaur on salient issues relating to the megatrend of digitalization and its political dimensions. Sachin

Digitalization

Gaur holds a Double Masters in mobile security and cryptography from Aalto University, Finland and the University of Tartu, Estonia. He has been a keen technology innovator. He holds 10 technology patents granted by the United States Patent and Trademark Office (USPTO). He has contributed to books on innovation and health care and received the prestigious top ten innovators award in India. He is active in the space of AI and information security in the areas ICT and in the health sector.

Interview with Sachin Gaur, MixORG

Q: Which political systems are best equipped to deal with digitalization? Will a digital world rather strengthen authoritarian or liberal democratic systems? To what extent does the digital revolution challenge the sovereignty of states?
Sachin Gaur: One thing to note is the attitude of the people toward privacy in a given country. In that sense, the EU countries should be at the top, while countries like India would be on the other end of the spectrum, as many citizens blindly trust companies and are not self-aware about how their data is used and sold. On the other hand, the type of governance is also important, as democratic states are currently struggling with regulation. As an example, a significant point of criticism against the GDPR is the fact that Microsoft has 1600 people employed, specifically to deal with its ramifications on the company, which basically costs them nothing, so you can see how too much regulation may even tilt the scales and favor these big companies. But again, in India for example too little regulation and/or punishment leads to constant data breaches, while authoritarian, undemocratic or one party states can freely introduce technology and reinforce the surveillance state. In China everything is monitored, and they have introduced this new social credit scheme, which is based on Big Data. Citizens who do not comply with rules could face serious consequences; for example, not being able to board a train or even leave the country. The proposed EU regulation of AI, for example, bans social credit assignment type of AI.

Q: How do you see the Digital Divide in India and on a global scale?
Sachin Gaur: If you look at the situation during the COVID-19 pandemic, overnight, everything went digital, from hospitals to schools and jobs, and those who did not have access to the internet, or a phone were immediately left behind. In the past it used to be the case that you could not go anywhere in life without an e-mail. Then WhatsApp came along, and this was now true for mobile phones, but I think that the human voice itself is the next big thing, which can help bridge that digital divide and allow people who may not be able to use the internet or a mobile phone, due to a disability or a lack of language knowledge, to be able to participate in society in a much more efficient way. There are smart speakers for example which can act like a mobile phone and can recognize your voice and adjust to your jargon and accent. In long term such a technology can allow you to be yourself, empower minorities and prevent a sort of technology-driven colonialism, which forces people to learn English for example in order to use new technologies.

Q: Do you think the Right to be Forgotten can exist and can be meaningfully implemented and what's your take on Digital Immortality?
Sachin Gaur: Not quite, since the internet is not a centralized place, you can't really enforce it. A company can destroy the data, but what happens if someone has made a copy of it somewhere on the other side of the world, since the internet has no physical borders? Also, what is culturally acceptable can change throughout time, so in 15 years you may be ok with a nude photo of yourself online as someone may post a deepfake of you and only your friends and family can attest that this is not you. Perhaps sooner or later people's identity online may even replace their real one, like authors in the past that changed their surnames, so there is a lot of possibilities for online identity in the future.

Q: How do you see the role of the internet in future geopolitics?
Sachin Gaur: There is already a divide going on, China is massively ahead in adoption of the internet in the population, while they are experimenting in ways that the West cannot even fathom. In

Digitalization

Singapore, I was stopped at the airport because a machine was 95 percent certain that I was a terrorist. This shows that there is a world in which human agency is completely removed from the decision-making and the type of harm that can be done even with a 5 percent error rate at a scale is scary! The internet more specifically can empower people—help them find jobs for example—but it seems like we are heading toward a world that is divided between the free population and one that lives under constant surveillance.

Digitalization offers a wide range of new business opportunities. The most valuable start-up companies—also known as unicorns once they reach a value of over one billion U.S. dollars—are based on digital business models. Tech companies make up for a growing share of stock markets, worldwide. Their value has rapidly grown over the past couple of years.

The top five companies in the powerful S&P 500 index are all technology companies—by a wide margin. The financial crisis of 2008 crashed many technology-based business models. However, the first wave of growing enthusiasm for technology-based business models was not the trigger of the crisis. The financial crisis of 2008 was caused by excessive risk-taking on the part of banks, combined with the bursting of the housing bubble in the United States (U.S.).

An old saying goes: "those who cannot remember the past are condemned to repeat it". The financial crisis of 2008 led to a series of new regulations of the financial sector, which has since experienced a period of steady growth until the COVID-19 shock of spring 2020. The market, especially most of the technology firms, recovered very quickly. The COVID-19 shock provided a push to many technology-based companies, the most prominent example being the fast rise of Zoom. The company provides the most convenient tools to organize online meetings and conferences and was the quickest to provide sufficient capacity to address the demand for video conferencing and online teaching. Microsoft and CISCO soon strengthened their efforts to catch up with the new trend and overhauled their video conferencing tools to meet the growing demand.

Another sector of digitalization also benefited from the restriction imposed in the context of the COVID-19 pandemic: financial services based on digital technology, such as Fintechs and cryptocurrencies. KPMG reports that in the first half of 2021, the global Fintech sector saw a record-breaking 52.3 billion dollars in venture capital investment, compared to the 22.5 billion dollars in the second half of 2020. These large investments are driven by the abrupt change in client expectations to be able to engage with companies digitally.[6]

The Sustainable Digital Finance Alliance was founded by UN Environment Programme (UNEP) and Ant Financial Services to address the potential for Fintech-powered business innovations to reshape the financial system in ways that better align it with the needs of sustainable development. Digital finance includes big data, Artificial intelligence (AI), mobile platforms, blockchain, and the Internet of things (IoT). Technology provides opportunities to make fast payments across the world and the COVID-19 pandemic only accelerated the adoption of digital payment.

Financial services have become cheaper, while the automatization of the financial sector provides huge opportunities. It provides for fast but well-researched choices on investments. The U.S. American investment company D. E. Shaw & Co., L.P., founded in 1988 by David E. Shaw and based in New York City — Jeff Bezos was the company's vice president in the early 1990s — pioneered sophisticated mathematical models and computer programs to exploit anomalies in the market through analysis of big data. "The world is embracing the Fintech revolution" writes Jeff Desjardins, the Editor-in-Chief of Visual Capitalist and a widely quoted expert on new business models and investing. The birth of Fintech companies, however, is concentrated in only a few countries: United States, China, Sweden, India, the Netherlands, and the U.K..[7]

Fintechs are a disruptive force for the banking industry which has long been considered a laggard in digital innovation. Fintech and the new technologies offered by services such as Bitcoin are

Digitalization

paradigm-shifting developments which have disrupted, and will continue to disrupt, existing financial systems.

Payment methods are also changing rapidly. All digital payment methods are on the rise while the use of cash is on a sharp decline. However, the usage of mobile payments varies greatly across countries. eMarketer research shows just how far ahead China finds itself as of 2021.

Figure 4.2: Mobile Payment User Share 2021, % of Smartphone Users (2021)

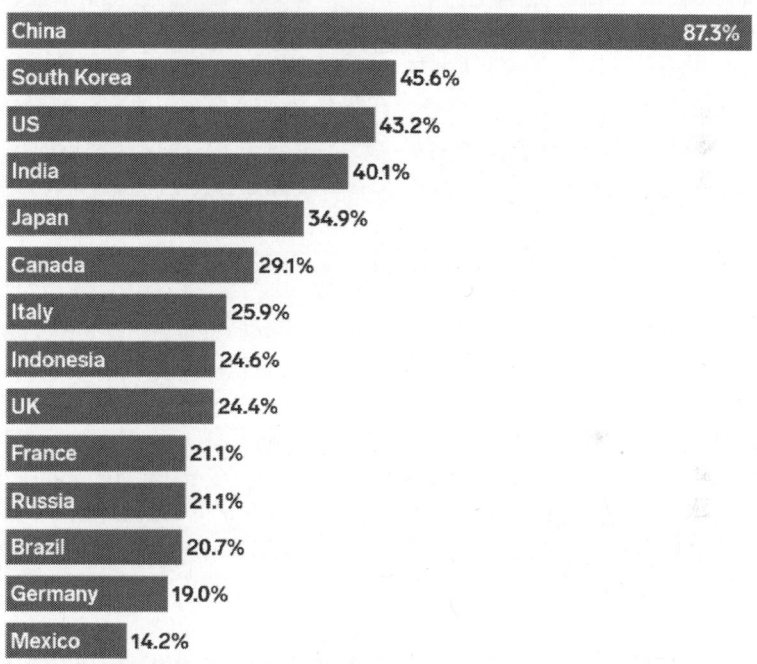

Source: emarketer.com/Insider Intelligence[8]

The trend is indeed particularly strong in China. The following table puts into perspective the growing market share of mobile payments in the country.

Global Perspectives on Megatrends

Figure 4.3: Market Share of Mobile vs. Non-Mobile Payments in China

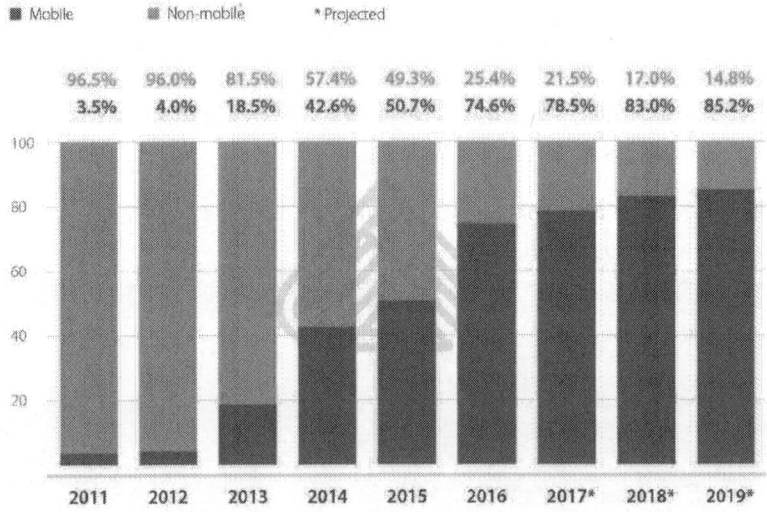

Source: Saarinen, Jeppe (2018). Asia Briefing – data from iResearch, WalktheChat.[9]

Wirecard quickly developed into one of the leading Fintechs. The German payment technology giant became a member of the prestigious DAX in September 2018 but collapsed less than two years later, at the end of June 2020, after years of accounting fraud. Wirecard was a very prominent company in Germany and showed the second highest market value after SAP in the year 2019. However, in general, Fintech companies are still less well known than other segments of unicorns with higher visibility for private customers.

The Wirecard scandal exposed the need for stricter control. It was no surprise that blockchain technology again experienced a rise in an atmosphere of mounting manipulations of financial transactions. Blockchains are a record-keeping technology, where multiple computers hold a list of prior records and new blocks are chained to the previous block. Bitcoin arrived in 2008 after the financial crisis, and early adopters of the digital currency made millions due to high fluctuations in value.

Digitalization

The future of cryptocurrencies is a complicated issue as it raises regulatory and highly political questions. Cryptocurrencies will need to preserve user anonymity without being a conduit for tax evasion, or money laundering; be technically complex to avoid fraud and hacker attacks; but easy for consumers to understand, as well as decentralized but with adequate consumer safeguards and protection.[10] The blockchain technology meets resistance from central banking authorities because it replaces central authority through a decentralized technology. In a way, owning bitcoin or other cryptocurrencies is holding a short position against the financial system as it escapes control of central banking authorities. The European Central Bank makes it clear that it considers Bitcoin a speculative asset, not a currency. No authority is backing the risk of losing investments.

The other great reservation against the use of Bitcoin stems from environmental considerations. Bitcoin mining needs enormous amounts of electricity arising from the creation of its proof of work (POW) protocols, which are described as "complicated puzzles". Bitcoin's energy consumption equaled that of Ireland in 2020. However, there are efforts underway to reduce energy consumption. Ethereum, an open-source blockchain featuring smart contract functionality and the second largest crypto currency, published plans to shift from the Proof-of-Work procedure to the much less power-hungry proof-of-stake procedure.

Companies that reach out to large sections of society, especially young people, are big drivers of the digitalization trend. Thus, e-commerce is at the core of the digitalization megatrend. There are many people, including us, who enjoy shopping in downtown areas. We personally love to spend time in bookstores. Even during the COVID-19 restrictions, bookstores could stay open in Berlin. A perhaps peculiar policy, but surprisingly few among the proponents of strict lockdowns resented it. In a way, the city of Berlin was fighting a small battle against the ravaging effects of e-commerce.

In the early years of the e-commerce trends, it required an innovative approach to attract customers. eBay, founded in 1995 as a marketplace for the sale of goods and services for individuals, was one of the early success stories. Their advertisement campaigns focused on auctions. This smart marketing approach served as a door-opener. Many new marketing strategies successfully promoted e-commerce, especially in China, where Alibaba made fortunes on the world largest online shopping day in the world. Alibaba shoppers exceeded 213.5 billion yuan (30.7 billion U.S. dollars) in total spending during 2018 Singles Day.

The Economist rightly pointed out that the future of e-commerce is being staked out in China.[11] Its market has about 850 million digital consumers, close to three times the number in the U.S. The mobile share of e-commerce is close to 90 percent, compared with little more than 40 percent in the U.S. China has only around one third of physical shop floor per person compared with the U.S. With consumption picking up more in the context of higher projected growth than in the U.S., online shopping will strongly benefit from it. Deliveries are easier to organize in more densely populated places, which again favors e-commerce in China compared to other countries.[12] In some cities, especially in Europe, there is growing concern about the future of retailers in city centers if e-commerce continues to grow. There are proposals to introduce a special tax for e-commerce companies that use city infrastructure to deliver their goods to keep retailers competitive and make city centers look attractive for tourists and locals. Bookstores are strongly affected by growing e-commerce with books. In most parts of Germany, bookstores could remain open during lockdowns as they would have otherwise not survived the rush to e-commerce.

The perception that China has copied business models of the West and that the Chinese models must be inferior is misleading. TaoBao exemplifies the great dynamic of Chinese online commerce. Founded by Alibaba Group in 2003, TaoBao facilitates retail by providing a platform for small businesses and individual entrepreneurs to open online stores.

Tencent, the other tech giant company in China, is operating the social media platform wechat which was started in 2011 and became the world's largest standalone mobile app in 2018, with

Digitalization

more than one billion users. Tencent is a multinational technology conglomerate holding company that is considered one of the world's most innovative and successful technology companies. It is the largest vendor of video games and offers online payment services. *Forbes*, the famous American business magazine, recently wrote about Facebook's effort to copy features of wechat.[13] Its move to introduce online payments linked to the app comes years after such a feature was available on wechat.

Toutia/Bytedance (video sharing social networking), Didi Chuxing (transportation platform, China) and Air B&B (accommodation platform, U.S.) are other companies that promoted the sharing economy and connect billions of people. None of the above major global platforms was founded in Europe. Katarina Stanoevska-Slabeva, Vera Lenz-Kesekamp, and Viktor Suter of the University of St. Gallen conducted a study on sharing economy platforms (SEP),[14] which offers some insightful analysis on the evolution of the sharing economy. The authors point out that "initially, the sharing economy was targeting private individuals as providers that share private goods and services on an occasional basis. However, the sharing economy has quickly proven to be interesting also for professional providers and the number of professional sharing-or private providers that share goods, not only occasionally, but more often or as main occupation, is constantly growing".

The distinction between private and professional provider has become a subject of controversy, particularly in Europe. This was one of the reasons that hindered the rapid growth of the sharing economy in the continent. Professional and tax regulations in Europe made the growth of the sharing economy more difficult than in other parts of the world. Air B&B and Uber faced accusations from the hotel industry and taxi driver associations of violating regulations.

In most parts of Europe, especially in Germany, concerns about regulations of small business tend to be higher than in the United States, China, and many other countries. It does not come as a surprise that Katarina Stanoevska-Slabeva and her colleagues conclude that "the platform analysis showed that the sharing economy in Europe, at least in some sharing categories, seems to be dominated by non-European platforms that have global operations". There are also European platforms that are globally active, however these platforms appear to be smaller than the global non-European SEPs. Their analysis also provides evidence that Europe will most probably not catch-up with the platform economy business models. Most of the big globally active platforms were founded before 2010, while the highest number of platforms was founded in the period from 2010 to 2015. After 2015 the growth of SEP seems to have decreased quickly.[14]

Airbnb and Uber are among the best-known platforms. Both have faced many challenges and restrictions in Germany. In 2017, Europe's top court ruled that Uber was a transport company rather than just a platform facilitating information exchange. German law says that private hire drivers must return to their company's base after completing a trip if they do not have another journey lined up. Drivers are not allowed to drive around or park somewhere waiting for a new job to come in, and, as such, Uber was subsequently banned in several big cities. In November 2019 London's transport authority, TFL, said it would not extend Uber's license to operate in the capital. Uber follows a double strategy to respond to such challenges. It appeals in the courts and simultaneously introduces modified business models.[15]

Airbnb also experienced a ban in Germany. The city senate of Berlin voted in a law in 2016 to limit the effect of such platforms on the long-term local housing market. Named "Zweckentfremdungsverbot" (law against misappropriation of housing space), this regulation threatens anyone who puts an entire flat up for rent with the intent of generating profit with a fine up to 100,000 EUR per violation. Any commercial exploitation must be sanctioned with a special permit from the city. This move received acclaim from many local actors who saw the end of abusive listings. However, since this law passed, we can still see many listings on Airbnb up to this date.[16]

4.2 Artificial Intelligence (AI)

Artificial Intelligence (AI) will have a growing impact on our lives, as it enables computers and machines to mimic the perception, learning, problem-solving, and decision-making capabilities of the human mind.[17]

The European Parliament defines AI "as the ability of a machine to display human-like capabilities such as reasoning, learning, planning and creativity".[18] The surge in AI development is made possible by the sudden availability of large amounts of data and the corresponding development and wide availability of computer systems that can process all that data faster and more accurately than humans can.

The use of machine learning and AI in the field of recruiting has started to guide recruitment of staff and has proved to be a lucrative field for start-ups. Algorithms facilitate the search for the right applicants.

AI systems were initially created to help us replace mundane and repetitive tasks. AI systems already clean houses, assist in farming, and serve up food and deliver groceries. They manage finances and assist in driving cars or drive us. Since the end of January, customers in Shenzhen, southern China, have been able to book self-driving taxis in everyday traffic for the first time. All you have to do is log into an app. There is no longer a safety co-driver in the car. AI will become more omnipresent. It is already completing our words as we type them. AI has already advanced to support us with our creative processes such as playing games, painting, and writing.

The performance of robots in playing chess and other games gives an idea about the rapid progress and huge potential of deep learning. Deep learning can leverage analysis based on huge datasets to inform us. In deep learning, the central learning method in AI, computers get to know the world as a hierarchy of concepts. In the course of a learning process, they are confronted with increasingly complex concepts, which they process on the basis of experience with the previous, simpler, concepts.

In a way, AI is imitating neuro networks to function like human brains. A former colleague of Berthold Kuhn used to wear a T-shirt bearing the words "not all intelligence is artificial". Many still consider AI as a hype. For decades, it was relegated to science fiction. Today, AI is part of our everyday lives. The capacity to manage large amounts of data and the wide availability of computer systems that can process all that data faster and more accurately than humans can, made this development possible. OpenAI developed a natural-language algorithm which will set new standards. Driverless taxis which have already been spotted in Phoenix, Arizona will be seen in many other places.[19] Governments are developing ambitious plans to support AI-related industries aiming to reduce international dependence. China aims to become the global center for AI by 2030. Currently 80 percent of the semiconductors processed in China are imported. By 2025, domestic production should account for 70 percent, and China aspires to become a global leader in all segments of the semiconductor value chain.

4.3 Data Protection and Cybersecurity

Digitalization makes it more difficult to protect our data. Sharing of data becomes a requirement for accessing a growing number of essential services and products, including health services. It becomes evident that we will not be able to escape digitalization if we want to live a modern life and access a wide range of services. In the age of digitalization, protection of personal data has become a key concern for many people. For good reasons, many people resent sharing information about their diseases and treatments but also about their circle of friends, their religion, or their ideological preferences. It is evident that we may expect disadvantages in our professional or private life if others know about psychological therapies or personal contacts, we had with people who have later been sentenced for crimes. If we enable others to make judgments based on our past, it will impact our scope of choices to develop into a new direction, to reinvent ourselves.

Digitalization

People evolve, and many make successful efforts to change the course of their lives. Being surveilled provides those who manage and analyze our data with the opportunity to draw conclusions and judge us based on a combination of personal data and our preferred online interactions. Such developments could potentially infringe on our freedom, lower the degree of our sovereignty in defining our identity, and provoke frustration, even leading to depression.

People's attitudes concerning identity management, data protection and privacy vary greatly across countries and cultures. The European Commission published its first big survey on attitudes on data protection and electronic identity in the European Union in 2011. This survey provided many insights into the concerns of EU citizens. Already ten years ago, Europeans showed considerable concern about the recording of their behavior via payment cards, mobile phones, and the internet. When asked, most people would say that they preferred to give the minimum required information to access online services in order to protect their identity in daily life. In practice, however, online services are designed in such a way that the most user-friendly and convenient user experience is coupled with the sharing of much personal data. Default settings in browsers make it possible to trace the history of the websites we accessed and to learn about our areas of interest and preferences. Combining such data in an intelligent way—for example, by comparing it with data of millions of other people—provides analysts with more precise information about us than most of our friends would have. Many people are concerned that our intellectual interests, our ideological preferences, and our health concerns are subject to the analysis of human resource managers of companies or public institutions with power to control and supervise our life.

Shoshana Zuboff, along with other contemporary thinkers and activists in the digital data world, has been sounding the alarm for a while now, with Zuboff coining the term "Surveillance Capitalism" to describe a radically different business model, which has altered the dominant mode of production itself and is all based on data extraction and selling. Zuboff has argued that it is not the data we might willingly supply that is of concern, but rather the

"Behavioral Surplus", that is the by-product of our online activities, which tech giants have utilized to create images of individuals that describe and know them better than they might know themselves. But even if this is the case, there is further critical distinction, as said data is then sold to third parties for advertisement purposes.[20] Readers will recall the most egregious of such cases in the Facebook-Cambridge Analytica scandal, whereby the data was used for political advertising in the 2016 U.S. presidential election.

Johann Hari, author of "Stolen Focus: Why You Can't Pay Attention",[21] even argues that, unless Big Tech moves away from the "Behavioral Surplus" model, we will not be able to take back control of our attention. Though there are not many longitudinal studies on the effect of social media on our minds, the goal of these social media platforms under the current operating model is to keep users engaged as long as possible. Many times, due to inherent biases found in humans, such as the negativity bias, the algorithms learn to show inflammatory content first, which elicits the greatest reactions and keeps us hooked.

Jillian C. York of the Electronic Frontier Foundation and author of *Silicon Values: The Future of Free Speech under Surveillance Capitalism* is also a staunch critic of the Big Tech companies, but instead focuses on their potential as unregulated gatekeepers of the online world. By allowing authoritarian regimes to control what their citizens can and cannot see on these platforms, and acting as mere intermediaries, companies like Facebook have been able to evade scrutiny and, more importantly, responsibility for their practices.[22]

In 2021, the Facebook Papers and the testimony of Frances Haugen, shed light on the type of practices that activists like York have been desperately speaking out against. While Facebook removes what it deems to be harmful content in the West, it is also genuinely responsible for inciting violence in other parts of the world due to negligence and the lack of sufficient ability to regulate content in other languages. In Ethiopia and India for example, glorified violence is endemic on the platform and has even led to real human suffering in the context of the Ethiopian Tigray conflict.[23] A lot of the work is automated and "Facebook's 15,000-strong content

Digitalization

moderation workforce speaks about 50 tongues, though the company said it hires professional translators when needed. Automated tools for identifying hate speech work in about 30."[24]

Jillian York joined us for an interview to present a more critical view of certain aspects of digitalization that may be overlooked in our excitement about this bright future.

Interview with Jillian C. York, Electronic Frontier Foundation (EFF)

Q: How could digitalization contribute to solving major challenges in health care? Do you see the global governance architecture sufficiently prepared and equipped to address major challenges arising from digitalization?
Jillian York: I see lawmakers globally being ill-prepared in catching up to changes in the digital world and protecting people. Health insurance is an example and a personal one as well, where I have low confidence that privacy concerns are being addressed the way they should be, especially during this pandemic. The German Corona app is one of the better ones out there in terms of privacy, and certainly much better than the one in the United States, as it uses open-source technology, while the latter has very real privacy concerns and a complete lack of transparency. As of this moment, I cannot endorse any sweeping technological improvements in the absence of a better General Data Protection Regulation (GDPR) and I am very skeptical of existing laws, as there is an ongoing trend, in which countries with weak democratic institutions and authoritarian tendencies, tend to copy the western archetype and use it as a form of oppression, as in the case of Turkey's copycat of the German NetzDG.
The UN, is as of this moment, not adequately prepared to face these challenges, as evidenced by its supposed strongest institution, the International Governance Forum, which "has no teeth". The greatest of problems with such approaches is the fact that it is all happening behind closed doors, leaving civil society groups completely on the outside.

Q: Will a more digital world strengthen authoritarian states and weaken liberal/democratic states?
Jillian York: Absolutely. Western countries are already selling these technologies to authoritarian states with truly little restriction and of course they are used for mass surveillance, especially against minorities.

Q: Is a fragmentation of the digital world likely or even inevitable?
Jillian York: It is already happening. In 2007, 65 percent of the world's population was living under some form of censorship, mainly due to the fact that large internet platforms readily comply with authoritarian states, while this trend is very likely to have accelerated ever since, considering the democratic backsliding.

Q: So, what kind of censorship is then acceptable, in your view?
Jillian York: I did write a book on this, which was released in March of 2021 and my answer is twofold here. First of all, any restrictions must happen under the oversight of the UN and must meet certain criteria: for example, the disturbance of public order, as in the example of anti-mask protests. On the other hand, there is this tendency of lawmakers to bring out the digital hammer as a solution, but we need to recognize that disinformation starts very early on, especially in schools. See, for example, I was taught that Columbus "discovered" America, meaning that we must tackle disinformation from the ground up, instead of trying to have technology fix our problems.

Q: You sound quite pessimistic about the future of the digital world.
Jillian York: I would say I am optimistic, as I am currently working with many people who are trying to put the power back into the hands of people — a user-powered movement, that is. As an example, the Digital Services Act was helped by my colleagues and I and was more transparent than other attempts in the past, but it remains to be seen what stays in there and what does not.

Q: What about the regulatory development in the EU and the U.S., which one do you prefer?

Digitalization

Jillian York: The EU is doing much better in this regard, due to the regulations being multinational, as I am quite critical of national measures, like those in France or Netherlands. On the other hand, I am also impressed by the contents of the DSA. The biggest thing it has going for it, as mentioned previously, is that it includes members of civil society and that it is designed to be future-proof and requires changes and incremental law-making process, and I hope that this will be the case with other technologies as well. The U.S., on the other hand, is as of this moment still reactionary, and in my view it can be largely attributed to a set news cycle, which has been stuck on section 230 for quite some time now and of course the lawmakers are not prepared at all to face these new challenges.

Q: What are some of the most important activist groups in the field?

Jillian York: The European Digital Rights Initiative (EDRi) puts out open letters and does consulting work in Brussels, the ACLU in the U.S., Access Now as well, Article 19 in the U.K., Amnesty International, which has a tech division based in Berlin. As for the rest of the world, in South-East Asia Singapore and Malaysia have many organizations; Ghana, Ethiopia, and Egypt in Africa, especially Egypt, which has a long history with such organizations that have now largely fled the country unfortunately; and as for Latin America, all countries have at least one strong organization, especially Chile, Brazil and Colombia. Other international organizations include the Internet Freedom Festival.

In many areas, people greatly benefit from digitalization and data sharing. At least theoretically, they also have a choice as to what extent and with whom they share their data. There is a growing number of initiatives to raise awareness on data protection, to work on standards for data protection and to promote a customer-centric approach to privacy. This is an important sub-trend of digitalization. For most people, there is no way to escape digitalization if they want to participate in modern life in technologically advanced societies. However, consumers tend to be more willing to engage with organizations if they can trust them with their personal

Global Perspectives on Megatrends

data. Some organizations aim to build trust by taking a more customer-centric approach to the way they manage customer data. Nonprofit organizations, such as consumer protection agencies, have raised awareness of the importance of trust and transparency in data management. Making use of data in an intelligent way has become a new business model. Collibra is an example of a data management company engaging with other companies and/organizations to promote trust and reputation.

Efforts for data protection may pay off for companies in the mid-or long-term perspective. Collecting consumer data is crucial for modern businesses, and the ability to access data from customers depends on trust. Efforts made toward data protection could contribute to build reputation of companies and brands. However, this perspective is quite idealistic if we look at the concentration of power in different industries. In the social media business, we face a monopolistic or oligopolistic situation.

4.4 Governance of Cyberspace and Anti-trust Legislation

The internet was initially built for research cooperation, not for business. It's very founding protocols are unsecure. They were designed for sharing, not for protecting data. The devolution of access from government and research bodies to individual private users has provided a gateway for cybercriminals. The initial enthusiasm about the opportunities provided by the internet and its very dynamic development outpaced international cooperation efforts to agree on governance principles and an institutional architecture to deal with the risks related to open internet use. The Internet Corporation for Assigned Names and Numbers (ICANN), a non-profit organization that operates the internet's Domain Name System (DNS), is an example of self-regulation with government involvement.[25] Jürgen Feick and Raymund Werle[26] observed that voluntary, private self-regulation coordinated the early architecture of the internet. For offline crime, police play an important role in investigation and prevention. However, a higher level of cooperation with states, the private sector and even individual users is required to tackle online crime. Governing risk through a national approach is no longer sufficient.[27]

Crime is widespread in cyberspace. Cybersecurity is a salient issue in the context of digitalization. Robeco investment group calls it a megatrend by itself[28] and points out that cybercrime has dramatically risen. In 2017, 6.5 percent of internet users were victims of identity fraud, losing 16 billion U.S. dollars, according to Javelin Strategy and Research. The market forecasters Gartner and IDC put the current size of cybersecurity at around USD 100 billion. Cybersecurity is providing ample opportunities for starting successful businesses though competition is fierce.

Next to cybercrime, the misuse of dominant market positions is a major challenge for managing cyberspace. The U.S. Congress's Subcommittee on Antitrust, Commercial and Administrative Law issued statements that Facebook engages in abusive market practices and stifles the market of social media services by not leaving users with many potential alternatives. We have also witnessed similar statements of public authorities targeting other tech giants such as Amazon, Apple, and Google in the United States.

In China, the confrontation between political authorities and Tech giants is more recent and became known to a larger public at the time when Alibaba launched the process of Initial Public Offering (IPO). The Chinese government flexed its muscles at the occasion of the planned IPO of Ant Group, otherwise known as Ant Financial and owner of massive Chinese payments app Alipay in late 2020. The IPO could not take place as planned. Instead, Chinese officials opened an antitrust investigation into Alibaba in December 2020, which heavily impacted on the stock market value of Alibaba.

At the level of the European Union, the Digital Services Act and Digital Markets Act encompass a set of rules applicable across the whole EU. These rules aim to create a safer and more open digital space by curtailing some of the powers of large gatekeeper firms on the internet. The Digital Services Act targets online intermediary services and the obligations of different online players are designed in such a way that they are supposed to match their role, size and impact in the online ecosystem. The Digital Markets Act (DMA) establishes a set of criteria for qualifying a large online platform as a so-called "gatekeeper". The Act aims to create a fairer business environment for business users who depend on gatekeepers to offer their services. The rules aim to create a better environment for innovators and technology start-ups by doing away with unfair terms and conditions limiting their development.[29]

The issue of digital governance also extends to the idea that governance itself can be digitized. We interviewed Heiko Vainsalu, who is an interoperability governance expert at the e-Governance Academy (eGA), Estonia and explored a number of aspects related to this.

Interview with Heiko Vainsalu, e-Governance Academy

Q: How does Estonia's e-governance help with citizen participation and decision-making?
Heiko Vainsalu: I think there are two aspects on this. For one, doing e-governance by default does not mean that it has to be citizen engaging, or that citizens are empowered to participate. Typically, e-governance is the way of working with digital tools and the digital mindset. The second aspect is that there are already several attempts in Estonia where these tools have been implemented in citizen engagement. The most illustrative example is the participatory budget in some major Estonian cities, but only on the municipal level, where citizens can vote on project ideas. There have also been several attempts in the governmental sector where these tools, polling stations, and so forth, have been made available for the wider audience to prepare proposals for the government, and people can vote to give their input. The tricky part as it stands is that these active participation tools do not work yet, but I would blame the mindset, not the tools. I respect the citizen that thinks they have elected someone to do the hard work of governance and that they should do that instead of asking them. I understand why it is difficult to engage in that sense.

Digitalization

To me, the key element with the highest impact is e-governance tools related to transparency, which build trust and promote better engagement from citizens. Ordinary citizens can give comments to regulations, and the policy making process has become so transparent with long-term decisions being made participatory. During COVID-19 decisions must be made fast, and these things do not work, but in a normal cycle they do and are important. I think part of the reason as to why Estonians trust the public sector, perhaps a bit too much, is the result of twenty years of this type of e-governance.

Q: How do you see e-governance developing in the next decade? Which were key factors of success in Estonia, especially during the COVID-19 pandemic? Where do you see limitations and challenges? How long did it take for people to adapt to the technological changes?

Heiko Vainsalu: Even though Estonians are technical-eager people, it took a long time for a basic level to be reached. Beginning in the 2000s with the digital ID, when it was introduced, people thought the best thing to do with it was to spread butter on bread. People were truly annoyed, and it took five to seven years depending on what indicators you are looking at. This five to seven years phenomenon is happening everywhere, and during that time the public sector begins using a lot of tools and building systems that will create a new type of legacy.

Moving on from here, I have participated in some workshops and tried to predict what comes next. One thing that I know for certain is that whatever people may think of Artificial Intelligence (AI), we need more of it. Everybody will be making decisions using AI, and the public sector will follow the private sector in doing so. The other thing is the creation of a technical legacy, and the stumbles in information security, which we can do nothing to avoid.

Q: Sharing of data becomes a requirement for accessing a growing number of essential services and products, including health services. How do you see data protection regulation evolving, in your countries, in the EU?

Heiko Vainsalu: I think the current approach to personal data protection is outdated, as regulations follow our notions of living in the past, and we are defining regulations for the 1970s or 80s, and neglecting the fact that information is shared at higher speeds than ever before. I think conflict will emerge from this very specific perspective that challenges all the regulatory aspects. The old approach is being bypassed by innovators and service providers. They are predefining their services so that even if you are getting a product, you are actually getting a service while they evade responsibility. Signing up for a service now means you are giving different set of privileges to the provider. To give you an example, in ten years maybe I do not have a fridge but a service of 365 days of fresh meat. The service is provided by means of a fridge, but I do not have the fridge itself. These things are being challenged by the private sector and as such the regulation has to be redefined in the future.

Q: To what extent is the cybersecurity threat from neighboring countries potent in Estonia? What lessons can be drawn from past experiences and have there been any large-scale incidents? Does digitalization in that sense hinge on cybersecurity considerations?

Heiko Vainsalu: There are smaller and different kinds of attacks, and the perpetrators are getting smarter. From a future perspective we have to redefine what neighboring means, as it has historically merely held a geopolitical meaning. Neighboring now means something entirely different. All over the world there are organizations or governments interested in having an impact on other countries and their economy without ever visiting. This model shifts our understanding of neighboring from geopolitical to a network type. The indications so far are obvious, but we haven't seen a very big cyber incident that has exposed this.

4.5 Digitalization and Sustainability

Digital technologies can make an enormous contribution to sustainable development and have a significant potential to abate

Digitalization

greenhouse gas emissions. However, digitalization has also its own carbon footprint. There are several studies and scenario developments about the potential contributions to sustainable development as well as on carbon dioxide emissions related to the use of digital technologies.

An example of a direct contribution of digital technologies to a more sustainable use of natural resources, is Global Forest Watch (GFW). This online forest monitoring and alert system uses crowdsourcing to allow anyone to create custom maps, analyze forest trends, subscribe to alerts, or download data for their local area or the entire world.[30]

Collaborative logistics, intelligent heating, demand side management, co-working, and car-sharing are areas concerning many of us. They offer a significant potential to reduce emissions according to a study by Lorenz Hilty and Jan Bieser of the University of Zurich in collaboration with SwissCom and WWF.[31] Their study focuses on Switzerland, but they draw several conclusions relevant to many countries and sectors.

Their study acknowledges the rising problem of big carbon footprints of information and communication technologies, especially at the level of the end user. However, they still conclude that "there is an unprecedented opportunity to take ambitious and targeted actions to implement ICT-based ("smart") low-carbon solutions, both in terms of technologies and business models..."

Econsense, the Forum for Sustainable Development of German Business, together with consulting company Accenture, produced a handbook for managers outlining "How Companies can Improve their Impact on the Sustainable Development Goals (SDGs) and Harness the Power of Digitalization".[32] Others emphasize the potential of digitalization to improve health services. Digitalization in health means more informed decision-making through access to pertinent patient information. A study of the Nuffield Trust identified seven opportunities to drive improvements in productivity and quality of care: more systematic, high-quality care; more proactive and targeted care; better-coordinated care; improved access to specialist expertise; greater patient engagement;

improved resource management; system improvement and learning. Digital health technology can help manage pandemics by providing an early signal to potential infection.[33] Reservations on digital health, however, are considerable as sharing of health information is particularly sensitive for many people.

Tim Unwin, Chairholder of the UNESCO Chair in ICT4D at Royal Holloway, University of London, is one of the outspoken critics with regard to the negative environmental impact of digitalization. According to him, "future projections relating to Smart Cities, 5G and the Internet of Things give rise to additional concerns over energy demand... e-Waste remains a fundamental problem for the sector.... Most of the sector is based on the fundamental concept of replacement rather than repair.... The hardware-software development cycle forces users to upgrade their equipment on a regular basis... Most digital technologies rely on rare minerals that are becoming increasingly scarce.[34]

The innovation and resource saving potential of digital technologies, however, should not be underestimated. Saving resources is a top priority of many current research activities on digital technologies. As mentioned above, the Proof-of-Stake procedure in using blockchain technology needs far fewer quantities of electricity to approve a transaction.

Chapter 5

Inequality

Inequality is a multi-faceted concept that can be viewed from different perspectives. The most common metrics are income and wealth inequality; however, one could also look at inequality of opportunity or inequality of risk exposure. It's yet further within this context that the digital divide stands as an increasingly salient dimension. Inequality also applies to aspects of vulnerability to environmental and climate risks, as the people most affected by climate change are often those who have contributed the least to and have the fewest resources to adapt to this blooming crisis.

How does inequality connect to the megatrend discourse? This chapter will mainly focus on inequality of income and wealth as these issues receive the highest attention in political discourses and inequality analyses. The Think Tank Avenir Suisse introduces its collaborative report on "Inequality and Equality" with a statement on the achievements of overcoming extreme poverty.[1] The number of people living in extreme poverty worldwide has been reduced to below ten percent, from around 45 percent in the 1990s. There are indeed still a handful of people who are skeptical of the idea that inequality matters in the face of rising prosperity, such as the authors of this collaborative report, who ask the questions: "why has the question of inequality become increasingly toxic on political agendas in the West?" and "how does one explain such widespread skepticism about distributional issues, while prosperity keeps growing worldwide?" The authors conclude: "A person's country of birth determines more than half the differences in his or her income even though inequality has been decreasing sharply between countries."[1]

As inequality gains political salience and is incorporated into national agendas in the West and worldwide, such findings are a stark reminder of the global wealth disparity, with the world's circa 2,150 billionaires holding more wealth than 60 percent of the entire human population.² In this light, it is helpful to distinguish between cross-country and within-country inequality. The former has been falling in the past 25 years due to immense gains in countries like China and India, while the latter has seen a worrying increase.³

Poverty and inequality are a part of the political agenda of nearly every government, even as large sections of societies in many emerging economies have become economically better off in the past few decades. China is often praised for having lifted about 800 million people out of poverty in the past 40 years,⁴ with Chinese political leadership having vowed to eliminate extreme poverty by the end of 2020.⁵ Official statistics confirm this accomplishment, but the country has nevertheless seen a sharp rise in inequality and a convergence in the share of total incomes of the bottom 50 percent and the top 1 percent.⁶ Although Thomas Piketty et al. find that Chinese income inequality is approaching levels the likes of which can be found in the U.S.,⁷ data for inequality measurements in China are incomplete, are scarce, and suffer from extreme underreporting, and they should be taken with a grain of salt.

Concepts and incidents of poverty and inequality greatly vary, and a differentiated analysis of income and wealth inequality is needed. While global inequality between countries has seemingly fallen in the past three decades, it has risen sharply within countries, especially in advanced economies and in some large emerging markets such as China, Russia, and India.

5.1 Dimensions of Inequality

Equality is at risk in situations of accelerated change, as we have witnessed in the context of the COVID-19 pandemic. A highly politicized issue, inequality is subject to fierce political debate and stands as a driver of ideological campaigns, social conflicts, and political unrest in many countries. Civil society movements across the world are putting inequality issues on the agenda. The Occupy movement, for example, emerged ten years ago as a powerful force uniting mostly young people in protest against social and economic inequality. Though most of these movements have lost steam, the spirit of inequality is either explicitly or implicitly included in most modern movements such as Fridays for Future.

At the level of academic discourse, Thomas Piketty pushed economic inequality to the forefront of scholarly, but also public debate through the publication of his "magnum opus" *Capital in the Twenty-First Century*.[8] The book presents a conceptual and factual background for interpreting changes in income and wealth inequality over time, and therein one finds the argument that when the rate of return on capital is greater than the rate of economic growth over the long term, the result is the extreme concentration of wealth. Such unequal distribution of wealth will, according to his findings, inevitably lead to social and economic instability. He proposes a global system of progressive wealth taxes to help reduce inequality and avoid a situation where the vast majority of wealth comes under the control of a tiny minority.

Richard Wilkinson, founder of The Equality Trust, is another leading academic expert on inequality. As a trained epidemiologist he extensively researched the impact of inequality on health-related issues, including psychological aspects such as depression, anxiety, and the unprecedented "deaths of despair". He has analyzed the impact of inequality on homicide rates, on the level of trust in communities and societies, and on psycho-social aspects related to shame and feelings of inferiority. According to him and The Equality Trust, status competition and consumerism are but consequences of unequal societies, in which people must always strive to accomplish more and actively seek to be on the level of those above them. People have a natural aversion to inequality, the Trust finds, but it is a deep-rooted phenomenon exacerbated by political and economic systems based on intensive economic and social competition.[9]

In *The Inner Level*,[10] Richard Wilkinson and Kate Pickett adopt a comparative approach and provide evidence for the inferiority of unequal societies in multiple metrics. They consider the dimension of the individual, arguing that inequality influences everything from life expectancy to social anxiety. These findings fall under the umbrella of "powerful psychological effects", which are shown to be more prominent where inequality reigns. For example, in places where hierarchies are the way of life, fibrinogen, a blood clotting factor, is found more frequently in people with lower incomes. Our own biology is a good indicator of our aversion to inequality and the significance of such findings.

In 2021, the information technology company Capgemini released its World Wealth Report on high-net-worth individuals (HNWIs), "defined as those having investable assets of USD 1 million or more, excluding primary residence, collectibles, consumables, and consumer durables".[11] Not only is the number of these individuals growing, but their investing activities are getting ever more sophisticated. A positive development can be said to be the increasing interest in Environmental, Social, and Government scores (ESG scores) by HNWIs under 40 years old. At the same time, 72 percent of those individuals have also invested in cryptocurrencies, highlighting what is usually left unspoken of in the world of cryptocurrency: the extreme inequality.[12]

As we will show in subsection 5.3, the narrative of trickle-down economics is seemingly breaking down, and thus the resulting siphoning of wealth to the top also poses the question of whether these individuals will choose to invest in socially desirable causes, and whether the gains will be distributed equitably. It is hard to argue that this can be the case without some form of government intervention and market-shaping. In this light, Mariana Mazzucato's thinking can go a long way, as she proposes that governments should look into a public-wealth fund (a concept which we will explore later in this chapter), but also asks the question "who gets what and why?"[13] Building on ideas like that of a public-wealth fund, or otherwise finding methods to socialize investment and thereby curbing the rise of HNWIs can aid in controlling and (pre-)distributing wealth in a more sustainable manner.

5.2 Measuring Inequality

How is inequality measured? The most important methodological reference is the Gini coefficient, developed by the Italian and

Inequality

sociologist Corrado Gini. It provides for an analysis of the distribution of wealth or income across different people or segments of societies. If income values are close to equal, the Gini coefficient will be close to a value of 0. A Gini coefficient of 1 expresses maximum inequality — for example, for a large number of people where only one person has most of the income or carries out the most consumption and all others have none, the Gini coefficient will be close to 1. Countries with an aging population, or with a baby boom, typically experience an increasing pre-tax Gini coefficient even if real income distribution for working adults remains constant. Undeclared incomes, high levels of social benefits spending, and prevalence of subsistence economies are factors which can distort the index. Thus, on occasion the index may be relatively far from accurately reflecting inequality among different countries, but it is still the best-established reference-point for measuring the phenomenon, and it is used by international organizations such as the World Bank.

The Elephant Curve, or the Lakner-Milanovic graph, represents the unequal distribution of income growth for individuals belonging to different income groups over the globe. The income growth depicted below, spanning 1980 to 2016, resembles the form of an elephant. For those between the top 45 percent and the top 20 percent, income growth was on a freefall. The lowest ten percent barely benefited, while the top 5 percent reaped the lion's share of the benefits of growth.

Figure 5.1: The Elephant Curve: Average Annual Wealth Growth Rate, 1995-2021

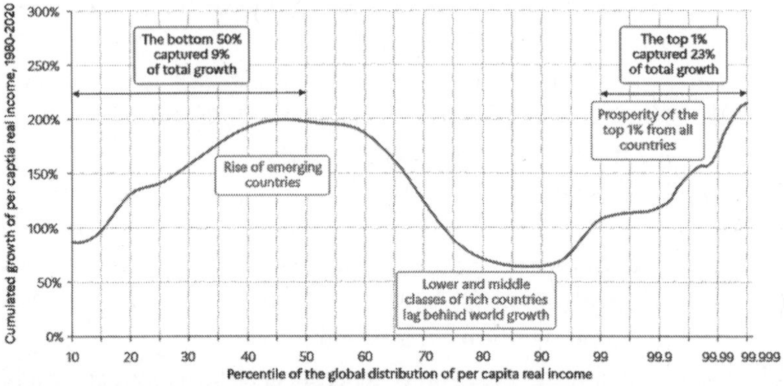

[Chart: Cumulated growth of per capita real income, 1980-2020, plotted against Percentile of the global distribution of per capita real income. Annotations: "The bottom 50% captured 9% of total growth"; "Rise of emerging countries"; "Lower and middle classes of rich countries lag behind world growth"; "Prosperity of the top 1% from all countries"; "The top 1% captured 23% of total growth".]

Source: World Inequality Report 2022[14]

5.3 Drivers of Inequality

Rising inequality constitutes a major risk for humanity. It endangers peace and harmony. A trigger of conflicts, it negatively affects the happiness of people and communities and the well-being of societies. The perceived risk of inequality sparks different kinds of actions based on diverse strategies. These range from explosions of violence to political and social reforms, and also include philanthropic and charitable activities.

Historically, the goal of the abolition of inequality in all its forms has fueled revolutionary movements, the overwhelming majority being violent ones, as Walter Scheidel points out.[15] The catch is that they have also been remarkably unsuccessful, with inequality rising almost immediately afterwards. Even in Soviet Russia, arguably the most extreme example of leveling, inequality soared after its collapse. Scheidel ends his book on a dire note, reminding those who care about the issue that any leveling has always come with sorrow, and that we must be careful what we wish for.

By looking at the history of inequality, we begin to realize that it is not a natural occurrence, but a result of human decisions and those of the institutions in place, largely driven by ideological convictions.[16] In the words of Emmanuel Saez, "...human societies can choose how much inequality they generate through social and public policy."[17]

From Hunter-Gatherers expelling or even murdering those who sought to accumulate power and wealth, to the modern passive acceptance and purposeful exacerbation of the immense gap between parts of society, the prevailing narratives at any given moment define our state of inequality.

Response strategies to inequality play out differently in different political systems and cultures, and as such there is no golden key that can magically close the gap. In the age of globalization, this trapped position has become self-evident, as countries have put on what Thomas Friedman has called the "Golden Straitjacket", a political position in which nations restrict their own policy options in exchange for a more favorable position in the global market, especially when it comes to taxation. This has led to a "Race to the Bottom", where countries have been gradually but steadily lowering their tax rates to attract workers, investors, or multi-national corporations, and thus remain competitive in the global market. As a result, according to the OECD, the average statutory corporate income tax rate has fallen from 28.3 percent to 20 percent in the last 20 years.[18]

This has been the consequence of a conscious change in the narrative around the responsibilities of firms and corporations in society. In the era of the "woke" and socially responsible corporation, this may seem outdated, but the economic practices behind the narrative shift have not necessarily been suspended. In crowning greed as a holy virtue and pursuing the maximization of shareholder value,[19] corporations were able to successfully lobby for lower taxation in the pursuit of the now ever-so-elusive growth that has for a long time now begun stalling.[20]

In the past few decades, many economists have been putting this theory to the test and are now trying to change this narrative. Nobel laureates Abhijit Banerjee and Esther Duflo loudly declare: "Tax cuts for the wealthy do not produce economic growth".[42] A 2022 paper by David Hope and Julian Limberg looks at "all major reductions in taxes on the rich across 18 OECD countries from 1965 to 2015".[21] The authors indeed find that in the aftermath of the tax decrease, the share of pre-tax incomes of the top one percent rose, and by extension, so did inequality, while in both the short and medium run the effect on GDP and unemployment is statistically indistinguishable from zero. Their findings are in line with previous research suggesting that lower tax rates allow richer individuals to bargain for greater personal compensation at the expense of those with lower incomes.[22]

The same principle seems to apply to lowered corporate tax rates. A 2021 working paper, a meta-analysis by Sebastian Gechert and Philipp Heimberger, in fact goes a step further and provides evidence that papers which argue the opposite — that is, that lowering corporate taxation does indeed lead to economic growth — are published more often. When correcting for this publication bias, the authors conclude a zero effect of corporate taxes on growth hypothesis cannot be rejected.[23]

The obvious caveat with lowering taxes is the fact that, in doing so, governments have had to look elsewhere, such as toward the welfare state, to fund their operations; nations thus step deeply into debt or into paths of taxing "low-hanging fruit".[24] They simply cannot afford to implement redistribution policies for fear of driving away both investors, but also their own citizens.

The most efficient way to tackle the problem of falling corporate tax rates is the global initiative supported by G7 and G20 countries to agree to a minimum corporate tax rate — in order to tackle the persistent offshoring of profits and to fight back against tax havens. The 2021 G7 and G20 meetings aimed to set a minimum rate of 15 percent, paving the way for a bright future of international tax cooperation. Ireland, a nation with a notably low corporate tax rate of 12.5 percent, and which has attracted over 800 U.S. businesses, signed on to the agreement in late 2021,[25] but it remains to be seen whether the efforts will be successful. With 137 countries signing on and a long-winded process finally looking like it will bear fruit, the first worrying signs came in December 2021, when the Biden administration failed to pass its tax bill, all the while the agreement still hinges on a unanimous acceptance of all EU member states.[26]

Inequality

The Tax Justice Network published a report in 2020 on the state of tax justice and concluded that "multinational corporations short-change countries out of 245 billion U.S. dollars in tax every year while people who move their wealth offshore short-change their governments out 182 billion U.S. dollars less in tax every year".[27] The same report finds that higher income countries are also responsible for 98 percent of the losses, while jurisdictions like the British Virgin Islands, Bermuda, Cayman Islands, the Netherlands, Switzerland and Luxembourg are some of the most prominent tax havens.

Understanding the limits of redistribution, as these limits relate to tax havens, is critical in tackling inequality. The Panama Papers shocked the world in 2016 by revealing the massive extent to which some rich individuals were hiding away their money in tax havens, though in the five years following those revelations, governments have managed to retrieve 1.36 billion U.S. dollars in unpaid taxes.[28] The Paradise Papers soon followed, while more recently the Pandora Papers,[29] the largest such leak in history, were released to the public, once more confirming the immense scale of the movement of capital and tax dodging practices.[30] In 2021, the investigative journalism organization ProPublica also obtained IRS files, which further established the fact that American billionaires pay little to nothing in income taxes. Between 2014 and 2018, the 25 individuals ProPublica investigated saw their collective wealth rise by 401 billion U.S. dollars, while they paid a total of 13.6 billion U.S. dollars in federal income taxes during the same period.[31] The report claims that Warren Buffet's true tax rate in fact amounts to a miniscule 0.10 percent.

It should be said that this is not necessarily illegal, but rather the result of a combination of finding loopholes in the tax code, the unwillingness to adequately tax these individuals, and the fact that many of these people simply do not receive any income. Jeff Bezos was able to pay no income tax in 2007 and 2011, while his net worth skyrocketed during both years; this was achieved by merit of the fact that, under U.S. law, there is no capital gains tax on unsold stocks. U.S. billionaires thus hold onto their stocks, while borrowing money at low interest rates, paying back said loans and evading federal income taxes.[32] To put it simply: billionaires do not play by the same rules as the average person.[33]

This has important implications for inequality. While the wealth that is created grows at a higher rate than the economy, as Piketty's aforementioned research suggests, the few who benefit from it are, as discussed, either siphoning their money to tax havens or preventing any of their gains from being shared by the rest. In theory, wealthy individuals should indeed spend more on luxury goods, which also carry high taxes, but this is not always the case, with regressive taxes like the VAT (Value Added Tax) disproportionally hurting lower income individuals. In this light, any attempt to redistribute wealth and income is almost futile in a vacuum, since countries risk losing revenue if they do not appease their wealthy taxpayers.

The inequality discourse often focuses on a rather western-centric context, largely due to the availability of good data. It can thus be hard to see why it is a global phenomenon, and we often neglect to consider how inequality manifests itself in other settings and countries. In view of colonial legacies, historical developments, geopolitical relations, and conflicts, one would not get far by using the same frameworks to study inequalities globally.

Though it is beyond the scope of this chapter to analyze each individual case, dissecting case studies, such as that of Bangladesh, one of the most unequal countries in the world, reveals just how differently inequality can rear its ugly head. Though the state of experienced relative deprivation may remain the same, economies globally are at different points and their inequality struggles reflect this fact. We thus spoke to Prof. Badiul Alam Majumdar, who provided us with a perspective on Bangladesh. He is an economist, development worker and political activist, with decades of experience in his field. He is also the founder-secretary of the civil society organization "Citizens for Good Governance", as well as the vice president of "The Hunger Project".

Inequality

Interview with Badiul Alam Majumdar, The Hunger Project

Q: How has the discourse and perception of inequality in South-East Asia, and Bangladesh, changed over the decades and what aspects have received more attention; for example, **the digital divide?**

Badiul Alam Majumdar: Awareness about inequality has been created with time, and lots of people are now interested in the ever-increasing inequality and the digital divide — more specifically in terms of the urban-rural divide. Urban areas, of course, have more employment and higher incomes, but there is also more growing inequality in urban areas relative to rural areas. It goes without saying that rural areas have less digitalization, less electricity access, and less internet connectivity. The pandemic made the urban-rural divide all the more obvious and serious as schools are closed, and the government encouraged students to stay inside and learn through online platforms. My own experience was different back when I was growing up — at that time disparity was not all that great — but overtime the quality of urban schools has increased, the opposite being the case for rural areas, which largely contributed to the inequality we see today.

Another cause is climate change, whereby some urban areas are not yet hit hard by it, but rural areas are bearing the brunt of it. There is also the gender dimension of inequality. In Bangladesh's patriarchal society, for example, women are subjugated, marginalized, and deprived, creating serious generational inequality between women and men. However, the living conditions of women have improved over time through the actions of NGO's, which empowered and supported women to be economic entrepreneurs, contributing to lowering poverty in the country; although the pandemic has to a great extent reversed the hard-earned gains made over the years. We must also not forget the effects of crony capitalism, which lets the rich and the powerful get unfettered access to resources and opportunities, and they are even allowed to loot banks without any consequences. This is facilitated by the fact that two thirds of

Bangladesh's MPs are businesspeople, who have access to power, and, with it, the money.

Q: Where do you see progress in reducing inequality in Bangladesh, South-East Asia, and beyond?

Badiul Alam Majumdar: If you look at evidence, Bangladesh is a much more unequal country than many others. In fact, people are growing rich at a faster rate in Bangladesh than any other country in the world. However, the pandemic worsened inequality in every country. The daily wage earners were the hardest hit everywhere while most of the rich became richer during the pandemic. It is clear that disparity and inequality are bound to increase unless governments intervene and address the market and policy failures. One of the countries which addressed inequality relatively more successfully is Taiwan. The generous social safety-net programs of Western countries make inequality more tolerable. In this regard, European countries have done better than the United States.

Q: What role does microfinance play in Bangladesh today? Is it still an integral asset in the fight against poverty?

Badiul Alam Majumdar: It has made enormous contributions, but it has limitations as well. It did free people from the clutches of money lenders and empowered many women to become small-scale economic entrepreneurs. NGOs played a big role providing microcredit to women and getting them out of the confines of their homes, which greatly contributed to Bangladesh's poverty eradication efforts. The ready-made garments industry owes its success largely to the availability of the stream of young women for operating sewing machines at relatively low wages. The women who were mobilized and empowered by NGOs through awareness creation and giving micro loans sent their children to schools, installed sanitary latrines, arranged safe water, and so on to improve their lives and their families's lives.

However, microcredit has its limitations. Amounts given as microcredits in most cases are low and not enough to start economically viable enterprises. Borrowing from multiple lenders has also now become a serious problem associated with microcredit. Many borrowers borrow from one lender to pay back another lender, using sort of a Ponzi scheme, and use the money for consumption rather than investment. This creates a "debt trap" for many borrowers. The pandemic has also badly hurt the microcredit industry. Because of loss of earning sources, many borrowers are now unable to pay their installments, putting the financial health of many lenders in jeopardy.

Q: How do you see future trends in inequality?

Badiul Alam Majumdar: While Bangladeshis are resilient people, there are dark clouds on the horizon. Bangladesh faces many serious challenges. One of the challenges originates from the fact that economic growth of the past has not created enough jobs and many of the jobs created are low paying. The jobless growth has failed to gainfully employ the large number of young people who enter the job market every year, making unemployment and underemployment a serious problem in Bangladesh. The pandemic has further accentuated the problem. The return of large numbers of expat workers from abroad, caused by the economic devastation worldwide, will further worsen the employment crisis as many of them will not be able to return to their former place of employment. The declining quality of Bangladesh's education also does not prepare its young people for the job market of the future, clouding their future. The high climate vulnerability of Bangladesh creates an additional challenge for the country. All these will only worsen the growing inequality in Bangladesh.

Q: In the West we observe quite a lot of adverse effects stemming from inequality, like lower life expectancy rates. How do these manifest themselves in Bangladesh?

Badiul Alam Majumdar: Bangladesh has one of the highest rates of diabetes and heart disease, but it is partly genetic and partly lifestyle-related, like consumption of processed and fatty food and sedentary living. There is also the "fetal programming" issue, meaning that a child born with low birth weight (less than 2.5 kgs), is likely to develop diabetes and heart disease later in life. This is because if an expectant mother is malnourished and is deprived of adequate nutrition during pregnancy, the fetus will develop only the essential systems needed for its survival—not the auxiliary systems needed for protecting it later from ailments such as heart disease and diabetes, as a result of which "normal" food becomes "abnormal" later in life, triggering those diseases. Thus, poverty can influence the health and well-being of the next generation because of genetic reasons, the root cause of which is deprivation, poverty, and malnutrition.

Life expectancy and health risks are also influenced by the "social determinants of health," which reflect the conditions in the environment where people are born, live, learn, work, play, worship, and age as well as the complex and interrelated social structures and economic systems that create discrimination and inequality. The growing inequality in Bangladesh, reflecting lack of opportunity and lack of resources, creates serious health inequalities which lower the life expectancy of the poor of Bangladesh.

A focus on inequality in the United States is natural, as the world often looks to the *city on the hill* for guidance or lessons to be drawn; but all over the world the causes of inequality differ, as we saw in the case of Bangladesh. In Greece, the Economic Adjustment Programs (EAPs) that the European Commission, the European Central Bank, and the International Monetary Fund implemented, saw the bottom quintile experience a 51.3 percent loss in its share of GDP from 2010 to 2017, compared to the top quintile, which saw its income fall by 36.2 percent.[34] Everyone experienced massive losses, while the cuts in health care led to many preventable deaths and an unprecedented rise in mortality,[35] but the austerity approach indeed hit the poorest the hardest.

In South Africa, a nation noted by the Wealth and Income Database as the most unequal country in the world,[36] has in fact seen a rise in inequality since 1994 in the context of gradual land reform and the remnants of apartheid.[37] This only goes to show that, in many contexts, colonial legacies persist to this day. To quote a massive recent analysis of inequality in countries that suffered under colonialism: "The situation of inequality just before independence weighed on postcolonial developments, even when European settlers had left".[38] In Tunisia, the urgent replacement of French civil

Inequality

servants saw an increase in wage inequality, while in 2021 the top ten percent held 41.4 percent of all pre-tax national income.[39]

Historical context is thus necessary to understand the present day in many parts of the world. This is also the case in Mexico, a country that Alexander von Humboldt in 1811 called "the country of inequality", possibly due to its historically weak institutional structure that promoted inequalities, as Acemoglu and Robinson have suggested.[40] At the same time, we need to be careful in framing inequality as an "economic destiny", as modern economic reforms in Mexico have seen the wealth of multimillionaires skyrocket, while "the top 1% of Mexico's high earners enjoy a whopping 21% of the national income in 2012".[41]

We spoke to Christian Joel González Cuatianquis, Executive Director of Analysis of Strategic Issues at the National Council for the Evaluation of Social Development Policy.

Interview with Christian Joel González Cuatianquis, National Council for the Evaluation of Social Development Policy

Q: Can you talk a bit about the primary drivers of inequality in Mexico specifically and how they relate to the rest of the world at large?

Joel González Cuatianquis: In my view, you have to go back in history to understand these developments. The classes that the Spanish elite once instituted went on existing way beyond their time, while a general unhappiness has accompanied all changes in land ownership in our past. Although there hasn't been any slavery per se, working people in this country have always had to work as such in order to make a living. Another aspect is the inequality between the big cities, which did evolve and industrialize and the rural parts, which were left behind. The welfare state was instituted at some point, but only for the formal sector, further exacerbating inequality, as a lot of work is of course informal. This is an inequality that has been accumulating over time, [with] the latest major change coming from the Washington Consensus, whereby development was once again concentrated in the big centers in the North, mainly driven by the automotive industry, as the small towns and villages were completely abandoned.

Q: More and more international institutions, national administrations, and political leaders, including such diverse actors as the IMF, the Chinese government administration, and also Joe Biden, are addressing the issue of inequality in a way like never before and seeing it as an urgent threat to our society's well-being. Why do you think this is, and what are the possible consequences of a world where it is not adequately addressed?

Joel González Cuatianquis: The Washington Consensus came with some promises of competition and prosperity, but over the past 30 years, not much has happened. The rich are richer, we work longer hours to be able to afford the basic necessities, and in 2008, every institution we believed in broke down. Even in the U.S., this ideal of freedom and opportunity is no longer the same, as people work 2–3 jobs to make ends meet. The welfare state on the other hand did not work in Mexico, while at one point, we even had the richest man on the planet — and people do notice, as they have done in the EU and the U.S., for example. They seek for someone to blame. In the U.S., Trump blamed the Mexicans, while the AfD blames the immigrants.

Q: Is the issue of inequality also more prevalent in more unequal countries — both politically as well as socially — or are there perhaps other elements directing people's attention to it?

Joel González Cuatianquis: It has to do with culture as well. In Mexico inequality is enormously high, and yet people seem to accept it somehow. Not only that, but usually people are not aware of their true place in the income distribution, mostly thinking they are middle class, no matter their true income. But Mexican people are remarkably aware of their standing, and yet they don't mind. In the U.S., there is also the idea of the American dream, and people justify their position like this, while the French will strike for anything and everything. So you can see the cultural aspect as well.

Q: What measures do you see as being successful in reducing different types of inequality, both in Mexico as well as the rest of the world, and what is lacking currently?

Inequality

Joel González Cuatianquis: There has been good progress on education—with children being more likely to graduate high school, the poverty trap has, to some extent, been disrupted through cash transfer programs. But there are also problems: there are no jobs afterwards. More importantly, indigenous people are also discriminated against, while these cash programs are not designed as well as they could.

The question of why income and wealth inequality have risen to such a degree over the past decades is still up for debate, with ideological convictions often getting in the way of productive discussions. Abhijit Banerjee and Esther Duflo have identified several potential factors.[42] Although said rise did indeed coincide with the Reagan-Thatcher years, less redistribution through lower taxation rates and cuts in welfare spending, though significant, could only be the sole explanations of the rise in inequality if everything else remained the same, which has not been the case.

As the labor share of income and GDP fell during the past decades, economists scrambled and quarreled to provide an explanation, seeing as it had been relatively stable in the past. One explanation is the rapid technological innovation and the rise of "superstar firms"—industry giants which take over the market and draw talent away from smaller ones further establishing their dominance. Autor et al. indeed convincingly argued that part of the fall could be attributed to the consolidation of these large superstar firms.[43]

A 2021 dissertation on superstar firm market entry, concentrating on Walmart in the United States, in fact found that "supercenter entry caused aggregate local employment to fall and workers to gradually exit the labor force. The employment losses were realized outside the retail sector, yielding greater local employment concentration in the retail sector...In fact, Supercenter entry caused earnings to fall".[44]

Still, this does not address the fact that the rise in inequality, though universal, has also been asymmetrical. As such, a second plausible explanation in the role of finance and CEO income comes into play. We spoke to Sarah Anderson, an expert on the topic, and the director of the Global Economy Project and co-editor of Inequality.org at the Institute for Policy Studies, a progressive center for research and action in Washington, DC.

Interview with Sarah Anderson, Global Economy Project

Q: Why has Inequality entered the policy agenda with such force in recent years and how have economists developed and adapted their thinking on the topic?

Sarah Anderson: The evolution of the field of economics has been fascinating for me. During the Cold War between the United States and Soviet Union, Americans who advocated for economic redistribution to reduce inequality were viewed as potentially subversive. So most U.S. economists shifted their focus to a "rising tide" of economic growth, which can "lift all boats". Kennedy first called for a cut in the top tax rate, but it was Reagan that slashed it drastically, arguing for a new trickle-down economics model, based on the theory that those at the top are the job creators and their wealth would "trickle down" to the rest. In the decades since, there has been voluminous research showing this is a failed theory. Rising inequality is not only seen through a moral lens, but also an economic one, as it is detrimental to growth. The rich can squirrel away their wealth, while lower-income individuals need to spend nearly everything they earn, which boosts the broader economy.

Research also shows that extreme inequality is bad for business. As the gap between CEO and worker pay gets bigger, it undermines worker morale and productivity.

So, why are we talking about this now? The 2008 financial crisis was surely a turning point, as wealthy Wall Street executives, who were once romanticized, drove the economy off a cliff. The Occupy movement that carried out prolonged protests near Wall Street popularized the concept of the 99 percent versus the 1 percent, and that has had lasting impact. The issue of extreme inequality has come even more into focus during the pandemic, as so many people have suffered while U.S. billionaires have added to their wealth and paid little to no tax.

Q: Inequality is and has been rising in the U.S. for the past 50 or so years. Which are the key discourses and topics in the U.S.? Who shapes the debates on inequality? Which issues are on top of the political agenda?

Sarah Anderson: Inequality dominated the 2020 Democratic presidential primary race, and that pressure, plus the impact of the pandemic, moved President Biden to go beyond his traditional focus on labor issues to tackle our country's extreme wealth and income concentration. Backed by strong support from labor unions, anti-poverty groups, and a growing number of progressives in Congress, he is now supporting some fairly bold increases in taxes on the wealthy and large corporations. An increasing important focus of the inequality debate is racial inequality. The Black Lives Matter movement has helped push these issues into the forefront. On top of all the issues around police brutality, every indicator of economic inequality grows bigger when you factor in race. There is an ongoing debate as to how to fight this problem, either indirectly through policies like canceling student debt and raising the minimum wage, or directly through reparations for slavery.

Q: There is a fundamental tension between the classic American dream and the type of inequality observed in the United States today, while the narrative around the rich has changed from "robber barons" to national superstars and living proof of an existing meritocracy. To what extent are these narratives true and could you add a little more nuance to the discussion?

Sarah Anderson: We call this the "myth of deservedness", which states that the rich deserve what they have, as they work harder and are smarter, while the poor are lazy. A significant part of the work against inequality is to combat this myth, as the Poor Peoples Campaign has done. Our recent Institute for Policy Studies report, "Silver Spoon Oligarchs", shows precisely how 50 families in the U.S. have become dynasties through inheriting incredible amounts of wealth, while the tax system allows them to do so. At the same time, CEO pay during the pandemic actually went up — not because top executives performed spectacularly, but rather because corporate boards took actions to protect their pay from pandemic risk.

Q: What are some realistic and effective policies that can be implemented in the next few years in the U.S. and in other countries? How do you rate the relevance of financial sector reforms in addressing inequality? The EU and Germany (with its new Sustainable Finance Strategy, May 2021) aim to become leaders in sustainable finance. How do you rate the relevance of sustainable finance initiatives and taxonomies for the social sectors in addressing inequality?

Sarah Anderson: The role of the finance sector should be to work for the real economy, meaning making credit available for families and businesses, and yet it is dominated by short-term speculation and high-speed trading that has no real economic value. In the U.S., as banks abandon low-income areas, people, particularly people of color, have to turn to predatory lenders and check-cashing firms that charge huge fees. On the policy side, a financial transaction tax is something we have been pushing since 2009, but negotiating such bold policies at the international level is difficult because of changes in governments and crises that distract from the focus, especially when the political will is weak. So we're pushing this at both the national and international levels.

If the sustainable finance agenda of the EU leads to an understanding by policymakers that we need stronger financial regulation to ensure environmental and social safeguards, that would be a positive step.

Q: What is the scope for individual countries, smaller and larger economies, to implement effective policies to reduce inequality in a globalized world? How do you see the potential of international cooperation to tackle inequality? Will the G7 or G20 take initiatives to address inequality issues?

Sarah Anderson: During the 2008-09 financial crisis, the G20 played a useful role in coordinating economic stimulus policies that helped lessen the pain for ordinary people. But this effort wasn't big enough and didn't last long. Also, a key factor was that the U.S. president at the time (Obama) could agree to the G20 deal, knowing

that he had a good chance of getting it through Congress, since his party had sizable majorities in both the Senate and House.
Today, there is an encouraging discussion in the G7 and the G20 around a global minimum tax on corporate profits. All countries suffer when global corporations use accounting tricks and tax havens to avoid paying their fair share of taxes. This enriches corporate CEOs and investors while sticking the rest of us with the bill. But in the United States we're not waiting around for an international agreement, for two reasons. First, Biden's party has only a razor-thin majority in Congress and under our system this means it would be very difficult for him to deliver on an international agreement. Second, an international agreement could take many years and we can do a lot domestically, especially in the current political moment, to crack down on corporate tax avoiders. Moreover, given the huge global footprint of U.S.-based corporations, unilateral action might also have beneficial effects elsewhere.
The United Nations is a critical body for establishing international standards on labor, environment, human rights, and other issues and facilitating international dialogue and cooperation. But most U.S. activism on inequality is focused on domestic policy. This is because of the UN's limited enforcement power and because we feel if we can "get our own house in order" it will have positive ripple effects globally.

Although high incomes have risen, it is the top incomes which have skyrocketed, suggesting that technological change can also not be the lone determinant of this explosion in inequality, as was examined by the aforementioned studies. The radical shift in finance, which has seen an explosion of short-term speculative activities, combined with what is often described as heavily rewarded rent-seeking, is now seen as carrying a heavy share of the blame.

Inevitably, any discussion on inequality must also lead to the question of redistribution and taxation. Equally predictable is the eternal question of tax rates in Scandinavian countries. The aptly named "How can Scandinavians tax so much" paper by Henrik Jacobsen Kleven provides some useful and largely counter-intuitive insights into what we conventionally know about taxes.[45] For one, Scandinavian countries raise a lot of revenue to pay for their programs by taxing everyone and implementing flat income taxes, which kick in at much lower incomes than in, for example, the United States.[46] This leads to a strange result, in that U.S. taxation is much more progressive than that of these countries, especially considering that Denmark, Sweden, and Norway have VAT rates of 25 percent—a tax which disproportionally hurts the poorest. Yet, said countries have remarkably low tax avoidance or evasion rates, while also having high incomes, normal employment rates, and are typically highly equal.

Although some of the above may seem counter-intuitive, one must always consider how countries spend their revenue. Social spending targeted at children and families and the provision of free goods such as childcare allows women to enter the workforce in larger numbers. Inequality of market income in the three aforementioned countries is high, as is the case with most countries, but it is the massive redistribution which leads to a more equitable distribution of disposable income.[47]

Figure 5.2: Inequality of Market/Disposable Income in Relation to the Gini Coefficient

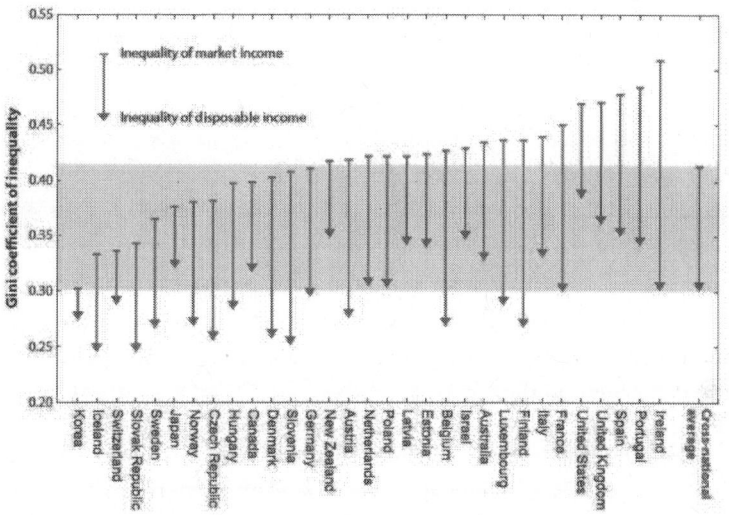

Source: Gornick and Smeeding (2018).[48]

But redistribution will clearly not suffice if market income is skewed so heavily to one side in an era where governments are severely constrained in their policy options. In fact, looking at the "New Labour" period of the U.K., an era during which Tony Blair and Gordon Brown led the British government toward a path of greater redistribution, we can see the paradox of successful efforts in redistribution combined with no changes in inequality. Largely driven by soaring top 1 percent incomes, redistribution indeed halted what would have been an explosion in inequality;[49] though the redistribution measures employed were by no means enough to reduce real inequality.

For this reason, we need to consider institutions and policies that bring about more equal pre-distribution, such as higher minimum wages, or stronger workers bargaining power and union participation. In fact, income and inheritance taxes are heavily correlated with unionization rates in 20 countries.[50] Considering the vast inequalities in voter participation, whereby poorer, disillusioned individuals elect not to participate in elections (although recent research suggests that income interventions, which bridge the civic participation gap are effective only in an individual's early life),[51] as well as the steady decline of trade unions, it makes sense that people are slowly being deprived of formal channels to express their grievances. A look into the protest participation literature also suggests that poorer individuals tend to participate less in non-violent protests, such as petition signing,[52] while Relative Power Theory posits that the wealthy use their resources to reduce the political salience of inequality and conserve their status.[53] Coupled with stagnant wages, a drop in progressive taxation, and the inferior quality of participation in democracy that less affluent individuals experience, it is hard to see how mere redistribution can alleviate inequality.

Figure 5.3: Mean Top Rates of Income and Inheritance Taxes in 20 Countries and Trade Union Density in Ten Countries, 1890–2010 (percent)

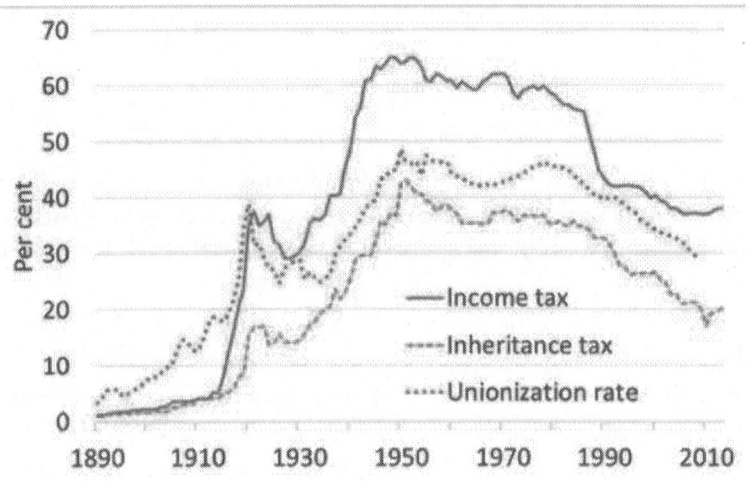

Sources: Scheve and Stasavage (2016.[54]

What appear to be insurmountable obstacles to fighting back against inequality may warrant feelings of pessimism or hopelessness, but there is a silver lining: those who care about inequality have access to better data than before and are able to show the extent of the problem in a much more comprehensive manner.

The collaborative World Inequality Report 2022 is the latest such project,[55] providing a clear picture of the existing disparities and sounding the alarm for what is to come. The findings are distressing with the global bottom 50 percent capturing only 8.5 percent of the income (at Purchasing Power Parity or PPP) and a mere 2 percent of the wealth. The authors find the trend of a falling between-country inequality to be continuing but warn that within-country inequality is reaching levels last seen in the early 20th century, at the peak of Western imperialism. MENA (Middle East and North Africa) is the most unequal region, while Europe is the only region, where the middle class has an overall higher share of national income than the top ten percent.

Figure 5.4: Bottom 50 Percent, Middle 40 Percent and Top 10 Percent Income Shares Across the World in 2022

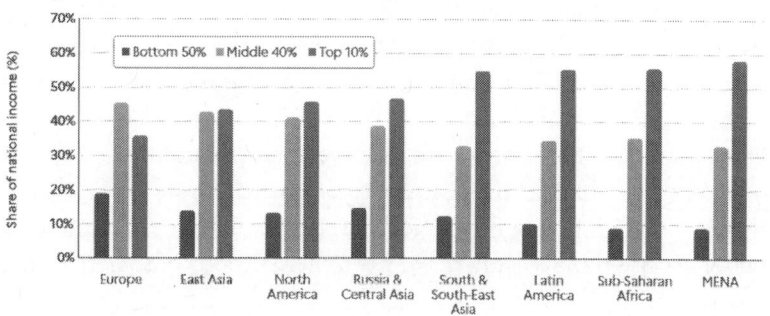

Source: World Inequality Report 2022[56]

The authors once again show that the benefits from the extraordinary growth of the past couple of decades have disproportionally landed in the hands of the richest of the rich, producing the all too familiar Elephant Curve.

Furthermore, the report shows global billionaire wealth to have reached 3.5 percent of global household wealth, while women globally are capturing a little less than 35 percent of income, up from 30 percent in 1990.[17] Meanwhile, the global ten percent is responsible for 48 percent of global carbon emissions, as opposed to the bottom 50 percent, which only carries a twelve percent share. We will explore the proposals of the authors in the next section, but first we must address the issue of wealth inequality in greater detail.

Inequality can be exacerbated by the increasing money supply, which has again risen in the context of the COVID-19 crisis and the resulting large state compensation programs. Interest rates remain low because debts of states are at a high level and economic growth is slow or negative. The speed of circulation of money shrinks in phases when the economy is not growing.[57] Therefore, we did not initially see a rapid rise of inflation even though the central banks flooded the markets with liquidity. Then demand began to rise as the economy rebounded, and supply chain bottlenecks saw the supply side unable to keep up with the skyrocketing demand, with many predicting that the ensuing price inflation would last well into 2022.

Another issue during the COVID-19 pandemic was a booming stock market, which saw wealthy individuals enrich themselves, even at times when the "real" economy was stagnant. Many people lack the financial means and/or knowledge to participate in the stock market, which is why we observe such inequalities.

We suggest that the inequality of participation in the rise of the financial markets can politically and socially be only, or at least better accepted if investments of the richer sections of society target companies with business models that bring particular benefits to the entire society and the environment — for example, developing new energy and recycling technologies — while also distributing the gains more equally. Hence, we are seeing a trend toward green and sustainable finance. For a long time, political supervision and guidance of financial markets were strongly resented by financial market players. Now, many investors consider the sustainable finance trend as a trend that provides the financial industry with higher legitimacy as the contribution of the financial industry to climate action is acknowledged.

Inequality

Another way to address this issue is to make the rest of the people shareholders as well. Two historically successful examples of citizen participation in financial markets—one of which has served to fund a universal basic income (UBI) project on a local level, as well as welfare state operations—are those of the "Alaska Permanent Fund" as well as Norway's "Government Pension Fund Global". A lot of attention is devoted to income inequality, but it tends to overshadow capital income inequality, which has historically always been high and has only gotten much worse. Matt Bruenig, founder of the "People's Policy Project" think tank, calculated that, in 2016 in the United States, "the top 1 percent had an average wealth of 26.6 million U.D. dollars, while the net worth of everyone in the bottom third combined was less than zero".[58] Instituting a national wealth fund which provides all citizens with an equal, non-transferable share of investments is nearly identical to Atkinson's approach of providing all citizens with capital upon reaching 18 years of age.[59]

Wealth inequality is traditionally conceived of as being different from income inequality, but a recent study by Yonatan Berman and Branko Milanovic has shown that the classic distinction in economics may be obsolete in terms of the division of individuals into "laborers and capitalists".[60] *Homoploutia* is their chosen term to describe the state of owning both large amounts of capital as well as receiving high incomes as an individual. Capital is already unevenly distributed, but the authors found that "[in] 1985, about 17 percent of adults in the top decile of capital-income earners were also in the top decile of labor-income earners. In 2018 this indicator was about 30 percent".

Before we move on to the next section, we need to once more remind ourselves that inequality is multi-faceted, and there are two more dimensions that need to be at least partially addressed here. Unfortunately, one can rightfully assume that whatever inequalities exist will be worse when it comes to gender and race; although we have made great improvements in these regards, and the setting in question matters. Nevertheless, we need to always be aware of the history and legacies of the systems in place, such as welfare states originally built to uphold Christian values,[61] which put, for example, single mothers at a disadvantage, or highways that divide black and white neighborhoods and perpetuate structural inequalities.[62][63]

In the U.K., a study found that 55 percent of the gender pay gap at the age of 25, or soon after graduation, can be explained by the difference in chosen subjects in school.[64] The Institute for Fiscal Studies has shown that women who studied economics, a field in which they are severely underrepresented, earn 75 percent more on average by the age of 30 than women who studied creative arts. Anna Stansbury, an assistant professor at MIT Sloan School of Management, along with Robert A. Schultz also recently showed that economics is the least socioeconomically diverse of all the major PhD fields,[65] which is beyond worrying, as economists pick and choose, create, and shape narratives that run through every aspect of our lives.

Traditional gender norms, and ideas about which subjects are "right" for women and men, end up creating unequal payoffs in a world that has historically been dominated by patriarchal archetypes. This is not to say that women should merely pick subjects that provide higher returns, as "attitudes toward risk, recognition for group work, hours worked, the propensity to bargain over wages and ask for promotions, and discrimination"[64] are all factors which hold women back in the workplace. In the United States, the compound effect of gender and race sees African American women lose around 14,300 U.S. dollars and 40,000 U.S. dollars annually in low and high wage jobs, respectively, compared to White men.[66]

Though we may consider certain inequalities a thing of the past, such as those of gender norms or stereotypes, we must be careful about proclaiming victory so soon. As a last remark on this topic, one may also consider the following findings: "Asian-American women performed better on a mathematics test when their ethnic identity was activated, but worse when their gender identity was activated",[67] while African Americans with stronger stereotypically "black" facial features receive longer prison sentences,[68] the two examples highlighting implicit/explicit biases, which produce inequalities.

Beyond effective policy choices, which we will explore in the next section, there is an urgent need to recognize that large scale changes pertaining to structural inequalities within societies cannot be merely ameliorated by law or legislation. Normative shifts in our thinking are required.

5.4 Tackling Inequality

Implementing effective policies means understanding the drivers of inequality and although we are still struggling to get a full picture of the root causes, combining said policies eventually brings us closer to a more equitable and sustainable distribution of wealth and income.

The Sustainable Development Goal (SDG) 10 pertains to reducing inequalities, and countries must evidently plan accordingly. China seems to be leading this race, switching its focus from poverty alleviation to reducing disparities through achieving what the CCP has called "Common Prosperity". The term was first introduced by former chairman Mao Zedong, but senior Chinese officials seem to be wary of the connotation that would contradict Deng Xiaoping's convictions to "let some people get rich first". In 2021, President Xi Jinping did indeed call for more regulation on high incomes and greater redistribution of gains.

On the other hand, trade unions have slowly been gaining ground, even in countries like China, where their existence is multi-layered and far more complicated than the Western "class-war" image may depict. As we have previously seen, union density has over the past 100 years moved inversely with income inequality.[69] Unionization is not some fringe policy outside the Overton Window (the range of mainstream and acceptable policies by a given population at a given time), and the United States seems to also be shifting its thinking when it comes to the structure of the economy. To quote U.S. President Joe Biden, "I believe every worker should have a free and fair choice to join a union".[70] Union participation is traditionally seen as having a "wage premium", which especially helps the less educated, while reducing wage inequality and contributing to pre-distribution.

Figure 5.5: Top 10 Percent of Income/Gini Coefficient-Share Unionized

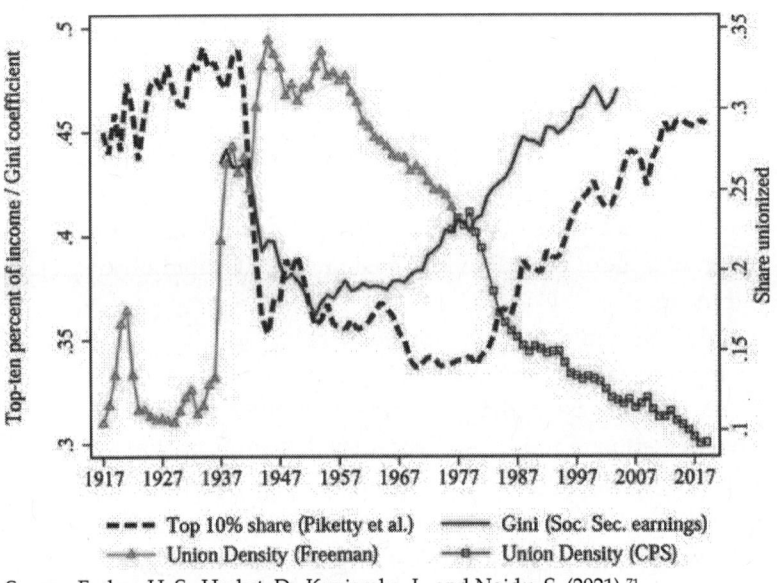

Source: Farber, H. S., Herbst, D., Kuziemko, I., and Naidu, S. (2021).[71]

A good-paying job, where the individual feels like they are contributing something to society and are respected is not a necessary evil; it is an integral part of our lives. Not only does job displacement correlate with higher death rates in the aftermath,[72] but it has also been shown to radicalize politicians in the jurisdictions where it was most prominent, with Autor et al. showing that, in the United States, the most conservative Republican candidates were elected in areas where the China Shock hit the manufacturing industries the hardest.[73]

A job guarantee (JG) in that sense, combined with protections offered by union membership could go a long way in the era of the gig economy, job computerization, and automation, but we should be mindful of creating further sticky economies that can lead to such outcomes. Still, having a job is not necessarily enough if the pay is not adequate, and so it must be coupled with a higher minimum wage above the poverty line.[74] A Job Guarantee or the pursuit of full employment is nevertheless not a perfect solution, but useful as a guiding light.

In such a world, the demand for jobs would be low and workers would have more bargaining power to set wages and demand better working conditions, which leads us to the concept of collective and sectoral bargaining. This type of bargaining does not merely affect union members, as in the case of France, where an eight percent union membership rate coincides with "95 percent of its workforce...covered by extensions of nationally negotiated collective bargaining contracts".[75] Because union density will take a lot of time to get back to anywhere near what it once was, while higher minimum wages can only benefit certain sectors and individuals, there is still a need for wage boards and sectoral bargaining, whereby the lowest wages and those in the middle are raised, lowering wage inequality.

While such ideas and plans are necessary changes, they should be gradual, as Arindrajit Dube notes, due to their effects on aggregate demand and price inflation.[75] But it is a fallacy to thus conclude that we should not implement any changes for fear of destabilizing the economy, as it can only get much worse on the current path.

We should keep in mind that economics is an empirical science, but it also has a strong social aspect, which influences what kind of research is done and what the theoretical foundations look like. Recently, it has become clear that the field is experiencing a transformation, which is not merely constrained in its theory, as new data is radically propelling the field forward. In October 2021, *The Economist* proudly ran a cover with the words "Instant Economics: The real-time evolution", based on the idea that said data will allow for new frontiers in policymaking and prevent economic malpractice.[76]

In 2021 there were also two important statements coming out of the Federal Reserve, an institution with a long history of inertia in its thought and actions. For one, Fed Chair Jerome Powell noted that "The historical record is thick with examples of underdoing it", referring to the Fed's response in previous crises.[77] In the same month, Jeremy B. Rudd of the Federal Reserve released a paper titled "Why Do We Think That Inflation Expectations Matter for Inflation? (And Should We?)", a caustic critique of the assumptions underscoring our current economic policy.[78] Rudd pointed out something simple: we are not always sure how inflation works, and it does not look like it has anything to do with the current economic axiom that expected inflation leads to a genuine rise of inflation. It may sound counter-intuitive, but our current understanding of the economy and of inflation is based on theoretical concepts like the Phillips-curve, which have in the past years begun to partially break down, and as such leave a vacuum in policymaking and narrative-setting.[79]

The transformation is massive, and is not merely constrained within the Fed, as evidenced by the 2021 Nobel Prize in economics, awarded to David Card, Joshua Angrist, and Guido Imbens, who changed the way we view and study labor markets.[80] For decades, the minimum wage has divided economists, as standard economic theory posits that setting the wage above market level will set off a fall in employment.[81] But now, study after study confirms that this just does not seem to be the case, provided the minimum wage is implemented in a manner guided by research; for example, tying the wage to inflation, or setting it to 60 percent of the local median wage.[82] Indeed, getting more money to consumers may even increase employment, as indirectly shown with U.S. states that cut unemployment insurance sooner than others having significantly slowed down their overall job creation and recovery during the COVID-19 pandemic.[83]

In regard to inequality, more and more economists are pointing to the shortcomings of a tunnel vision type of optimization of growth at the expense of a more equitable distribution. The Labor government in New Zealand has also conceptually moved on from measuring economic success in terms of GDP growth, and instead uses a "Wellbeing Budget" that tracks and promotes the well-being of its citizens.[84]

The idea for a long time has been that a trade-off between growth at the expense of equality is necessary. However, developed countries have now been struggling to justify this ever-increasing inequity as they experience hampered growth rates. By lowering interest rates, there has been notable compensation, but GDP growth has now substantially slowed down, and aggregate demand has lagged behind.[85] This makes sense considering that the gains are going to the top decile, which tends to spend less of their income than the rest, while the top one percent and especially the top 0.01 percent use tax loopholes and have been noted not to participate in the real economy.[86]

This slowdown is now largely attributed to inequality by institutions like the IMF,[87] and the OECD,[88] while Thieß Petersen of the Bertelsmann Foundation believes that there is an inverted U relationship between inequality and growth, [89] whereby countries like Germany are more than likely on the wrong side of it. The important thing to keep in mind is that there are pragmatic and ambitious solutions to inequality. If countries want to meet their citizens' demands as well as their SDGs, there are viable options in their policy arsenal.

The authors of the World Inequality Report 2022, for example, recommend a global progressive wealth tax and point out that there is no justification for the current wealth taxes remaining flat, even though taxes on income are progressive and capital accumulation progresses faster by the day.[17] The tax would target 62 million individuals globally (1.2 percent of the total population), as it would kick in at a million dollars, and have 6 brackets of progressively higher taxes. If there is one important takeaway from the report is that any solution will require international cooperation, which we know works, because previous programs like the Foreign Account Tax Compliance Act (FATCA) in the U.S. and the DAC (Directive on Administrative Co-operation) in the European Union work, or at least they work better than no cooperation would.

Before we dream this big though, there are still things we could do tomorrow to alleviate inequality. Homelessness is one of the problems which is likely to be tackled as deservingness criteria fall apart in the face of numerous studies showing that a lack of money or a lack of housing can only be solved if said necessities are provided.[90] Homelessness in Finland has almost disappeared after a genuine declaration of war against it, and in Canada a one-time payment of 7,500 Canadian dollars saw those who received the payment find housing after an average of 3 months, while "spending on alcohol, cigarettes and drugs went down, on average, by 39 per cent",[91] contrary to what many people might expect to be the case.

This is not to say that handing out checks or that raising taxes is going to solve every problem. Indeed, Piketty himself concludes his aforementioned book by acknowledging that a global tax regime requires unprecedented international cooperation, and that investment in education, knowledge, and non-polluting technologies is also a necessary step toward greater equality.[92]

Tackling the global network of tax havens will be critical, as governments begin to seek new ways of raising revenue that does not hinge on regressive taxation. In Germany, a country that is considered to have a progressive tax system, the poorest ten percent see 30 percent of their income go to the state, while the top one percent pay only about 40 percent of theirs in taxes, mainly in income and wealth taxes.[93]

At the same time, the Bertelsmann Foundation finds that wage inequality keeps increasing in Germany, a large part of which can be explained by a drop in collective bargaining agreements.[94] International trade has very little effect, unlike "The shift to higher education and age groups [which] explains around 10 and 20 percent respectively of the total rise in wage inequality from 1996 to 2010".

Figure 5.6: Development of Wage Inequality in Germany

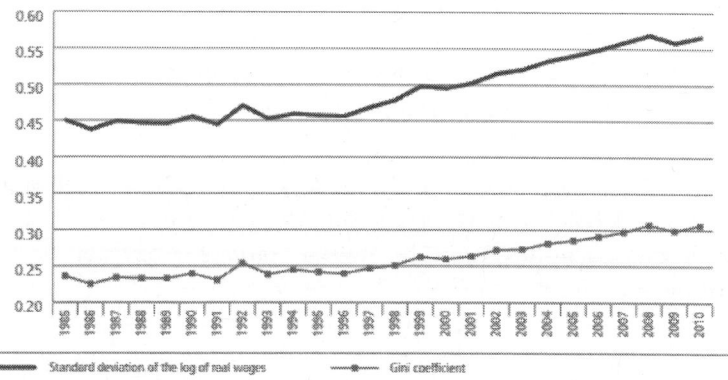

Source: Felbermayr and Lehwald (2015).⁹⁵

Considering and implementing all these ambitious plans may seem frightening at first. Nevertheless, one can only wonder why we see little to no change, even while we understand the massive scale of the problem. Before we move on to the next chapter, it is useful to consider the lack of implementation from both the supply and the demand side.

From a purely ideological perspective, one would expect that parties considered to be on the left of the political spectrum, which traditionally campaign in favor of more taxation and redistribution, would act upon these beliefs while in power. Beramendi and Rueda instead find that social democratic parties have, in the past, implemented regressive taxes, e.g., the VAT, to finance their operations.⁹⁶ The authors find that stronger corporatism is associated with these constraints, but it is worth noting what is now a fundamental law in our globalized world: capital and individuals are increasingly mobile. Attempting to raise taxes in a vacuum seems catastrophic, as people will merely seek to shift their wealth elsewhere. Hakelberg and Rixen in their 2021 study do confirm that international cooperation to prevent tax competition has helped prevent capital flight.⁹⁷ They note that since 2009, these efforts have seen a reversal of tax cuts, due to the successful fight against tax evasion, usually concentrated in the top one percent, which allows for greater progressivity in taxation.

But there is a deeper problem at the heart of the inequality discourse, and in our view, it may be the catalyst for achieving progress: the sheer and unequivocal lack of information a given person possesses about their position in the distribution of income is the invisible restraint to an already invisible force. There is an urgent need to reframe the discourse and provide people with factual information, as well as try to be more ambitious in our policy. As it stands, half of all Americans want the pandemic child benefits to not be a permanent measure,[98] effectively lowering societal welfare in favor of vague ideas of individual success and deservingness.

Information shocks, which provide people with critical knowledge they lacked before, do seem to have an effect. The two examples come from the Panama Papers and Norway. The former is almost a natural experiment, seeing as it is an exogenous shock. A 2020 study found that not only did people's redistribution preferences change in the aftermath – the change taking place mainly in those who identified as being on the right of the political spectrum – but such individuals also became more likely to vote for parties which supported redistributed policies.[99] Meanwhile, in Norway in 2001, citizens were suddenly allowed to view others's tax records,[100] granting the Norwegians what economists would call "perfect information". The results were staggering, as "income comparisons accounted for 22 percent of the happiness that individuals in Norway derived from their incomes during the period of higher transparency".

People have false assumptions about their position in the income distribution ladder, and their redistributive preferences have more to do with their perception of inequality rather than the actual levels.[101] In short, everyone thinks they are middle class.[102] Norwegians are in fact quite accurate when asked to describe the income distribution in their country, but this is less true of other nationalities.[103] The U.S. is the classic case of people massively underestimating the levels of inequality, which may be driven by either ideological beliefs in equal opportunity and deservingness criteria, trust in government, or simply a failure to connect policy with its outcomes, such as the contradictory support for redistribution as well as Bush-era tax cuts.[104]

A 2019 study ran four experiments to test how invisible inequality affected redistribution preferences, and showed how such knowledge can be useful in altering beliefs,[105] but other studies like a 2019 survey in Australia find that the effect is often times constrained in specific groups of people, such as right wing voters.[106] It should be noted, though, that these were lab experiments and, as we have seen in the case of the United States, ideology and framing play an important role. Indeed, in 2015, the Swiss had the chance to vote on raising taxes on the rich but elected not to do so due to powerful campaigning by business interests, which were able to portray the raise as hurting the economy.[107]

"Shocking" people with information just does not seem to be enough, as there are other important factors at play, such as trust in government. The lower the trust in government, the lower the support for redistribution no matter the information provided to them, while connecting said information to concrete policies and showing how it affects people's livelihoods does indeed raise their support for redistribution.[108] Perceptions of social mobility, diversity and immigration also play a role, and importantly do not have to be informed by factual information; for example, when participants in a study were made to think about immigration, which then lowered their support for redistribution.[109] Finally, rising inequality may in fact make such information shocks more powerful, as those who overestimate their position in the income distribution and are then informed of their misjudgment have been shown to be more likely to support redistribution, while those at the top do not alter their preferences.[108]

Thus, it is not enough merely to provide information to people; narratives which are not based on reality must also be torn down. Creating a sustainable and ethical economy is of utmost urgency and ideology should not get in the way, as the future of social cohesion hangs by a thread. Guided by empirical facts and lessons from the past, governments need to implement ambitious reforms and cooperate to effectively communicate their goals and subsequently tackle inequalities. The reluctance to massively overhaul current economic structures is understandable, and we should not throw the baby out with the bathwater — but if we are serious about tackling inequality, the current path is not only unjust, but also unsustainable.

Chapter 6

Demography

Population studies have a long tradition across the world. Anticipating demographic trends has always been a subject of interest for international cooperation experts. The Malthusian[1] argument that countries will face famine or war as population growth outpaces food supply, has proved to be wrong. Karl Marx and Friedrich Engels argued that Malthus failed to recognize that humans are a distinct species, and that humanity is able to push scientific and technological progress beyond the effects of population growth.[2]

However, the Malthusian argument has continued to remain a reference point for debates on demography for a long time. While the concept of biopolitics is still fresh in people's minds due to the COVID-19 pandemic, it is also a useful lens through which we should analyze this argument, as it can have subtle and dangerous undertones.[3] The idea that low birth rates are a problem in the West and a trend that needs to be reversed, but that high birth rates in other parts of the world should be constrained in the name of environmental protection is enough of an indicator to show the true colors of those who praise Malthus's "foresight".

Today, demographic developments are covered by most megatrend researchers, including Megatrends Watch, a foresight think tank based in Barcelona. It features Declining Population Growth rates, Urbanized World, and Ageing Societies as key contemporary demographic trends. On population growth, Megatrends Watch summarizes:

> "The world's population will rise to 9.7 billion in 2050 from the current level of 7.7 billion, and India is set to overtake China to become the most populous nation by 2030 with 1.5 billion people. The focus of demographic growth will be on developing countries, as their populations will grow 6 times faster than that of developed countries."[4]

The Economist pointed to the fact that the decline of fertility rate has accelerated in emerging economies. This would have profound implications for the global economy: "interest rates may become more entrenched, returns on assets could drop and global imbalances widen."[5]

Demography changes are highly relevant for policymakers. The effects of population growth or decline affect all kinds of policy areas, including labor markets, welfare state policies, energy and resource consumption, and the changing composition of consumer demand. The study of this relationship between politics and population change is called political demography. The American sociologist and political scientist Jack Goldstone is considered as the father of this emerging academic discipline. Today, the population Association of America and European Association for Population Studies (EAPS) are important research networks.

Moreover, Government offices, such as the German Federal Statistical Office, regularly publish reports and analysis demography trends. In September 2021, the German Federal Statistical Office published an analysis saying that "there will be considerably more people of retirement age in Germany by 2035.... Between 2020 and 2035, the number of people aged 67 or over will rise by 22% from 16 million to an expected 20 million."[6] The share of the world population over 50 will rise from 25 percent today to 40 percent in 2100.[7]

The European Commission published a Demography Report that says that the share of Europe's population in the world is shrinking and by 2070 it will account for just under 4 percent of the world's population. The first recommendations state that Europe's working-age population is shrinking, and ways to sustain economic growth by increasing employment rates and productivity need to be found.[8]

Overpopulation also attracts significant attention by media and activists. The Population Media Center conducts mass media campaigns to help achieve the stabilization of the human population at a level that can be sustained by the world's natural resources. In mainly Western countries, we have seen a surge in populist style social media attention focusing on immigration-led ethnic change supposedly altering the composition of a country, region or city's population.

This demonstrates how demographic issues remain politically sensitive. Anti-natalist birth policies—for example the one-child policy in China lasting from 1980 to 2015—invited much criticism by liberal-minded people. Reproductive health and family planning are highly politicized issues both on global and national levels. They are subject to continuous contestations, arising from questions about gender and equity, human rights, morality, religion, and cultural norms. Reproduction issues mobilize strong sentiments and carry great symbolic value.[9] The issue of abortion for example is highly divisive in many countries and will continue to be so. Abortion is fiercely objected to by many conservatives, especially in the United States, where the first states legalized the practice in 1967. Since then, there have been about 61.7 million abortions performed in the U.S. public support for legal abortion has fluctuated in the past decades but has remained relatively stable over the past five years. Currently, 59 percent of U.S. citizens say abortion should be legal in all or most cases, while 39 percent say it should be illegal in all or most cases.[10]

On a global institutional level, the United Nations Population Funds (UNFPA) supports reproductive health care for women and youth in more than 150 countries. Its latest strategy focuses on South-South and Triangular Cooperation projects to accelerate results in the areas of sexual and reproductive health and rights, gender equality, youth empowerment, and population and development. The Club of Rome's famous publication Limits to Growth, a 1972 report on the exponential economic and population growth with a finite supply of resources[11], eloquently stressed the linkage between population growth, resource consumption and environmental impact. Climate change has revived such debates, emphasizing the significance of demography as a future megatrend. Today, demography trends are mainly discussed in connection with prospects of economic development and scarcity of resources. We shall address such aspects but also analyze the relationship between demography and social changes with focus on social and cultural diversity in affluent societies.

6.1 Diversity of Demography Trends

Demographic developments have gone through several stages. The world population remained relatively constant until about 150 years ago, reaching one billion in 1800. The modern expansion of human numbers started thereafter, especially after the end of the Second World War. During the second half of the twentieth century population growth rates accelerated to historically unprecedented levels due to several interlinked processes: Mortality rates fell sharply, especially among infants and children in developed countries. Meanwhile, many countries witnessed a baby boom. The absence of wars and major pandemics reinforced longevity.[12]

We currently observe the following trends: low birth rates and high life expectancy lead to a shrinking population and an ageing society in advanced economies; high birth rates and short life expectancy lead to a population increase in poorer regions, even though some of them are affected by outbound migration of younger people, degradation of natural resources, and deadly local conflicts, especially in parts of sub-Sahara Africa. In West Africa, the population is expected to almost double from 402 million to 797 million until 2050. A report of the Berlin-Institute points to opportunities for cooperation with religious organization. According to the report, representatives of religious organizations enjoy a high level of trust in West Africa and many of them have become more open to advice families on birth-control.[13]

Global population trends are clearly presented by the 2021 *World Population Data Sheet*, published annually by the Population Research Bureau (PRB). It found that the total fertility rate (TFR) — or average lifetime births per woman — has declined from 3.2 in 1990 to 2.3 in 2020. However, large variations exist, ranging from 4.7 in sub-Saharan Africa to 1.3 in East Asia and Southern Europe.[14]

Demography

With regard to the effects of the COVID-19 pandemic, the PRB concluded in August 2021 that we don't have enough information to fully understand COVID-19's global demographic impact. The pandemic is likely the cause of an increase in crude death rates in some countries around the world and a dip in life expectancy in the United States."[15] We see many arguments in favor of larger and smaller populations. Recently, an analysis of age-dependent effects in the transmission and control of COVID-19 epidemics suggested that societies with younger populations have an advantage in coping with pandemics.[16] Christa Wichterich, an expert affiliated to the Heinrich Böll Foundation, pointed out that the rise of China and India has given way to a change of perception on countries with large populations, especially young populations.

> "China and India, the new major powers, are now proving that a large number of young people — precisely those who, in the discourse of 'overpopulation', had been deemed expendable — are by no means an obstacle to growth and economic advancement. On the contrary, today sizable populations are seen as an economic advantage in global competition."[17]

Let us have a closer look at the key factors affecting demographic change. Low birth rates, increasing life expectancy, and an influx of migrants are considered major population trends in economically advanced countries, though there are also exceptions; for example, life expectancy has not increased in the United States, while migration to Japan remains low. In poorer countries, higher birth rates, lower life expectancy, and out-migration are some of the key factors.

This indicates how population developments are subject to strong regional differences. Even though the world population increased from around 2.5 billion people to 7.6 billion people between 1950 and 2018, population growth varied greatly from region to region: While the total population of Europe grew by only 35 percent during this period, it increased by 460 percent in Africa.[18] This clearly demonstrates the diverging population trends in different parts of the world. In most parts of Africa populations are growing, while advanced economies are characterized by aging societies.

Interestingly, both trends tend to lose momentum. Migration is one key factor for it.

Nevertheless, experts point out that a rapidly shrinking and aging population can create stress for the welfare state and the social security systems. The relationship between aging and population shrinking and sustainable development are, however, complex. Experts argue that "a diverse set of context-specific technological, socioeconomic, institutional and governance interventions would be needed to leverage effectively the opportunities and minimize the risks posed by ageing and shrinking urban populations for long-term sustainability."[19]

The Bertelsmann Foundation, one of the leading think tanks in Germany, therefore identified demographic change as one of three megatrends and investigated how it relates to digitalization and globalization, the two other prioritized trends of the foundation.[20] The foundation argues that the demographic structure of a country shapes its integration into the international division of labor. Western industrialized countries like Germany, which have relatively few workers compared to the rest of the world, specialize in products which require little work but a lot of capital and technology. According to the foundation, labor shortage is seen as an incentive to develop labor-saving technologies through advancing digitization. Broadly speaking, this assessment is largely correct; however, we see some important exceptions. China faces no labor shortage but still pursues ambitious digitalization policies in the context of Made in China 2025, including the expansion of the use of robots. Other factors and strategies also matter, especially technology and education policies.

Demographic change and population policies have also shaped debates on the ethical legitimacy of anti-natalist birth policies. At times, almost 75 percent of the world population was affected by birth policies of different natures, including anti- but also pro-natalist policies.[21] The member states of the United Nations report regularly to the Population Division of the United Nations on pro-active birth policies.

Demography

Population-wise, policies of the most populous countries matter a lot. In January 2015, the Chinese government officially announced the end of its one-child policy, ending the most extreme state birth control project in history after 35 years. The policy reduced the growth rate of the population to close to zero. China is now incentivizing families to have a second child, with limited success, as the number of newborns has dropped by 15 percent in the year 2020.[22] With 7.52 births per 1,000 inhabitants, China recorded another record low birth rate in the year 2021, the lowest since 1949.[23] India on the other hand, is set to cross the number of 1,4 billion people and overtake China as the most populous country around the year 2026. India and China are on top of the list of countries that are set to have a population of more than 150 million people by 2030:

Figure 6.1: Countries with more than 150 million people by 2030

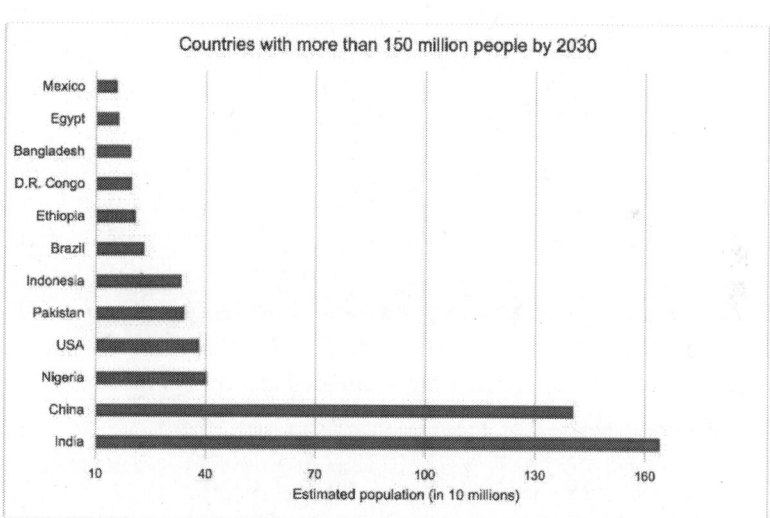

Source: Data from PopulationPyramid.net (2021).[24]

Europe's total population is shrinking because it features a particularly low birth-rate. In two-thirds of EU regions, the population is projected to decline until 2050.[25] Eurostat, a Directorate General of the European Commission, recognizes that "such developments are likely to have profound implications, not only for individuals, but also for governments, business and civil society, impacting, among others: health and social care systems, labor markets, public finances and pension entitlements."[26]

Figure 6.2: Europe's Total Population

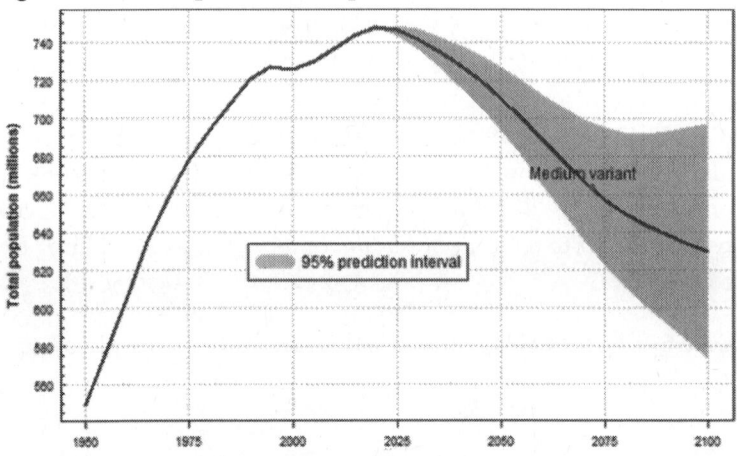

Source: United Nations (data and projections of 2019)[27]

We talked to Dr. Catherina Hinz, the Executive Director of the Berlin Institute for Population and Development, a leading European think tank on population studies, about which trends she foresees for different world regions and how she looks at the complex nexus between population dynamics and development, especially in Africa. We also asked questions on the legitimacy of anti-natalist birth policies and on promising strategies to address the challenge of aging societies.

Interview with Catherina Hinz, Director of the Berlin Institute for Population and Development

Q: Which population trends do you foresee for different world regions? To what extent do we see a consensus among demography experts? Where do we see diverging forecasts?
Catherina Hinz: We are currently experiencing the largest demographic imbalance in history. One thing we all agree on is the

Demography

declining fertility rates since the 50s–60s, as well as the slowdown of global population growth. At the same time, there is no consensus on when the plateau will be reached, or when world population will begin to shrink. Another aspect is the huge variation of trends across countries and regions; for example, youthful populations, the high fertility rates and resulting population growth in some African countries, in contrast to the aging societies and declining populations in Europe and elsewhere in the West. In general, the consensus is that the plateau will be reached some time close to the end of the century, but at what level and when exactly, that is where opinions differ. In general, medium-term projections like those of the UN, which look 30 years into the future, have been and will be more accurate than long-term projections into the more distant future.

Q: You have worked on the complex nexus between population dynamics and development in Africa. Could you please elaborate on some of your key hypotheses/findings?

Catherina Hinz: If we look at Africa, there are diverging trends even within the continent. In countries like Tunisia or South Africa, there has been a rapid decline in births, even though the population of the continent as a whole is still projected to double in the future, as some countries like Niger are currently experiencing birth rates as high as seven children per women. There is a need for more family planning, which especially benefits women of all ages, as well as an acceleration of fertility decline, in order for countries to move to a more favorable age structure and eventually reap the demographic dividend and bring about more development, through a young and productive majority, and a healthy and educated population. We can only hope that these countries will enter this window of opportunity soon. While some like Tunisia have already done so, others need to be prepared and keep up their efforts, like the Ethiopian government, which has already invested in technologies and infrastructure to make health care and family planning easier available for its citizens. Policy makers in African countries must engage today to shape tomorrow. Investments in human capital through three key sectors are vital for that: Health, Education, Agriculture.

This means improving people's access to essential health care services, especially those for family planning. The need to educate children, youth and particularly girls properly to equip them with the skills to find a decent job and take control of their own lives. And the need to provide sufficient food to generate healthy and prosperous populations.

Q: Demographic change and population policies have shaped debates on ethical assessment of the legitimacy of anti-natalist birth policies. What is your take on such policies? Which trends do you observe?

Catherina Hinz: The landmark Cairo Program of Action of 1994, reaffirmed in Nairobi back in 2019, has influenced a lot of contemporary policymaking and thought on the topic, and has put a focus on the individual, instead of top-down policymaking. The truth of the matter is that when you place women's rights at the center, everyone benefits, from families to states themselves. Women respond by having fewer children, simply out of their own choice, as they can exercise their rights and make their own choices and decisions. Now, the document itself is by no means binding, but it is reflected in all development frameworks of today. Looking at the millennium development goals, as well as SDGs, health, education, and gender are closely interconnected and always taken into account.

Q: What are some promising strategies, if there are any, to address aging societies? Is migration a key remedy, a realistic strategy (given the political resistance in many countries) and how may it, positively or negatively, impact social cohesion and economic development?

Catherina Hinz: Research suggests that societies need migration to prevent their shrinking, while migration in itself is beneficial for all if well managed. The problem of course in the EU is that there is a strong skepticism around the topic at large and governments must make a strong case for more migration, and paint it in a good light, by refuting common misconceptions, such as the fact that migrants receive more welfare than they contribute to the economy, which is simply not true, as they contribute a great amount in taxes. At the same time, we must get the facts straight to prevent fearmongering.

Demography

One example is the fact that, while surveys may show that one in three people in Sub-Saharan Africa say they would like to live in another country, in reality very few will ever migrate. Only one percent have concrete plans to move and 0.12 percent actually migrate per year. And a majority of them do not actually come to Europe; four-fifths of migrants worldwide migrate to neighboring countries.

6.2 Aging Societies

According to the United Nations, Population aging is a global phenomenon: virtually every country in the world is experiencing growth in the size and proportion of older persons who make up their population. Population aging has been fastest in Eastern and South-Eastern Asia, Latin America, and the Caribbean.[28] The below graph provides a picture of the future for these countries.

Figure 6.3: Countries or Areas with the Largest Percentage Point Increase in the Share of Older Persons Aged 65 Years or Over Between 2019 and 2050

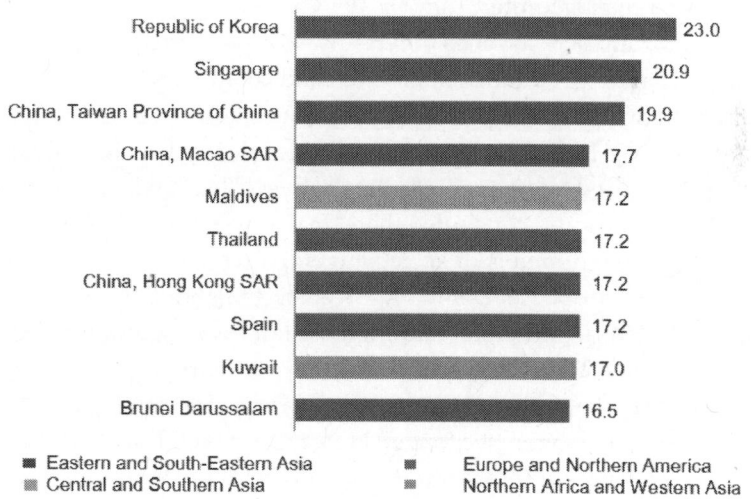

- Eastern and South-Eastern Asia
- Central and Southern Asia
- Europe and Northern America
- Northern Africa and Western Asia

Source: United Nations, Department of Economic and Social Affairs, Population Division (2019); World Population Prospects 2019.[29]

- 169 -

Global Perspectives on Megatrends

Global population trends suggest a global parity between seniors and children in terms of their putting stress on social welfare and elderly care systems. The challenge of aging societies hits countries in different continents at different times. For example, in recent decades, Brazil doubled its percentage of older people three times as fast as France, the United Kingdom, and Spain, which are already known for their inhabitants's longevity.

What are the economic consequences of a growing percentage of elderly people of a given population? One commonly used indicator is the old-age dependency ratio (OADR) which is defined as the number of old-age dependents (persons aged 65 years or over) per 100 persons of working age (aged 20 to 64 years). This metric approximates the implied economic dependency associated with a growing share of the population at older ages.[30]

European countries affected by aging populations address demographic change quite proactively by providing a series of incentives to encourage parenthood, ranging from direct payments, and significant tax advantages to the extension of childcare facilities and the introduction of generous regulations for parental leave. Success, however, remains limited.

Aging impacts societies differently, as a study in the *The Lancet Healthy Longevity* found. Cynthia Chen and co-authors from the Research Network on An Aging Society constructed a multidimensional Ageing Index to account for gender differences in societal aging. They used latest available data between 2015 and 2019 for 18 OECD countries and concluded that: "In every country, gender differences in key domains of societal ageing favour men. Countries in northern Europe (ie, Denmark, Sweden, Finland and Norway), the Netherlands, and Japan had high overall Index scores for both genders, whereas many eastern and southern European countries (eg, Hungary, Poland, and Slovenia) performed less well." Statistically speaking, women live longer. However, in their last years they are more often poor, more often sick and feel more alone, also because male partners die earlier.[31]

Theoretically speaking, aging societies need more migration to halt the trend of shrinking populations. For instance, Japan with a relatively low migration influx has the oldest population in the world: 28.7 percent of the population are 65 or older, with women forming the majority. By 2036, people aged 65 and over will represent a third of the population. Since 2011, the Japanese population has also been shrinking.[32] But migration continues to be a subject of political controversy, as it is seen to challenge the social cohesion of societies. However, migration remains a strong trend for various reasons which are difficult to control or anticipate, such as wars, political conflicts, and natural disasters. Climate change is likely to accelerate the migration trend as livelihoods become threatened in more parts of the world.

The proliferation of research journals on aging societies is an indicator of the topic's growing relevance in academic discourses. *Ageing & Society* is an interdisciplinary and international journal devoted to the understanding of human aging and the circumstances of older people in their social and cultural contexts. The *Journal of Population Ageing* examines the broad questions arising from global population aging. The *International Journal for Equity in Health* publishes research which improves the understanding of issues that influence the distribution of health and health care within populations. These journals feature contributions from around the world and provide insights into what issues are worth addressing to enable societies to better understand and adapt to an aging population and the role of the elderly in different spheres of life. Some examples: Co-authors Srivastava and Muhammad looked at changes in living arrangements and subjective well-being among older adults in India. Their findings suggest that change made in living arrangements in late life that is associated with low subjective well-being among older adults indicates a need for developing an appropriate home environment for older adults where they can find life satisfaction and self-esteem and live the rest of their life in happiness.[33]

Two researchers from the National Taipei University, Tsui-o Tai and Hsien-Chih Tu, investigated the effect of grandparental care on men's and women's parenting practices in Taiwan.[34] Their findings suggest that, while grandparents are an important source of care help, the differences in child-rearing practices between generations might entail inconsistent parenting practices.

6.3 Demography and Other Megatrends

Demography is deeply entangled with many other megatrends and, thus, is for good reasons part of most megatrend analysis. Let us focus on the three megatrends climate action and sustainability transformation, digitalization, and inequality to illustrate how they are entangled with demography issues.

In the context of climate change, demography trends have attracted renewed political attention. Leading international organizations and experts—some of them inspired by the controversial work of Garrett Hardin who coined the term "the tragedy of the commons"[35] –have emphasized that humanity is unlikely to succeed in creating an ecologically sustainable world unless we further reduce worldwide population growth. The renowned Club of Rome, a leading environmental think tank, argued that it would be helpful if society could shrink its population growth, ideally turning it negative. One of its reports even called for a massive pay out to childless women as way to curb population.[36] The recommendation is unrealistic as well as controversial, especially in the context of growing problems for aging societies.

It is beyond doubt that a rising population puts more pressure on the scarce resources of Planet Earth. The environment, especially biodiversity, would greatly benefit from reduced human economic activities, especially polluting industries. However, it is a fine line the Club of Rome and others are treading if they argue for far fewer people in the world and we do think that it is a dangerous argument to make, especially if combined with calls for rigorous birth control measures.

The more people who live on Planet Earth, the more ambitious climate action must be to prevent Planet Earth from heating up. However, rapidly shrinking populations would pose so many threats to humanity that such a scenario is far from desirable. It could trigger multiple conflict scenarios which will probably make

Demography

it impossible for humanity to act in a responsible way and address the challenges of climate action and sustainability transformation in a serious way by concluding and properly implementing ambitious global agreements, practicing responsible behavior, and developing innovative technologies to significantly reduce emissions and scaling up carbon capture projects.

Demography is also entangled with digitalization. Aart Jan De Geus, the Chairman and CEO of the German foundation Bertelsmann Stiftung pointed to the intersection of demography with digitalization in a talk with SITRA, the Finnish Innovation Fund registered as an independent public foundation which operates directly under the supervision of the Finnish Parliament. "Demographics is the most predictable of megatrends. Other trends may have unforeseen Black Swan events, but we know what to expect in demographics.... Digitalization is intersecting demographics. For the first time in human history, we have reached a state where the life cycle of a human being is longer than the lifecycle of a profession."[37] This means that societies need to cope with innovations in all spheres of life. Old people will have to engage in life-long learning if they want to remain productive for society. Young people need to become experts in knowledge management and keep themselves ready for new ventures.

The relationship between demography and inequality has also been subject to many critical analyses. The key components of population change—fertility, mortality, and migration—influence patterns of inequality.

For instance, countries with the highest fertility rates such as Niger, Mali and Chad are among the poorest. Low-fertility countries tend to be rich. *The Economist* looked at the intersection between demography and inequality and found that "when people respond to lower mortality rates by having smaller families, economies change fundamentally, usually for the better."[38]

However, there are exceptions. The case of China does not quite fit into this logic. For a long time, low fertility rates did not correspond with a high per capita income. Nevertheless, this is changing now. Fertility rates remain low but China's per capita income increases. The government is now worried about its aging society and relaxed birth control. However, the effect of this policy change is very limited. In China, it was mainly the intra family division of tasks which helped China to catch up. The young generation focused on paid work while the elderly looked after their grandchildren. Many parents compensated for the lack of time with their children by heavily investing in the upbringing of their single child. This benefited the private education industry and improved the skills of children. The psychological consequences of the one child policy are yet to be fully analyzed. For instance, in big Chinese cities, the number of marriages is significantly declining which will in turn affect the fertility rate and lead to an aging society. *The Economist* also referred to the work of David Bloom, David Canning, Gunther Fink and Jocelyn Finlay at the Harvard School of Public Health who came to the conclusion that lower fertility rates may exacerbate higher inequality.[39]

"Empirical analysis using the American Community Survey confirmed that households residing in more unequal metropolitan areas tend to have fewer children than households residing in more equal metropolitan areas".[40]

These examples indicate how demography is closely intersecting with other megatrends, affecting the global future in its specific as well as combined consequences.

Chapter 7

Urbanization and Smart Cities

Why do so many people want to live in cities? From a global perspective, the trend toward urbanization is uninterrupted. It is driven by natural population increase and by rural-urban migration. People are attracted by better employment and business opportunities; better access to education and health care; and high-level sports and cultural events. Urbanization will remain strong even though COVID-19 restrictions and progress in digitalization have provided the educated middle-class with new options to exchange small city apartments for individual houses outside the city.

The United Nations estimates that the number of people in urban areas overtook the number in rural settings in 2007. For most of human history, the majority of people across the world lived in small settlements. By 1800, over 90 percent of the global population still lived in rural areas. Now more than 4 billion people representing more than half of the world's population live in urban areas. Most people prefer to live close to good infrastructure. Cities are hubs for education, business, and cultural inspirations alike. They are laboratories for new trends in managing habitats. We see a strong trend toward urban modernization, including strategies to link cities to rural areas better, and toward greater emphasis on sustainability The 2020 State of World Cities report focuses on the value of sustainable urbanization[1] With an increasing urban population, creating safe, resilient, and sustainable cities is at the top of the agenda.

Northern America (82 percent), Europe (79 percent), and Latin America (75 percent) are today the regions with the highest urbanization rates. Unlike Northern America and Europe, Latin America will show dynamic urbanization in the coming decades. By 2050, 90 percent of all Latin Americans will live in cities. Urban planners initially struggled to keep up with this growth. Due to a series of innovations in the field of the Internet of Things (IoT) and connectivity, however, many cities are now able to transform themselves into smart cities with a higher quality of life.

The rates of urbanization have increased almost everywhere, but the speed has shown variations between countries and regions. Relatively good historical data is available.

Figure 7.1: Urbanization over the Past 500 Years, 1500 to 2016

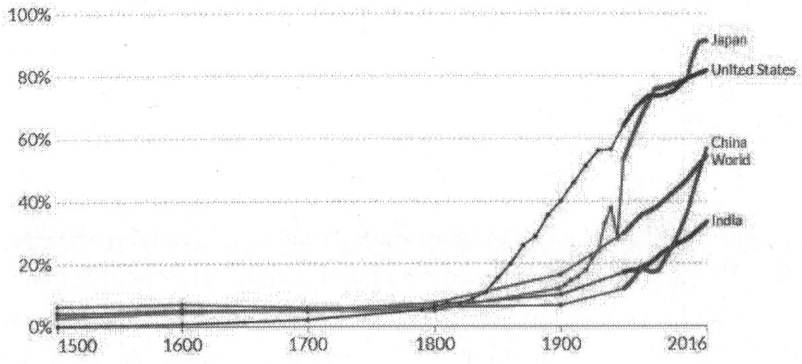

Source: Our World in Data (2016)[2]

The rate of urbanization has developed fastest in Japan. Urban shares in Japan were low until the 20th century. They are now above 90 percent. Urbanization rates are still relatively low in India. However, India has witnessed a steady rise to one-third of the population now living in cities.[3] China's rate of urbanization increased rapidly over the 1990s and 2000s. Over the past 30-year period its urban share has more than doubled to 58 percent.

Urbanization remains in full swing in China. By 2035, 75 percent of the population will live in cities, up from 64 percent in 2021. This means that more than 150 million people will move from rural areas to urban environments.[4] Two forces are driving urbanization in China: rural-urban migration and rapid suburbanization through the integration of towns and villages into integral parts of urban economies.

Africa is one of the least urbanized places in the world but its urbanization rates will continue to grow among the fastest of the world regions. In 1950, Africa had an urban population of 27 million people; today it is approaching 600 million people. By 2050,

Africa's cities will be home to an additional 950 million people. Much of this growth is taking place in small and medium-sized towns.[5]

7.1 Drivers of Urbanization

There is a strong and persistent relationship between urbanization and economic growth. Cities have always been hubs for talent, capital and innovation, according to an analysis offered by Blackrock, the world largest asset management group.[6] Cities make up for more than 70 percent of global GDP, over 60 percent of global energy consumption and over 70 percent of greenhouse gas emissions, as well as 70 percent of global waste.[7] One would expect these percentages to rise in the coming decades, but perhaps not in unison. In many countries, there are efforts underway to relocate environmentally harmful practices to rural areas where fewer people are directly affected and public anger is unlikely to fuel protests.

The urbanization drivers—the positive, but also the negative aspects of urbanization—have been subject to analysis by many scholars over decades. Edward Glaeser of Harvard University and Bryce Milet Steinberg emphasized the benefits of density and proximity in terms of lower transportation costs, increased specialization, opportunities for learning, and the production of new ideas. Adam Smith argued that urbanization enabled specialization, while in "*the highlands of Scotland, every farmer must be butcher, baker and brewer for his own family.*" With regard to the benefits of urbanization, some far-reaching hypotheses have been tested, including whether urbanization promotes democracy. The conclusion of Glaeser and Steinberg is that there is mixed evidence of the impact of urbanization on democracy building. The hypothesis that urbanization increases the demand for democracy could not be confirmed by empirical analysis.[8]

China has been a key driver of urbanization in the past decades by adopting a more pro-active approach to urbanization though it still maintains the strict household registration policy in its megacities. City-planners in China and elsewhere are now paying much attention to middle-tier cities and the urban-rural nexus.

China's new urbanization policies are driven by efforts to reap the benefits of densely populated or planned agglomerations, especially in terms of connectivity and the advancement of smart city development.

Technology companies, consulting firms, the construction industry, architects, and real estate companies are among the most important drivers of urbanization. We have seen major projects in different countries related to the planning of entire new cities, including capital cities. Brazil planned a new capital in the 1950s after deciding to move it to a more central location than Rio de Janeiro. Brasília was planned and developed by Lúcio Costa, Oscar Niemeyer, Joaquim Cardozo, and landscape architect Roberto Burle Marx. The design divides the city into numbered blocks and sectors for specific activities. Brasília is Brazil's third most populous city. It also has the highest GDP per capita among major Latin American cities. Abuja, a centrally located city in Nigeria, is a planned city built mainly in the 1980s. It replaced Lagos as the capital in December 1991. Naypyidaw, officially spelled Nay Pyi Taw, is an entirely planned city which became the seat of the government of Myanmar. Naypyidaw officially replaced Yangon as the administrative capital of Myanmar in November 2005. It hosts the Union Parliament, the Supreme Court, the Presidential Palace, the official residences of the Cabinet of Myanmar, and the headquarters of government ministries and military. One of the biggest city development projects underway is Xion'an, which started in 2017 in the Baoding area of Hebei province in China. It is located about 100 km southwest of Beijing. The purpose is to make it a development hub for the Beijing-Tianjin-Hebei (Jingjinji) economic triangle. "*Non-core*" functions of the Chinese capital are expected to migrate here, including offices of some state-owned enterprises, government agencies, and research and development facilities. Real-estate prices started to increase rapidly, and the local government imposed a temporary ban on new property sales. Other planned cities include Canberra in Australia, Washington, D.C. in the United States, and Islamabad in Pakistan.

An ongoing major project of a planned city is Neom in Saudi Arabia, dubbed *I Line*. It is projected to cover a total area of 26,500 km^2 and will extend over 460 km along the coast of the Red Sea. The massive global advertisement campaign of the Kingdom of Saudi Arabia[9] focuses on many sustainability features, especially green and smart city technologies. It states that all basic facilities would be within 5 minutes walking distance. Analysts refer to its visionary design and its potential positive impact on relations with Israel and other countries in the Middle East. Others point to the risks that it could become another White Elephant project of the Kingdom of Saudi Arabia. It remains an open question whether it could attract the earmarked 1 million residents and become a prime tourist destination. Walking may prove not be fun in a place heating up to well above 40 degrees Celsius in summer.[10]

The Chinese technology giant Tencent released plans for the Net City project in 2020. Net City will be home to about 80,000 people and should cover an area of about 2 million square meters (equivalent in size to Monaco) situated on a stretch on the Pearl River Estuary adjacent to Shenzhen. It will be an almost car free city. The plan centers around a *"green corridor"* designed for buses, bikes, and autonomous vehicles. It will include office buildings, parks and recreational zones, shops, schools, and entertainment venues. It will be interconnected, smart, and green, and the perfect hub for innovation.[11]

The Ellen MacArthur Foundation and ARUP, a city planning firm, published a guidebook for promoting circular economy in cities. It includes a series of good practice examples, including in London where circular economy principles were integrated into the preliminary draft local plan for the regeneration of the Old Oak and Park Royal districts. The plan aims to create more than 25,500 new homes and 65,000 jobs in 640 hectares of residential and industrial area, while at the same time ensuring optimal local material circulation to develop an "exemplary world class neighborhood underpinned by new business.[12]

7.2 Smart Cities

Smart city is a widely used term for holistic development concepts that aim to make cities more efficient, more technologically advanced, greener, and more socially inclusive. Smart city concepts are based on technical, economic, and social innovations with a focus on big data, connectivity, and energy management. Today, the term smart city guides city planners all over the world. The platform digi.city provides a series of definitions for smart cities.[13] In short, "smart cities leverage information technologies and state-of-the-art urban planning to improve efficient management and provision of services for citizens."

IoT analytics have extensively researched the current developments of smart cities and identified seven aspects that set the leading cities apart from the rest:[14]

- holistic smart city development
- citizens-come first mindsets
- alignment with government initiatives
- long-term vision
- sustainability as top priority
- public-private partnership programs
- open, city-wide, data bases and platforms

The global megacity network C40 is seen as a key facilitator for exchanges on smart city development strategies with a focus on climate action. C40 Cities connects 97 of the world's greatest cities, representing 700+ million citizens. In the last ten years, the smart city trend has become a truly global phenomenon.

In June of 2015, India's Prime Minister Narendra Modi launched the Smart Cities Challenge, a competition among Indian cities designed to accelerate and inspire more sustainable, citizen-centric, and effective urban development.

Many cities run smart city initiatives. The Smart City Berlin Network is an alliance across all sectors of more than 160 stakeholders from business, science, research, and administration. It brings together the stakeholders of Smart City Berlin in various communication and cooperation formats with the purpose of making Berlin an intelligent, innovation-oriented, citizen-focused, and resilient city.[15]

One of the most innovative smart cities is Shenzhen, located within the Pearl River Delta, which borders Hong Kong to the south. Shenz'en's economy surpassed Hong Kong's for the first time in 2018. The concept of Smart City, where almost everything is networked, is consistently implemented. Shenzhen is a young metropolis and received significant support and freedom from the Chinese central government. As early as 1979, Deng Xiaoping declared Shenzhen a *Special Economic Zone* with the purpose of boosting innovation and entrepreneurship. The motivation to rival and overtake Hong Kong is one of many factors explaining the city's ambitions. The city is at the forefront of several technological developments. All buses and taxis are electric vehicles.

Many young people from China and the rest of the world arrive in Shenzhen to fulfill their dreams and wishes there. This creates a particularly creative climate in the city.

In 2021, to guide investments in ecosystem conservation and restoration, Shenzhen officially adopted the use of gross ecosystem product (GEP), a measure that summarizes the value of the contributions of nature to economic activity, to guide investments in ecosystem conservation and restoration. As a new ecological accounting system that measures ecology status, GEP refers to specific indicators to measure the total economic value of all ecosystem products and services supplied to humans as part of their well-being. Ecosystems that will be measured include natural ecosystems such as forests, grasslands, wetlands, deserts, freshwater and oceans, and artificial systems that are based on natural processes like farmland, pastures, aquaculture farms and urban green land.[16]

Smart city developments are not confined to the technologically most advanced cities. Many large and medium-size cities refer to the concept in the process of modernization. We talked to Prof. Xanin García of the Municipal Planning Institute in the Mexican city of Saltillo, the capital and largest city of the northeastern Mexican state of Coahuila, which has close to 800,000 inhabitants.

Global Perspectives on Megatrends

Interview with Xanin García, Saltillo Planning Institute

Q: Where do you see urbanization heading in the next decade in Mexico, what are the key response strategies, and could you compare them to other countries?

Xanin García: As far as we can tell, around 83 percent of the population in Mexico will grow up in large cities, but there are challenges facing us like informal settlements, high levels of inequality and the lack of planning in cities. The smaller areas also do not have the resources to move forward in a coherent way and they are also up against threats like excessive pollution within their cities, and these are all problems that are for the moment, not getting enough political attention on a state level.

Q: Where would you say that most change comes from? Is it from the central government or do local governments play a bigger role?

Xanin García: On climate change as an example, the government is doing nowhere near what it should be doing, as evidenced by its working together with the fossil fuel industry, its lack of investment in renewable energies, and so forth. On the local level, we just do not have the capacity to implement large-scale changes, due to a lack of technological knowledge, information, resources, and funds. In Saltillo's case, the city I work and live in, we receive such help from the international civil society that we are able to have a concrete city planning strategy in place. But you can clearly tell that this is not enough, as some problems like water waste or pollution have no borders, and as municipalities begin drafting plans with no help or guidance from the federal level, they stumble upon such problems. A federal strategy is thus much needed, but obviously nowhere to be found.

Q: How does international cooperation and city-networking help Mexican cities and what are some of the shortcomings?

Xanin García: It is definitely of incredible value to the cities and especially to Saltillo, which belongs to many such organizations. The problem with this is the ensuing inequality between big cities, which do have access to such programs due to more advanced technologies, and the smaller ones, which are left behind and do not receive the necessary help to catch up, which again, is also a failure on the federal level.

Q: What does the future for smart cities in Mexico look like? Who is pushing for changes, such as big data or energy planning?

Xanin García: Of course, as with all else, there is no federal strategy on this. On a local level, there is also no long-term strategy, and it depends on how high the issue is on the given elected government's priority list, as there are also budget constraints, which are slowly becoming worse by the year, with the overall budgets on a local level being gradually reduced. The problem is also the inequity between the cities, as some do not even have access to the internet, Saltillo as an example ranks high in the competitiveness of its students and the educational level of its citizens, but only 17 percent of people have access to the internet. You can think of the whole thing as a vicious cycle, where there is no smart city, so there is no money, and because there is no money, there is no smart city.

Q: What about sustainability, how important is it?

Xanin García: The first step is to reduce inequity in the case of Saltillo, where the automotive industry is the primary employer, while the city must have human resources that are able to work in these places. Cities in Mexico have to first deal with poverty and inequality and facilitate development, which is why it is hard to focus on sustainability. That is why it is necessary to work on models that strengthen local economies that are sustainable.

Q: Which countries does Mexico cooperate with—say for example, China, India, Brazil, and so forth— and how important are these relationships?

Xanin García: Mexico cooperates with several countries. This linkage takes place between state secretaries. At the subnational level, such as municipalities, they can be chosen to participate in cooperation projects through calls for proposals. However, the preparation of local governments for cooperation is very scarce. Recently, training has been provided to assist cities in their internationalization. In the case of Saltillo, due to its economic dynamics, we have links with several cities. Saltillo has a sister city, namely Austin,

Texas, which is an immensely important relationship to us, as we are able to compare and provide one another with invaluable information. Saltillo is currently part of the Morgenstadt City Initiative, a global project, working in coordination with Kochi, India, and Piura, Peru, and we are working on a triangular cooperation project with Asunción, Paraguay.

7.3 Urbanization and Other Megatrends

Urbanization brings about significant changes in all spheres of life and is closely connected to other big megatrends. The interactive platform *Urban Hub* publishes stories about urban landmarks, innovative technologies, and future ideas for the sustainable development of cities and buildings worldwide.[17]

Digitalization will change the way cities are managed. Cities will pioneer the implementation of new intelligent systems such as innovative mobility solutions, real-time adaptation of traffic signals, air filtration, and electronic services for citizens. Cities will attract digital business and digitally-minded people and will experiment with new and fast forms of mobility, communication, and cooperation in many spheres of life.

The European Commission started the Intelligent Cities Challenge (ICC) initiative to promote technological transformation, build a green Europe and foster intelligent and sustainable growth across European cities with the purpose of supporting 100 mainly small and medium-size cities across the EU to advance digitalization.

Urbanization is closely related to climate action and sustainability transformations. Rapid urbanization is making people more vulnerable to the impacts of climate change. Cities will further step up efforts to promote urban resilience and to protect residents by supporting a robust physical and social infrastructure. Record heatwaves in June and July 2019 in France, globally known for its mild Mediterranean climate, caused the deaths of 1,435 people in 2019, many of them in the capital city of Paris. During the summer of 2021, red alerts—the most severe warning category—were issued in several areas of France. A brutal heatwave nearing 46°C hit southern Europe in August of that year, causing large fires, while the Northwest heat wave in the U.S. saw excess deaths rise beyond the peaks of the pandemic.[18] In Oman, temperatures reached an unfathomable 55°C. Southeastern Europe was experiencing one of its worst heat waves in decades, especially in Greece, Italy, Croatia, Albania, and Turkey. Athens thus appointed a chief heat officer in 2021, the first such appointment in Europe after life in Athens was seriously disrupted throughout long periods in the summer. While Greece experienced its worst wildfire season since 2007,[19] Sicily, Italy, recorded the highest temperature in the history of Europe with a staggering 48.8°C.[20] It should also be noted that in Greece's case, the intersection between the trends was even more striking, as evidenced by negligent planning regulations as well as notoriously deficient environmental protection standards.[21]

The urban poor are particularly exposed to the increased intensity and frequency of extreme weather events. City and municipal governments are under pressure to diminish risks through comprehensive city planning based on resilience criteria. In a study featured by the Mercator Research Institute on Global Commons and Climate Change, Carl Pierer and Felix Creutzig recommend that growing cities should ideally develop a star-shaped form, with interstices for green spaces. The experts point to inherent goal conflicts for city developers:

> "Climate change has given rise to a conflict of goals. On the one hand, cities should be maximally compact so that traffic and buildings produce as little greenhouse gases as possible; yet on the other hand, they should be less densely built as a way to cope with potential climate impacts, such as heat waves."[22]

The old European cities, such as Córdoba, which are characterized by narrow walkable streets and protected from sunlight through trees and buildings, can be a guiding light for city planners, while ambitious technologies are constantly being developed to improve cities's resilience to warming temperatures[23]. One of these more promising technologies seeks to halt the relatively low survival rate of urban trees by using censors in the soil to let people know when a tree needs watering.

Many smart cities with green and sustainability features are currently being planned and marketed across emerging economies. Emerging market governments are particularly fond of "greenfield" smart cities where problems like pollution, slums, and crime that plague existing cities do not have to be tackled. City planners love to indulge in urban utopia dreams.[24] The Forest City project, in the Iskandar Malaysia economic region built by Chinese investors, is a prime example. However, in many cases, including in Forest City, most of the sustainability and smart-city features have been added on later and are primarily driven by marketing purposes as critical analysis of experts revealed. The Forest City project has received heavy criticism for various reasons, especially related to the loss of biodiversity and other environmental problems.[25]

The urbanization trend often exposes inequality in a drastic and visible way. The Organization for Economic Cooperation and Development (OECD) sponsored a series of analyses on how urbanization accelerates inequality. Ricky Burdett from the London School of Economics found that social inequality is becoming increasingly specialized.[26] At least a quarter of the world's urban population is living in slums and informal settlements. In many low and middle-income nations, urban growth has been accompanied by the rapid expansion of unplanned, underserved neighborhoods with high concentrations of poor people.[27] Many urban projects contributed to a physical reinforcement of inequality. Gated communities and enclaves are seen to proliferate and promote inequality in a very visible way.

Inequality has produced different kinds of frustrations of city dwellers. In Berlin, public anger has been growing over affordable housing and practices of stock-listed housing companies, especially Vonovia and Deutsche Wohnen. Berliners voted to expropriate large landlords in a public referendum on 26 September 2021. Though the results were not binding for the government, it sent a strong signal to policymakers to address affordable housing in urban planning. In view of the referendum and in the context of their planned mega merger, Vonovia and Deutsche Wohnen offered the Berlin Senate 20,000 apartments for sale.

Urbanization impacts on health and nutrition. To cater to busy urban lifestyles, cities offer access to a wide variety of food prepared outside the home, including street food and food served in restaurants and kiosks. The International Food Policy Research Institute (IFPRI) issued a warning that diets are changing with rising incomes and urbanization. People tend to consume more animal-sourced foods, sugar, fats and oils, refined grains, and processed foods. Urbanization would fuel a "nutrition transition" that causes increases in overweight and obesity and diet-related diseases such as diabetes and heart disease.[28] At the same time, cities also host many sustainability and innovation-minded people who advocate for new low-carbon diets. Vegan diets tend to be more popular in modern cities than in rural areas. According to Google-based research by *The Guardian*, the interest level around vegan — restaurants, recipes, dog food — is highest in Bristol, followed by Portland, Edinburgh, Vancouver, and Seattle.[29] Others regard Tel Aviv as the vegan capital of the World. Berlin is also widely known for its many vegan food stores and restaurants.[30]

Urbanization is also strongly connected with migration trends. The migration portal developed by the International Organization for Migration (IOM) explains that migration, both national and international, has always driven the growth of urbanization. The number of foreign-born residents is particularly high in capitals and megacities. IOM sees municipal authorities becoming key actors in managing migration by including migration in their urban planning and implementation.

Talks about modern cities as "climate havens" entered discourses in different parts of the world. With growing parts of the world becoming uninhabitable, people will inevitably seek refuge in places where they can feel safe. This poses tremendous challenges to cities, as they must urgently begin to adapt to such an influx of people and make cities more resilient to climate change. The concept of sponge city has become popular, especially in flood-prone areas. Typical features of sponge city programs include the building of contiguous open green spaces, interconnected waterways, and channels and ponds across neighborhoods that promote biodiversity and create cultural and recreational opportunities. Green roofs are also typical features of sponge city programs as they can retain rainwater and naturally filters it before it is recycled or released into the ground.

The four million-strong Chinese city of Xiamen is a flagship city in the promotion of the sponge city concept. Xiamen has already carried the label of low-carbon city for more than ten years. It has a superb beachfront area and is a major hub for tourism. The city started its ambitious sponge city program in 2015. Expenditure amounted to more than one billion U.S. dollars through 2020. Activities included the construction of a new 221 km rainwater pipe network and renovation of buildings. Also part of the program was a series of porous design interventions across the city, such as construction of systems to detain run-off and allow for groundwater infiltration; porous roads and pavements that can safely accommodate car and pedestrian traffic while allowing water to be absorbed, permeate, and recharge groundwater; and drainage systems that allow trickling of water into the ground or that direct storm water run-off into green spaces for natural absorption. Compared to other cities in China, Xiamen also has abundant open green space, including one of the world's largest botanical gardens.

7.4 The Greening of the Construction Sector

The building and construction sector makes a significant contribution to CO_2 emissions worldwide, as buildings are, of course, a key component in the fabric of cities. The Global Status Report 2017 constituted a first landmark for analyzing the potentials of greening the building and construction sector. It was prepared by the International Energy Agency (IEA) for the Global Alliance for Buildings and Construction (GABC). According to the report, building and construction activities together account for 36 percent of global final energy use and 39 percent of energy-related carbon dioxide (CO_2) emissions, when upstream power generation is included.[31] Thus, greening the production and the maintenance of buildings is one of the most important areas of intervention to address climate change. A more intensive use of buildings would also make contributions to reduce overall emissions.

New approaches could reduce the carbon-intensity of cement production and lessen concrete's broader environmental impact. Cement, the critical glue that holds concrete together, is so carbon-intensive that if it were a country, it would rank fourth in the world as a climate polluter.[32] The Global Cement and Concrete Association committed to zero emissions by 2050.

UNEP launched the Sustainable Buildings and Climate Initiative (SBCI) in 2006. It promotes and supports sustainable building practices on a global scale with a focus on energy efficiency and GHG emission reduction. The World Green Building Council (WorldGBC) has issued a bold new vision for how buildings and infrastructure around the world can reach 40 percent less embodied carbon emissions by 2030 and achieve 100 percent net-zero emissions buildings by 2050.[33]

There are several certification systems for the building and construction industry, including LEED (Leadership in Energy and Environmental Design), DGNB (Deutsche Gesellschaft für Nachhaltiges Bauen e.V.), and BREEAM (Building Research Establishment Environmental Assessment Method). IFC has launched an innovative green-building certification program in Vietnam. EDGE (Excellence in Design for Greater Efficiencies in East Asia markets) aims to help developers reduce their buildings's energy and water consumption by 20 percent while lowering greenhouse-gas emissions. Different building certificates have different approaches and focuses. LEAD is strong in marketing and well recognized in the U.S. Carbon neutrality was recently incorporated. The German nonprofit system DGNB focuses more on the life cycle and is popular in Germany. In the Global South, many challenges remain to going through certification systems, as access to specific materials, processes and documentation requirements could be challenging for some real estate developers.

The Ellen MacArthur Foundation has supported a series of projects focusing on greening the construction sector by referring to f circular economy practices and investment opportunities to make the construction sector more environmentally friendly. Recommendations pertain to the renovation and upgrade of buildings, building materials reuse and recycling infrastructure.[34]

We talked to Thomas Fritsche, founder of thomasfritsche architects (tfa). Since 2005, tfa is based in Shanghai and operates an office in Cologne. Tfa designed more than 175 projects and completed mor than 85 buildings. Thomas Fritsche is involved in many sustainability and smart city networks in China and Germany and has earned himself a reputation as a visionary and well-networked sustainable building and workplace expert.

Interview with Thomas Fritsche, thomasfritsche architects tfa, Shanghai and Cologne

Q: You have designed and realized projects as business parks, buildings for work and workplace interiors. Which is the most important smart-city trend in practice from the perspective of an architect?

Thomas Fritsche: Smart city is a very present catchword in Shanghai. Most Shanghainese are technology savvy, and open to technological innovations and change, eager to try new solutions. First, smart city promises better energy management, improved flow of traffic and a more convenient and pleasant use of urban space. It is also relevant for designs of buildings, in terms of energy efficiency and the use of construction material. There is also scope to improve the efficiency of work place facilities, e.g. elevators, design of offices and conference rooms, etc. Shanghai has swiftly improved livability. Smart planning is typically initiated by new government policies and regulations but executers at different levels promptly adopt new regulations. There is significant scope to improve consultation processes at the outset of major planning exercises and in project design. Adjustments at a later stage are costly and much less efficient.

Q: How does the sustainability and zero carbon trend impact smart-city development, buildings for work, and workplace interiors? As you work from Shanghai and also have an office in Cologne, how do you compare developments in China and Germany/Europe?

Thomas Fritsche: The building industry uses great quantities of raw materials that also involve high energy consumption. The long-term trend is to regard building as material depot. The sustainability and zero carbon trend will translate into new regulations. At the moment, there are few zero carbon buildings and passive houses in China. Some real estate developers have established sustainability departments. They would be open to comply with new regulations regarding better material efficiency and looking to use more sustainable building materials. We now see more wood constructions in the building sector and a trend toward better use of space. Technical skills of workers are still comparatively low in China which affects the quality of the construction. There is also much scope to improve co-ordination and consultation processes in China to enable cleaner production which in turn reduces resource use and/or pollution at the source. End-of-pipe technologies to curb pollution emissions by implementing add-on measures are usually less effective.

Q: Which are the key drivers or influencers to promote green buildings in Asia, in Europe, other parts of the world? How do you see the development of certification systems, and labels?

Thomas Fritsche: Government policies and regulations are key to setting new sustainability standards. Compliance will be high in China even though regulations are drafted and implemented in top-down fashion. Certification systems also play an increasingly important role. There is a growing number of real estate funds which only invest in certified buildings. It is also a matter of prestige and reputation for major companies to own a zero or low-emission building. LEED is well established on the large U.S. market and also popular in Shanghai. It is a for-profit organization with a strong marketing arm. The German Sustainable Building Council (DGNB) is a nonprofit initiative with increased recognition in

China. It has released an updated version of its certification system for buildings in use in 2020. Under the new system, property owners, operators and users can plan sustainable property strategies for existing buildings, simultaneously laying emphasis on climate protection. DGNB covers the whole life cycle of buildings.

Thomas Fritsche stresses the complexity of the smart city development process. He advocates for a holistic, visionary, and inclusive approach to city development, the use of renewable and reusable materials, and the promotion of the circular economy. He expects a trend toward more consideration of green space development, prefabrication and standardization of construction elements and a push for collaborative efforts to raise the quality of urban designs.[35]

Chapter 8

Health and Nutrition

Health is synonymous with a good life. Preventive and curative health both witness growing importance, and the COVID-19 pandemic has only further accelerated this trend. Humans have increasingly become better at making sure that their physiological needs are met, while the Sustainable Development Goals are heavily focused on aspects, such as health and food (see SDGs 2 and 3).[1]

Life expectancy is the most commonly used measure to describe a population's health.[2] Knowledge of the human body and its functions is growing steadily, and it is easy to forget that just 200 years ago, human life expectancy ranged from 26 years in Africa to 35 years in the Americas.[3] In 2015, the number stood at 80 years for North America and 61 years for Africa.

The World Health Organization (WHO) presents a series of visualized data on the significant marks of progress in various fields of health: "From declining mortality rates to ending epidemics of infectious diseases, the world has made significant forward strides. But there is much more to be done."[4] The health megatrend is not only influencing the private sphere of individuals, but also shaping the world of business and work. It is a trend that appeals to everyone worldwide, though attitudes and practices differ across countries and regions.

Many leading futurologists and think tanks, including the German Zukunftsinstitut (The Future Institute), define health as a megatrend.[5] Health care is one of the largest economic sectors. In Germany, the sector accounts for more than 7.5 million employees and exports in excess of EUR 126 billion.[6] It is Europe's largest medical technology market and ranks third internationally. Kantar Consulting, meanwhile, ranked health as the number one consumer trend in German speaking countries in 2020.[7]

8.1 The Globalization of Health

The COVID-19 pandemic has made it very clear that health is an issue of global concern and that more international cooperation is urgently needed to curb pandemics and advance research through global exchange of data and expertise. The institutional infrastructure needed for this massive change is by no means complete, but the COVID-19 pandemic has highlighted our current shortcomings, paving the way for its rapid development during the next decade.

The work of the WHO has gained much recognition in the context of the COVID-19 pandemic. The WHO has been on top of the global health agenda for many decades but did not receive due attention, mainly because of geopoliticization of health issues and nationalist attitudes toward management of global health challenges.

The WHO's 2020–2024 digital health strategy underscores the linkages of health policies to other global agendas and to other megatrends, such as climate action, digitalization, and inequality. The strategy builds on the ideas introduced in the United Nations Sustainable Development Goals (SDGs), and aims to "…accelerate human progress, to bridge the digital divide and to develop knowledge societies…" [8] It reiterates previous goals such as providing universal health care access to one billion more people, better protection from health emergencies for another billion, and a greater well-being for a further billion people, as part of WHO's triple billion targets. It also sets out new goals and puts strong emphasis on health data security in our new information economy, whereby protection against misinformation, monetization of health data, and human rights violations are at the center of the transition. WHO envisions people-centered health systems, achieved by each country developing a national digital health strategy framework, and ramping up national investments in health that will lead to primary health care and universal health coverage and the achievement of relevant SDGs. Health data will be subject to international health data regulation and will be seen as a global public health good and shared accordingly to develop best practices as well as improve upon *Artificial Intelligence* (AI).

This kind of international data and information sharing is particularly important in regard to one of the greatest emerging threats to humanity: antimicrobial resistance. The rise of superbugs (including microorganisms such as bacteria, fungi, viruses, and parasites) which mutate to possess genes that protect them against antimicrobial drugs presents a grave danger to all countries, as these microorganisms know no borders. [9] In 2018, WHO detected "...widespread occurrence of antibiotic resistance among 500 000 people with suspected bacterial infections across 22 countries.".[10] Penicillin, the world's first antibiotic,[11] is becoming less and less effective at treating pneumonia, with resistance ranging all the way up to 51 percent in some countries.

In order to gain more perspective on the relevance of international cooperation in the field of health, on antibiotic-resistant microorganisms, and on other health challenges, we talked to Dr Sonu M. M. Bhaskar, a clinician-scientist, board director, and academic neurologist with a specialization in vascular neurology and neuroradiology; and a researcher with a strong focus on global health, clinical neurology, and health systems, with a proven track record in governance, policy-making, social innovation, and systems-level growth and strategy.

Interview with Sonu Bhaskar, Director of Global Health Neurology and Translational Neuroscience Lab

Q: Health care is conventionally thought of as a national issue, but what role can international cooperation play in the future of the sector.
Sonu Bhaskar: Although conventionally thought of as a national issue, health care is increasingly drawing international cooperation underscored by several infectious disease outbreaks such as COVID-19 forcing health systems globally to cooperate. Besides, taking a leaf out of the changes incorporated in the National Health Service (NHS), U.K. over the last decade; learnings from developing countries have informed health system design, strategy, and planning. The notion that developing countries learn from

developed ones unidirectionally is being challenged, as over the past 30 years, the experience gathered from countries such as Sudan has also informed, and transformed, the health systems in developed countries vis à vis NHS. During the COVID-19 pandemic, the deficiencies in strategy to curb or contain the virus outbreak were exposed, as several nations, including from the developed world, lacked a national, coherent, and integrated approach. While the COVID-19 response of countries such as South Korea, Taiwan, Singapore, and India have had a fair share of challenges, a cooperative and integrated approach, drawn from their previous experiences of tackling infectious disease outbreaks, offers an opportunity for cooperation and mutual learning to the rest of the world.

Q: Was the COVID-19 pandemic an outlier, a once-in-a-century pandemic, or should we expect more and more frequent similar instances?

Sonu Bhaskar: COVID-19 is by no means an outlier; rather, a significant addition, causing global concern, to the list of a number of infectious disease outbreaks like Ebola or H1N1 we have witnessed in recent years. Pandemics have existed in the past, like the 1918 H1N1 great influenza pandemic, and are likely to further emerge given the ongoing challenges to the ecosystem; for example, through rampant deforestation, allowing viruses to cross over to humans more easily.

Beyond the infectious disease outbreaks, another pandemic that looms is the growing epidemic of antimicrobial resistance around the world.

Q: Exactly, so what do the future of antibiotic-resistant microorganisms and the danger they pose to humanity hinge on? What measures can humanity take to prevent the worst outcomes?

Sonu Bhaskar: The world is interconnected like never before, and these new resistant strains pose a threat to all. Personally, I'm an advocate of preventative medicine and traditional public health measures such as educating people about hygiene, washing hands, and increasing awareness among primary care physicians on risks of long-term resistance with antibiotics, and the need to limit or moderate antibiotic use as and when applicable. In developing countries, the use of antibiotics among children is a major concern. Research shows that early exposure to antibiotics causes resistance in bacteria, hence posing as a major public health problem.

The problem with the broad use of antibiotics goes beyond humans, with implications to livestock, agriculture, and veterinary practices as a major public health threat. This has caused the expansion of multidrug-resistant organisms (MDROs) globally, including in children, making the current practices of antibiotic use unsustainable.

Q: How do we ensure the health of children everywhere and what are our current shortcomings? How does childcare differ in that regard from other health care policies?

Sonu Bhaskar: A critical element influencing the health of children everywhere is to do with the social determinants of health such as malnutrition, poverty, and so forth that mediate individual life course and long-term health outcomes. The ongoing COVID-19 pandemic has negatively impacted the health and well-being of children. Mental illness, including social ideation and depression, are growing challenges and need interventions specially tailored for children at risk.

Q: What looks to be the next big breakthrough in health and what is the biggest challenge holding it back? How will it affect people's lives?

Sonu Bhaskar: Firstly, the emergence of mRNA technologies including vaccines, artificial organs, telemedicine, robotics and the use of AI and machine learning in health care are some exciting developments that offer the potential to address overarching challenges in health care

Secondly, the future of medicine will see rapid development and deployment of open-source technologies or innovations. This is important to ensure the benefits of medical innovations reach one and all—toward an equitable framework. Although the software or computing industry has been an early adopter of open-source development; health care has been rather late in leveraging and applying such platforms or frameworks.

Thirdly, there is a shift toward social and ethical health care innovations. Increasing attention is being paid to what the needs of the community are and how innovations can address them. Ethics should not be an afterthought; rather, they should be considered at the conception and design stage of the innovation pipeline. We must ask ourselves what our communities require, want, and how can we make technologies or innovations socially responsible? One major concern here is the commercial determinants of health and conflicts of interest. The escalating health care costs are unsustainable. This has also come to the fore during the COVID-19 pandemic when we witnessed growing disparities in vaccine access and availability. We witnessed how some manufacturers escalated the costs making it furthermore unaffordable to low-resourced countries. Commercial determinants of health are a major issue that merits global attention as this is likely to exacerbate the global-North-South divide, including in the developed nations, as socio-economic disparities continue to deepen between geographies and communities.

Q: How do these ideas work in practice? Are the current institutions capable of bringing about the kind of world that you are envisioning?

Sonu Bhaskar: As a global health practitioner and clinician working at the coalface of medicine, community, and academia, I believe that there is an increasing need for independent think tanks. Think tanks can present governments and international bodies with differing perspectives on policy, planning and implementation, hence preventing the waste due to bureaucratic inefficiencies and policy and innovation stagnation due to echo chambers within the institutions. They can also act as a bridge to community and community service organizations. At Rotary Sydney, we created a flagship "parliamentary Friends of Rotary" to allow bi-partisan support and collaboration involving political executives and leadership and Rotary-led community and global initiatives/projects. Initiatives like this cross political lines and support projects with broader societal and community impact.

Health and Nutrition

For ideas and policies to have a tangible impact, it is critical to involve institutions, including political leadership. A collaborative approach facilitated by domain experts from think-tanks can facilitate as well as expedite the translation of ideas to make them work in practice.

The provision of health services will undergo significant changes in the next decade. In Silicon Valley, investors are bracing for a future where AI will replace doctors, perhaps as soon as 2035. [12] Making fewer errors while being able to analyze vast amounts of data, these AI systems should in theory be able to improve health care for all. Conversely, they could also be detrimental to high-risk patients, as the system itself is dependent on the kind of data that is fed into it. Were we to neglect human errors and biases that run through and define such data collections, we would be merely systemizing and anchoring dangerous practices that disproportionally hurt minorities.[13]

Global warming is an example of how the megatrends of climate action and health are intertwined. Heat waves are associated with increased hospital admissions for cardiovascular, kidney, and respiratory disorders, while certain regions may become fully uninhabitable, posing an existential risk to local inhabitants. In the American west, 20,000 extra COVID-19 cases and 750 deaths were associated with the 2020 wildfire season that plagued the country.[14]

Inequality and health are also strongly connected. As we've previously seen, inequality negatively correlates with differences in health status. The Equality Trust's research suggests that life expectancy is longer in more equal societies, while rates of adult mortality, infant mortality, mental illness, and obesity are lower.[15] At the same time, as status anxiety and competition rise, tasks with a form of "social evaluative threat" (tasks whereby others may judge us) become harder, and stress levels, which correlate with rising death rates, also rise.[16]

The growing sensitivity on health is associated with the consequences of industrial development, especially increased pollution levels. Growing evidence of the harmful effects of environmental degradation caused by industrial developments contributed to further boost the health trend. A 2021 study on air pollution had the researchers questioning their own findings, when they discovered that 8.7 million deaths worldwide in 2018 could be attributed to air pollution.[17] All the while, their findings suggest that ceasing fossil fuel emissions would raise the global life expectancy by more than a year.

Demography and health also go hand in hand, with aging societies in the West creating unmistakable challenges to their governments. At the same time, prevalence of disease in old age has risen over time and disability has fallen, while people are also living longer.[18] Nevertheless, health systems are transforming, and demand is rising, while prices are clearly mirroring this trend, which begs the question of how countries will respond.

The future of work and health are unmistakably intertwined, as there is plenty of evidence that long working hours, the intake of fast food, and the lack of physical exercise trigger health problems. WHO, in collaboration with the International Labor Organization (ILO) are categorical about this in a 2021 study: long working hours were associated with 745,000 deaths from stroke and ischemic heart disease in 2016.[19] The threshold for the increased risk stands at a mere 55 or more hours a week—meanwhile, the COVID-19 pandemic has also caused an increase in working hours.[20] It is no wonder that countries like Iceland are introducing a four-day workweek.[21]

It is thus understandable that people have become more sensitive to their health status. According to the Boston Medical Center, "an estimated 45 million Americans go on a diet each year, and Americans spend 33 billion U.S. dollars each year on weight loss products. Yet, nearly two-thirds of Americans are overweight or obese."[22] We have talked about obesogenic environments for a while now: environments wherein individuals are forced to live an unhealthy lifestyle, but we are slowly beginning to realize that our societies may be structured that way as a whole. Obesity itself is by no means constrained to the West: 2.1 billion people worldwide, according to the World Population Review, are classified as obese, with three million people dying of related health issues each year. The "worldwide obesity rate has tripled since 1975" and is still rising.[23]

An example of this is found in the intersection between urban planning and food security, manifested in the form of food deserts. "Food deserts are geographic areas where residents have few to no convenient options for securing affordable and healthy foods — especially fresh fruits and vegetables. Disproportionately found in high-poverty areas, food deserts create extra, everyday hurdles that can make it harder for kids, families, and communities to grow healthy and strong."[24] The discourse originated in the United States, and often comes hand in hand with racial segregation, especially in predominantly black neighborhoods,[25] but there have been attempts to investigate the issue in other contexts as well. In Germany, Ulrich Jürgens using a novel approach to consider "mental" food deserts, found that people may also inadvertently create such settings by refusing to buy local.[26] Using geo-big data, researchers looking at the Shenzhen province in China found patterns describing a food desert, largely driven by "lower density of healthy food stores {and} limited transportation convenience {in} socioeconomically disadvantaged districts".[27]

Meanwhile the List of Psychological Disorders has already grown in length in recent years,[28] partly due to the sheer recognition of existing disorders and the accumulation of knowledge around them. For instance, it now includes 15 categories of psychological disorders, including stress-related disorders. This development has posed a scientific and social dilemma: is mental illness on the rise, or are we merely finding new names for already existing behaviors?

Lucy Foulkes, author of *Losing our Minds: What Mental Illness Really Is*, explores precisely this question.[29] For one, the field is currently experiencing a massive case of "concept creep"; that is, a vertical and horizontal expansion or compression and even removal of concepts. Sometimes this makes sense, as in the case of the removal of homosexuality as a disorder, but overall, it has led to a large disagreement between scientists as to the actual number of disorders, ranging from 298 all the way to 541. At the same time, the growing awareness around mental health has also meant that people may misuse terms like "OCD", "panic attack", "PTSD", "social anxiety", "depression", along many others, to describe their own experiences, draining said words of their meaning with no malintent. On the other hand, Foulkes claims that whatever link can be found between social media usage and mental health issues is based on inadequate research, and often on cross-sectional instead of longitudinal studies. A combination of poor information and the media's propping up of certain findings with no context has meant that there is an understandable confusion around trends in mental health research.

8.2 The Impact of the COVID-19 Pandemic

It should be noted upfront that we cannot and will not know the true impact of COVID-19 for years to come. Data can be invalidated within days of the emergence of new variants and unforeseen developments.

Figure 8.1: Confirmed COVID-19 Infections by Region

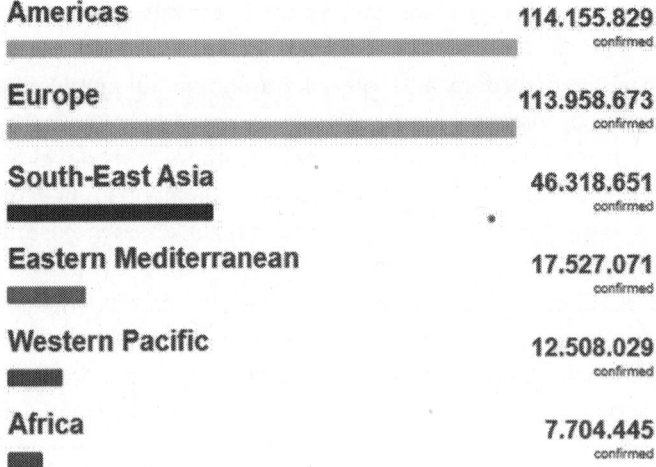

Source: WHO (January 13, 2021).[30]

Health and Nutrition

The COVID-19 pandemic led to massive research efforts in developing a vaccine. The success of the "messenger RNA" technique behind the Pfizer-BioNTech and Moderna vaccines shows how science continues to empower medicine and health. Humans are increasingly able to bend biology to their will,[31] but it is no coincidence that mRNA was an idea 30 years in the making.

The vaccines were found to be remarkably effective against death and prevented or eased hospitalization. In August 2021, of the 163 million people vaccinated in the United States, 6,587 ended up being admitted to the hospital or dying (0.004 percent).[32] Surveying 25 states, the Kaiser Family Foundation found that "the share of deaths among people with COVID-19 who are not fully vaccinated ranged from to 96.91 percent in Montana to 99.91 percent in New Jersey".[33] In September 2021, the CDC also found that unvaccinated Americans were eleven times more likely to die, but also ten times more likely to be hospitalized from COVID-19.[34]

In November/December 2021, the Omicron variant started to rage through the world. It featured a higher transmissibility and greater breakthrough infections, but a lower severity. Many countries lifted COVID-19 restrictions as hospitalization rates dropped.

Three questions largely remain unanswered: for one, the tilted playing field of vaccine distribution, which has favored the richer, Western countries; second, and more urgently, the impact of so-called Long COVID; and third, vaccine hesitancy among the population.

As rich countries bought and hoarded vaccines in the early stages of the pandemic, they got a head start with the less affluent countries not being able to keep up even months afterwards.[35] The Delta variant, first identified in India, spread rapidly through its population and caused high fatality rates and unprecedented suffering. Many health experts tried to sound the alarm, but the political ambitions of the Indian government to declare the battle won, while also promoting its non-dependency strategy meant that crucial time was lost.[36] The first signs of the variant were there by February 1, 2021, and yet the authorities suppressed them until March 24, when India's health ministry confirmed the double mutation.

All the while, independent voices have pointed to a severe undercounting of the death toll. In July 2021, the authors of a report for the Center of Global Development, claimed that the reported 400,000 death toll at the time was actually closer to three or even five million.[37]

Not only was the situation catastrophic in India, but the Delta variant soon came to the Western countries, which had loosened restrictions and were hopeful that they could now return to "normal" life. When it also hit said countries hard, the irony of what has been since called "vaccine apartheid" became all the more evident.

There were some attempts to counteract this grim reality. Covax, a program backed by the UN, tried to help by buying and then distributing doses of vaccine to low-income countries, but repeatedly failed to hit its targets, especially when it most mattered: during the surge of the Delta variant.[38] In late December of 2021, the Independent Allocation of Vaccines Group (IAVG) of COVAX also called for a "70 percent coverage with COVID-19 vaccines in all countries as a global imperative".[39] Meanwhile, there were some independent, valiant efforts, such as those of the Texas Children's Hospital Center for Vaccine Development (Texas Children's CVD) in partnership with the Baylor College of Medicine, who developed the CORBEVAX vaccine and sought no personal gain or patent.[40] The Indian government immediately approved it and/ordered 300 million doses.

The second and long-term problem is that of so-called Long COVID. The issue received scarce attention initially, until its effects were detected in people of all ages and health status, as well as in many elite athletes.[41] Whether Long COVID's effects are in fact ongoing symptoms of COVID-19, which have been shown to last for four to twelve weeks, or are indeed a form of longer term "Post-COVID Syndrome", remains to be seen, though patients supposedly recovered from COVID-19 report themselves as unable to concentrate at work, as experiencing unprecedented fatigue, and as having to either stop work much earlier, or work even longer to make up for their lost productivity.[42] Others have reported experiencing parosmia — a condition that causes foods and drinks to taste like, in the words of some, "garbage" or even "sewage".[43] It is nevertheless clear that Long COVID can only be understood thoroughly in a post-pandemic world, when the time and resources to do so are available, but there is already some promising research.[44]

The final problem that has become increasingly clear — one which had been brewing in the shadows, but which came to the forefront during the pandemic — is the triumph of conspiracy theories, and the complete and utter denial of science exhibited by a significant number of people in our societies. Trust in government continues to plummet in national settings,[45] while populations are acclimatizing to the slow and unsettling reality of polarization. Populist sentiments also go hand in hand with vaccine hesitancy; "In a recent German poll, half of the unvaccinated respondents had voted for the far-right populist party, Alternative für Deutschland, in the recent election. Anti-vaccine sentiments are also most common in the populist areas of Austria, France, and Italy."[46]

Political leaders during the pandemic were thus faced with a tough challenge: play the role of the benevolent dictator and mandate vaccinations to protect the health of their citizens while taking an enormous political risk, or sit idly by and protect what Isaiah Berlin would see as people's "Negative Liberty"; that is, the freedom from constraints from external sources. French President Emmanuel Macron, faced with a constituency in which 30 percent of the population were outright refusing to take the vaccine at the time,[47] took a major political gamble and made "…the anti-coronavirus shots virtually unavoidable for anyone wanting to live a normal social life".[48] New York followed a similar strategy, but vaccination rates still lagged even months after the implementation of such policy — but such was the case in the entirety of the West. Widely accessible vaccines saw a fierce resistance from 20–30 percent of the American population.[49]

It is vital not to confound the reasons people are hesitant, and to recognize that such reasons are complex and multi-faceted. One theory suggests that it is the denial of death itself that causes people to fiercely defend their beliefs,[50] while the 5C's model presents five different possible drivers:[51]

- Confidence: the person's trust in the vaccine's efficacy and safety, the health services offering them, and the policy makers deciding on their rollout
- Complacency: whether or not the person considers the disease itself to be a serious risk to their health
- Calculation: the individual's engagement in extensive information searching to weigh up the costs and benefits
- Constraints (or convenience): how easy it is for the person in question to access the vaccine
- Collective responsibility: the willingness to protect others from infection, through one's own vaccination

As climate change causes temperatures to rise, and as biodiversity continues to crumble, scientists have begun to realize that in the 21st century, pandemics might become all the more common. A 2021 paper authored by Rodó et al. proposes that zoonotic spillover, "the multilevel process by which pathogens (e.g., SARS-CoV-2, Ebola virus, human immunodeficiency virus and avian influenza viruses) manage to overcome a series of natural barriers and infect other animal species", might be accelerated through indirect ways, such as "forest fires, droughts, floods, famines and migrations".[52] Drawing lessons from the COVID-19 pandemic, the authors claim that Japan might not have experienced a third wave were it not for temperature effects, but also intervention measures, such as lockdowns. Still, they are careful to point out that overall, "climate should be seen mainly as a necessary but not sufficient factor that contributes to disease emergence."

The COVID-19 pandemic has also accelerated the adoptions of digital technologies in medicine, including telemedicine. Countries that had a significant digital infrastructure in place were able to protect their citizens to a greater degree, as services were provided online, instead of in person. The International Finance Corporation (IFC) has reported an overall increase in the "…use of digital infrastructure compared to pre-crisis levels".[53] Although the evidence is limited, it increasingly looks as if people will indeed shift toward doing more of their shopping, news consumption,

Health and Nutrition

schooling, and so forth, online, which begs the question of whether the health sector can adapt quickly enough.

Depressive disorders also skyrocketed within the world's populace, and so-called essential workers were "...more likely to report symptoms of anxiety or depressive disorder (42 percent vs. 30 percent), starting or increasing substance use (25 percent vs. 11 percent), and suicidal thoughts (22 percent vs. 8 percent) during the pandemic".[54]

The impact of the COVID-19 pandemic truly cannot be overstated, and it will take a while to get a coherent picture of the true scale of the damage caused to our health.

8.3 The Future of Health Systems

The future of health care is dependent on how the industry will decide to adapt to several emerging challenges. While costs are exploding, people are increasingly demanding universal access to health care, and for good reason. It is no coincidence that Norway and Finland topped Bloomberg's Covid Resilience Rankings.[55]

Traditionally, we distinguish between four models of health care: the Beveridge model — characterized by a nationalized system and free access; the Bismarck model — privatized, but high in regulation; the National Health Insurance model — in which the government pays private firms and provides its citizens with insurance; and finally, the Out-of-Pocket model, where citizens must provide for themselves and the government does not intervene, unless absolutely necessary.[56] Said systems come with tradeoffs, such as efficiency, availability, and greater freedom of choice — but decades of experience and research have helped us realize that some of these trade-offs might be obsolete. Consider an example from the United States, the Affordable Care Act or "Obamacare", as it is sometimes called. It currently offers 174 different plans, even though we are fully aware of the consistently unsound decision-making that goes into choosing a health care plan.[57] Health systems should thus be wary of overwhelming people with choices and withholding benefits, unless the patients themselves choose to enroll into such programs. Inertia in health care is a given, and defaults matter, with one study finding that the limited degree of active choice that is present is mostly random.[58]

We thus expect health systems to transform slowly, but in radical ways in the next decade. The authors of "The Future of Health Systems to 2030: a Roadmap for Global Progress and Sustainability" analyzed 57 case studies, which cover 152 countries and 90.5 percent of the world's population, and subsequently identified five large trends which will define and shape the future of health care.[59] According to this study, sustainable and affordable health care systems need to be built by supplementing their workforce and keeping up with new technologies, while also remaining accessible; *the genomics revolution* is not going anywhere, moral and privacy issues notwithstanding; *emerging technologies* related to e-health will change the way that services and information are provided to the patients; *global demographic dynamics* will also clearly influence health systems, especially as people begin to move more often, either to seek refuge or simply to find better job opportunities, all the while the global population will keep increasing and aging; and finally, *new models of care*, partly resulting from new technologies, pose new challenges, such as accessibility in rural areas, which are falling behind the curve.

As the number of people who have access to health care increases, so will budgets allocated to the sector. Budgetary estimates for 195 countries and territories from 1995 to 2016 range from a low of 10 percent all the way up to 42 percent,[60] while efficiency per patient is expected to rise and costs per capita to fall by as much as 28 percent.[61] As we have discussed previously, data and analytics are integral to the future of health, and a large share of the launch forward will be carried out by tech companies, posing a threat to biopharma companies. As many have said, the disruption in the sector will only be capitalized on if these companies are willing to disrupt themselves and change their business models to unlock new opportunities. In the words of PricewaterhouseCoopers (PwC): "This shift will require transformation in every part of the existing healthcare system. Physicians and caregivers will need to

Health and Nutrition

redefine their roles; regulators will have to create acceptable frameworks for digital health solutions and the sharing of sensitive data; and payers will have to account for new types and ways of spending".[62]

Deloitte is investigating precisely what the current radical shifts in the health sector are. At large, the identified shift in thinking can be attributed to the COVID-19 pandemic, with spill-over effects due to the rapid digital transformation, including demand for ownership of one's personal data, a focus on disadvantaged communities, but a focus also on preventive health measures.[63] Virtual visits are here to stay, although patients have begun voicing their disagreements to their doctors amid this distinct shift. Better educated patients in charge of their data should also gradually transform the current health-care delivery models, though this keeps the issue of interoperability at the forefront. In terms of prevalent technologies in the sector, AI, cloud computing, and virtual health (for example, shifting from inpatient visits to more outpatient) are currently dominant, with Chinese companies having made great strides in their development already. As we've seen previously, AI can be tremendously useful, with the accuracy of diagnosis increasing up to 83–87 percent in certain cases[64] — we can assume that this rate will only get better as time goes on, but the success of these technologies will always rely on the quality of the data. The emerging data value chains — which will be unlike anything we have seen before, with sensors on the body and in our personal spaces[65] — create a fundamental tension. The behavioral surplus extracted from such activities — that is, data which can create accurate predictions about our actions and sold to third parties and fed back to us in the form of advertisements — must be taken into account.[66]

8.4 The Future of Food and Eating

Healthy nutrition plays a critical role in preventive, but also curative health care. The food trend is developing an enormous dynamic, especially in affluent societies. The number of people following a vegetarian or vegan diet has significantly risen.[67] The Economist went as far as to name 2019 "The Year of the Vegan".[68] Although the United States and Europe are largely driving the trend, with 9.7 million people in the United States leading a plant-based lifestyle,[69] the global vegan food market is expected to have grown "from 14.44 billion U.S. dollars in 2020 to 15.77 billion U.S. dollars in 2021 at a compound annual growth rate (CAGR) of 9.2 percent."[70] Should this type of exponential rise continue, it has been suggested that one in ten people might be vegan in the next ten years,[71] but we see this as extremely optimistic.

On the other hand, the Good Food Institute's China Plant-Based Meat Industry Report 2018 estimates that the plant-based meat industry has been growing at a rate of around 15 percent yearly,[72] while the pandemic supply bottlenecks provided an opportunity for many companies to introduce their plant-based products into the Chinese market.[73] There are economic factors, such as the rise of the middle class in China and the ability to include environmental concerns into one's daily decision-making, but there are also obvious cultural and religious differences in food choices. In India, according to a recent Pew Research poll, 81 percent of people restrict their meat consumption, but only 39 percent of them describe themselves as vegetarian.[74]

In terms of the environment, the kind of food we eat also causally relates to our carbon footprint, with red meat, cheese, and butter having a significant carbon footprint. Animal-based foods have an overall higher footprint than plant-based foods. In total, land use and farm-stage emissions account for more than 80 percent of the footprint for most foods, but transport accounts for a smaller percentage; usually for less than ten percent.[75]

Abinet Tasew joined us to talk about the lessons to be drawn from the pandemic, but also about what we can expect from the continent in the future. Abinet Tasew is a Senior Gender and Livelihoods Technical Advisor for the Gender, Youth, and Livelihoods team of the Food and Water Systems unit at CARE USA. She has over 13 years of experience in the fields of gender, agriculture, nutrition, education, and child protection. She is an advocate for

Health and Nutrition

gender equity and equality, and has previously worked with Addis Ababa University, FHI360, and UNICEF. Abinet is a 2017 Mandela Washington Fellow; a flagship program of the Young African Leaders Initiative.

Interview with Abinet Tasew, CARE USA

Q: How did, or how does COVID-19 and the restrictions in place affect the nutrition and health situation of vulnerable communities in Africa?
Abinet Tasew: It is of course known that nutrition contributes to the immune system's strength and helps reduce the impact of a potential infection. Maintaining a healthy diet is thus extremely important in fighting the virus, but what we have seen is that, unfortunately, this has become harder and harder for people during the pandemic, as lockdowns restrict access to markets, as well as the availability of essential foods with short shelf lives like vegetables. At the same time, some inaccurate messaging has meant that mothers are afraid to breastfeed their children for fear of exposing them to the virus, depriving them of necessary nutrients.

Q: Which are the key nutrition challenges for improving the health of mothers, new-borns, and children in Africa?
Abinet Tasew: Nutrition challenges can be inferred from achievement or low performance on global nutrition indicators. The following indicators, in terms of prevalence among the populations are helpful to achieve our targets., while the 2020 global nutrition report on Africa has given us a glimpse into the current figures: anemia in women of reproductive age (39 percent); low birth weight (13.7 percent); under five stunting (being too short for age – tall for age), which stands at 29.1 percent, compared to the global average of 21.3 percent; under five wasting (being too thin for one's height), which is lower than the global average of 6.9 percent by 0.5 points; under five overweight (4.7 percent); adult female obesity, whereby 18.4 percent of women and 7.8 percent of men live with obesity; adult female diabetes (8.6 percent for women, 8.3 percent for men); and the rate of exclusive breast-feeding, with the

estimated average prevalence of infants aged zero to five months who are exclusively breastfed currently standing at 43.6 percent.
Q: Do you think the situation will improve or worsen in the next decade?
Abinet Tasew: It depends. If we are intentional about understanding the root cause of the problem and introduce and implement integrated gender transformative food systems programs with strong coordination and collaboration between the public, private, and NGO sectors, the situation could indeed improve. We need a systems thinking approach, where we think about the food from the first moment of production, until it finally reaches our plate; but this would still not be enough, as restrictive social and gender norms stand in the way of our goals. For example, stopping intergenerational malnutrition requires tackling early marriage, while exclusive breastfeeding in the first six months is held back by competing information and women's poverty struggles, as they take on multiple roles with no support. Even encouraging and offering different dietary options does not change much if the purchasing power and the change in restrictive social norms is not there. Furthermore, not all who afford nutritious meals could be taken for granted without a tailored behavior change intervention.
Q: How will climate change impact nutrition and health in Africa? Which communities will be hit hardest?
Abinet Tasew: Food systems and the climate are intertwined and as such climate change would directly affect nutrition and health. Climate change severely affects the poorest of the poor as they do not have the means to cope with its impacts. Twelve million smallholder households in Ethiopia, accounting for an estimated 95 percent of national production—their land holding being 1 hectare on average—rely on traditional, rain-fed, subsistence-oriented, low-yield production systems to generate income and feed their families. Climate change could quickly make food insecurity and malnutrition a reality for these households, all the while women lack access to productive resources.

Health and Nutrition

Q: How do you rate the importance of global agreements—for example, 2030 Agenda for Sustainable Development, and international partnerships—in addressing health and nutrition issues?

Abinet Tasew: I see global agreements like the 2030 Agenda for Sustainable Development as important accountability frameworks for member states. It is important that goals are set, as they determine where we want to go; and international partnerships can get us there. Health and nutrition are global issues with a strong need for global commitment. Leaders should be held accountable for not meeting their targets and such platforms make partnership and collaboration possible for proven approaches and models to be adapted and scaled in different contexts.

Q: How much does Africa need international support? Could it do with less? Which factors matter most? Which strategies are suitable to addressing nutrition challenges in Africa?

Abinet Tasew: Africa could do with less international support if the continent is set on good governance and democracy. When we become intentional about building strong institutions, using our human and natural resource equitably, when we are not leaving anyone behind and work with women and men, and use the wisdom and capacity of old and young, we can start addressing our nutritional challenges. According to CARE, there are three major underlying causes of poverty; gender inequality and lack of women's voice, weak governance, and increasing frequency and impact of humanitarian crises, all of which are still prevalent in Africa and halt progress. The reality is that international support is still needed until solutions to these problems can be found, while a recent FAO report indicates that 34 African countries in crisis require external assistance for food and are expected to lack the resources to deal with reported critical problems of food insecurity.

Food culture and systems are clearly distinct in different parts of the world. In her book *Sitopia*, Carolyn Steel makes the point that our taste is shaped by culture to such an extent that it is incredibly rare for our concept of what is and is not edible to change.[76] As such, though insects like the black soldier fly are gaining traction as feed for animals,[77] it is yet to be seen whether "entomophagy", the consumption of insects by humans, will expand beyond cultures where such foods are already part of their cuisine. Nevertheless, we now know that insects are great substitutes for meat and fish, rich in protein and fatty acids, as well as fiber and micronutrients, such as copper, iron, and magnesium.[78]

The Meat Atlas 2021, a report from the Heinrich Böll Stiftung, provides some context to global meat consumption: "the richer a country is, the more meat its inhabitants consume. But other factors, like climate or religion, also influence per capita consumption".[79] Overall, meat production is still going up, although two-thirds of people in some of the world's biggest economies have reduced their red meat consumption specifically to combat climate change.[80] Dr. Lukas Paul Fesenfeld, the researcher behind these findings, points out that unless there are market distorting policies, such as "higher taxes on meat, labels to reflect the sustainability of products", the narrative of consumer responsibility may lose us precious time in the fight against climate change.

A lot of companies like Beyond Meat or Impossible Foods were created with the explicit goal to transform our diets[81], and have been assuming a dominant market position, as the economies of scale kick in, but also as consumers begin to realize that humans cannot have their cake and eat it (literally). The difference in CO_2 emissions, liters of water, as well as land use between conventional meat production and the type that is produced in the lab is massive, with conventional beef emitting 99.5 kg of CO_2/kg, using up 1,451 liters of water/kg and 326m² of land, while the same values of the Beyond Burger are 3.5, 9.7, and 2.7, respectively.[82]

How can we ensure healthy and sufficient nutrition for future generations? This question guides a transdisciplinary research project funded by the Germany Ministry of Education and Research and implemented by Freie Universität Berlin. The world produces more than enough food, but, as discussed, food habits should change, and food quality must be improved; meanwhile distribution needs to be taken into account. Food4future, the aforementioned project, conducts sociological and anthropological studies

Health and Nutrition

and focuses on different extreme future scenarios. The purpose is to identify possible challenges of future food security and subsequently drive innovation. Myriam Preiss, who led this program for some years, and who is an expert on the future of nutrition, helped us create a better picture of what this might look like.

Interview with Myriam Preiss, former research project leader at Freie Universität Berlin

Q: How do you see diets evolving globally in the next 10-15 years?
Myriam Preiss: In the West there is definitely a growing interest in a healthier and more sustainable diet, which is also a more individualized one, according to a person's tastes and preferences. Diets in general will be more diversified, depending on which social class someone belongs to. As such, we will initially see a shift to a more sustainable and healthier diet in more progressive and educated parts of the population, characterized by ethical considerations about both the planet and the well-being of animals. As for the time frame, ten years may be too little for such changes to occur, but the next generation will surely be the one to facilitate these changes. Now, in other countries, specifically developing ones the numbers are clear and the picture is quite different. If production is possible, there will be more meat consumption, mainly due to the perception of meat as an indicator of wealth and a good diet. It is also important to mention that due to the unequal distribution of wealth during the COVID-19 pandemic, this trend has decelerated.

Q: What role will insects play in our future diet?
Myriam Preiss: Insects will be part of our diets, but do not necessarily have to be sold as stand-alone products. Rather, they could be ingredients of processed foods, if the large producers behind said products find that it is indeed worth it to substitute their old ingredients, and if more knowledge on how to actually use these insects is produced.

Q: Do you think there is great potential for research in this sector?
Myriam Preiss: Yes, if we believe in the idea that the private sector goes where the money is, then absolutely.

Q: What about products like vegan burgers? Will they substitute the real thing?

Myriam Preiss: Perhaps in the distant future, but we need to consider the competition in place. For example, there is already a restaurant in Singapore selling burgers with meat grown in the laboratory, so there are different alternatives to just vegan variants.

Q: Are you optimistic that the carbon footprint from diets will be reduced and that these new and more sustainable diets will contribute to combating climate change?

Myriam Preiss: First, there is already research out there showing that people have begun to choose their food based on surrounding temperatures, which is encouraging, but it's hard to tell if that will be enough, if people just close their eyes to the impact that their diet is having on the environment. There is a strong potential influence that people can have out of their good will and the changing diets due to rising temperatures, which makes me hopeful.

Now, am I optimistic? Yes, because countries are already reducing their food waste, which is massively reducing the carbon footprint, while the younger generations are choosing different diets, and if of course the availability is scaled up, meaning that there aren't merely meat alternatives, but also dairy ones, then that could help. Overall, though, it seems that globally the carbon footprint will unfortunately rise, due to what we discussed previously.

Q: Who are some of the most important stakeholders in this sector?

Myriam Preiss: I would go with retailers. If we want to see actual change, they are the key to everything, as they are the ones who are putting these new products on their shelves. On the flip side, it's the investors, who are looking into alternatives, perhaps not so much in Germany at the moment, but rather in the U.S.

Q: So these investors are anticipating a rising demand, otherwise they would not be taking such risks.

Myriam Preiss: Exactly. Whether it's plant-based protein, or meat/dairy alternatives, they seem to think that people want such products.

Health and Nutrition

Q: Going back to the point about diets being tied to class, what could social cohesion at danger look like in the West?
Myriam Preiss: In the U.S. at least, malnutrition and obesity numbers occur at the same places, whereas educated people are fitter and slimmer than the rest of society, something entirely unprecedented in human history. If people do not have access to knowledge about healthy food and the government is not stepping in to help, there will be no actual counterweight to this, and diets will keep drifting further apart.
It's important to stress the role that schools play in this, as there is the danger that if parents don't have a specific routine, then there is nowhere else from which the knowledge can come from in regard to the child.
Q: Based on what you mentioned previously about the role investors will play, as well as the interaction of government and the schooling system with people's diets, do you think this supports Mazzucato's theory of the Entrepreneurial State, and furthermore, does this mean that providing healthy school meals will be more important than ever?
Myriam Preiss: There is definitely something to Mazzucato's thinking, as a lot of the research and groundwork for changing diets was not done by private investors. But now that the private sector is investing so heavily into this emerging market, there might be even more good coming out of it. As for the school meals, there needs to be a balance between control of food-intake and personal choices, as that can easily backfire. Imagine for example a child that eats healthy in school and then goes home to a completely different diet. This is why education on food, perhaps included in the curriculum itself, is so important.

So, what will food consumption look like in the coming years? Some claim that our current products will be engineered to be more nutritious, for example, banana hybrids with extra provitamin A, or corn and rice with more protein, and DNA from external sources spliced into other conventional foods.[83] Seeking to overcome our ignorance around the food we eat, companies have also come up with convenient food scanners, which can enormously help people with allergies.[84] Intuitive eating and nutrigenomics, both based on listening to one's body and the idea that food affects people differently,[85] are gaining traction and might end up shaping our individual diets in ways unfathomable to us now.[86]

Our food waste will also be used to aid sustainability efforts. In Seville, the company municipal water company Emasesa has pioneered a system where thousands of oranges that are now polluting the city's streets can be recycled and turned into electricity.[87] Milan has taken a different approach building "hubs", which are supermarkets stocked with food donated by local businesses and supermarkets to help prevent food waste.[88] With current food systems representing 34 percent of total Greenhouse Gas (GHG) emissions,[89] such innovative solutions will inevitably be needed.

This is precisely why urban farming is also gaining traction. A 2008 study found that urban community gardeners consumed more fruits and vegetables on average.[90] Vertical and rooftop farming seem to be the most promising methods, while the resulting schemes like Community Supported Agriculture drop the boundaries between the supplier and the consumer,[91] as well as bring people together in ways that modern society can sometimes restrict. Plant Factories with Artificial Lighting (PFALs) are part of this transformation in food production, and are surrounded by claims of incredible efficiency, but must still improve in terms of environmental impact and energy use, were they to be widely implemented.[92]

Food and agricultural systems will face many challenges in the years ahead, while global health will forever be transformed after the COVID-19 pandemic, which still has no end in sight. Both the health and food sectors will be characterized by radical transformation and innovation, incorporating digital technologies and promoting sustainability, while being largely focused on moral issues, such as tackling malnutrition and famine and providing health care to as many people as possible. International cooperation can accelerate these trends, and countries must be prepared to make decisions and set trends on the path to sustainability.

Chapter 9

Green Economy

Safeguarding clean air and water, biodiversity and halting climate change are among the biggest challenges facing humanity. Business and investment activities that are ignoring planetary boundaries[1] contribute to destroying the safe operating space for humanity and undermine the basis for a flourishing global economy. Instead, an inclusive green economy recognizes and nurtures nature's diverse values.[2]

The green economy is a widely referenced and powerful megatrend meeting the criteria of the Pentagon Model. With regard to research, there is a significant number of book publications and specialized journals on the concept of the green economy. *International Journal of Green Economics*, *The International Journal on Green Growth and Development*, *Green Economy Journal*, and many development journals or journals carry sustainability in their name as well as publish special issues on green economy issues.[3] The Global Green Growth Institute,[4] headquartered in South Korea, also published a Green Growth Index in December 2020, which we will briefly introduce later.

The UN Environment launched the Green Economy Initiative (GEI) in 2008, a program to motivate policymakers to support environmental investments. The concept of the green economy has since gained traction with many governments, international organizations, and the business community. At the United Nations Conference on Sustainable Development (Rio+20 in June 2021), governments agreed that green economy was an important tool for sustainable development.

Environmental harm caused by business activities, including activities of multinational companies, is a global phenomenon. The most devastating economic activities have often taken place in countries with poor environmental standards and with weak legal systems or in conflict-ridden areas with limited state sovereignty, in so-called "failed states". In the face of several environmental disasters, such as the serious water pollution in Nigeria's Ogoniland and in Zambia's Copperbelt region as well as the Amazon deforestation in Brazil), the concept of green economy has gained traction in the past decade and will continue to do so.

The United Nations Environmental Program (UNEP) regards the green economy as an alternative to today's dominant economic model, which exacerbates inequalities, encourages waste, triggers resource scarcities, and generates widespread threats to the environment and human health.

The World Bank and the Organization for Economic Cooperation and Development (OECD) are also engaged in the promotion of the green economy though they put more emphasis on growth aspects. A study of the World Bank states that "growth and equity can be pursued without relying on policies and practices that foul the air, water, and land."[5]

The Global 100 list published by the Corporate Knights, a media, research and financial information company based in Toronto, Canada, ranks corporations with revenue in excess of one billion U.S. dollars based on key metrics of sustainability, among them their carbon footprint. The French electricity company Schneider Electrics topped the ranking in 2021 after committing to a sustainability program. The Denmark-based renewable energy provider Ørsted topped the list in 2020.[6] These are just two examples selected from a large number of start-up companies which represent a growing green economy. Governments across the world are setting incentives and offer prize money to green business models. For example, the EUREF Campus in the heart of Berlin hosts Climate Knowledge and Innovation Community (KIC). It presents itself as the world's largest accelerator for green start-ups. A multi-stage funding program accompanies young companies in the first phases of their founding in developing a solid cleantech business model, opening up markets for the products and going on a growth path.[7]

Though we have not traced statistics across the globe, many experts around us agree that media coverage on green economy issues has also significantly increased. We also witness a growing number of social enterprises aiming to blend green business with social and ecological purposes.

The green economy trends are also supported by many nonprofits and social movements. The Green Economy Coalition is one of the world's largest alliances for green and fair economies. It is hosted by the International Institute of Environment and Development in London and Finance Watch in Brussels and regroups more than 50 member organizations, uniting multilateral agencies, civil society, businesses, think tanks, youth and citizens' movements. It organizes dialogue events, publishes papers, and networks with international organizations, including the United Nations. But what is the concept of green economy and how is it linked to green growth?

9.1   Green Economy and Green Growth

The green economy concept is based on an understanding that policies stalling or reversing growth are unlikely to attract widespread support from the mainstream business community or win democratic elections. Instead, green growth concepts are based on the hypothesis that it is theoretically and practically possible for economies to grow in a green way, without harming the environment in a significant way or accelerating climate change. It is presumed that a decoupling between growth and carbon emissions is possible and that even energy consumption could be cut back by new business models and through efficiency gains. Countries in Asia and the Pacific had already pioneered the concept of green growth in 2005.[8] The concept of green growth has spread around the world but also invited a lot of criticism.

Jason Hickel and Giorgos Kallis argue that "there is no empirical evidence that absolute decoupling from resource use can be achieved on a global scale against a background of continued economic growth, and absolute decoupling from carbon emissions is highly unlikely to be achieved at a rate rapid enough to prevent global warming over 1.5°C or 2°C, even under optimistic policy conditions." They have examined many studies on historical trends and model-based projections and conclude that "green growth is likely to be a misguided objective, and that policymakers need to look toward alternative strategies."[9]

It is obvious that the promotion of the green economy would imply a series of drastic changes in many countries. For instance, energy taxes and subsidy reforms are key to achieving the objectives of decarbonization and access to affordable energy. The OECD—regrouping 37 countries with high per capita income—points out that in 44 countries—members of OECD and/or G20 countries—around 70 percent of energy-related emissions are untaxed.[10]

As far back as May 2011, the OECD delivered its first Green Growth Strategy to Heads of State and Ministers of over forty countries with a focus on expanding economic growth and job creation through more sustainable use of natural resources, efficiencies in the use of energy, and valuation of ecosystem services.[11]

The OECD presents a series of arguments on why green growth is needed to re-balance economic development in view of emerging environmental crisis and climate change scenarios. It acknowledges that "natural capital, encompassing natural resource stocks, land and ecosystems, is often undervalued and mismanaged. This imposes costs to the economy and human well-being."[12]

We share the OECD's assessment of green growth as a subset of sustainable development rather than a concept replacing or rivaling sustainable development. The OECD has provided such clarification because economic growth is subject to many controversies. It is critiqued by many social scientists and a few economists working on sustainable development with focus on degrowth concepts. For example, the Club of Rome report on "The Limits of Growth" has set the agenda for a growing number of experts advocating for less growth to save Planet Earth. Fundamental criticism of economic growth gained popularity in mainly Western countries while not receiving much attention in emerging markets apart from Asia.

Green Economy

In Asia, the concept of *Green Growth* enjoys much popularity. United Nations, Economic and Social Commission for Asia and the Pacific (UNESCAP) even stated that the concept emerged from the Asia-Pacific region.

The Republic of Korea, for instance, was an early adopter of green growth strategies. It designed a national strategy and a five-year plan for green growth as early as the period 2009—2013. It allocated two percent of its gross domestic product to invest in several green sectors such as renewable energy, energy efficiency, clean technology, and water. The South Korean government also launched the Global Green Growth Institute (GGGI) which aims to help countries (especially developing countries) develop green growth strategies.[13] Which issues are today on top of the agenda, do we see different approaches in different parts of the world, and how is the trend of the green economy related to other megatrends? We talked with Emily Benson of the Green Economy Coalition about key discourses, global agendas, and stakeholders promoting the green economy.

Interview with Emily Benson, Green Economy Coalition

Q: Which discourses shape today's green economy agenda, and how did they evolve over time? How do interpretations of the green economy vary among countries and regions?
Emily Benson: The green economy emerged from a number of discourses. It is rooted in the discourse around sustainable development but informed by more recent climate science, the concept of planetary boundaries, and the principle of climate justice. Firstly, as laudable as the concept of sustainable development was and is, it was struggling to make an impact within national strategies. Pockets of sustainability in, say, Indonesia, Nepal, or Costa Rica, were not enough among the sea of brown economic activity. Tiny efforts in an extractive economic model really showcased the limitations of sustainable development. The second driver was the political deadlock emerging in the international climate change negotiations, exemplified by the failure of the COP15, as poorer

countries felt their own development was being curtailed by climate change targets and rich nations were reluctant to pay their fair share. The green economy offered a chance to reframe the transition to one that offered opportunities for green jobs, poverty alleviation, and small enterprise development. A third driver was the discourse around planetary boundaries and limits to growth, which seemed to have been disproven in the 1970s due to the Green Revolution but turned out to be accurate and relevant as the data on ecosystems improved. At the core of the green economy is the question of how to bring green and fair together, and in order to take that to scale we need to tackle the economics. Doing sustainability right means rewiring the economy.

As for the differences between countries, one of our initial fears was that this model would mirror the Washington Consensus in being a "one size fits all" approach, but this could not be further from the truth. Green economies are all context-specific and are emerging along different pathways. For example, Trinidad and Tobago are quite dependent on oil and, as a set of tiny islands, financial shocks have huge impacts, which they have to consider during their transition. In South Africa, a significant mining economy, and the questions of which materials will be used, as well as that of job creation and unemployment are the ones driving their own transitions, while India, on the other hand, has a myriad of tiny businesses. These economies could not be more different, so each of their transition pathways are unique. Yet they share the same foundations of moving away from an extractive and exploitative economic model toward a regenerative and more distributive model.

Q: How do we measure "green"? Do you see the risk of greenwashing? Is there already a proliferation of green labels and certificates across sectors? Is this the way forward to win investors and customers trust? What are your recommendations?

Emily Benson: Measuring "green" is hard. A macro perspective has to be informed by environmental limits, taking into account biodiversity and natural assets, and whether natural capital is increasing or decreasing. As such, greening does not stop at whether resources are being used a little more efficiently, but rather whether those natural stocks and flows (be they ecosystems or biodiversity or natural processes) are recovering and replenishing or not.

Unfortunately, many claims in green marketing and green financing are misleading, but I see it as a positive that companies like Amazon, BP or Blackrock are finally starting to engage in green metrics of progress. As heinous as greenwashing is, when it is discovered, companies can then be held to account. For example, when so-called socially conscious fashion retailers such as GAP and Benetton, were exposed for poor labor conditions they had to transform their practices very quickly. VW is another example, as they are now looking to be a leader in electro mobility after the emissions fraud scandal.

As for certificate schemes, I am worried that the multitude of different standards in different countries and sectors may make the life of producers harder in trying to meet said standards, but it is definitely a positive development that consumers are demanding such schemes.

Q: How do you see the relationship between green economy, green growth, and degrowth or post-growth discourses?

Emily Benson: The degrowth movement criticizes economic growth on all levels, but looking at different countries and contexts, where poverty is still an enormous challenge—for example, Uganda or Peru—it is not morally, politically, or socially acceptable to prevent countries and regions from growing their economy. Now, from the Green Economy Coalition's point of view, we do believe that rich countries must indeed contract their economies, not just to do more with less, but rather to reduce the net amount of consumption. Green growth tends to emphasize the energy transition and resource efficiency and has been so busy with making the political and business case that historically it has not always prioritized issues of distribution or fairness. The green economy, on the other hand, was pioneered by the UN and recognizes distribution, biodiversity, and participation. By no means do I want to demonize green growth, as it is still trying to tackle the dominant, linear models of extraction and resource use, but I do see it to have a narrower logic than green economy.

Q: Which sectors have come into the focus of new business models and investors?

Emily Benson: When people think of green economy, they think of energy and wind turbines or solar panels. However, for me, what is more exciting is the kinds of innovations we are seeing both on the ground and in the policy space. From the off grid green energy revolution that is starting to build across the African continent; or the innovation we are seeing all over the world, as small enterprises use waste to produce new goods and services; and indeed, even the multinational companies like IKEA, H&M, which are finally taking responsibility for the full life cycle of their products. I am also really excited by the innovation we are seeing in finance, for example, where larger investors are working with small, locally rooted banks and finance providers to bundle up different green investments in order to reduce the risk the portfolio.

However, while some sectors such as fashion and energy are showing huge innovation, the same cannot yet be said for mainstream construction or industrial agriculture yet. They need to be the great next frontier.

Q: How is green economy related to other megatrends, such a climate action and sustainability transformations, digitalization, and inequality which we consider as some of the most powerful global trends?

Emily Benson: When the opportunity of a green economy first emerged, we undertook wide consultation with over 500 networks all over the world to understand what it meant to them. By talking to labor groups, community organizations, businesses big and small, local authorities and non-governmental organizations, we discovered that a green economy was so much more than wind turbines or solar panels. Rather, it was a holistic approach to rewiring our economies to deliver different results. It was founded on principles of well-being, justice, sufficiency, planetary boundaries, and good governance. We also discovered that it was not limited to a single sector, such as energy, but required transformation across our housing, food, and infrastructure; it required a mass change in financial flows; and it tackled how. This bigger systems approach can feel overwhelming at times because it embraces so many megatrends. The way that we choose to run our economies shapes how we produce or share goods and services (digitalization), how financial and natural resources are distributed (inequality), and how we tackle carbon emissions (climate change). Until we tackle the economics, we will really struggle to achieve change at scale.

9.2 Green Growth versus Degrowth

Degrowth is a term that encompasses a set of theories criticizing the paradigm of economic growth. It is viewed by its proponents, including many social scientists, as a concept to re-define human well-being beyond material growth.[14] A crucial element of the degrowth concept is the decoupling of individual contentment from material prosperity. Happiness research has found that individual happiness is determined only up to a certain point by income, material assets, and consumption of resources. Instead, equality in society plays a role in subjective contentment, especially for one's sense of justice. Stress due to constantly increasing competition is one of the main causes of individual unhappiness.[15]

Experts argue that degrowth would be an adequate strategy to avoid disaster through overuse of natural resources. "Degrowth — by design or by disaster", asked Christiane Kliemann in an article published by the Zukunftsinstitut (The Future Institute), one of the leading German think tanks on future research. She points to the rebound effect and other dynamics of economic development that negate efforts to decouple growth from the degradation of natural resources.[16]

The concept of degrowth goes hand in hand with a critique of the Gross Domestic Product (GDP) as an overarching reference framework for development. Philipp Lepenies, professor at Freie Universität Berlin, recounted the history of GDP's political acceptance and eventual dominance in his book *The Power of a Single Number: A Political History of GDP*[17]. He explained "how the GDP has become the world's most powerful statistical indicator of national development and progress..."and "why "practically all governments adhere to the idea that GDP growth is a primary economic target."[18]

We must admit that degrowth discourses do not resound much in emerging markets and developing countries. Globally speaking, degrowth is still a niche concept, while green growth has received widespread recognition by international organizations, including the United Nations and the G20.

We have at least seen a proliferation of initiatives and index projects aiming to replace the GDP as the dominant concept of well-being. In his popular book *Less is More*, Jason Hickel pointed to initiatives of scientists calling on the European Commission and governments of this world to shift from GDP growth and to focus on human well-being and ecological stability instead.[19] The National Welfare Index (NWI) is one index project which has been presented at many international environmental conferences. It was developed via a research project founded by the German Federal Ministry for the Environment, Nature Conservation and Nuclear Safety (BMU) and Federal Environment Agency (UBA) as a contribution to the debate on a more sustainable economy. The index is the sum of 20 monetarily assessed components. The most important one is real consumption expenditure weighted by the distribution of income using the Gini coefficient. Other welfare-enhancing components are housework, volunteer work and expenditure for health and education that have a positive impact the NWI, whereas negative activities are subtracted, such as environmental damage or crime.[20]

There is growing recognition, especially within the sustainability and inequality research community, that the GDP does not provide an adequate account of social and economic progress. Economic activities leading to environmental degradation are part of the GDP as much as investments in environmental protection and costs of repair. Reports and index projects on happiness and livability[21] have made us aware that we need to shift our attention to the quality of growth rather than the quantity of it. Proponents of degrowth are particularly vocal on highlighting the need to create socially just and ecologically sustainable societies in which the concept of well-being replaces the GDP as the indicator of prosperity.

Green Economy

Catch words of the degrowth community are autonomy, care work, self-organization, commons, community, localism, work-sharing, happiness and conviviality. Many proponents of the degrowth discourse would question the ability of capitalism to cope with climate change risks, pointing to incentives of externalizing environmental costs and rebound effects. Some question the ability of capitalism to cope with climate change altogether.

The Swedish researcher Andreas Malm of Lund University proposes another perspective on the relationship between capitalism and climate change. He argues that "vested interests" are preventing climate action by referring to the century-long structural intimacy between fossil fuels and capitalist systems. His popular book *Fossil Capital. The Rise of Steam Power and the Roots of Global Warming* explains how the demand for steam power by British cotton manufacturers gave rise to a sharp increase in coal use and the take-off in greenhouse gas emissions.[22] It is historical irony that the United Kingdom's (U.K.) leftist coal unions lost influence on political decisions during Margaret Thatcher's time in power in the 1980, especially after the miner strike in 1984 and 1985. Thatcher's firm stand on cutting subsidies, which eventually resulted in phasing out coal production in the U.K. earlier than elsewhere. Naomi Klein's *This Changes Everything: Capitalism vs. the Climate*[23] is another bestselling book which bashes capitalism, neoliberalism, and corporate elites in particular. Do capitalist structures really stand in the way of climate action? Klein has a point when arguing that powerful and well-financed rightwing thinktanks and lobby groups lay behind the denial of climate change in recent years. However, the attention paid to climate action and the net-zero pledges of multinational companies in the past years must raise serious doubts whether climate action remains marginalized in the further development of capitalism in the coming decade. Hartmus Elsenhans, a renowned German political economist, argues that "the shift to environmentally safer production constitutes no threat to capitalism; in fact, it is the most advanced frontier of capitalist growth."[24]

In reality, market-mechanisms are about to become effective in stimulating climate action in many ways, especially if complemented by command-and-control initiatives and a series of legal and regulatory reforms. Even the Chinese Communist Party (CCP) embraces many market-based mechanisms in their strenuous efforts to promote green technologies and a green transition of the economy. The merit of the degrowth argument is perhaps that it strongly points to the need for changing business as usual. Indeed, it is not sufficient to develop greener technologies. We also have to design and agree on exit strategies for dirty industries. This is often a huge challenge as it could lead to massive job loss in areas which are hugely dependent on old industries. This applies to many provinces in the North of China. The Chinese Ministry of Industry and Information Technology released a five-year plan aimed at the green development of its industrial sectors in December 2021. The plan calls for cutting carbon emissions by 18 percent and achieving 1.7 trillion U.S. dollars of economic output in the environmental sector by 2025.[25]

Most countries face big challenges in developing their structural adjustment policies. The German government and regional leaders agreed on a deal to phase out coal-fired power stations by 2038, involving compensation of about 40 billion EUR. The end date for burning brown coal (lignite) — the dirtiest type of coal — could be brought forward to 2035. There are three brown coal mining districts left in Germany: the Rhenish district in North Rhine-Westphalia (NRW), the Lusatian district in Brandenburg and Saxony and the Central German district in Saxony and Saxony-Anhalt. Local politicians advocated for higher compensations and an extension of the use of coal-fired plants. Climate activists heavily criticized the plan, pointing out to the huge climate impact of coal mining and the increasing number of workers in the renewable energy sector which already outnumber those working in the coal sector by far.

Facing the complexity of these issues, OECD Secretary General Angel Gurría has appointed a high-level group of experts to develop reform proposals for economic policy. The guiding principle: to see growth not as an end in itself, but as a means of achieving social goals such as ecological sustainability, equal opportunities, and individual and global well-being.

9.3 International Cooperation in Support of the Green Economy

Green economy concepts are supported by a wide range of organizations across continents. The Green Economy Coalition unites 50+ member organizations, including multilateral agencies, civil society, businesses, think tanks, youth and citizens' movements. It entered into partnerships with major institutions including the Organization for Economic Cooperation and Development (OECD), United Nations Environmental Program (UNEP), United Nations Development Program (UNDP), the International Labor Organization (ILO), International Finance Corporation (IFC), Global Green Growth Institute (GGGI), World Wide Fund for Nature (WWF), the Capitals Coalition (CC), and many more, and is recognized as a key player by many more institutions and experts.

The GGGI is a treaty-based international and inter-governmental organization that supports developing country governments's transition to a model of economic growth that is environmentally sustainable and socially inclusive. GGGI was established in 2012 at the Rio+20 United Nations Conference on Sustainable Development and is based in Seoul, Republic of Korea. Membership in GGGI is open to any member state of the United Nations or regional integration organization that subscribes to the objectives of the Institute. GGGI supports its members in mobilizing green finance needed for meeting their National Determined Contributions under the Paris Agreement and green growth targets. It leveraged 2 billion U.S. dollars of climate finance for 60 projects during 2015–2020.

The GGGI developed the Green Growth Index Framework (GGIF) in collaboration with a wide range of stakeholders. The engagement process was initiated in 2016 and completed in early 2019. The GGIF emphasizes four closely interlinked concepts that support green growth and sustainable development:

- Low carbon economy;
- Ecosystem health,

Global Perspectives on Megatrends

- Resilient society;
- Inclusive growth[26]

Figure 9.1: Green Growth Index Framework

Source: GGGI (2019)[27]

The International Finance Corporation (IFC), part of the World Bank Group with headquarters in Washington, is another major promoter of the green economy, especially in emerging markets and developing countries. IFC works with the private sector, companies, and banks across the world. Projects typically focus on infrastructure, agrobusiness, and manufacturing. IFC has been piloting green finance models in China, Ukraine, and in Latin America. It has invested more than two billion U.S. dollars in energy-efficient construction. IFC and the World Bank Group have created the Lighting Africa initiative to develop commercial markets for safe, clean, and affordable lighting alternatives for the 500 million Africans who currently rely on dangerous, polluting, and expensive fuel-based lighting. IFC also granted a new credit line of 350 million Mexican pesos to the Mexican eco-construction company VINTE to develop 26,000 sustainable homes across Mexico varying the EDGE certificate.

Also, many international cooperation agencies have launched projects in support of the green economy. One of them is the Green

Economy Transformation project of the Deutsche Gesellschaft für Internationale Zusammenarbeit (GIZ). The project uses green economy approaches to strengthen the capacities of key public sector actors to implement the Sustainable Development Goals (SDGs) and the National Determined Contributions under the Paris Agreement more systematically. The project pays special emphasis to financial incentives for a green economy and on knowledge management and transfer. Partner countries include Argentina, Costa Rica, Indonesia, Peru, South Africa, and Uruguay. National efforts are linked up with international networks.[28]

The partnership between the International Cooperative Alliance (ICA) and the European Commission, created in 2016, is another initiative in support of the green economy. It aims to illustrate how the cooperative movement could function as a model of ecological equilibrium by incorporating the values of cooperation, solidarity, self-management, and democracy in planet-centered development approaches. The joint report "Cooperation for the transition to a green economy", published in 2021, highlights connections and interlinkages between cooperative enterprises and positive environmental outcomes.[29]

However, the many relevant international cooperation activities in support of the green economy cannot obscure the fact that international environmental rules are often vague and lack binding effect. There is also a considerable lack of uniformity across countries and regions, a condition which allows multinational corporations to choose strategically where they will face the least opposition to environmentally harmful production. Next to developing a system of incentives, monitoring and evaluation mechanisms in support of environmentally friendly production and consumption, it is also important to address international law as well as legal and governance issues. Legal scholars such as Professor Karin Buhmann, Head of the Center for Law, Sustainability and Justice of the University of Southern Denmark, have been working on business and human rights issues and have challenged the state-centrist conception and operation of international law in an effort to raise legal obligations of corporations. The promotion of the green economy is therefore a project including a very wide and diverse range of stakeholders and expanding over different academic disciplines.

Chapter 10

Sustainable Finance

The trend of green and sustainable finance has gained strong traction. It is driven by various factors matching the criteria of our Pentagon Model. We have seen a proliferation of research publications on green and sustainable finance in recent years. Some academic papers — including one of the Hamburg based researchers Gunnar Friede, Alexander Bassen and Timo Busch — made widely quoted contributions to this trend by providing evidence for good financial performance of sustainability-oriented funds.[1]

Figure 10.1: Green Finance Publications and Annual Absolute Growth of Green Finance Publications, 1990–2020.

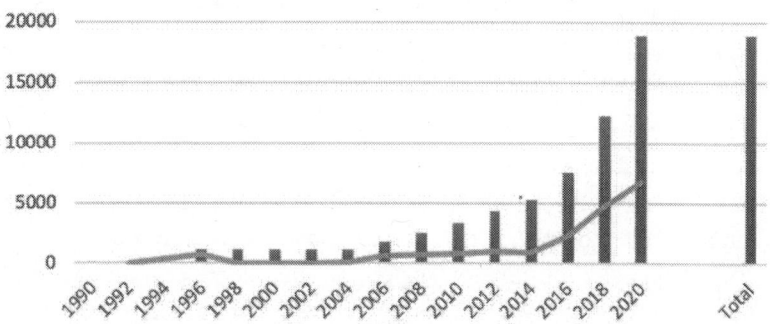

Bar Chart: Green Finance publications per year;
Line: Annual growth of Green Finance publications
Source: Stemshorn (2021) based on Freie Universität Berlin primo data.[2]

Momentum is growing to align the financial system with sustainable development. The trend has been further consolidated since the COVID-19 pandemic in 2020. We have witnessed a big push for sustainable and green finance policies in the past years. The European Commission, national governments and regulatory authorities are discussing and enacting new regulations on classifications of assets according to sustainability criteria with far-reaching consequences for the investment community.

Bjarne Steffen of ETH Zurich, one of our interview partners in this chapter, presented a comparative analysis of green financial policy outputs in OECD countries from 2001 to 2019, based on an inventory of 136 policies from 29 countries and the European Union. The results clearly show that policy output accelerated rapidly after the Paris Agreement. Key instruments included carbon disclosure requirements, low-carbon investment policies for public funds and green state investment banks.[3]

We see a strong growth in sustainable investments: an annual increase of 55 percent per annum in the year 2021 amounting to about 726 billion U.S. dollars.[4] The Glasgow Financial Alliance for Net Zero (GFANZ), chaired by Mark Carney, UN Special Envoy on Climate Action and Finance, brought together over 160 firms collectively responsible for assets of more than 70 trillion U.S. dollars across the financial system to accelerate the transition to net-zero emissions by 2050 at the latest.[5]

The term *sustainable finance* primarily refers to the integration of Environmental, Social and Governance criteria (ESG) in investment decisions. Environmental criteria consider how a company performs as a steward of nature and contributes to addressing climate change. Social criteria examine how a company manages relationships with employees, suppliers, customers, and the communities where it operates. Governance deals with a company's leadership, executive pay, audits, internal controls, and shareholder rights.[6]

Furthermore, sustainable finance approaches are associated with a series of so called "exclusion criteria" related to various concerns of business and investment practices: for example, production of or trade in controversial weapons; violation of human rights resolutions; social and labor standards and animal welfare; and gambling.

Companies listed on the stock markets witness strong incentives to perform better on the ESG criteria as a growing number of institutional investors such as pension funds and city governments apply ESG criteria in asset management.

Perspectives of different stakeholders on sustainable finance are quite diverse. Some well-established banks and asset managers still aim to respond with minimal adjustments to a new trend in finance. Others adopt a more proactive approach. Some advocacy-oriented nonprofit initiatives focus on 'naming and shaming' of companies and point to greenwashing of investment strategies. Rating agencies and consulting firms are involved in developing criteria and standards for evaluating the performance of companies and providing guidance to investors.

We are confident that mainstreaming of sustainable finance will continue. Many initiatives from different types of stakeholders, ranging from financial industry associations to civil society organizations, contribute to the mainstreaming of sustainable finance in many countries. The European Commission presented a comprehensive sustainable finance strategy in 2018 with a focus on green finance. The new Sustainable Finance Disclosure Regulation (SFDR) came into force on March 10, 2021.[7] It introduced new transparency and sustainability-related disclosure requirements for financial market participants with a view to preventing greenwashing and ensuring comparability.

There are many international initiatives aiming to push the green finance agenda. One of them is the Carbon Tracker. It introduced the concept of stranded assets to get people thinking about the implications of not adjusting investment in line with the emissions trajectories required to limit global warming.[8] Media coverage on green and sustainable finance has significantly increased as more institutional investors and retail customers are asking for sustainable investments. Investment advice becomes more regulated and more complex. In Germany, one of the daily newspapers, the *Frankfurter Allgemeine Zeitung* (FAZ), frequently covers issues related to sustainable finance. *The Financial Times* (FT) launched a new initiative—Moral Money—in 2019. It explores the fast-growing, international shift toward ethical, sustainable, and responsible investing—which, according to its editor-at-large Gillian Tett, is "the next big thing."

The number of business associations and nonprofit advocacy groups that focus on green and sustainable finance issues has significantly increased. There are specialized organizations such as the Forum for Sustainable Investment (FNG), covering Germany, Austria, and Switzerland, and more traditional nonprofits, such as the World Wide Fund for Nature (WWF), that started to work on issues related to green finance in order to complement their environmental action agenda. This also applies to city governments, which are under political pressure to shift funds to more sustainable investments, sometimes with mixed results. The city of Berlin aims to be a frontrunner city in climate policies. It runs the Berlin Energy and Climate Protection Program 2030, declared the "climate emergency" in 2019, and aims to consider sustainability criteria in its investment decisions. The index in which the state of Berlin invests around 20 percent of its assets applies a series of exclusion criteria. The composition of the fund, however, has invited criticism.[9]

The process of mainstreaming sustainable finance gained further momentum in the context of the implementation of the 2030 Agenda for Sustainable Development and the Paris Agenda from 2015 onwards. The establishment of the EU Action Plan "Financing Sustainable Growth" in 2018 was an important milestone and strongly impacted new policies and regulations in EU countries. The regulation of the EU's Action Plan led to activities at all levels of the financial industry, including asset management companies, insurance companies, financial advisors, and rating agencies. The sustainable finance trend will go on. However, the "reinvention of finance will not eliminate hubris"[10]. Stock market performances of companies depend on a complex set of factors, including expectations on profits and market shares of companies as well as monetary policies, macro-economic, political, geopolitical, and psychological factors. Sirio Aramonte and Anna Zabai cautioned in a paper published in the *BIS Quarterly Review* that "historical lessons from the investment volume and price dynamics in rapidly growing asset classes could be relevant for ESG securities. Assets related to fundamental economic and social changes tend to undergo large price corrections after an initial investment boom."[11]

10.1 From Ethical Investment to Sustainable Finance

How could sustainable finance be defined, and how could the term be distinguished from related terms and concepts? The term sustainable finance is mainly used by those concerned with political supervision, regulation, and macro-management of the financial sector. The rationale behind the concept of sustainable finance is that the sustainability transition requires enormous investments. Re-directing investments from fossil fuel industries to clean technology industries requires political guidance, new laws and regulations, and a series of stimuli. The term ethical investment is mainly used by institutional and private investors whose backgrounds are religious (churches) or philosophical (anthroposophical movement) or which have specific ethical concerns, such as those related to animal welfare.

In Germany, the pioneers of ethical responsible investment included some church-affiliated banks and other specialized banks. They showed early concern for investment practices and agreed on exclusion criteria for their own investments, such as investments in weapon manufacturing companies or others suspected of violating social and labor standards.[12] The early proponents of ethical investment could hardly have dreamed about the emergence of a global trend that pays attention to environmental and social concerns.

The climate change debate eventually called for action to make investors, including large pension funds, accountable for the environmental and climate impact of their investments. This development triggered political and regulatory action at different levels. Meanwhile we have witnessed a proliferation of terms and concepts related to investment that is not only concerned with financial returns but also with ethical concerns: responsible investments, green finance, ethical investment, and impact investment have all gained traction in the investment community.

The term *responsible investment* is particularly popular with investors and companies. Many mainstream investors are still not in favor of comprehensive regulations of the sector and tend to remain skeptical about sustainable finance policies. However, they are keen to highlight their own pro-active contributions to make the world a better place. Responsible investment receives good attention as it is used by a United Nations-supported international network of investors, the Principle for Responsible Investment Initiative (PRI). The PRI initiative supports signatories to incorporate six key principles into their investment decision-making and ownership practices and, thus, contribute to the promotion of sustainable finance.[13]

Green finance is sometimes used synonymously with *sustainable finance* but strictly interpreted, would exclude social and governance criteria from screening investments. Sustainable development is the broader term that addresses aspects of green development but also focuses on social and economic aspects, driven by the 2030 Agenda and the 17 Sustainable Development Goals of the United Nations. The World Conversation Congress organized by the International Union for the Conservation of Nature (IUCN), a leading international nongovernmental organization working in the field of nature conservation and sustainable use of natural resources, makes strong statements in support of green finance. Chris Buss, IUCN, noted at the IUCN world conference in Marseille in September 2021 that mobilizing public finance is crucial to upscaling private investments in nature conservation, highlighting the importance of quality assurance mechanisms like the IUCN Global Standard for Nature-based Solutions (NbS Standard).

Impact investment focuses on the investor's perspective and motivation to make a difference with his or her investment. For example, by focusing on the economic development of vulnerable groups or on environmental protection, the investor can make positive contributions to certain sections or the whole of society.

10.2 Mainstreaming of Sustainable Finance

Large-scale investment will be needed to advance the sustainability and climate action agenda across the globe. Article 2.1c of the Paris Agreement sets the goal of making financial flows consistent with a pathway toward low greenhouse gas emissions and climate-resilient development. This commitment is widely acknowledged. The World Resource Institute (WRI), the Rocky Mountain Institute (RMI), and Third Generation Environmentalism (E3G), three influential international nonprofit organizations, consider it to "break new ground."[14]

According to the EU's European Green Deal, sustainable finance is among the priority areas of EU climate action. The EU website on sustainable finance highlights the transition to a low-carbon, more resource-efficient and sustainable economy through meeting climate action benchmarks. Specific reference is made to the 2030 Agenda for Sustainable Development and the Paris Agreement.

The war in Ukraine will—in the short run—lead to a revaluation of fossil fuel and other assets violating standards of ethical investment. However, we shall see even stronger efforts to quickly transition towards renewable energies in many Western economies, which could in turn raise interest in green finance.

We have seen a proliferation of investment funds and investment strategies that integrate green, social, and other ethical considerations into the investment process. At the same time, we have also witnessed advocacy activities to end public investment in fossil-fuel infrastructure. The value of social, sustainability and green bonds has significantly increased since 2015. Definitions of green, sustainable, and social remain somewhat blurred. However, green is the top priority as a table published by MSCI ESG research illustrates.

Figure 10.2: U.S. Dollar Value of Social, Sustainability and Green Bond Issuances 2015–2020.

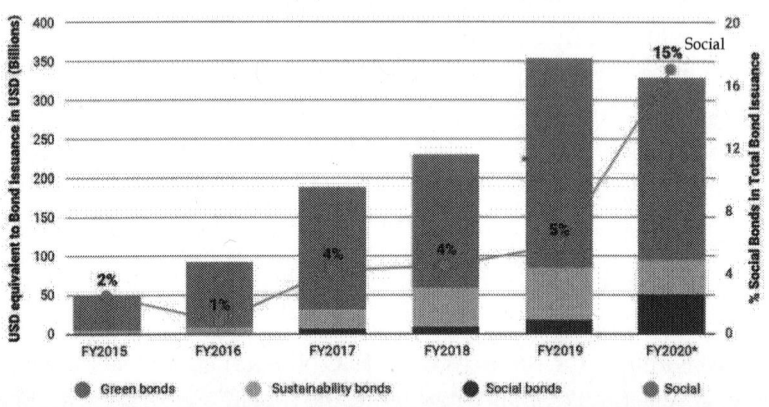

Source: Climate Bonds Initiative, MSCI ESG Research (Dec. 7, 2020), Data as of October 15, 2020.[15]

MSCI ESG Research defines social bonds as bonds that aim to finance projects or operations with social benefits and green bonds as bonds that aim to finance environmentally beneficial projects. Sustainability bonds incorporate both social and environmental elements. Such bonds can facilitate the transition toward a more sustainable European economy. However, experts point to a lack of transparency and suggest a series of measures to make effective use of the European Green Bond Standard (EuGBS).[16]

Mainstreaming of sustainable finance is underway. Digital finance will be instrumental in pushing the trend as it makes large amounts of data available at high speed and low costs. This increases opportunities for more sustainable lending and investments through greater information and transparency.[17]

ESG criteria stand out as a reference framework for sustainable finance. In recent years, the bulk of attention paid to sustainable finance focused on green finance, in particular climate change.

The European Commission established a High-Level Expert Group on Sustainable Finance (HLEG) in December 2016. The group provides advice on how to 'hardwire' sustainability into the EU's regulatory and financial policy framework and how to mobilize more capital flows toward sustainable investment and lending. The EU set up a Sustainable Finance Action Plan in 2018 and is in the process of completing a classification system, the EU Taxonomy on Sustainable Finance. Its purpose is to establish criteria for sustainable economic activities. The regulatory initiatives at the EU-level will result in a comprehensive taxonomy which defines sustainable investments with a view to providing guidance to investors and to setting incentives for investments that meet environmental and social criteria. Next to the taxonomy, the EU intends to issue a total of 250 billion euros in so-called green bonds by 2026. Money invested in green bonds can only be used for climate protection measures in the member states.

The taxonomy is considered the most important enabler to scale up sustainable investment across Europe and to implement the European Green Deal. It is supported by major sustainable finance stakeholders. However, it has also invited criticism. It is evident that the EU's sustainable finance policy is predominantly focused on green finance, in particular climate change. It remains to be seen if the EU could also agree on social criteria and, thus, offer a wider coverage of ESG criteria for investors.

Controversial issues related to the taxonomy include the question of whether to consider nuclear power and natural gas as climate-friendly technologies. This question has divided the EU for more than three years.[18] Austria, Germany, Luxembourg, Italy, Greece and Cyprus want nuclear out of the taxonomy. There were also other controversial issues among EU member states related to the coverage of the taxonomy and to regulations for disclosure of investments. Meanwhile, the WWF and other environmental non-profits proposed a taxonomy which gives every economic activity a ranking from dark green to red.[19]

There are also fundamental critics of the taxonomy project though they constitute a relatively small minority of larger asset management companies. One of the most outstanding critics is Bert Flossbach, the founder of Flossbach von Storch AG.[20] He warns that sustainability demands might create a new "bureaucratic monster".

According to the PRI, the EU taxonomy offers myriad benefits to investors. It can help to (a) identify investment opportunities which meet a high standard of sustainability, (b) construct taxonomy-aligned portfolios and monitor their impact, (c) strengthen and enable more focused dialogue between investors and companies on investment impact, and (d) support communication between fund managers and asset owners, particularly resource-constrained asset owners that may struggle to develop deep environmental expertise.[21]

The investment community looks at the EU Action Plan from a risk perspective, meaning that certain investments, especially in fossil fuel industries, could be seen as anachronistic, undermine sustainability transitions and, thus, put such investments at risk. Investors already anticipated the growing demand for sustainable finance, including pension funds, cities, and retail clients. A series of new regulatory changes are in the making at the level of public investors.

The German Bundesbank acknowledges that the sustainable finance market in Europe has seen dynamic growth in the past few years. In Germany, the volume of sustainable investment rose by more than 70 percent between 2014 and 2018. Investors have started to shift trillions to more sustainable investments and have withdrawn funds from fossil fuel assets. Similar developments, though still less ambitious, are underway in other parts of the world, too.

China issued new regulations in June 2021. The regulations require companies to disclose their climate impact. However, publication of environmental data is only mandatory for some key polluting enterprises listed on the stock market. There is still work to do for the China's Securities Regulatory Commission to comply with good practices elsewhere. Jiang Chiang, environmental analyst at the consulting firm Trivium China, says: "The existing disclosure requirements are useful, but expanding mandatory environmental information disclosure to all listed companies would be a huge step forward in improving the comparability of greenness among listed companies." He is, however, optimistic that the climate impact of green investments will change soon, as there is

Sustainable Finance

"increased political impetus driving the growth in green finance with a focus on ensuring that funds are impactful".[22]

Switzerland is one of the leading financial centers in Europe and the world. Swiss banks are anchored in the region and have excellent international networks. We conducted an interview with Bjarne Steffen and Florian Egli of ETH Zurich and asked them about the sustainable finance initiatives at the level of the EU in order to capture perspectives from researchers outside the EU.

Steffen and Egli have done extensive research on sustainable finance. Steffen is the head of the Climate Finance and Policy Group (CFP) at ETH. In his research, which is published in high impact journals, he analyzes policies related to the low-carbon transition in the energy and financial sectors.

Egli is a Senior Researcher and a Lecturer at ETH Zurich. His dissertation titled "*The role of finance in mitigating climate change: Insights for public policy*" won the ETH medal for outstanding doctoral theses and the best dissertation award from the Swiss Association of Energy Economics (SAEE).

Both highlight the relevance of the EU taxonomy for other financial centers and the importance of broadening and deepening sustainable finance to support sustainability transitions. They confirm that sustainable finance will be important for sustainability transitions in different sectors and are moderately optimistic that the sustainable investment movement will gain further traction. They also point to a growing interest on the part of family service centers and children of high-net-worth individuals.

Interview with Bjarne Steffen and Florian Egli of Eidgenössische Technische Hochschule (ETH), Zurich

Q: In the past two years we have observed tremendous growth of assets aligned with criteria of sustainable investment. Will this trend continue? How dependent is the trend on the overall performance of stock markets and the commitment of big players who may be driven by motivations to greenwash their image?
Bjarne Steffen: Sustainable finance will be incredibly important for sustainability transitions in different sectors. Much research is

required to develop more low-carbon technologies. A lot of new infrastructure is needed. This will require massive funding.

Florian Egli: Exactly, and though we do not know if this a bubble or not, we should make the most of it, whatever the motivation of some companies may be. An interesting point to add is that we also witness growing engagement of policymakers and regulators with this trend. More and more institutions are acknowledging the coherence between the real world and the financial system and are passing new legislation, regulations, and action plans.

Q: Do you see sustainable finance, as well as ethical finance, moving into the mainstream?

Bjarne Steffen: I agree with the analysis that it is trending in that direction. I should also mention that ethical considerations had started way before the climate movement, for example in the context of banning Apartheid in South Africa. There are, in my view, two main steps in mainstreaming: on one hand, the climate risk, meaning the realization that the physical climate risks are highly relevant and necessitate policies to regulate them; on the other hand, more recently, investors have also begun seeing "climate opportunities". The question is/remains what this means for sustainable finance. There is definitely a need for minimum standards and the EU taxonomy seems to be the most likely leader, which will be a guideline for other countries to follow suit.

Florian Egli: I agree with this and hope that the ones which will come afterwards will be more ambitious. I would also like to add that what determines whether or not such measures are successful is the pressure from civil society and that investors and politicians are exposed to such information. Social movements have recently begun being more active in this sector and are actively developing concrete ideas and advocating for them, like in Switzerland for example.

Q: Speaking of Switzerland, how do key actors respond to this trend, as they will not be directly affected by the taxonomy? Is there serious opposition? Are they afraid of bureaucracy?

Florian Egli: The finance sector in Switzerland is placed very well to play a big role in the transition. Switzerland is still an attractive place for asset and wealth management due to its long-lasting experience. The problem is that Switzerland has traditionally held a hands-off approach, but without proper regulation, progress will be slow. In all likelihood we will see a "wait and see" approach, as they observe what happens in EU jurisdictions.

Bjarne Steffen: Yes, it is still seen as voluntary and is left up to the industry, but Switzerland will have to comply with regulations to maintain access to markets. The Swiss sector is diverse, not uniform. You can see that even though the green parties made gains in the last election and there has been a CO_2 law, the principle of voluntariness has persisted in the sector, but the truth is that they will have to comply with the EU taxonomy in the end if they want to keep selling their products across Europe and the world.

Florian Egli: Exactly, I have personally seen banks and asset management firms in Switzerland which are now calling for more transparency and information, as the EU regulations influence their business. It can have an effect on legitimacy, large players want to be part of international decision-making, because it has an effect on the national level.

Q: Is this trend truly global or are there certain regions that are not affected?

Florian Egli: There are definitely differences, but the world is interconnected. The trend cannot only hinge on the good will of the investors. This is an even more pressing question in the time of the COVID-19 pandemic, as states have indebted themselves to an extreme level.

Bjarne Steffen: I am moderately optimistic that the sustainable investment movement will gain more traction. We see a growing interest by family service centers and children of high-net-worth individuals. Here at ETH Zurich—in cooperation with the Initiative for Responsible Investment at Harvard Kennedy School—we offer training programs which equip the next generation members of ultra-high-net-worth families with skills needed to move assets toward impact. Since its inception in 2015, the program has trained more than 130 alumni—and counting.

10.3 Greenwashing of Investment Strategies

Part of the green and sustainable finance boom is inflated by "*sustainability washing*" or "*green washing*". Sustainability washing refers to abusive marketing practices where the sustainability benefits are exaggerated or misrepresented. Green washing refers to the exaggeration of environment friendly investments. As the sustainable finance and ESG trend is mainly driven by green finance, greenwashing is particularly widespread. The ESG criteria, however, remain the key reference framework for the financial industry. The Deutsche Bank's investment arm, DWS, claimed that the ESG integration process applied to half of its 900 billion U.S. dollar assets under management. Leaked internal documents and statements made by Desiree Fixler, the company's former Global Head of Sustainability, contradicted this analysis. Fixler declared that she was fired after objecting to inconsistencies between the company's public statement and its ESG integration processes and policies. It was one of the first examples of whistleblowing on ESG matters.[23] The U.S. Department of Justice, the U.S. Securities and Exchange Commission and the German financial regulator Bafin have started investigations of DWS practices, according to reports in the *Wall Street Journal* and Reuters.

Pressure is increasing on managers of ESG-labeled investment funds to show that they are being truthful with customers about what they are selling, reports Green Bloomberg.[24] The London-based nonprofit InfluenceMap claims that more than half of climate-themed funds are failing to live up to the goals of the Paris Agreement. The Global Sustainable Investment Alliance erased two trillion U.S. dollars from the European market for sustainable investments after anti-greenwashing rules were introduced in March 2021 by the European Union.

BlackRock, the world's largest asset managing company, is trying to champion the sustainable investment movement. However, civil society initiatives targeted BlackRock and other investment groups for greenwashing their image. The nonprofits Reclaim Finance and Urgewald published a report in January 2021 that said

BlackRock has 85 billion U.S. dollars invested in companies on the Global Coal Exit List. The list, compiled by the German group Urgewald, mentions companies around the world that have some sort of exposure to the coal industry. The authors conclude that "BlackRock remains a massive investor in coal companies and even in companies planning new coal projects."[25]

The road to green investments will be bumpy. However, the mainstreaming of the trend is clearly underway. Based on information from the UNFCCC, *The Economist* counted 30 financial firms with net-zero targets in November 2020, moving up to 160 in April 2021 and to 450+ in November 2021. The Economist also summarized a few challenges which stand in the way of making the trend work for massive climate action. First, major state-controlled companies such as Coal India or Saudi Aramco do not operate under the sway of institutional fund managers and private-sector bankers. Second, there is ample scope to improve methodologies behind attributing emissions to financial flows. Emissions from a barrel of oil could be allocated to different companies involved in the production and supply chains.[26] However, we believe that the sustainable finance trend will make significant contributions to shifting assets away from fossil fuels. Many investment firms have set up funds that are specifically focused on companies that consider the environment, social justice, and good corporate governance, or ESG, in their daily operations. Such funds are subject to analysis by professional sustainability rating agencies and, in some cases, even scrutiny of nonprofits. The knowledge on finance, especially sustainable finance, is rapidly growing in many countries. The market capitalization of many green technology companies and companies with low emissions or high energy efficiency has significantly grown in the past decade and is likely to continue though it is hard to generalize across sectors and industries.[27]

Chapter 11

Democracy and Governance Innovations

It is a difficult and controversial though truly relevant endeavor to cover democracy and governance innovations in the analysis of major trends. Democracy remains a powerful reference concept in international relations and a key element in legitimizing political rule. It is a powerful reference framework used by political leaders, academics, activists and even strategy consultants. Roland Berger, a leading German strategy consulting firm, covers it in its megatrend analysis.[1]

Democracy literally means rule by the people. The term is derived from the Greek *dēmokratia*, which was coined from *dēmos* ("people") and *kratos* ("rule"). Having a closer look at democracy practices in ancient Greek, however, the concept of the people was limited to adult male citizens over the age of 20. Therefore, it was a direct rather than a representative democracy. Though democratic ideals and processes did not survive in ancient Greece, they have been influencing politicians and governments ever since.[2]

The term governance, on the other hand, became popular from the 1990s onwards when international organizations, especially the World Bank, started to attach growing importance to good governance in the process of issuing loans and supporting development processes in the Global South.[3] In a way, the focus on good governance covered up concerns for democracy. Today, the support of democracy is again a very sensitive topic in international cooperation, as the concept of democracy is ideologically charged, quickly seen as interference in domestic politics and internal affairs. China and the United States were tussling over President Joe Biden's democracy summit in December 2021, especially over the invitation of Taiwan. Just before the summit, the P.R. China's State Council Information Office presented a new White Paper on Democracy called "China: Democracy That Works" which dwells on the term "whole-process people's democracy" and criticizes chaos and populism in parliamentary democracies.[4]

The quality of democracy and governance is today subject to many research projects. We have witnessed a proliferation of democracy and governance index projects that—based on complex sets of criteria—aim to measure the quality of different dimensions of democracy and governance, including checks and balances of political power, conduct of elections, and scope for citizens participation. We will briefly introduce some of these indexes and their critique.

The ongoing social and political negotiations of these questions by international institutions, social movements, the media, and academic research emphasize the significance of democracy and governance issues as a future megatrend. The claim that democracy is strongly related to values and norms remains at the core of democracy debates. Cultural aspects of political rule matter and practices of democracy and governance are deeply rooted in historical developments shaped by socio-economic as well as religious influences.

This chapter explores questions related to the appeal of democratic governance in the context of rising authoritarianism in many countries and regions. It puts special emphasis on participatory and consultative forms of democracy and governance and discusses concepts of input versus concepts of output legitimacy.

We argue that—against the backdrop of identity politics—we will see a trend in many liberal democracies toward making democracy and governance more inclusive. In authoritarian states, we shall witness growing cultural and national assertions.

Democracy and governance trends will play out differently across the spectrum of political systems of liberal democracies, ranging from a push to more consultations with experts from different professional backgrounds at national levels to a push for more public participation and inclusiveness in planning at the level of city governance.

For authoritarian political systems, it is particularly difficult to predict the future because access to critical information on the popularity of government is severely restricted. Authoritarian systems also greatly vary in terms of legitimacy, political stability, and consistency of policymaking. From our point of view, it is therefore not helpful to group countries with very different political features, such as China and Russia, in the same category of authoritarian political systems.

Prospects of regime change depend much on economic factors. Nationalism will continue to shape political developments in China and India but there are good chances that their continued integration into the global economy will prevent the political leadership of those countries from overstretching nationalism. In retrospect, the America First policy of the Trump administration and the Brexit policy of the United Kingdom will not be regarded as success stories though some elements of them — for example, reducing dependency on foreign countries — will remain powerful narratives in policymaking processes.

11.1 Concepts, Discourses, and Political Trends

In the context of the collapse of the Soviet Union and communist regimes in Eastern Europe (1988-1991), the American political scientist Francis Fukuyama proclaimed, "the end of history" and the victory of liberal democracies over authoritarian forms of governance[5] New democracy movements in Arab countries, especially the major Arab spring movement which started in December 2010 and went on until around mid-2012, had fueled hopes of liberal democrats that the wind of political change could spread to several Arab countries and across the world. But the wind of change did not last. On the contrary, in many Arab countries, political freedoms soon declined. For some time, Tunisia — where the Arab Spring originated with the suicide of a local vendor — seemed to be the only democracy to emerge from the Arab Spring movement. In 2021, the situation in Tunisia turned again into "a mess" or, more formally speaking, into "an institutional conflict, pitting the presidency against the parliament."[6]

Around the millennium, there was also hope in Western countries that the integration of China into the World Economy — China accessed the World Trade Organization on December 11, 2001 — would translate into a process of political liberalization in China. It was argued that China's integration into the world economy would have an impact on its political system. Indeed, the political leadership in China seemed to be open to experimenting with pluralist governance mechanisms in the early years of the 21st century, involving private sector and civil society organizations in the management of economic and social affairs, and also testing electoral-style democracy at the local level. In fact, many Western experts believed that China would not be able to sustain its economic development without political liberalization. From today's perspective, such hopes have not materialized. Nevertheless, China has not completely stopped local-level experimentation with new forms of governance. In the social welfare sector, nonprofits play a significant role in reaching out to vulnerable communities. However, under the rule of Xi Jinping, the Chinese Communist Party stepped up its efforts to reinstate the party rule and disseminate ideological leadership in policymaking and management of public affairs. Moreover, confrontational policies in the West, especially under the Trump administration, may have contributed to China's assertiveness and growing reference made to its own political traditions and values. These are just two examples demonstrating that Fukuyama's claim of the victory of liberal democracies has not been realized.

Democratic legitimacy from a citizens' perspective has become an important strand of research in political science. Michael Strebel from the University of Zurich, together with his colleagues Daniel Kübler and Frank Marcinkowski of the University of Duesseldorf in Germany, has advanced the debate on 'input-oriented' versus 'output-oriented' legitimacy with empirical evidence from European countries. Input legitimacy is based on the concept that citizens have a strong and intrinsic preference for meaningful participation in collective decision-making. Output legitimacy presumes that citizens care mainly about the substance of decisions and their economic and social consequences, but much less about the procedures leading to them. Striebel and his colleagues analyzed data from 5,000 respondents in eight metropolitan areas in France, Germany, Switzerland, and the United Kingdom which focused on preferences for different governance arrangements. They found that output evaluations are the most important driver for citizens' choice of a governance arrangement. However, they also found strong evidence that democratic input and throughput[7] remain important secondary features of democratic governance and non-negligible factors of citizen satisfaction with political rule.[8]

In democracy discourses of Western countries, free and universal elections involving political parties of different orientations are the most critical aspects of the democracy concept. Rivalry between political parties is fierce. We have even seen entrepreneurial-like initiatives to start new political parties. In his book *Political Entrepreneurship*, Josef Lentsch, the Austrian entrepreneur and co-founder of NEOS, a centrist Austrian political start-up, outlines how political entrepreneurs can drive political change and presents a series of tools and methods for successful political entrepreneurship. In the preface of this book, he writes that politics is an exhilarating but often bruising team sport, played 24 hours a day, 7 days a week.[9] Digitalization will heavily impact election campaigns at different levels and new political marketing opportunities and risks of simplification and manipulation of content will come along with it.

The extensive reference attached to the criterion of high-paced competitive multi-party competition, however, has also invited criticism, especially as election processes exhibit flaws and we see a great deal of variations in the quality of democracy at work. In substantial parts of Africa for instance, democracy has been misconceptualized as voting on Election Day. As in the U.S. and other countries with "free" elections, money heavily influences election outputs. While authoritarian socialist rule in the Soviet Union and Eastern Europe has discredited practices of socialism over many decades, the rapid political ascension of Donald Trump in the United States and Javier Bolsonaro in Brazil to the positions of

President and numerous other examples, including in EU countries, have negatively affected the reputation of electoral democracies.

Democratic backsliding is therefore seen as a major threat. Lentsch pointed out that "what was previously a struggle between the Left and Right has turned into a struggle between open and closed societies and economies". Some of the most successful political entrepreneurs of late are representatives of the aspiration for closed societies—UKIP in the U.K., PiS in Poland, the PVV in the Netherlands, M5S in Italy, AfD in Germany, and Donald Trump in the U.S.[10] Achim Schäfer and Michael Zürn, two renowned German political scientists, have therefore rightfully drawn our attention to the declining quality of democracy in countries which have long been considered "consolidated democracies", including the United States (U.S.) and Poland. Schäfer and Zürn point to electoral autocracies which have limited the chances for democratic renewal through election processes.[11]

Politicians trumpeting short-term goals to win over voters, the influence of big money on elections, unrealistic electoral promises, aggressive advertising campaigns including personal attacks of opponents, and the spread of fake news have severely damaged the high-flying image of electoral contests as the backbone of modern democracy.

Moreover, the political unity of the West has significantly suffered from the Trump presidency. When Trump refused to recognize the election results, it was not only Americans who started to worry about their democracy. Europeans were shocked alike. A survey by the European Council on Foreign Relations carried out in eleven European countries at the end of 2020 shows that the view of the U.S. political system is predominantly negative: 61 percent of those surveyed in all countries described the U.S. system as completely or partially dysfunctional; in Germany, 71 percent did so.[12]

Social cohesion has been undermined by fierce electoral contests not only in the U.S. and Brazil, but also in Europe. In many European countries, effective policymaking has suffered from unstable coalition governments. Nationalist parties have won a significant number of seats. Political parties and social movements of the extreme right, and in some cases of the extreme left, promoted hate sentiments against the political establishment. Such political developments have made Western democracy concepts less attractive. In the U.S., the Biden administration aims to repair the image and to re-establish the supremacy of liberal democracy by focusing on the democracy and human rights deficiencies of China, in particular the violations of political and civil rights, and by making efforts to build alliances with other countries, especially in Europe.

China, in return, will continue to blame the U.S. and the EU for interfering in China's domestic affairs and reproach political leaders for instrumentalizing sensitive political issues for geopolitical power games. The Chinese government stresses its high legitimacy by praising its accomplishment in lifting several hundred million people out of poverty and in safeguarding economic and social rights. China aims to further increase its influence in the United Nations in order to forestall attempts by the U.S. and Europe to blame China for curtailing political freedom in Hong Kong, restrict religious freedoms and suppress cultural practices in Xinjiang and Tibet. The U.S., Britain, and the EU will intensify efforts to protect Taiwan against tightened political and potential military interventions while the one-China-policy will remain a corner stone of Chinese foreign policy. However, we shall also see more efforts to challenge it, such as recently observed in Lithuania. China immediately recalled its ambassador to Lithuania on August 10, 2021, over the Baltic nation's move to allow Taiwan to open a diplomatic outpost in Vilnius.

With regard to democracy discourses, the Chinese leadership remains assertive. It offers the concept of consultative democracy inspired by socialism with Chinese characteristics. This concept of consultative democracy stresses the importance of gathering expertise from various sources, including researchers, all kinds of associations, and business consultants in the policymaking process while also taking sentiments of the public into deep consideration in order to foster harmony and avoid confrontation.

The Center for China and Globalization lists the strengths of the Chinese democracy with reference to consultative democracy: "For a long time, under the Western conception of political parties and democracy, China's political system was seen as lacking electoral democratic competition. But in fact, the Chinese system ensures the scientific and democratic nature of its policies through extensive political participation and deliberation under consultative democracy, allowing for systematic long-term policymaking that is consistent and stable."[13] China's success story of economic development and poverty eradication gripped widespread attention, especially in the business community and among the top political leadership. It made the Chinese model attractive to many developing countries with an interest in state-led development and a focus on infrastructure. The governance style of China's administration is sometimes compared to governance styles of major corporations where fundamental decisions are taken by a small circle of leaders and implemented in a hierarchical fashion.

Even beyond developing countries and emerging economies, government administrations seem to have become more affirmative. Even *The Economist*, known for its liberal editorial stands, reckoned in January 2022: "After decades in retreat, the state is back in business. From growth in regulation — covering competition policy, climate, worker rights and much else — to a renewed zeal for industrial policy, governments around the world are becoming bossier with regard to the private sector."[14]

The Chinese concept of consultative democracy under strong party or state leadership exhibits obvious limitations and deficits in public participation when confronted with claims of minorities, especially demands for more political and religious freedom.

What accounts for good governance then? Good governance, though not explicitly related to democracy, exhibits a set of criteria that enables us to make judgments on the quality of policymaking and decision-making. It focuses on the improvement of transparency, accountability, and the ability and capacity of the government to involve business and civil society stakeholders in policy-making processes. The World Bank as well as other institutions engaged with research networks to develop a series of criteria for measuring governance.

After the collapse of the Soviet Union and the regime changes in Eastern Europe in the late 1980s/early 1990s, it became the credo of political scientists and economists alike that the quality of governance and institution is of utmost importance to promote economic and social development. This is exemplified by Douglass C. North's Nobel Prize lecture in 1993, when he stated that "institutions form the incentive structure of a society and the political and economic institutions, in consequence, are the underlying determinant of economic performance."[15]

Democracy and governance support therefore became a priority of EU development cooperation in many parts of the world, especially in Africa but also in parts of Asia. But the world has witnessed a resurgence of authoritarian regimes in many countries and a growing ideological confrontation between the U.S., Europe, and China in the past ten years. Russia and India have also developed more nationalist features in domestic and foreign policymaking.

This trend also shows in the efforts of development cooperation: the support provided to democracy and civil society movements has faced a series of setbacks. Cambodia and Myanmar are two examples in South-East Asia where authoritarian rule has crushed emerging democracy and civil society movements.

Nevertheless, the EU continues to support democracy, good governance, civil society, and human rights in international cooperation, while China's engagement in the Global South—for example, in the context of the Forum for China Africa Cooperation (FOCAC) and the Belt and Road Initiative (BRI)—has focused on the realization of big infrastructure projects and increased trade. In fact, China became the biggest investor in Africa and in many other parts of the world challenging the democracy and governance-based dialogue model of EU engagement with developing countries. Notwithstanding, there are mutual efforts between Germany and China to harmonize development cooperation, especially in the context of promoting the implementation of global agendas. For instance, China and Germany run the Sino-German Center for

Sustainable Development, which was established on May 11, 2017, as a joint initiative between the Federal Ministry for Economic Cooperation and Development of the Federal Republic of Germany (BMZ) and the Ministry of Commerce of the People's Republic of China (MofCom). It aims to promote Sino-German Dialogue on Development Cooperation, triangular Cooperation Projects, and partnership with businesses.

The wind for change toward participatory democracy which has shaped the last decade of the 20th century has been dispersed in many countries, especially in those experiencing democracy movements in the context of the Arab spring. According to the Human Rights Foundation's research, led by the former Russian chess champion and democracy advocate Garry Kasparov, authoritarianism is one of the largest challenges – if not the largest – facing humanity.[16]

In view of assertive nationalism in China and India, however, the U.S. and Europe will step up efforts to unite and capitalize on the freedom and opportunities that the educated middle-classes enjoy in liberal democracies. However, the support to interventionist foreign and security policies could decline in the West while soft power policies will rise again. Index projects ranking the quality of live and promoting more qualitative growth models will flourish and might replace the focus on GDP growth.

11.2 Empirical Democracy Research and Proliferation of Index Projects

As a starting point for modern empirical democracy research, Robert Dahl's model of polyarchy – published in 1971 – remains a landmark.[17] His concept of polyarchy attempts to develop an empirical definition of democratization. For that, he proposed a set of criteria to decide whether or not a political system can be counted as a democracy focusing on how authority is effectively controlled by societal organizations and civil associations. The more they can and do operate autonomously and independently from the state, the higher the quality of democracy.

Democracy and Governance Innovations

Since then, the measurement of democracy and governance has seen an upsurge from the 1990s onwards. Many projects engaged in comparative analysis of democracy, governance, and the conditions of rule of law in different countries and developed indices. Among the most well-known ones are the Freedom House Index, the Bertelsmann Transformation Index (BTI), the Varieties of Democracy Index, the democracy index of the Economist Intelligence Unit, and the Rule of Law Index of the World Justice project which we will briefly introduce in the following.

The popular Freedom House rates people's access to political rights and civil liberties in 210 countries and territories through its annual Freedom in the World report. It is founded on the core conviction that freedom flourishes in democratic nations where governments are accountable to their people.[18]

The BTI, by contrast, analyzes political and economic transformation processes and publishes a governance index based on a complex set of criteria and expert opinions. The results are visualized in form of an atlas. The BTI 2020 concludes that "the quality of democracy, market economy and governance in developing and transformation countries has fallen to its lowest level in 14 years ..." According to the BTI 2020 "democratic regression, rampant corruption and deepening polarization are interlinked and mutually reinforcing each other in many of the 137 states surveyed."[19] The 2022 edition of the biannually published BTI which came out a few days before finalizing this manuscript, "for the first time since 2004, counted more autocratically governed states than democracies."[20]

Varieties of Democracy (V-Dem) is an approach to conceptualize and measure democracy. It was launched by the V-Dem Institute, a research institute founded by Professor Staffan I. Lindberg and headquartered in the department of Political Science, University of Gothenburg, Sweden. It provides for a multidimensional and disaggregated dataset that reflects on the complexity of the concept of democracy as a system of rule that goes beyond the simple presence of elections. The V-Dem project distinguishes between five high-level principles of democracy: electoral, liberal, participatory, deliberative, and egalitarian, collecting data to measure these principles. It also claims to have a truly global International Advisory Board and team: The index is produced by a team of over 50 social scientists on six continents and engages with more than 3,200 country experts.[21]

The V-Dem project developed into the one of the most popular index projects on democracy. It produces the largest global dataset on democracy involving 202 countries from 1789 to 2021. Its graphs receive widespread attention, including from the British Broadcasting Corporation (BBC)[22], and are referenced by megatrend analysts such as Roland Berger, a leading German strategy consulting firm. One of the most striking features of its latest reports was the downgrading of India which has now become an 'electoral autocracy'.

Figure 11.1: Democracies and Autocracies

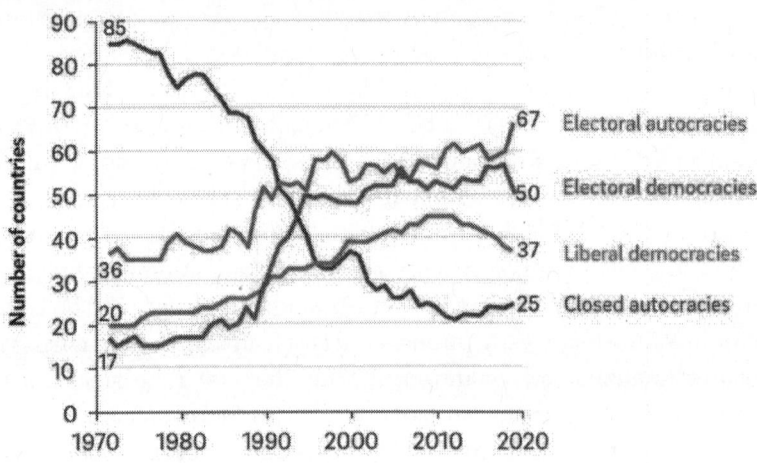

Source: V-Dem Democracy Report 2020, Roland Berger (2021).[23]

This graph of the V-Dem Democracy Report 2020 shows a clear increase of electoral autocracies and closed autocracies while electoral democracies and liberal democracies are in decline. The key findings of the latest V-DEM Democracy Report 2021 further accentuate such developments:

- The global decline during the past ten years is steep and continues in 2020, especially in the Asia-Pacific region, Central Asia, Eastern Europe, and Latin America.
- The level of democracy enjoyed by the average global citizen in 2020 is down to levels last found around 1990.
- Electoral autocracy remains the most common regime type. Together with closed autocracies they number 87 states, home to 68 percent of the world population.
- The world's largest democracy turned into an electoral autocracy: India with 1.37 billion citizens.
- Liberal democracies diminished over the past decade from 41 countries to 32, with a population share of only 14 percent.[24]

There are, however, positive developments in different categories. For example, according to the latest V-DEM data, the political participation of women has significantly increased in the past decade.[25] According to V-DEM, "women's political participation is understood to include women's descriptive representation in the legislature and an equal share in the overall distribution of power. India had already introduced reservation quota for women in the context of the 73rd Constitutional Amendment in 1993, the *Panchayati Raj Act*. Evidence has been collected that such reforms matter. Berthold Kuhn concluded in his book on *Participatory Development in Rural India* that "the reservation quota, in particular the reservation for chairpersons, provided women with a tremendous opportunity to partake in village, block, and district level politics which they would have otherwise not have obtained."[26] In India, "the number of drinking water projects in areas with women-ledcouncils was 62 per cent higher than in those with men-led councils"[27].

Progress has been made globally in women's political participation, but there is much more work to be done. In 2020, the share of women in the EU Member States' single/lower houses of parliament average stood at 32.7 percent.[28] In 2021, there were 26 women serving as Heads of State and/or Government in 24 countries,[29] while 25 percent of national parliamentarians were women.

The Economist Intelligence Unit's (EIU) Democracy Index publishes an annual survey, which rates the state of democracy across 167 countries based on five measures — electoral process and pluralism, the functioning of government, political participation, democratic political culture, and civil liberties.

The EIU 2021 report concluded that liberal democracy continued its decline. Almost 70 percent of countries covered by the index recorded a decline in their overall score, partly because of lockdowns to protect lives from the novel coronavirus.[30]

According to the EIU 2022 report, the number of people living in a democracy fell to less than 50 percent. The western Europe region recorded another drop and Spain was downgraded from a "full democracy" to "flawed democracy."[31]

The World Justice Project's (WJP) Rule of Law Index covers 139 countries and jurisdictions and relies on national surveys of more than 138,000 households and 4,200 legal practitioners and experts to measure how the rule of law is experienced and perceived worldwide. The 2021 report concluded that "more countries declined than improved in overall rule of law performance for the fourth consecutive year."[32]

Index projects have flourished in political science and gained significant media attention. However, they have also invited criticism on numerous grounds. In a publication in 2011, Berthold Kuhn pointed to the strong normative bias, the limited involvement of regional expertise and some other deficits of the Freedom House and the BTI and the mostly uncritical use of their index results in academic papers.[33]

Thamy Pogrebinschi, one of our interview partners for this chapter, also adopts a critical view on some of the index projects. Professor Pogrebinschi is the coordinator of LATINNO (Innovations for Democracy in Latin America), the most comprehensive database on democratic innovations that evolved in 18 countries of Latin America between 1990 and 2020. Her team comprises of over thirty PhD and master students who collected and assessed around 3600 cases of democratic experiments involving deliberation, citizen representation, digital engagement, and direct voting. The project has been funded by the Open Society Foundations and the Open Society Initiative for Europe and is based at the WZB Berlin Social Science Center. She and her team had a closer look at the functioning of democracy in Latin America which mostly scored badly in indexes and opinion polls designed to measure and compare democracies around the world. They conducted extensive empirical research and conclude that democratic innovations have grown steadily since 1990 throughout Latin America. However, after reaching a peak in 2015, they slowed down rapidly after 2016. The COVID-19 pandemic seems, however, to have reversed this downward trend—at least temporarily—in 2020.[34]

We have talked to Thamy Pogrebinschi on democracy index projects, on democracy innovations in Latin America and on the future of liberal democracies which—according to her concluding statement—"may become less liberal, without necessarily becoming less democratic."

Interview with Thamy Pogrebinschi, senior researcher at the WZB Berlin Social Science Center

Q: We have seen a proliferation of index projects measuring the quality of democracy, governance, and the rule of law. To what extent do they shape discourses, stimulate debates, and feed ideas into policymaking processes?

Thamy Pogrebinschi: These indexes receive significant attention by the academic community and the media, but they are far from perfect. Some exhibit more obvious flaws than others. Most rely on concepts and methods that tend to be biased toward Western liberal democracies. Some select experts for their opinion or design questions for their surveys without paying enough reference to more nuanced aspects of a given country, such as practices of participatory democracy. They still measure participation, for example, mostly by looking at party affiliation, voter turnout, membership to associations, engagement in protests, petition signing, and so forth, while citizen participation and civil society engagement have assumed many other forms in the last years. In some countries, like in most of Latin America, for example, there are hundreds of participatory institutions, processes, and mechanism which play a relevant role, engage thousands of CSOs, sometimes millions of citizens, but are overlooked by those indexes. There are truly major innovations in democracy and citizen participation happening in Latin America, but you would never know if you only look to those standard measures of quality of democracy which only show you part of a more comprehensive picture.

Q: How do you rate the importance of interactive governance for democratic legitimacy?

Thamy Pogrebinschi: What is called interactive governance or participatory governance is very important and very much needed, as it results in more legitimate policies and a more responsive government. The higher the interaction between state and civil society, the closer political decisions tend to be to citizens' preferences, engendering more democratic and legitimate policies. However, participatory practices do not always work the way they are supposed to and while citizens are "included" in the process, their preferences are not reflected in the outputs. This can lead to the legitimization of authoritarian regimes, like in China, or in Venezuela under Chavez, where participatory processes tended to favor his supporters.

Q: How do you analyze the proposed trend of democratic backsliding in different parts of the world? Is it likely to be a short-lived trend? Which opportunities do you see to counteract this trend?

Thamy Pogrebinschi: Had there not been the COVID-19 pandemic, which allowed some countries to gain perspective on what it really means to have populist, non-democratic governments in power, this trend could have become even stronger. I think the pandemic contributed to slow down this trend in some countries (like the U.S. and Brazil), while in others it enabled political leaders to advance more authoritarian measures (like in Russia, Hungary, Philippines, or El Salvador). In Brazil, the COVID-19 pandemic opened an opportunity for a reversal of such a trend, with Bolsonaro increasingly losing public support due to his handling of the crisis. Another important thing that the COVID-19 pandemic seems to have brought

to democracy is the perception that, especially in highly unequal and low state-capacity countries, governments should resource more to civil society in order to address public problems.
Q: Would the indexes show such changes though?
Thamy Pogrebinschi: Maybe in the U.S. and Brazil if there is indeed a reversal.
Q: How could liberal democracies respond to challenges of political fragmentation and disintegration? Will liberal democracies regain ground in the near future?
Thamy Pogrebinschi: If we consider liberal democracies as full democracies, which are not affected by populism or polarization, then they should gain more ground after the pandemic. Something that needs to be said though is the fact that the very idea of a liberal democracy is undergoing changes. Liberal democracies may become less liberal, without necessarily becoming less democratic.

11.3 Practices of Participatory and Consultative Democracy

The issue of participation is at the core of democracy and governance debates. Digitalization offers citizens more options to become involved in policy- and decision-making processes and might contribute to reducing the democratic deficit. Information and communication technologies make existing participatory arrangements easier to implement and provide alternative as well as cheaper ways of eliciting participation. For example, e-petitions (the online version of petitions, by which citizens can directly submit a policy for consideration of representative institutions) have been a popular e-participation channel in the past two decades, with many countries adopting such systems.[35]

Online participation could also be viewed as the safer option for engaging with politics. Observed in Thailand, for example, young people who are scared to demonstrate post their voices on Facebook to stimulate pressure on the government for improvement of democracy.

Based on Sherry Arnstein's analysis[36], several degrees of participation are usually distinguished. In the participation literature, a common reference is the International Association for Public Participation (IAPP) scale. The scale has five steps: information; consultation; collaboration; involvement; and empowerment.[37]

From such qualitative analysis of practices of participation, it becomes evident that multi-party elections alone are not considered sufficient to establish principles of democratic rule. For instance, public referendums become increasingly popular. Switzerland is a well-known example of a country that practices direct democracy in parallel with representative democracy. However, critics of public referendums refer to the complexity of political decision-making and the need to protect the rights and interest of minorities from policymaking based on the opinion of the majority. An example of this was seen in March 2021, when Switzerland voted in favor of banning face coverings in public, including the burka or niqab worn by Muslim women.

In the field of governance, we have witnessed a proliferation of planning and evaluation tools promoting public consultation and participation. Next to the classic participation mechanisms of direct democracy such as referendums and citizens' petitions, a series of innovative forms of citizen participation has been observed worldwide since the 1990s.

Examples include the EU conference on the Future of Europe, the citizen participation processes conducted by Missions Publiques in France, consensus conferences on the assessment of technology impacts in Denmark, Citizens' Assemblies in the Canadian state of British Columbia, participatory budgeting in Porto Alegre (Brazil) and local initiatives to promote civic engagement in disadvantaged neighborhoods in many European and North American cities. In cases which exhibit strong conflicts of interest, civic participation often plays a role in counterbalancing the interests of organized groups or mitigating concerns voiced by radical groups. Genuine citizen participation, however, presupposes that policymakers and senior staff in public administration are willing to overcome top-down decision-making practices and be prepared to deal with open exchange and participation processes in a competent manner.[38]

We have talked to Marie Jünemann, the young spokeswoman of Mehr Demokratie! (More Democracy!), a German grassroots association registered in Berlin which is involved in numerous citizens' initiatives and democracy campaigns on good practices of democracy, democratic backsliding, and citizens' assemblies in Germany and across Europe. She highlighted opportunities to involve citizens more deeply in democratic decision-making and also referred to constraints and ways to possibly address them.

Interview with Marie Jünemann, spokeswoman of Mehr Demokratie!

Q: Democracy is a multi-faceted concept with numerous definitions and characteristics. On which aspects and good practices are you focusing in your work?
Marie Jünemann: There are two key components for me, such as better transparency laws and strong opportunities for public participation. To have a good democracy, you need all the different instruments and varieties to be working together, meaning that citizens must be informed on how decisions are made and how they can participate. More concretely, a bad example of this is Germany, where requests for release of information to the citizens have a fee and no specific date of release, all while the country is behind in digitalization. In other countries—for example, in the U.K.—you can just search online and find such information from the comfort of your own home and with no fees. I am also big on citizens' assemblies through a random selection method that reflects the given society, where people that do not usually participate in democracy can meet outside their bubbles and make recommendations to politicians. This was the case in Ireland, a very religious country, in 2017 whose citizens' assemblies' recommendations on same-sex marriage and abortion were overwhelmingly adopted later in two referenda by the population.

Q: What do you think about the phenomenon of democratic backsliding? What are the threats to democracy and what are some positive developments?

Marie Jünemann: There are different results from different indicators; for example, the economist one shows increasing participation but also a decreasing functioning of governance, so it is hard to assess these findings. Looking at individual cases helps, like Uruguay or Switzerland, since countries have different political systems, but one thing that is worrying is the dwindling trust in democracy itself, as seen in the U.S., Turkey, or Poland, where fundamental aspects of democracy are questioned like the separation of powers, and so forth. The only way for Western democracies to protect themselves from such tendencies is to be brave and try out new participatory instruments.

Q: Especially during the COVID-19 pandemic, there is a strong anti-intellectualism movement and a resentment of experts. What is your take on this?

Marie Jünemann: Scientific findings are absolutely necessary in policymaking, but they are not enough, as we have seen in the case of measures against the pandemic; therefore, the ethical, psychological, economic sides should all be considered. In the end what seems to be clear is that we need a compromise in such situations of crisis between rash and representative government decision-making, which is why I think that these decisions should be primarily left to the parliament, or at least reviewed as soon as possible, otherwise a lot of possible debate never takes place in public. Parliament Reservation, where the government decides on measures, which are reviewed by the Parliament after 4 weeks and can be reversed is a good way of dealing with this.

Q: What about on the EU-level?

Marie Jünemann: It is of course difficult, and I really like the transparency laws in relation to Germany, as well as how clear the decision-making process can be, but in the end itis the same thing; you can clearly see how some interests are better represented, which is why Members of Parliaments (MPs) should discuss and bring opinions to the table and in the end, be the ones to decide on legislation.

Q: And if there were a sort of assembly on a global level, outcomes would surely be underrepresented and the outcomes would be widely different, right?
Marie Jünemann: It would be really good. There are some initiatives right now, which are dealing with the unequal distribution of vaccines globally, for example, because the crisis will not end if we just vaccinate our own people, so such an assembly could challenge this and try to solve this conflict, while all relevant views are represented.
Q: These Citizens' Assemblies, though, they can be very time-consuming. Surely some people would not have the time to participate, correct?
Marie Jünemann: The way to circumvent this is to do everything in our power to enable citizens to participate, meaning providing compensation for lost work/income, helping with child-care and even having the event take place digitally. What we also found in our case, was that our experiment in Germany brought together an incredibly representative sample of the population, outside mid-education individuals.
Q: What do you think about social selectivity?
Marie Jünemann: It's something that can be observed in all institutions, like the fact that the composition of the parliament is not representative of the population. Citizens' assemblies based on random selection are a good way to balance this problem in the political system. On the other hand, direct democracy is a good way to circumvent this, as it allows people who care for singular issues and would not participate in the general election to cast their vote for something they care about. In Switzerland, over time more than 70 percent of citizens take part in referenda.

Chapter 12

Multipolar World Order and the Future of Multilateralism

Geopolitics is on a trajectory toward a multipolar world order. We are entering a period of history which is evidencing a reconfiguration of the balance of power and a new geopolitical positioning of countries and institutions. The former United Nations Secretary-General Ban Ki-moon stated as far back as 2013 at Stanford University that we had begun to "move increasingly and irreversibly to a multipolar world." Parag Khanna concludes in his book *The Future Is Asian: Commerce, Conflict and Culture in the 21st Century*, "Asia dominated the Old World, while the West led the New World — and now we are coming to a truly global world."[1]

In this chapter, we shall explore the prospects of an emerging new world order, the rise of China, old and new geopolitical alliances, the impact of the COVID-19 pandemic on geopolitics, and finally the future of multilateralism, including the role of international organizations and non-state actors. The chapter includes interviews with renowned experts from different countries and world regions.

One of the early outspoken proponents of 'a new world order' is Kishore Mahbubani, who served as Singapore's permanent representative to the United Nations for many years. The academic and former career diplomat has published a series of books that have shaped discourses on the term new world order. Those using the term are usually more outspoken on the declining global influence of the United States (U.S.) than proponents of a multipolar world order. Mahbubani's latest book carries the title *Has China Won? The Chinese Challenge to American Primacy*.[2] He emphasizes that the combined GDP of three Asian powers — China, India, and Japan — is greater than that of the U.S. and the European Union (EU), and that China continues to consolidate its pursuit of regional free trade agreements. The middle-class population of Asia continues to expand. On the new emerging world order, he argues that the "U.S. is in a pitiful state, has actually already gambled away its claim to global leadership — and a much more rational and better organized China stands ready to step into the gap. The leadership style, however, will be different: China does not want to change the world or even improve it in a missionary way. China will not get tangled up in unnecessary wars like Iraq or Syria."[3]

"Westlessness" was the title of the Munich Security Conference's annual report (Münchner Sicherheitskonferenz) in 2020. The conference of the leading German foreign and security policy think tank, attended by top-level political leaders, issued a wake-up call to decision-makers in the West. The report elaborates on new power configurations that are making the world less Western. It further explains that Westlessness also refers to the West itself becoming less Western.[4] Other think tanks and global conferences refer to the rise of Asia, too. The Bloomberg New Economy Forum, held in Singapore in November 2021, pointed to Asia's growing share of the world's Gross Domestic Product (GDP) (31 percent) and its growing stock market capitalization (31 percent), as *The Economist* reported. The Forum also highlighted the intense interdependency of the U.S. economy with Asian economies in times when political rhetoric suggests decoupling is on the agenda.[5]

Zaeem Hassan Mehmood wrote a short but insightful analysis of the multipolar world order in *Modern Diplomacy*, a journal reaching audiences across the Middle East, Africa, and Asia. He argues that China's economic growth is anticipated to translate into increased diplomatic influence and power. He also assumes that a resurgent Russia is expected to wield considerable military might. Mainly in the U.S. and Western Europe, such analysis is met with resentment. Doubts are raised as to whether political systems which exhibit such authoritarian features are ultimately able to flourish and cooperate with societies where citizens enjoy a higher degree of personal freedom.

There is no consensus among leading scholars and analysts on whether multipolarity will be more unstable than bipolarity or unipolarity, which is a popular belief.[6] When it comes to strategic approaches to world politics and global risks, Parag Khanna, a leading global strategy advisor, forwarded the argument that countries, especially smaller and medium-size countries, would be well advised to practicing multi-alignment."[7] However, Russia's military invasion of Ukraine will make it difficult for any country to practice multi-alignment. China and India, however, will go along this path. They abstained from voting on the U.N. resolution condemning Russia's invasion of Ukraine and will not join calls of the U.S. and the EU for sanctions.

12.1 Hegemonic Shift?

Hegemonic shift is a category of political analysis for Freedomlab in Amsterdam, a future studies think tank affiliated with the investment company Dasym. The think tank points out that "since the Iraq war, the protection of Western values has become a controversial theme in the rest of the world. It is, however, likely to gain more momentum in the coming years."[8] Dasym experts also noted that "among Asian countries, there is a growing policy of hedging, or triangulation, an attempt to create ties with both the U.S. and China, balancing them against each other and in this way extracting the maximum benefit for themselves."[9] Such strategies will become difficult in the context of growing confrontation between the U.S. and China. The extent to which the EU will align with U.S. foreign policies in different parts of the world is uncertain. The new German government has emphasized a reinforcing of ties with the U.S. However, the humiliation of the U.S. and its Western allies in Afghanistan has seriously questioned American leadership, competence, and credibility.

When analyzing the U.S. National Security Strategy, it is evident that China has moved to the center of attention since the Trump presidency. Donald Trump and his "Make America Great Again" strategy intensified and accelerated conflicts with China and moved the U.S. away from some of its closest allies, especially in Europe. The trade war between the U.S. and China culminated in rising tariffs, escalation over the control of 5G with the Huawei controversy at its core, and the battle over the World Trade Organization (WTO). Trump's strategy proved ineffective, and in fact counterproductive. The poor management of the COVID-19 pandemic in the U.S. and Europe opened space for China's assertion across the world and intensified debates on hegemonic shift. However, two years since the outbreak of the pandemic, China's success in combating COVID-19 might turn out to be less impressive than initially thought. In the medium term, China may have paid a high economic price for its zero COVID-19 strategy by initiating new lockdowns and imposing extensive quarantine regulations for international travelers for a very long time.

The Biden administration is making efforts to repair the damage and re-engage in multilateralism. The U.S. is sending signals to China that the U.S. will not accept co-leadership of global affairs, with the notable exception of climate action. It seems, however, unrealistic to limit cooperation with China to climate action. China has deepened and broadened its investments across sectors and its efforts to forge new alliances in the past decades, especially in the Global South. Many of China's accomplishments in diplomacy are overlooked or underestimated by Western pundits who are sometimes locked into past perspectives on geopolitical power distribution shaped by the economic power of the U.S. and the EU. The hegemonic position of the U.S. is largely due to the dominance of the U.S. dollar in international trade, and its huge stock markets. China is strongly pushing for the globalization of the Renminbi as a currency for international trade and seeking to expand its stock markets. Its efforts to reduce the international influence of the U.S. dollar will lead to new conflicts, adding to a series of controversial issues.

The U.S. is calling upon the G7 countries to line up behind it in order to counter China's rise on the grounds of its authoritarian rule, its human rights abuses, its restrictions of press freedom, and its shrinking of spaces for advocacy-oriented civil society organizations and academics.

In the short term, China will be able to capitalize on its continued economic growth, which will outpace growth in the U.S. and

Europe. However, if the U.S. can modernize its economy along the lines of a Green New Deal, develop a smart strategy of building alliances with other strong economies in transformation, and arrive at a realistic analysis of China's strength, China's chances of China dominating global economics and politics will shrink. Compared to the U.S. and the EU, China risks being unable to forge strong and sustainable alliances with other strong economies and being locked into internal power struggles over the succession of Xi Jinping, once his age begins to affect his personal leadership abilities and make the Chinese political system look ossified.

Much will depend on domestic policy dynamics in the U.S., the EU, and the United Kingdom (U.K.). It is hard to predict whether liberal democracies will be able to address the mounting challenge of social cohesion and be able to adjust their foreign policy initiatives to a more realistic vision of an emerging multipolar world order.

Public opinion matters in electoral democracies in Europe. A study by the European Council on Foreign Relations (ECFR) concluded, "In today's Europe, there is no dream of a return to a bipolar world in which the West would face off against China and its allies as it once did against the Soviet Union."[10]

We interviewed Prof. Shada Islam from the College of Europe about the prospects of multipolar world order. Having grown up in Pakistan, she has traveled the world and is a well-known Brussels-based commentator on EU affairs who now works independently as an advisor, analyst, and strategist on questions related to Europe, Africa, Asia, geopolitics, trade, and inclusion. Ms. Islam is a member of the European Policy Centre's prestigious Strategic Council and a senior adviser for its Europe in the world program. She is the former head of Friends of Europe, a Brussels-based think tank, and a correspondent for over 20 years for Asia's leading news weekly *The Far Eastern Economic Review*.

Global Perspectives on Megatrends

Interview with Shada Islam, professor at the College of Europe, former Executive of Friends of Europe (FOM)

Q: How do you evaluate the discourses of hegemonic shift and multipolar world order? Which other terms would best describe likely future scenarios of geopolitics and international relations? How would different scenarios play out in terms of geopolitical stability and multilateral cooperation?

Shada Islam: I am concerned with Europe-centric world views, ideological divisions, and hegemonic thinking. Such perspectives have a long tradition rooted in colonial history and overplay conflict and confrontational scenarios. They ignore the fact that countries — even small countries — have agency and do not want to be dragged into a calamitous new Cold War or even worse, into a real war between the Great Powers. Countries want to be able to navigate between cooperation and competition modes in international relations. They are pragmatic and choose their partners freely, depending on their capacity to tackle global and regional challenges, such as peace and security issues, trade, technology, combating the pandemic and climate change. In an interconnected and interdependent world where there are no "good" or "bad" countries; foreign and security policymaking initiatives designed to openly confront or aimed at containing countries, especially China, will not work. Sanctions can make policymakers feel virtuous because they are responding to human rights violations but in many cases, they don't really lead to a change of behavior on the part of the country accused of such violations. Instead, they can be counterproductive. It is also wrong to link human rights and geopolitics because countries which are targeted by sanctions can argue they are politically motivated. Sanctions can also hit middle-class consumers by limiting their access to essential goods. They lead to job losses, often affecting women and underprivileged groups disproportionally. They seldom produce the desired political change or benefit the local population. If applied, they should be well targeted and focus on selected political elites involved in specific crimes. Let's not forget also that multinational companies have a significant role to play by monitoring supply chain management and respecting social and labor standards.

Q: How should the EU balance its relations with the U.S. and Asian powers?

Shada Islam: Both under Donald Trump and now under the Biden administration, the EU has made it clear that it agrees with the U.S. on many aspects of the strategic challenge posed by a more assertive China—but does not always agree on the best way to address it. While Washington foresees an uneasy relationship with China shaped by either "cooperative rivalry," "managed competition," or "competitive co-existence," the focus in Brussels—despite recent acrimonious tit-for-tat sanctions with Beijing—remains on dealing with China as a partner, competitor, and systemic rival, with EU heavy hitters like German Chancellor Angela Merkel and French President Emmanuel Macron warning against setting up a united front against Beijing.

These transatlantic divergences are likely to persist, giving an added significance to how the EU approaches the Indo Pacific's geographical, economic, and geopolitical complexities. The EU should be careful not to over-romanticize its friends and over-vilify its competitors. Also, while looking at Asia, the EU should not make the mistake of putting China and India on the same economic level.

In my opinion, China is economically still far more potent than India. Its market is also more important for Europe than the Indian market. India has made remarkable progress in some sectors, but it is still in catch-up mode and faces some serious internal problems on the way to superpower status, especially deep-rooted poor governance and flawed democracy. In particular, exacerbated Hindu nationalism and human rights issues in Kashmir, as well as discrimination against its Muslim citizens, tend to be overlooked by Western pundits in the context of geostrategic considerations. Also, while the EU's embrace of India as a key "like-minded" Indo Pacific actor is good news, the new strategy must not make the geopolitical mistake of neglecting the opportunity to deepen Europe's engagement with other South Asian countries, including Bangladesh, Pakistan, Afghanistan, Sri Lanka, and Nepal.

Q: How do you see the prospects of the BRICS (Brazil, Russia, India, China, and South Africa) alliance and cooperation between emerging economies and the Global South? How much political weight will China gain through the Belt and Road Initiative (BRI)? Will China and also India be able to play a stronger role in geo-economics and geopolitics, for example, through agenda-setting in the context of G20 or G10 summits?

Shada Islam: The BRI is emblematic of China's rise and a label of China's extensive collaboration across the world. Its global involvement in global supply chains and its engagement with other countries is the better alternative to an inward-looking China. The BRI is a fluid initiative of almost global scale that encompasses economic, geo-strategic, and diplomatic aspects and underscores China's commitment to stay engaged in different parts of the world. The BRI is far more popular in Africa and Asia than Europe and the U.S. tend to think. Italy, Portugal, and other EU countries have also embraced BRI projects. Additionally, while U.S. hard power will certainly continue to matter for countries in the region, as China's BRI reaches deeply into countries across Asia (and Africa and Latin America), the real struggle will be about who gets to set standards, rules, and regulations for — inter alia — global trade, connectivity, and data exchanges.

The Shanghai Cooperation Organisation is of relevance for peace and security issues even beyond Asia. It should not be underestimated. The G10 idea is unlikely to develop much traction. The G20 and G7 summits showcase multilateral exchanges but its summit meetings will not shape the world as much as some political elites or think tanks want to make us believe. The composition of the G7 is especially obsolete, as it only has one Asian economic power. The G20 is more representative but lacks organizational structures. Talk of an "alliance of democracies" ignores the depressing fact that democracies are fragilized and under threat also within the EU.

12.2 The Rise of China: How Long Will it Last?

A huge proliferation of books and political analyses have focused on the rise of China. China's ascent has remade the landscape of global politics and will continue to shape geopolitical conflicts as well as international cooperation.

In the U.S. but also in Europe, the academic community has collected enormous knowledge on Greater China, which includes the People's Republic of China, Hong Kong, Macao, and Taiwan. However, there are very few experts who understand the P.R. China's role in the world and its relations with other countries. Many China experts underestimate the influence of China in other world regions, especially in the Global South.

China experts in the United States and Europe often know few other countries except their own country and China. Thus, they are tempted to compare China with their own country rather than adopting a wider perspective in comparing developments in China with political and economic trajectories in other countries. Broader and diverse perspectives matter. Berthold Kuhn knows China as a former resident professor of Tsinghua University and Xiamen University, as a consultant, project evaluator, conference speaker, investor, traveler, and husband of a Chinese wife and father of children with German as well as Chinese identity.

Ties Dams, research fellow at the Clingendael Institute, one of the Netherlands's leading independent think tanks, acknowledges that China has succeeded in projecting a strong, positive image in different parts of Africa by training thousands of journalists, opening dozens of Confucius Institutes, and investing deeply in diplomatic ties. According to him, "China has successfully carved out a narrative space for alternatives to Western modernity, sometimes to the detriment of Europe's soft power, but at the very least to relative gains in legitimacy of China's model of development."[11]

However, doubtful views of China's rise continue to shape political debates. Maximilian Mayer, a junior professor of international relations and global politics of technology at the University of Bonn and Emilian Kavalski, professor at the Jagiellonian

University in Krakow, have boldly stated, "One thing is clear, Beijing's influence is currently in decline. To take one prominent example, China's signature infrastructure project, the Belt and Road Initiative (BRI), has been underperforming for some time." They also refer to China's relations with Eastern European countries and argue that the 17+1 bloc is in decline while relations with the U.K. have become strained and foreign relations with many other countries suffer from a lack of trust.[12]

What they largely ignore in their analysis is China's steady rise in economic power, its technological and infrastructure development at home and abroad over recent years, its growing cohort of engineering talent, and the growth of its educated middle class. Economic growth and China's growing influence in the world are key sources of legitimacy for the Chinese political leadership. According to many Chinese, the Middle Kingdom (a name for China derived from the translation of its native Chinese name, Zhongguo) is on the way to regain the position it deserves in the world.

Figure 12.1: Percentage of Global GDP 1820–2012

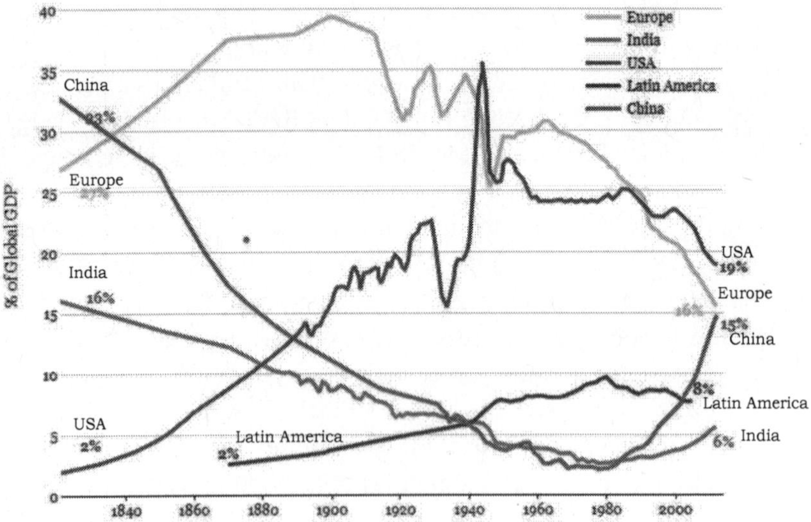

Source: Maddison/OECD (2013).[13]

Multipolar World Order and the Future of Multilateralism

China faces challenges such as widening inequalities, an aging population, growing fiscal imbalances, and public debt as well as confrontations over some of its territorial claims, but there are currently no signs that the economy will dwindle or that influential political groups and large sections of the society want to topple the regime. In the 2022 Edelman Trust Index, China saw the biggest gains and the trust of the Chinese people in government reached 91 percent.[14] The interviews and surveys conducted by the U.S. based global communication firm are considered a credible source of reference by many experts.[15] They largely confirmed the results from a long-term public opinion survey of the Harvard Kennedy School Ash Center, which concluded that "compared to public opinion patterns in the U.S., in China there was very high satisfaction with the central government.[16] The "zero Covid" pandemic strategy, however, could pose a risk to China if it is to be continued for much longer. The leading German economist Marcel Fratscher, president of the economic research institute Deutsches Institut für Wirtschaftsforschung in Berlin, also points to the risks of a future financial crisis triggered by China.[17]

There are lots of reasons to be critical of political and economic developments in China. However, one mistake many China experts have made in recent decades is to greatly underestimate China's political and economic resilience. Many failed to predict China's enormous success in technological development. At the same time, China's continued rise and even political stability are not guaranteed forever. If the economy becomes seriously crippled, the legitimacy of its political leadership to continue ruling the country in an authoritarian way will be affected. Leading experts, including star U.S. economist Stephen Roach, have long defended the future viability of China's tech sector. But the crackdown on innovation leaders and tech firms by the government has him, among others, doubting, and not without reason. He argues that "the Chinese government has taken dead aim at its dynamic technology sector, the engine of China's New Economy." He sees signs of a clampdown on many other leading Chinese tech companies, including Tencent (internet conglomerate), Meituan (food delivery), Pinduoduo (e-commerce), Full Truck Alliance (truck-hailing apps Huochebang and Yunmanman), Kanzhun's Boss Zhipin (recruitment), and online private tutoring companies like TAL Education Group and Gaotu Techedu. And all of this follows China's high-profile crackdown on cryptocurrencies.[18]

However, we must acknowledge that China's efforts to recalibrate economic and political stability are mostly underestimated, as are its efforts to tackle pollution, environmental degradation, and climate change. The pollution crisis seriously plagued Chinese cities before Premier Li Keqiang declared "a war on pollution" in 2014.[19]

There are growing signs that the Chinese political leadership is overstretching. Chinese nationalism is becoming a visible threat to other countries and is likely to produce repercussions. China's efforts to become an economic powerhouse, however, will make it difficult for other countries to challenge the rise of China. China is the largest trading partner of close to two-thirds of all countries. We would argue that military power and, unfortunately, soft power tend to be overrated; economic power and infrastructure development matter much more for the rise of countries in the modern world.

Beginning with its entry into the World Trade Organization (WTO) in December 2001, China has rapidly transformed its economy from a low-cost 'factory to the world' to a global leader in advanced technologies. China's emergence as a global economic powerhouse has created tensions. Early expectations that China's integration into the global economy would lead to liberalization at home and moderation abroad have proven overly optimistic, especially since President Xi Jinping rose to power in 2012.

China and its influence in world politics, including in the United Nations and other international and regional organizations, is still underestimated by many political leaders in the West. Policies to counter the influence of China are on the rise.

China's key initiative to increase its global influence is the BRI. This global infrastructure and connectivity strategy was adopted by the Chinese government in 2013 and is closely associated with

President Xi Jinping's vision of China-centered economic development initiatives across Asia and the world. The BRI was incorporated into China's Constitution in 2017. The BRI comprises the Silk Road Economic Belt and the Twenty-First Century Maritime Silk Road. The number of countries that have joined the BRI by signing a Memorandum of Understanding (MoU) with China has risen to 140. Not only developing countries (DCs) but also industrialized countries (ICs) have signed MoU. The initiative has received criticism because of a lack of transparency, especially regarding loan agreements, and its heavy carbon footprint, because of continued investments in coal-fired plants and large steel projects. However, China's pledge to stop financing new coal plants abroad, announced by President Xi Jinping at the United Nations summit in September 2021, could improve the BRI's reputation. The BRI International Green Development Coalition (BRIGC), which was established after the second Belt and Road Forum in April 2019, continues to lobby for greening the BRI.

Other criticisms of the BRI relate to the rising debts of poorer countries that have signed loan agreements with China. China is not a member of the Paris Club comprising major creditor countries whose role is to find coordinated and sustainable solutions to the payment difficulties experienced by debtor countries. It is, however, a major, if not the largest, creditor to quite a few developing countries. There may be competition over the repayment of loans to China and Western creditors. While some BRI-related investments and projects might provoke criticism, it is also evident that part of the harsher criticism of the BRI is motivated by the foreign policy orientations of the U.S. and Western countries. Western experts consider the BRI an instrument to increase China's dominance and influence in several world regions and fear that the BRI will be a geopolitical game-changer. Australia announced on April 21, 2021, that it would withdraw from the BRI completely.

While the BRI is its flagship initiative, China pursues a multi-pronged strategy in terms of foreign policy, investment, and trade: First, China maintains involvement in existing international organizations. Second, it aims to gain more influence in existing international organizations like the WTO and the World Health Organization (WHO). Third, it begins new initiatives such as the BRI and takes on the (co-)establishment of new organizations and initiatives in which China plays a leading role. Heike Holbig, professor at the Goethe University Frankfurt in Germany, points out China's new strategy of engagement with international organizations: from joining, to reforming, to initiating.[20] China was chiefly involved in starting the Asian Infrastructure Investment Bank (AIIB) and the New Development Bank (NDB) of the BRICS countries. Both banks focus on investments in infrastructure projects. The idea to launch the AIIB as a new regional development bank was first voiced by the vice chairman of the China Center for International Economic Exchanges, a Chinese thinktank, at the Bo'ao Forum in April 2009. China's President Xi Jinping presented the initiative at the occasion of a state visit to Indonesia in 2013. The bank began operations on December 25, 2015. The bank has 104 approved members and several prospective members from around the world.

The NDB was first proposed by India at the 4th BRICS summit in 2012, held in Delhi. BRICS leaders agreed to set up this new development bank at the 5th BRICS summit held in Durban, South Africa, on March 27, 2013. The Agreement on the New Development Bank entered into force in July 2015. The Bank's Articles of Agreement specify that all members of the United Nations could be members of the bank; however, the shares of BRICS nations can never equal less than 55 percent of total voting power. BRICS countries hold equal shares.

China has significantly increased its political clout in global politics even though the process has not been linear and is increasingly challenged. On the way to more global influence, China will encounter a lot of criticism and strong resistance from Western states, especially from the U.S., but also from the EU, Australia, and Canada. Bilateral confrontations with countries in Africa and Latin America are unlikely to escalate, partly because the U.S. is losing influence there. Based on our own analysis and talks with experts, including experts affiliated to the Dialogue of Civilizations Research Institute, we assume that in the coming years, China's relations with Russia and Central Asian countries will continue to improve but will not equate to the power of an alliance of liberal democracies, like the G7 countries. China's relationship with India will remain a risk factor. China's authoritarian and nationalistic drive is expected to translate into a stronger military presence and involve engagements in security issues, especially in Africa, where it has already been involved in numerous military exercises.[21]

12.3 Old and New Western Alliances

After the Biden administration assumed office, it soon began, rhetorically, to place strengthening democracy abroad at the center of its foreign policy. The U.S. government organized support for combating authoritarianism, advancing human rights, and combating corruption in December 2021. U.S. think tanks provide strategic advice to the Biden administration on how to curtail China. Brookings, one of the leading think tanks, put the following advice forward:

> "First, it [the U.S. administration] should bolster core institutions of democracy in strategically important countries. Second, democracy strengthening, and democracy protection should be coupled to enable countries to prevent and counter Russian and Chinese interference. Third, it should support a positive vision for how technology can deliver on democratic principles and pushing back against digital authoritarianism. Fourth, it should recommit to working with allies to shore up democracy abroad. Finally, it must back these initiatives with forceful and principled diplomacy to stand with democratic activists and speak out against dictators and tyrants."[22]

The U.S. is increasingly concerned about the Indo Pacific region. The United States, United Kingdom, and Australia launched the AUKU.S. (Australia-Canada-U.S.) alliance in September 2021, a historic security pact in the Asia-Pacific which is seen as an effort to counter China. The pact will let Australia build nuclear-powered submarines for the first time, using technology provided by the U.S. The decision prompted a diplomatic row between the U.S. and France. France's foreign minister accused Australia and the U.S. of lying over the new security pact and Paris even recalled its ambassadors.

Global Perspectives on Megatrends

From the perspective of the United States, South-East Asia, and not Africa, is likely to becoming the primary venue for the U.S.–China power struggle, even though Africa remains important due to its rich mineral resources. South-East Asia, however, is economically more important, if the U.S. aims to advance decoupling its economy from China. Vietnam has received increasing attention as an alternative manufacturing hub to China, even though its political system and human rights record is not in line with freedom-oriented political thinking. African leaders are understandably concerned they will once again be swept up in great power rivalry, this time between the United States and China.

The EU has pledged to raise 300 billion EUR for the "Global Gateway" infrastructure initiative to counter China's BRI. One third will come from different EU instruments (grants, loans, export guarantees), the rest is supposed to be raised by the private sector. The plan is to globally invest in digitalization, green technologies, and transport links and to provide partner countries with an alternative option for infrastructure investments.[23]

The strategic response of the U.S. and the EU to the rise of China will be an important factor shaping a new world order. It is difficult to predict how China-U.S. relations and China-Europe relations will develop in the next decade, as multiple factors will influence strategic considerations. U.S. President Biden will use diplomatic tools and invest much effort in forging alliances, especially with the EU and major EU countries. However, he is realistic enough to understand that China's influence is not easy to contain and that the U.S. will provoke a series of reactions that could harm the U.S. more than China. Despite years of conflict with massive mutual punitive tariffs, former U.S. President Trump failed to reduce the U.S. trade deficit with China. In October 2021, just before the U.S. elections, China's trade surplus with the U.S. rose to a monthly record of 42 billion U.S. dollars, exports surged by about 30 percent from one year earlier. Imports increased by almost 17 percent. The U.S. remained China's largest trade partner on a single-country basis.[24]

Multipolar World Order and the Future of Multilateralism

The European Parliament is known to be adopting critical positions on China and putting China's human rights violations on the agenda frequently. A long-time advocate for containing China is Reinhard Bütikofer, the chair of the delegation for relations with the People's Republic of China in the European Parliament. The former Maoist has turned strongly against China and is on China's list of sanctioned EU politicians. In March 2021, China imposed tit-for-tat sanctions on ten EU individuals and four entities that it accused of seriously offending China's sovereignty regarding Xinjiang abuses.

"Americans and Europeans together against China? Not a good idea," said Emmanuel Macron in a guest lecture at the U.S. Atlantic Council think tank on February 4, 2021. He warned that a united front against Beijing could result in China reducing cooperation on combating climate change and tightening its regional agenda in Asia.[25]

The outcome of the struggle between different EU institutions and leaders of member states on how to engage and confront China is hard to predict and will probably result in a series of back-and-forth strategies which will not be helpful to increasing the image and influence of the EU in China. EU member states seem to tolerate the fact that European institutions, especially the Parliament, adopt a far more critical attitude than most individual EU member states. At the bilateral level, EU member states tend to be more afraid of a deterioration in economic relations.

The coalition agreement between the newly elected German government comprising the Social Democrats, the Greens, and the Liberals, includes some strong language on China by highlighting human rights issues in Xinjiang and urging Beijing to respect the one-country-two-systems treaty arrangement on Hong Kong. The text also refers to Germany's possible acceptance of Taiwan's participation in negotiations on technical issues at the international level. Beijing reacted promptly with a warning to the new German Chancellor Olaf Scholz. While such language resounds well with part of the electorate and much of Germany's mainstream media, the EU and Germany might indeed overstretch their foreign policy ambitions and harm their industries, which are highly dependent on China, including industries of relevance for the energy transition and digitalization strategies.

Herfried Münkler, professor emeritus of Humboldt University Berlin and a renowned German political analyst, regards the withdrawal of U.S. troops from Afghanistan as proof that the West has overstretched its foreign policy ambitions. He concedes that "in the foreseeable future, the liberal values of the West will only apply in the West and in the areas belonging to it."[26]

The North Atlantic Treaty Organization (NATO), however, is making a remarkable comeback in the context of Russia's military invasion of Ukraine. Security cooperation between the three Baltic states and NATO will further intensify. Finland and Sweden may consider to join NATO. Russia will continue its strong engagement in Central Asia. However, we agree with other experts that Kazakhstan and other countries in Central Asia with authoritarian leadership are likely to be a source of problems for Russia.[27] Protests in Kazakhstan and instability in Afghanistan will probably lead to stronger military presence in the region. Protest movements in the region as in other Asian countries will be hard to silence. Those who oppose and protest against authoritarian regimes will continue to receive international attention and support, especially from the U.S. and some EU countries.

In the early morning of February 24, 2022, Russian armed forces invaded Eastern Ukraine and launched attacks in other parts of the country after a prolonged military buildup at the border and the Russian recognition of the self-proclaimed Donetsk People's Republic and Luhansk People's Republic. The authors refrain from making sweeping statements on the future of the conflict and instead point to the possibility of a new type of response from the U.S. and Europe in acting together and implementing massive sanctions. The response to the Ukrainian crisis will define future conflicts in the continent, and we will see Europe's fight to preserve, if not reconstruct and modernize its sovereignty. A potential refugee crisis could provoke divisions among EU countries.

Though it is too early to tell which side will come out victorious, it is nonetheless becoming evident that there are no victors in modern warfare. An ill-equipped Russian army is seeing tens of thousands of losses in both equipment and human lives, while committing crimes against humanity under international law. Millions of Ukrainians fight for their lives and flee their country towards a European Union, which welcomes them with open arms, a stark contrast to past refugee crises. Inside Russia people do not have access to information about the war, the word itself being banned, while consuming government propaganda inside an authoritarian nation, whose leadership can only survive the breakdown of its economy by consolidating power and leaning into more autocratic tendencies. The emergence of the "Z" movement, which finds wide support in the Russian population and echoes Nazi Germany is worrying, as well as a stark reminder that the internet is a powerful tool against authoritarian governments.

The authors are not optimistic that Vladimir Putin's regime will be toppled any time soon, but Russian oligarchs are seeing dire losses, while the Russian population will have to live under a new reality of Western sanctions. As such, the government will have many questions to answer, including providing a justification for the immense cost of the war at the expense of the livelihoods of its people. It is inconceivable that Russia will be able to quickly build trust with the West once more. The EU's status quo is inevitably disrupted, and the authors see the next few years as an opportunity for the Union to become independent in its energy production. The next decade will see the rise of a new geopolitical power in a (possibly expanded) European Union, much to the dismay of Russia.

12.4 The Geopolitical Impact of the COVID-19 Pandemic

Richard Higgott, a seasoned political scientist, emphasized early on in the pandemic that the global COVID-19 outbreak would bring about shifts in international economic and political power. He predicted that "in the wake of COVID-19 pandemic the U.S. — and to a lesser extent Europe — is the major victim of COVID-19 in both real, economic, and diplomatic terms."[28]

Simon Frankel Pratt and Jamie Levin have argued in *Foreign Policy* that rich democracies are easily winning the domestic vaccination race,[29] but at the price of extending any coherent influence in the rest of the world. This tends to reinforce perceptions that these countries are little rich enclaves, primarily preoccupied with domestic politics, the balancing of which depends on keeping the rest of the world at arm's length.[30]

The COVID-19 pandemic has revealed mutual economic dependencies. Europe has critically depended on Chinese imports for the pharmaceutical, chemical, and electronics sectors, mostly for components produced in technologically less sophisticated areas of the value chain. The European Commission's Policy Department for External Relations has published an insightful study on "The geopolitical implications of the COVID-19 pandemic," which takes stock of patterns of geopolitical change and reflects on some of the worries of EU leadership. It stated the following:

> "COVID-19 erupted into a landscape of change: even before the pandemic unfolded, 'uncertainty' became the defining marker of these times. This perception of the unknown was the result of several changes occurring simultaneously in the international system: from relations with China to those with the U.S., from a change in international trade patterns to an increase in disinformation campaigns, because these shifts occurred over several years consistently in a certain direction, they can be called trends: a pattern of change."[31]

Throughout the year 2021, it looked as if China could emerge as a winner of the COVID-19 pandemic even though COVID-19 broke out in Wuhan in late December 2019. China witnessed relatively few deaths and the economy recovered more quickly after a massive lockdown policy was implemented for several months. Its Zero-COVID strategy, however, resulted in long-lasting restrictions for international visits and foreign travel. The Omicron variant started to rage through the world from end of November/early December 2021 and reached China in January 2022, just ahead of the Beijing Winter Olympics.

Multipolar World Order and the Future of Multilateralism

Will globalization ever be the same? Adam Tooze, a British historian and professor at Columbia University, predicted a "perfect storm", acknowledging that "the COVID-19 shock has raised globalization angst to a new pitch" and that "the broader vision of the flat world of globalization is dead."[32] Efforts are underway to restructure supply chains. Many countries will engage in tightening border controls. International exchanges will suffer for a considerable period of time. Much will depend on geopolitical relations between the U.S. and China and their impact the global trade regime. Some signs do not bode well. However, we see many forces at play which will push for a recovery of international exchanges and multilateral cooperation, even though nationalism will be on the rise for some time and cause multiple setbacks for international cooperation.

We interviewed Dr. Huiyao (Henry) Wang, the founder and president of the Center for China and Globalization (CCG), a leading Chinese non-governmental think tank that ranks among the top 80 think tanks in the world, on how multipolarity will play out after COVID-19 and how China is positioning itself in the new world order. Dr. Wang is an adviser to the Chinese government, having been appointed as a counselor for China State Council, China's Cabinet, by the Chinese Premier in 2015, and is a globally renowned expert on China and globalization, global trade and investment, China's international relations, and China-U.S. trade relations.

Interview with Huiyao (Henry) Wang, Founder and President of the Center for China and Globalization (CCG)

Q: You have developed the argument that the COVID-19 pandemic will reinforce the trend of increasing multipolarity that we have seen over the last two decades. Given the trajectories of the pandemic and policy responses in different countries and regions, how do you see the trend of multipolarity playing out in the coming years and over the next decade?

Huiyao Wang: The world has, over the last 200 years, undergone an ever-accelerating transformation and has become increasingly intertwined, like never before, but it is also gradually breaking into blocs and moving away from the traditional unipolar/bipolar model. I consider the nuclear war option to be off the table, as it would completely paralyze the world as a whole.

The multipolar world order will be strengthened. In sum, we shall see more treaties, agreements, and cooperation between the big players and also between bigger and smaller players, even though disputes will catch political attention and may temporarily lead to some delays or smaller setbacks. The EU and the U.S. will seek to forge cooperation based on common political values and ideologies. Economically, however, the EU will be inclined to continue its strong cooperation with China.

Q: You framed the term "multispeed globalization," explaining how COVID-19 will impact processes of globalization. While you acknowledge concerns around decoupling that may lead to some degree of "decoupling" and "reshoring" you also identify opportunities for ecological globalization to strengthen. Please explain and comment on China's strategies to re-engage in ecological globalization.

Huiyao Wang: We shall not ignore challenges that could make the world drift apart, because of conflicts about the use of technologies, power-shifting, the Thucydides Trap, and ideological differences. This obliges us to do our best to address global challenges together and to deepen cooperation on common issues, like pandemics, climate change, and most importantly, to rebuild the trust that has been lost. No country is safe from these threats, and it is very encouraging to see President Biden tell the G7 that we should get rid of vaccine patents. In many countries this initiative has been welcomed and from China's point of view, it is exactly the type of mutual cooperation and consensus that we require in this fractured world.

Q: The WTO's negotiating function has been nearly moribund at the multilateral level for more than a decade. Similarly, the dispute settlement function of the WTO is in a state of crisis. How do you see the future of WTO in the next decade? What reforms are needed to restore the relevance of the WTO?

Huiyao Wang: There are reforms needed, absolutely, but high-level talks to revive the WTO are gaining traction again. The WTO is not idle. For example, the Informal Dialogue on Plastics Pollution and Environmentally Sustainable Plastics Trade took place on March 29, 2021, and focused on enhancing transparency and international cooperation. On many WTO issues, China has been at the forefront of trying to facilitate and support reform processes. What makes me hopeful is that the new leadership of the WTO is competent and sufficiently diverse and of course the fact that President Biden is eager to return to multilateralism, so let us see what comes out of this.

Q: China is pushing the globalization of the Renminbi as a currency for international trade and seeking to expand its stock markets. Will its efforts to reduce the international influence of the U.S. dollar intensify conflicts with the U.S. and how could such conflicts be mitigated?

Huiyao Wang: I think so, absolutely and we should remember that we are talking about a multipolar world order. From this perspective, the global dominance of the U.S. dollar does not reflect the weight of other nations in international trade, especially China. China maintained its position as the world's largest trading nation in goods for the fifth year running in 2020. China will seize the opportunity to introduce digital currencies and will aim to increase its weight in the global currency market. China already has a massive digital economy, almost 50 percent of which is present in big cities, and I personally cannot even remember the last time I used cash, so we are setting an example. And another thing is that the digital infrastructure and the market potential is extraordinarily strong in China. As for the stock markets, China has not even reached its peak potential and is currently on a path to reach eight percent growth or even more, while enjoying remarkable stability, so the synergy and stability is there, and this will be reflected in the stock market and growing market capitalization of some of its leading companies.

Q: What about Bitcoin? Do you see banks backing it up in the future?

Huiyao Wang: Probably not, since it is so incredibly volatile and also not many people have it in China or Asia in general, while it is not used in international trade.

Q: Who stands to gain more from the comprehensive trade agreement between China and the EU?

Huiyao Wang: Obviously, the EU, since its economy is still rebounding, while China even saw GDP growth in 2020. As an example, companies like Mercedes Benz, BMW, and so forth, all made profits in China, the third-largest automobile market, while they made enduring losses in the EU.

Q: Which markets in emerging economies and developing countries will gain more weight in the coming years? What are the opportunities and risks for China in engaging more deeply with these countries and regions?

Huiyao Wang: China is specifically looking at Africa and for good reasons. The African Continental Free Trade Framework Agreement has been signed by 52 African Union member states. It is now operational with the necessary 22 ratifications after only three years of free trade negotiations. We expect a boom in the region in the next 10–15 years. It is such a young continent, with the median age being around 20 years old. The other area of interest for China is India, as there is a long history between the two countries and a lot of similarities as well, so economic cooperation will also help to tone down unnecessary conflict.

12.5 The Future of Multilateralism

The benefits of multilateral cooperation are obvious in an increasingly globalized world. Mounting challenges for humanity—climate change, the loss of biodiversity, pandemics, financial crisis, cybersecurity, poverty, and other issues of transnational relevance—require close collaboration between states, multinational corporations, transnational research networks, and civil society organizations across the world. States are not the only important actors in multinational cooperation but play a key role in fostering peace, and drafting laws and regulations for economic development, trade, and environmental protection. If we learn our historical lessons, we should be very serious about expanding multilateral cooperation rather than focusing on the threat of mutual dependence. For a brief moment after World War One and the 1918 pandemic, the international community came together in the League of Nations. The effort failed, and humanity endured the far bloodier World War Two and the Holocaust.[33]

Multilateralism has been crucial in maintaining peace and prosperity in many regions of the world, especially in Europe. However, more, not less, effort is needed to sustain the benefits of international cooperation. Key institutions such as the United Nations, the International Monetary Fund (IMF), the World Bank, and the World Trade Organization have found it difficult to exercise their ambitious mandates. Their legitimacy is being challenged. Critics consider them unable to implement adequate reforms to refocus their mandate and become more inclusive. The political discontent with multilateralism is very noticeable in the United States and is associated with the failure of the post-Bretton Woods system to adequately solve challenges arising from economic and financial crisis situations worldwide. China and other emerging economies do not think that they are adequately represented in the IMF, World Bank, and other institutions and have created new institutions, such as the Asian Infrastructure Investment Bank and the New Development Bank of the BRICS countries. The Global Solutions Initiative, a Berlin-based think tank focusing on the work of the G20, concludes that "resulting disillusionment with formal multilateralism has led to the consideration of various alternatives, such as the parallel pursuit of bilateral deals or cooperation that is limited to like-minded or geographically proximate countries."[34] The G20 has established a working group on the future of multilateralism, which focuses on enlarging consensus on the traffic rules needed to achieve adequate multilateral cooperation and coordination while ensuring that the multilateral system remains democratically legitimate and politically sustainable. This task is very challenging in view of deep-rooted lines of conflict and confrontation between the U.S., China, Europe, and other nations. Experts are discussing the trend of "decoupling" between China and the Western world. There is indeed evidence of increasing separation in the fields of technology and data governance. However, looking at capital markets, cross-border portfolio investments into and out of China are growing fast, despite some setbacks.[35]

While the entanglement of the Chinese economy with Western countries seems hard to reduce, we have witnessed an upswing of political assertions between China and Western countries. In China, new political discourses that emphasize the power of cultural and civilizational roots are in vogue. The focus is more on the differences between civilizations rather than what they have in common. "Culture is the new currency of power" is Cristopher Coker's thesis advanced in his book *The Civilizational State*.[36] Instead of political ideologies, cultural identities are now the focus of disputes. The term "Civilizational State" was first used by scholars in the 1990s and has subsequently gained popularity amongst political leaders outside the West. The Chinese President Xi Jinping, Russian President Vladimir Putin, and Turkish President Recep Tayyip Erdoğan have all referred to it on multiple occasions. India has also been proposed as an example of a civilization state. The concept resounds well with the political leadership of the ruling Bharatiya Janata Party (BJP). The popularity of the concept in the East has discredited the concept among political elites in Western countries. The thesis of "culture as a new political currency" relates to the global debate initiated by Samuel Huntington on the "clash of civilizations"[37] and to debates about exceptionalism (Chinese exceptionalism vs. American exceptionalism).

Samuel Huntington's *Clash of Civilizations* (1996) is probably the most widely referenced political science book in recent decades.[38] He argued that the fundamental source of conflict in this new world will not be primarily ideological, nor economic. The great divisions among humankind and the dominant sources of conflict will be cultural. Nation-states will remain the most powerful actors in world affairs, but the principal conflicts of global politics will occur between nations and groups of different civilizations.

Multipolar World Order and the Future of Multilateralism

The clash of civilizations will dominate global politics. The fault lines between civilizations will be the battle lines of the future.[39]

Huntington has been criticized from different perspectives. One of the most valid criticisms relates to the argument that Huntington's civilizational groupings are fraught with their own internal cultural divisions and conflicts. Michael Kennedy argues that Huntington alluding to unity among civilizations is invalid.[40] Adrian Pabst of Kent University refers to Huntington when he argues that China and Russia define themselves not as nations but civilizations – in opposition to the liberalism and global market ideology of the West.[41] Coker points to the difference between civilizations and clashes of civilizational states. This distinction reminds us of how cultural (and religious) identities could be manipulated by powerful political elites.

The debate on civilizations and civilizational states has definitely influenced views on the future of multilateral cooperation and brought more pessimistic scenarios to the fore. A G20 publication co-authored by Homi Kharas of the Brookings Institution, Dennis Snower of Global Solutions Initiatives, and Sebastian Strauss acknowledged that "over the last 75 years, multilateralism has been a strong driver and pillar of global integration, peace, and prosperity....recently, however, disaffection with globalization and current forms of global governance has emerged, threatening the very edifice of the rules-based multilateral order, partly because of competing economic models."[42]

We interviewed Parag Khanna,[43] a leading global strategy advisor and bestselling author on the future on multilateralism.

Interview with Parag Khanna, Founder of FutureMap

Q: How do you see relations between civilizations and geopolitics and what do you make of the argument of the rise of the civilization state and Christopher Coker's argument that culture has become the primary currency of politics?
Parag Khanna: On Chris Coker's argument specifically, I may praise his contributions to the debate but would like to critically

dismiss his thesis, which dates back to Huntington around 30 years ago, as it conflates civilizations with empires. The fact that there are ethno-nationalist "civilizational states" does not change the fact that power remains the currency of politics and that empires (not civilizations) should remain the primary unit of analysis. As with Huntington, it is dangerous to assume that the model which he describes is applicable to the West, Islam, or Christianity and if we try to measure the fundamental metrics in geopolitics or ask ourselves how uniformly those units operate, the answer is clearly, not all that much.

Q: The concept of the civilization state is quite popular in India and China, so what do you make of it?

Parag Khanna: Well, China and India were civilizations before they were states and do not need to be told things like this, as they understand that their civilization is bigger than their state, but still, they do operate in a world of states, but seem to be using this concept in order to weaponize it to their advantage. A notion that is applicable in such limited circumstances is far from a universal theory.

Q: How will the hegemonic struggle and/or the trend of multipolarity play out in the coming years and the next decade? What do you think of the Thucydides Trap?[44]

Parag Khanna: First off, this is the first time in history that we have a global distribution of superpowers (with sustained global influence), as Japan in the 1930s doesn't really count. Now, within this multipolar world order, there are also regional powers, like India, Japan, Australia, and Russia, so it's not just China. The challenge now for China is to prove, in the next decade, that it can overtake these competitors, likely in the way that colonial powers have done in the past. The example of the U.S. monopolizing influence over certain areas and wiping out competitors is the obvious one, so China must show that it is capable of reaching that level and cannot really call itself a hegemon yet. As for the Thucydides Trap, almost all the conflicts used in the theory apply only to the West, whereby the countries involved share an intense geographic tension, which obviously cannot be said for China and the U.S. Not only that but accepting a multipolar world and focusing on two rivals just doesn't make sense in a multipolar order.

Q: How do you see the future of multilateralism with reference to agenda-setting power and influence of some key institutions, especially the G7, G20, the UN bodies, the WTO, and the WHO?

Parag Khanna: I want to emphasize that multilateralism is not the sum-total of global governance. There are many private-sector and non-state actors that exercise significant influence on world economics and world politics, from multinational companies to major nonprofits like Oxfam, WWF, and Greenpeace. Their agendas also impact multilateral cooperation at different levels. I don't quite believe in reforming the big UN institutions. Look at the UN Security Council which has been subject to many reform initiatives, and they are still ongoing. Its decisions are often close to irrelevant and also non-binding. Even if it disappeared tomorrow, global governance would still go on. The WTO for example, which can be said to be the most successful multilateral institution in history as it has brought global tariffs down 90 percent; most of what it represents is today written in law and, again, were it to disappear tomorrow, trade would still go on, so let's not confuse the institution with the issue. I am an outcome-based person and I don't see the G20 or the UN organizations having a very significant impact in the world and then of course if you look at the IMF, another great candidate in terms of impact, only three countries in all of Asia have some sort of deal with it, so it can also be said to be much less significant than some governments believe or expert or some analyses suggest. Multilateral bodies should be measured only by how, where, and in what issues they are successful.

Q: Will we see deepened and broadened multilateral governance on energy and sustainability issues in the next decade or will we see sharpened differences in approach, focus, and speed of climate policies which may in turn trigger new conflicts?

Parag Khanna: Well, I would like to point out that countries sign up to agreements if they are watered down and the goals are achievable due to the country's current trajectory, so if you look for example at the SDG's, every country joined. The Paris Agreement is a bit of a different picture and certainly a kind of a breakthrough in global climate action though — legally speaking — it leaves ample room for countries to comply with it at their own speed and submit more or less ambitious targets. Environmental, social, and governance (ESG) commitments have an actual impact the other hand, for example, when the Norway Pension Fund decides to divest from coal, this has ripple effects in global supply chains. And if you compare the UN Global Compact with the World Business Council, the difference is night and day, right, so the hard work is done in the background and then these agreements tend to be just residuals to me. I have to say that I support people like Greta Thunberg and Luisa Neubauer and the Fridays for Future movement as they inspire many young people in mostly Western countries, but is there a Greta in China or India or are there many school strikes in support of climate action? Clearly not, so, it is simply true that Walmart or Amazon, and industries more generally, altering their courses is just far more impactful than social movements in the West could ever be.

The emerging multipolar order will transform multilateral cooperation. Multilateral cooperation will become a more pragmatic affair. The rise of the G20 reflects the trend. The G20 has become a pillar of multilateralism. It promotes global dialogue, debate, and — most importantly — economic problem-solving. Finance ministers from 20 of the world's largest economies agreed in July 2021 to set a minimum tax rate for corporate income of 15 percent, an initiative which has been joined by many more countries thereafter. By October 2021, more than 130 countries had agreed to implement a 15 percent minimum corporate tax rate in a bid to force large multinationals to pay taxes in countries where they operate.

High-level political debates and media coverage of multilateralism are usually focused on interstate relations. However, globalization has facilitated exchanges at all levels. Multinational companies exercise significant influence over global debates. Non-governmental organizations (NGOs), such as the World Wide Fund for Nature (WWF), Oxfam, CARE, World Vision, and Transparency

Multipolar World Order and the Future of Multilateralism

International operate in a large number of countries across continents. Kofi Annan, United Nations Secretary-General from 1997 to 2006 and co-recipient, with the UN, of the Nobel Peace Prize in 2001, launched the Global Compact in the year 2000 to engage more with multinational companies and the business sector.

This initiative was instrumental in opening up the United Nations system even more to dialogue with business and non-state stakeholders. The United Nations has recognized the importance of working with multinational corporations and non-state actors. The number of NGOs which have been accredited to participate in United Nations sessions has gradually increased in recent decades. Global summits, especially the climate summits, unite a large number of multiple stakeholders, involving representatives of cities, business, and grassroots environmental and social movements.

In its efforts to promote multilateralism, the UN pursues a two-fold strategy that consists of deepening, as well as broadening engagement with multiple stakeholders. With regard to deepening the understanding of climate change, the UN cooperates with leading scientists across the world. With regard to broadening, the UN has further stepped up its efforts to involve important stakeholders and to engage in new partnerships.[45]

Civil society and religious organizations have greatly shaped civilizations across the world. Berthold Kuhn has highlighted the valuable contributions of civil society organizations to international and development cooperation in African and Asian countries.[46] Matthias Helbe has investigated the possible ways that religion influences international trade patterns. The results of his research indicate that religious openness boosts national trade performance.[47] Faith-based groups play an important role in promoting transnational dialogue and engage in peace initiatives. At the same time, they are often seen as agents that instigate or exacerbate conflicts. Yitzhak Reiter argues that the significance of religion within ethnic and religious conflicts has risen steadily in recent decades, and especially so within the Israeli-Palestinian conflict.[48]

Talking about the future of multilateralism with reference to the role of the United Nations, superpowers, and multinational corporations but not analyzing the role of civil society and religious organizations and the prevalence of deep-rooted conflicts in some parts of the world would be a very limited perspective.

We interviewed Dr. Peter Makari on the role of churches and civil society groups in shaping multinational cooperation. We also asked him about the role of churches in ethnic and religious conflicts and the Israeli-Palestine conflict, which is one of the most enduring conflicts in recent history. An Egyptian-American, Peter Makari has served as the executive for the Middle East and Europe with the Common Global Ministries Board of the United Church of Christ and the Christian Church (Disciples of Christ) since July 1, 2000. He serves on the U.S. National Council of Churches's Interreligious Convening Table, of which he is a co-convener.

Interview with Peter Makari, Executive at Global Ministries of the Christian Church and United Church of Christ

Q: When we talk about multilateralism, there is strong emphasis on interstate relations and the global governance architecture evolving around the United Nations, and the G20. How do you see the role of religious communities and civil society organizations in advancing global understanding on key challenges and trends affecting people and communities across the globe?

Peter Makari: From a U.S. church perspective, the historical engagement of mission boards starting in the nineteenth century has had a tremendous impact on Americans, and American churchgoers more specifically, as it has brought to them a wider perspective on the world and on faith traditions, beyond the usual media headlines. In addition, the rise of international institutions coincided with the advance of global ecumenism, for example, the establishment of the World Council of Churches, which was founded just three years after the United Nations, and so it can be said that these two paths mirror one another. Now, David Hollinger has put forward the thesis that Protestants abroad and the rise of the mission movement have led to the rise of advocacy for human rights and have changed U.S. foreign policy and social engagement itself. The relationship between the church and the state is both complementary and at odds, as churches have the obligation to lift up theological values, principles, and motives, instead of political and commercial interests and so the church can play a significant role in advocating for more human rights and human equality, for climate justice, and other aspects of peace and justice.

Q: Ethnic and religious conflicts are key sources of interstate wars, civil wars, terrorism, and the most serious human rights violations. How do you see the potentials and limitations of civil society organizations and religious communities in contributing to conflict resolution and peace settlements?

Peter Makari: There is no consensus among faith communities on war and peace, but the truth of the matter is that, while some religious institutions or leaders promote peace based on faith and conviction, others, including political leaders, appropriate religious ideas to justify conflict and oppression. What better example than that of the U.S., where white Christian nationalism emerged, as it justified historical oppression using theology. Now, of course, we are at a time of reckoning, where some want to keep holding on to their privileges, while others want to lift up principles of equality and justice for all. This is also the case globally, as oppression is justified through certain readings of scripture, while others seek to focus on the parts that can promote good values and change. And a last point to make is that the church may act in less visible but sometimes effective ways to promote conflict resolution, engaging with the grassroots, as well as advocacy with political leaders, to foster peace and justice.

Q: U.S. churches do have diverse views on the conflict in the Middle East, is that right?

Peter Makari: Diversity is the experience of America and that much is also true in our churches, where many people from different backgrounds come together, but there is an important distinction to be made. We need to distinguish between the ecumenical churches, or those which are committed to the unity of the Church and which are eager to engage with other churches, and in the case of Israel and Palestine, listen to the voices of Palestinian Christians and churches, and lifting up the values of human justice and dignity for all people; and many among the evangelical community, with a lowercase "e," that is, evangelical in the American sense (not the German "Evangelical" or traditional Protestant), conservatives, who interpret the scripture differently and support Israel regardless of any wrongdoings, based on a literal interpretation of scripture called Christian Zionism (or pre-millennial dispensationalism).

Q: The Israeli-Palestine conflict has claimed 14,000 lives since 1987 and is one of the most enduring conflicts in recent history. The conflict erupted again in May 2021. *The Economist* **(May 29, 2021) wrote "instead of imposing peace in one top-down stroke of diplomatic brilliance, a more realistic aim would be to build it patiently from the bottom up." What could be realistic options for a roadmap for conflict settlement from your perspective?**

Peter Makari: For many, the Israeli-Palestine conflict is a religious one, a conflict between Muslim and Jewish people, and as such, one that cannot be resolved, as the region will always feature different religions. The religious framing is a false framing. For one, it ignores the Christians living in the area, who have been there for over 2000 years, but just as importantly, it ignores the basic political/social/economic rights of the indigenous people on self-determination, land, access to resources, religious sites, the right to move, to return to places one has fled, and so forth. The conflict is often deliberately framed in exclusively religious terms in order to claim certain lands and expand control, while also garnering support, specifically from the U.S. evangelical community, whose reading of the bible is unequivocally supportive of Israel. At the same time, this interpretive lens tends to be antisemitic, as it theologically results in either the conversion of Jews to Christianity or their eternal damnation to hell. Of course, the church has a bottom-up approach in trying to educate its members as well as the broad public on these issues, but a top-down approach is also necessary, as the U.S. government must be held accountable for its unconditional support for Israel and injustices must be called out. Take the recent assault on Gaza as an example. When the U.S. supplies Israel with military aid

to purchase and develop weapons, some of which are built in the U.S., to destroy buildings and lives, and pledges funds to help in the reconstruction, that is simply hypocritical and counterproductive to a just and lasting peace.
Q: Is there any hope for a two-state solution anymore?
Peter Makari: There is a growing recognition that this is less and less possible, if not already impossible, due to Israel's insistence of expanding settlements, evicting people from their homes, and denying basic human rights, while also denying self-determination to the Palestinians. A solution, and part of what we and other churches are advocating for as well, is a rights-based approach and advocacy for justice, peace, and equal rights, and based on international law.

The future of multilateralism is certainly one of the most complex scenarios to analyze given the diversity and multitude of actors involved in shaping international cooperation. We have focused much on the U.S. and China, which we consider the key players in international relations in the next decade. Other regions and institutions, including the European Union, because of its complex power-sharing arrangements and internal struggles, will often remain reactive rather than proactive in world politics matters. France, however, has attempted to change this, especially under the leadership of Emmanuel Macron.

The U.S. will re-engage in foreign affairs and prioritize the Indo Pacific region, trying to forestall the influence of China and its winning of support across Europe and in Asia. It will be less engaged in other geographical areas, including the Middle East.

The EU will be preoccupied with its own ambitious policy agendas, especially with the Green Deal and with catching up on digitalization. Its influence on conflicts in other parts of the world will remain limited as its foreign and economic policy stance will remain unpredictable. Toward China, the EU's political rhetoric will tilt between systemic competition and engagement for the protection of the global commons, while it will prove very difficult to reduce economic dependency on China. Asian powers, especially

India, will exercise an autonomous and also pragmatic foreign policy. Russia will continue to remain a strong regional power. Its involvement in internal and regional conflicts will weaken its ability to strengthen economic development and influence global business trends. The G20 meetings will gain further profile and cooperative attitudes will prevail in promoting and implementing the UN 2030 Agenda for Sustainable Development while more disputes are expected in the field of climate action in the context of loss-and-damage claims by countries of the Global South.

Will we see tendencies toward an 'aristocratic world order' or a "feudal world order" with a few economies at the top level dominating global politics? The interplay of a few superstates in form of quasi-empires, substate entities and regions will require a multi-level and multilayered multilateralism which might be more pragmatic and more ad-hoc.[49] Such a multipolar world order would not necessarily make global politics more democratic, but it could at least add to balancing powers and enriching perspective in tackling future challenges.

Chapter 13

Civilizational Developments: Diversity, Individualization and Loneliness, Gender Shift, and Identity Politics

The term *civilizational development* encompasses emerging trends in the social and cultural spheres of life. We see different as well as diverging trends in the areas of civilizational development across the world. This makes it challenging to speak about megatrends in the field of social and cultural change. Both authors were born and currently live in Europe, but we have worked and traveled in many countries. We are mindful that social and cultural trends play out very differently across the world. Huntington's theory of "the clash of civilizations"[1] — though often criticized — remains a reference point in the analysis of assertions of social and cultural identities.

Changes in social life and cultural practices are subject to a wide array of research activities in social sciences and related academic disciplines. Several megatrends identified by the German Zukunftsinstitut (The Future Institute) relate to social aspects, such as individualization, gender shift, and silver society.[2] Other future research institutes have dwelled on civilizational trends, too. Attitudes on social and cultural issues impact strongly on political preferences of people and communities as well as on consumer behavior.

There is a lot of political and social science research on changing social and political attitudes and how they relate to voting preferences in elections at different levels. The Washington-based Pew Research Center is one of the leading think tanks that inform the public about the issues, attitudes, and trends shaping the world. It conducts public opinion polling, demographic research, content analysis, and other data-driven social science research on a large number of topics, including political, social, and religious attitudes.[3]

Marketing research on new consumer trends done by multiple consulting firms also provides insights into social megatrends.[4] New trends in product design, clothing, food, and the leisure and tourism sector are highly relevant for investors. Diversity management is a key term for human resource development managers of larger and smaller companies, especially multinational companies. Political regulations require boards of directors and top management to become more diverse, especially in terms of increasing the number of women in top positions. Diverse and inclusive workplaces are perceived to be more ethical and good for business. Investors are increasingly looking for companies which have good diversity and inclusion ratings.[5] Social movements advocate for power shifts and greater diversity in politics and business and make valuable contributions to international cooperation. The Berlin-based International Civil Society Center engages with futurists and forward thinkers to inform their member NGOs on advocacy opportunities and social campaign strategies to change the world for the better. Berthold Kuhn has highlighted the often privileged access of civil society organizations to marginalized communities and their contributions to inclusive development.[6]

After talking to several think tanks and experts, we have prioritized four aspects that will shape civilization developments in the next decade and thereafter: diversity, individualization, gender shift, and identity politics.

13.1 Diversity Trends

Increased diversity offers new opportunities and more freedoms for self-realization. This trend affects politics, polity, business, and many other spheres of life and is reported to enhance innovation potentials and creativity of societies. However, we also witness growing concerns — especially among people with little exposure to other cultures — that diversity undermines social cohesion and leads to more conflicts within societies. As such, populism is on the rise. However, we do not consider populism a global (counter-) trend by itself because its features are configurated by sentiments

Civilizational Developments

of specific local or national identities. Its rise has provoked powerful response strategies across the world, including in the United States, and has not resulted in slowing down multilateral trade and cultural diversity trends in any significant way.

The major diversity trends in affluent aging societies relate to growing cultural and religious diversity, individualization, gender shift, and identity politics. How are these intertwined trends connected to population development?

We shall put special emphasis on the impact of demography trends on diversity. While exploring the impact of changes in demography on social structures, it is worth noting that there are other factors, especially economic and political ones, which are influencing social change. Demography-related trends play out differently in countries of different geographical regions, different levels of economic development, and different political cultures and systems, and thus produce even more diversity between countries. However, demography trends do not impact societies in similar ways. Japan, though it is an old-aged society, has still not become an immigrant-friendly country despite the fact that it has relaxed some immigration rules in recent years. Entrants are temporary "guest workers" who will eventually return home. This applies to refugees, too.[7]

Theoretically, aging societies would depend more on migration from poorer countries to fill demand for low-paid jobs, including elderly care. This argument is forwarded by many experts, including Parag Khanna.[8] Migration leads to greater cultural and religious diversity of populations. Aging societies would also need to create a significant number of well-paid jobs to account for the growing number of retired people. Women spend less time on family care and become part of the work force, while claiming equal payment and other rights. In this way, demography trends influence gender equality discourses.

Countries in sub-Sahara Africa have the youngest populations and account for a high number of refugees, as employment opportunities are scarce. Aging societies should thus have an incentive to welcoming young migrants; however, we experience significant differences across countries and political systems.

The growing shortage of elderly care workers has been accelerated by the COVID-19 pandemic, which focused attention on the chronically understaffed hospitals and elderly care institutions in a dramatic way. A series of start-up and other initiatives have tried to mobilize migration of young health workers, but success remains limited due to political and legal restrictions as well as language challenges.

The COVID-19 pandemic has shed light on the vulnerability of societies with older populations. Elderly people are more vulnerable to diseases and death and require special measures of protection and care which produce huge economic costs for societies. Such situations bear a potential for growing conflicts between generations. For example, restrictions in times of pandemics are least popular with young people. They are less vulnerable but are governed by older people and they find themselves in a position, where they must make costly contributions, not only in terms of payments to pension funds, but also in terms of overall health costs.

In young societies, youths are considered particularly vulnerable due to limited employment opportunities and limited political participation, especially in economically less advanced countries governed by authoritarian leadership in a hierarchical fashion. The more authoritarian the leadership is, the more limited the turnover of leaders and the stronger the trend to exclude younger people from political participation. The same applies to women and minorities.

Economic development in advanced economies is fueled by technological innovations and growth of the service sector. We witness growing professionalization of services, especially related to elderly care and all kinds of customized services for affluent people.

We also see more diverse family and social structures in richer countries, especially in those with more open political systems. Higher levels of affluence increase freedom of choice, which in turn leads to more diversity, especially among young people. Diverging preferences, however, challenge social cohesion which in turn risks producing social and political conflicts.

How do high degrees of social freedom impact social cohesion? The impact is probably most significant when it comes to parenthood. Starting a family is no longer the main option available for young people in search of independence and identity building. In affluent societies, few young people opt for early parenthood and children. Their life will differ from those who focus on career development, indulging in hobbies or partying. As a result, traditional family models tend to become less popular in younger age groups, however, such change in preferences — opting for more individual lifestyles — tends to be limited to younger age groups who can afford to value independence more than social bonds. People living in a traditional family structure tend to have more children. We acknowledge that children remain deeply influenced by their parents. In this way, traditional family values will not disappear and may even surge in the context of growing anxieties due to economic insecurities, and fear of loneliness. COVID-19 restrictions have seen such feelings of anxieties rising among young people. Thus, it is difficult to identify overarching mid-term or long-term social trends. We observe that certain trends produce countertrends which, in turn, lead to greater diversity and lack of social cohesion.

We interviewed the founder and chief executive of Cultural Infusion, Greek-Australian Peter Mousaferiadis, and his Harvard-educated Spanish colleague Máximo Plo, who runs the operations of the organization in Europe. Cultural Infusion is Australia's leading culture-in-education provider and hosts the Diversity Atlas project, which provides a world-first definition and measurement of cultural diversity, along with the knowledge and insight necessary for inclusive strategies. Both are committed to change the narrative of diversity.

Global Perspectives on Megatrends

Interview with Peter Mousaferiadis and Máximo Plo, Cultural Infusion

Q: How do you see the relationship between demography and diversity? Are demography issues drivers for diversity? Which other drivers are important?
Peter Mousaferiadis: All societies undergo demographic changes. In Europe, our society is aging, and therefore we need migration to be sustainable. However, although migration is good from an economic point of view, it challenges the way of life of certain people. As demographic changes increase the diversity of our societies, we need to create spaces in which people can learn the identities of each other to facilitate social cohesion and the confluence of cultures, which has historically been a driver of progress.
Máximo Plo: To add to this, we need to keep in mind that diversity is inherently a negative thing, and it is only when we possess the knowledge of how to foster and manage it, that it can be said to be a net positive for our societies, which is precisely the goal we should be striving for. Simply put, demography, comprising two ancient Greek words means how we describe people. Diversity is central to demography and allows for us to understand the richness of our societies and the differences that make them up.
One of the reasons why the increase in diversity is challenging is because of the way that we teach history in schools. Each country fosters a sense of national identity, a *Volksgeist*, which can lead to unfortunate frictions between members of different cultural groups. The book *Confluences: Forgotten Histories From East And West* reminds us that all of our national cultures are the product of confluence with other cultures. We would do well to remind people about this to prepare them for ever more diverse societies.
Q: How do changes in demography, such as aging societies and migration, impact civilization developments and social structures?
Peter Mousaferiadis: As I said, we need plans to embrace and foster diversity or tensions will keep on growing. Interestingly enough, we can look at history for examples, like the Ottoman

Empire, which was a safe haven for many religious expressions, Jews, Christians and Muslims representing a range of denominations. Furthermore, fostering interaction between diverse groups also leads to innovation. Knowledge is a diversification of ideas.

Máximo Plo: There are also examples of successful intercultural management today, like Singapore, in which every neighborhood and every building is ensured to be intercultural and diverse. Bad examples of intercultural management have been social policies that have put minorities in ghettos, like France did with its *banlieues*, which have led to marginalization and radicalization.

Many societies are worried that demographic changes pose a threat to their identity, their "civilization". France tried to preserve its idea of "France" by identifying it with the concepts of *liberté, égalité et fraternité*. However, this homogeneity is a construct because French people experience those three words differently depending on their lived experience, which is defined by the intersection of their cultural and demographic attributes. After decades of forbidding measuring beliefs and cultural heritage, France is now debating whether they should measure diversity in institutions to spot gaps and foster participation of underprivileged groups.

Q: **How will diversity trends play out in different parts of the world? Which are the perceived benefits and challenges?**

Máximo Plo: For one, I can tell you that it is big in LinkedIn at the moment, as a simple search reveals hundreds of thousands of inclusion/diversity managers, a position which is becoming all the more common and integral to organizations across the world. On the other hand, there is a lot of confusion around specific identities and the terminology associated with them because of conflation. Globally, we are seeing the conflations of race and ethnicity and gender and biological sex, which are creating confusion and division. These are examples which need to be disaggregated so policies can be targeted to specific needs of people The current approach is perpetuating inequality and difference and having a disproportionate impact individuals as highlighted during the pandemic of COVID-19.

Peter Mousaferiadis: The main challenge is that our societies are not built around spaces that bring people together. We need to intentionally create these spaces to spark dialogue between people that are different. Otherwise, we are going to continue seeing an increase in polarization and lack of trust in our societies.

Q: Why is dialogue on diversity so important for peace and conflict resolution? How can cultural diversity in national and international policies foster social inclusion and equity?

Máximo Plo: There is some conflating of dialogue and debate, especially during COVID times, where an attitude of "our way versus theirs" has prevailed. Language very much defines the reality we live in. Harsh language has simply not helped our cause. Dialogue means sensitive, underpinned by compassion, understanding the other, embracing one another and meeting them in the middle rather than language that alienates and instills fear in the other.

Peter Mousaferiadis: There is extensive literature about the benefits of positive intergroup contact. If you were to ask people what they think of, say, Muslims, they might hold negative attitudes, while at the same time acknowledging that the one Muslim person, they know is wonderful. Dialogue and positive intergroup interaction is the path to peace and social cohesion. To achieve a socially inclusive and equitable world we also need to ensure that everyone has a real chance to participate in political, social, and economic institutions. The only way to evaluate how representative are these institutions of the different cultural and demographic groups in society is through diversity measurement, which is what we do with Diversity Atlas.

Q: What is your attitude on quota systems as means to promote diversity?

Peter Mousaferiadis: Quota systems in particular are generally good; however, we need to be mindful of unintended consequences. In the UAE and Qatar, quota systems for gender parity have led to a surge in depressions and suicides by men. These unintended consequences are not isolated to the Gulf. In places like Sweden, encouraging women to strive for medical positions has meant that there won't be any male doctors left in the next 15 years.

At the same time, diverse groups have often been found to bring about better outcomes than ones composed of experts, so there are clear benefits, if done well.

13.2 Individualization and Loneliness

Individualization is a result of the growing diversification of society and the accentuation of diverging interests. The trend of individualization relates to the disengagement of the individual with family life and community life. However, complete disengagement of individuals from social groups seems to contradict human nature. Individualization is a key characteristic of affluent societies though there are still enormous differences between different countries and cultures. Many old people are looked after in professional institutions. The younger generation, men and women, are busy involved in earning high incomes and transfer parts of their income to increasingly complex social welfare schemes and pension funds. In affluent societies, elderly people are financially more independent but less integrated into family structures. Career development in competitive professional settings requires a strong commitment of time and energy of the working population. Mobility also increases in a more specialized job market with higher incomes which affects care for older family members but also relationships between younger people.

The number of marriages is declining in many countries. People tend to marry later. The trend, however, greatly varies across countries. In some countries — for instance, in Germany — it tends to lose momentum. We also witness a trend of "decoupling" of parenthood and marriage in many industrialized countries.

Figure 13.1: Number of Marriages in Each Year per 1,000 People in the Population

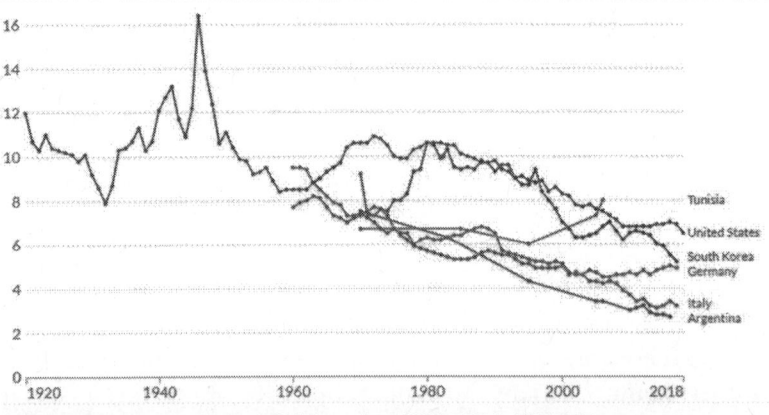

Source: Our World in Data (2022) based on OVID, UN; OECD, Eurostat.⁹

We also see a growing number of distance relationships among young people. When young people—or those who feel young—meet a person living at another place, they tend to see the advantages first. They are thrilled to engage in new discoveries and enjoy traveling to other cities or countries in to meet their beloved partner. Once they envisage spending more time together, starting a family, and having children, they realize the challenges and disadvantages of living at two different places which involves higher costs and more time on the rail, road, or plane. Given the difficulties of finding accommodation in global cities, moving together presents big obstacles.

High mobility, mostly related to distant workplaces, has a significant impact individualization. We see career-oriented double income no-children couples (DINCS) who have two apartments in different cities or countries and regularly commute to see each other. Parents engage in regular traveling to different places, even countries, to see their children after separation. Divorce rates have increased in all societies on their way to more affluence, reaching up to 50 percent in some countries.

There is also a growing number of people who have been living outside any family structures for many years and have few contacts with their family members. This tends to erode family values over time though not everybody might be conscious of it. People accommodate themselves to the situation, practically and spiritually, and find it more difficult to integrate into family structures once they have lived by themselves for many years. More and more people look for alternative arrangements and share flats or houses with like-minded people. The turnover in co-shared places is often high, especially among younger people in big cities who move from one place to the other for their studies or early career development.

The easy and quick access to digital platforms creates the illusion that it is easy to make new social contacts at any time, to find roommates, sex partners, or soulmates in the universe of the internet. Especially young people are thrilled by the quick access and the great number of potential contacts within quick reach. However, building relationships and trust takes time. This is obviously in contrast to the business models and cultural practices dominating the platform economy. Platforms facilitate a high frequency of changing social contacts.

Looking at the current business models of companies like YouTube, TikTok, the Meta platforms, and especially dating apps, there is a fundamental tension between short, cheap, and instantaneous gratification and the everyday experience of human relationships, which take time and effort to develop and sustain.

An unintended consequence for many users, unconsciously perhaps, is that they are getting used to it and may find it gradually more difficult to find a partner to live with, settle down with, and invest in the relationship with, even though this might have been their initial motivation to join the platform.

Driven by their own dreams and ambitions, as well as the given beauty and personality standards of the time, people can spend enormous time and energy to increase their market value on dating platforms. Their profiles may not match with reality. People cover up their disadvantages. This can lead to large-scale user disappointment when they meet their contacts face-to-face. All these factors contribute to discontent and disengagements at different levels and, ultimately, to loneliness.

Awareness of the negative impact of individualization, especially loneliness, has risen first among elderly people. Aging in diverse affluent societies has become a lonely affair. There are government loneliness strategies in England, Scotland, Wales, and many other countries. The United Kingdom appointed a Minister of Loneliness, an appointment born from a 2017 report that said nine million of the country's 67 million people feel lonely some or all of the time. The German Federal Ministry for Family Affairs, Senior Citizens, Women and Youth supports 29 model projects that address loneliness.[10]

The situation in other affluent societies is similar and has much aggravated in the context of COVID-19 restrictions. Individualization creates an array of problems and explains some forms of identity politics, including identity affirmations resulting in exacerbated nationalism, a proposition shared by other contributors to the loneliness debate, such as Jessica von der Schalk who works for the Amsterdam based think tank FreedomLab. "Although many new initiatives help to strengthen the position of the individual and hence his autonomy and personal freedom, it is questionable whether people are able to live with their "fear of freedom" (a term coined by Erich Fromm). Especially in our times of crumbling communities, accelerating social life and the loosening grip of tradition, the rapid process of individualization also creates new problems (for example, new forms of loneliness or, paradoxically, new forms of nationalism).[11]

With regard to politics and social activism, we observe a tendency to overcharge individuals and to very critically evaluate individual action. For those receptive and sensitive to such evaluations, this will lead to frustration, in extreme cases to depression. Mark Kaufmann, a science reporter at Mashable, takes a more offensive approach in his article on the "the carbon footprint sham".[12] He argues — with reference to communications of British Petroleum (BP) and other companies — that company and media attention on carbon-footprint calculations for individuals aims to divert the attention away from big industrial polluters and much-needed political action for structural changes toward low-carbon infrastructure and development.

13.3 Gender Shift

The number of well-educated women joining the workforce has significantly increased. However, the rise of women is unevenly spread across sectors and occupations. The International Labor Organization (ILO) compiled information from countries across the world and concluded in a frequently referenced analysis that women are most likely to hold managerial positions in human resources, administration, finance, marketing, or public relations — areas the organization defines as business support functions.[13]

In liberal democracies, women exercise power through their votes. All major political parties face pressure to increase the number of women in leadership positions and in their party ranks. Governments across the world have put gender issues on their agenda, focusing, for example, on persistent gender pay gaps. The gender trend has provoked some critical reactions, especially if promoted by Government-led affirmative action policies. Gender mainstreaming policies are widely adopted in Western Europe and North America. However, many conservatives regard it as an attack on traditional family models. People and communities who put emphasis on traditional family values stress that many women rejoice doing care work in family structure when their role is valued by society. Liberals have pointed out that state bureaucracies should promote equal opportunities but not get involved in the repartition of work through quota regulations. In countries with advanced gender equality in professional life, gender equality in childcare has sometimes not progressed with the same pace. Fathers still take less paternity leave. Unmarried fathers point to persistent legal and also practical gender inequalities.

Gender roles are deeply rooted in most societies and linked to family values. The question to what extent gender roles are linked to biological differences is subject to controversial debates. Many affluent countries apply quota systems to reach gender equality.

Young men realize that women applicants are given priority by some employers until quota requirements are met, especially in the public sector. We observe a gradual change in the division of family work and education of children. Men spend less time than women with children but much more time than their fathers did in raising children. The assimilation of gender roles sparks new developments. Men are now also required to balance the responsibilities of work and family.

One important reference framework for measuring gender equality is the Gender Equality Index of EIGE.[14] Since 2013, the Gender Equality Index has been recognized by EU institutions and Member States as a key benchmark for gender equality in the EU. The 2021 report though partly based on 2019 data still provides ample evidence of the pandemic's negative repercussions on women in the domains of work, money, knowledge, time, power, and health.[15]

The Gender Equality Index score for the EU is 68.0 points out of 100. It is an improvement of 0.6 points compared to the 2020 edition and of 4.9 points in total since 2010. The summary reads that "...even that minimal progress on gender equality is threatened by the impact of the COVID-19 pandemic." According to the report, "overall progress in gender equality between 2010 and 2019 was largely driven by advances in the domain of power, in particular improved gender balance on company boards and in politics".[16]

Civilizational Developments

Figure 13.2: Gender Equality Index 2021

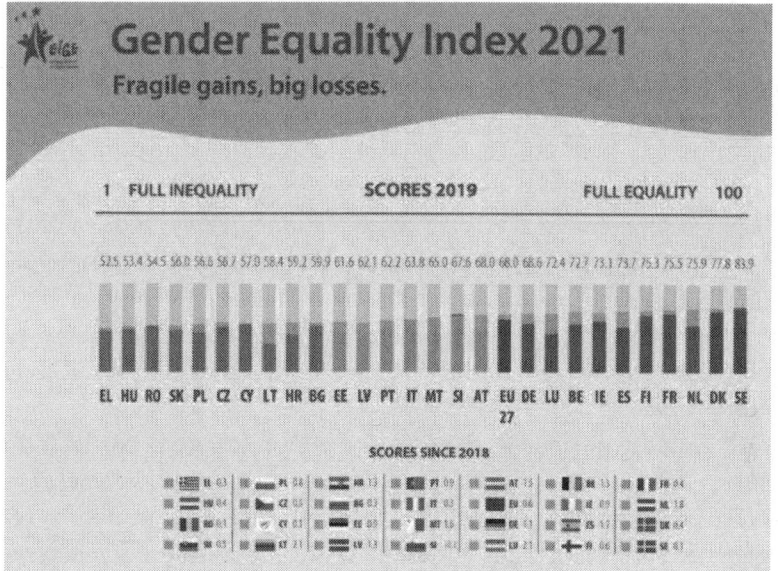

Source: EQUALA-EU.org (2021) partly based on EIGE data.[17]

We also witness that some societies are increasingly moving past gendered identities and toward a post-binary understanding of gender.[18] A third gender, described as "diverse", was created for civil status purposes in Germany in December 2018. The United States (U.S.) printed a passport that has a third option of gender identity in October 2021. Post-binary definitions of gender still face opposition in many societies, especially when it comes to the education of children or transgender medicine. In the U.S., transgender medicine gets entangled in cultural conflicts. More and more doctors are offering puberty blockers and cross-sex hormones to children. More than sixteen states have introduced legislation to ban the prescription of such drugs to people below 18 years.[19]

On a global scale, a large majority of the world's population wants children to have a female mother and a male father. China and India, by far the most populous countries in the world, are considered to uphold traditional family values though they play out differently in each country. In China, we see a strong focus on nuclear families. In India, extended family concepts are still popular. Most marriages are officially arranged by parents. This is accepted by most young people.

Today, women empowerment and gender equality are goals that are pursued at the highest level of global political action. They are promoted by international and supranational institutions as well as national and subnational governments. The third Sustainable Development Goal of the United Nations 2030 Agenda for Sustainable Development focuses on gender equality. A gender-sensitive perspective is increasingly being included in climate-related environmental and development projects across the world. More and more gender analyses are being conducted as part of projects and programs.

In affluent open societies, we continue to see a particularly strong movement on gender equality and diversity. Women are making enormous progress in education, including in poorer regions of the world. Signs bode well that gender inequality is in retreat in most parts of the world. However, strategies to achieve this goal greatly vary between countries and institutions.

The Zukunftsinstitut (The Future Institute), founded by Matthias Horx, is Germany's leading think tank on future research. We interviewed the Institute's Lena Papasabbas on the gender shift trend, which is one of the top trends identified by the Institute.

Interview with Lena Papasabbas, Zukunftsinstitut (The Future Institute, Germany)

Q: What are some of the key characteristics of Gender Shift?
Lena Papasabbas: Gender Shift is one of the biggest and most relevant changes happening in the world right now — it's also one of the most underestimated ones. We define the Gender Shift as a megatrend. Megatrends are interconnected and as such, its drivers are other trends like Individualism, Connectivity or New Work. It is characterized by a pluralistic model of society, whereby individuals have a singular pluralistic concept of the self, distancing themselves

from traditional roles, values and images connected to the binary and heteronormative idea of gender.

Q: Would you say that Gender Shift is a sub-trend, then?

Lena Papasabbas: No, it's a megatrend itself, as it has its own logic and dynamics — and such a huge influence on a wide scope of issues in society and the way that it is structured, like on topics such as consumption, work, family, identity, even the way we are building our cities, and so forth. We are seeing this binary thinking slowly dissolving. This affects all parts of society: politics, economics, and everyday culture.

Q: Can you talk a bit about Gender Identity?

Lena Papasabbas: Gender Identity specifically influences how people live, consume, look like, behave, and so forth. The concept of gender greatly influences our choices in partners, jobs, goods we consume, foods we eat, clothes we wear and so forth. Especially younger people seem much freer from narrowing ideas of femininity and masculinity. They think about themselves in a post Gender Identity world. It starts with seemingly unimportant aspects like claiming clothes, haircuts or items of pop culture from "the other side".

But these surface phenomena are just the tip of the iceberg of dissolving the many determinations and inequalities concerning the traditional gender roles. For example, people begin to look into careers that were not traditionally "meant" for them. Motherhood and fatherhood are being redefined. New relationship models are being tested. Activism against all kinds of discrimination from "gender pay gap" to "orgasm gap" are rising everywhere.

Q: Does this all apply globally? Say, for example, does one observe these fluid genders in more traditional societies like India or China, and is there strong opposition?

Lena Papasabbas: The West is not necessarily the most progressive part of the world concerning this topic. Take Rwanda's government, for example. Or the strong Me Too Movement in India. Or if you look at platforms that younger people use, like TikTok, you will find a lot of very progressive feminist subcultures, often represented by male users from African countries. In Germany for example male feminists are harder to find.

But: Every strong trend creates counter currents, in the West as well, so there is a lot of conflict and friction and countertrends, but to futurists this is a sign of change underway since there will always be unease to such a radical change.

Q: How will Gender Shift affect the raising of children?

Lena Papasabbas: There are some obvious differences, like the fact that children will have a wider range of choices to pick from for their private and professional life. We will also see the traditional family structure change, with children not necessarily being raised by a man and a woman living together in one household. Families are already diversifying into different shapes, like patchwork models, same sex couples, polyamorous constellations, living with peers instead of relatives, Co-Living projects including three generations and many more.

Q: How do you see the connection of Gender Shift and the economy?

Lena Papasabbas: There have been a lot of studies, which show that companies, organizations, and so forth with diversity in their board of directors are more resilient, competitive, and profitable, so the pursuit of diversity and gender equality is driven more and more by economic motivations as well. The pandemic also showed that countries led by men, representing the typical conservative concept of masculinity, like Trump, Orbán, or Bolsonaro, do seem to be much less resilient in the case of crisis.

If you want to look at countries as a unit, the most progressive and resilient countries seem also to be the ones that exhibit the most Gender Shift.

Q: How has COVID-19 impacted Gender Shift?

Lena Papasabbas: There are multiple impacts of COVID-19, not all of them are yet perceptible or even studied. There seems to be quite a backlash concerning the question of domestic work versus paid work, financial discrimination against women, and also the sad topic of domestic violence. But then, also a lot of positive cultural change has happened during the pandemic. Female leadership has proven itself to be capable in volatile times. The image of the female leader has been loaded with new power and trust, not just in Germany. The value of traditionally female jobs, like nursing and medical care, has increased in the times of the lockdowns. Applauding the nurses and cleaners going to work every day from our balconies, while being at home all day, made many of us realize how extremely important (and underpaid) care work is for the functioning of society. Also: many men suddenly found themselves working in the home office, having their kids around all day, while trying to work. These kinds of experiences change the way people see unpaid work and the effort and energy it demands — work which is traditionally assigned to women.

13.4 Identity Politics

Identity politics are on the surge. Identity politics play out very differently across the world. India — soon to be the most populous country in the world — is a place where society is particularly shaped by identity politics, primarily based on caste but also on religion and class, as it has been for many centuries. One among many striking examples of identity politics in India is the Dravidian movement in the Southern Indian state of Tamil Nadu inspired by the thoughts and actions of Erode Venkata Ramasami Naicker, called Periyar. Nobel Prize Winner V.S. Naipaul has written an insightful chapter on the conflict between Brahmins and anti-Brahmin communities in the chapter "Little Wars" in his global bestselling book *India. A Million Mutinies*.[20] The chapter describes the lifestyle of a traditional Brahmin man who indulges in spiritual simplicity. By remaining faithful to traditional Brahmin practices, he distances himself — unintentionally — from social and community life. Naipaul illustrates that co-existence of diverse communities is at stake in a politically charged environment shaped by the Dravidian movement in Tamil Nadu.

For many people in Western countries, especially the younger generations, it is evident that identity politics have empowered vulnerable groups in several countries and led to legislative changes, especially for people belonging to the LGBTQ+ community, an abbreviation for lesbian, gay, bisexual, transgender, and queer (or questioning), plus other sexual and gender identities. Identity politics have mobilized a new generation of activists who have challenged institutional policies and structures. Identity politics have also legitimated the presence of dissident subcultures.[21] However, identity politics of underprivileged groups have also backfired on some communities. In most countries homophobia and anti-feminism have not disappeared. Identity politics and the struggle for recognition will continue to shape political debates, especially in liberal democracies.

Francis Fukuyama wrote one of the most widely quoted books on identity, carrying the subtitle "Contemporary identity politics and the struggle for recognition".[22] He discusses identity politics in the context of the democratization of dignity and observes that "dignity has been democratized as political systems have progressively granted rights to wider and wider circles of individuals."[23]

Many social activists, including some feminists, point to the achievements of assertive identity politics. They would argue that progress in protection of rights of minorities was only possible through articulation of collective interests and formation of pressure groups. They tend to look at identity politics as a process of exploring and promoting communalities with a purpose to empower members of social groups. However, there are also critical feminist voices. Joan D. Mandle, Professor at Colgate University, writes: "the hegemony of identity politics within feminism, in my view, has helped to stymie the growth of a large-scale feminist movement which could effectively challenge sexism and create the possibility of justice and fairness in our society.... identity politics makes the coalitions needed to build a mass movement for social change extremely difficult. With its emphasis on internal group solidarity and personal self-esteem, identity politics divides potential allies from one another."[24]

The trend of individualization appears to contradict the trend of identity politics. However, we observe that they are reinforcing each other. Human beings are a social species that relies on

Civilizational Developments

cooperation to survive and thrive, and cooperation lies at the heart of human lives and society. People look for acceptance and recognition. Individualization sharpens identities but does not remove the desire of people to relate to each other. Social media make it easy to identify and connect to like-minded people. Thousands of small diverse sub-groups emerged in social media, including some promoting distinct cultural or political identities.

We see a growing amount of critical analysis of identity politics that points to its divisive impact on community life and political culture. Identity politics would, in this reading, divide society into communities with diverging values and in distinct political classes and declare them to be antagonistic to each other's interests: blacks against whites, women against men, gays against heterosexuals. Amy Chua, the author of *Tiger Mom*, is one of the proponents of the argument that "America's identity politics went from inclusion to division". "Whites and blacks, Latinos and Asians, men and women, Christians, Jews, and Muslims, straight people and gay people, liberals and conservatives—all feel their groups are being attacked, bullied, persecuted, discriminated against." She points out that leading liberal philosophical movements in American history were group-blind and universalist in character. The dominant voices were expressly group-transcending, framed in the language of national unity and equal opportunity. According to Chua, this has changed. She observes "a shift in tone, rhetoric, and logic...toward exclusion and division. She concludes that "once identity politics gains momentum, it inevitably subdivides, giving rise to ever-proliferating group identities demanding recognition."[25]

The Somalian-Dutch-American intellectual Ayaan Hirsi Ali shares such critical analysis of identity politics in an interview with the *Neue Zürcher Zeitung* (*NZZ*). She points to the emergence of a kind of an aggressive new age movement which would view Western societies only through the lens of capitalist and colonialist exploitation and moved away from principles of enlightenment, the European intellectual movement of the 17th and 18th centuries that emphasized the use of reason to advance understanding.[26] Sahra Wagenknecht, the longtime chairwoman of the socialist Left Party in Germany regards identity politics in her widely referenced but also often criticized book *Die Selbstgerechten* (The Self-Righteous) as an ultimately divisive, anti-egalitarian and anti-enlightenment "elitist tribal thinking" in a context where minority and victim groups claim privileges and funding support.[27] The book has contributed to her declining popularity within the Left Party in Germany which has been shaken by diverse political and social attitudes in recent years and scored poorly in the 2021 general elections.

Identity politics draw on distinct cultural roots or lifestyles as defining features of solidarity and political action. "Culture is the new currency of power" is the thesis of Christopher Coker, which he puts forward in his book *The Civilizational State*.[28] We have introduced his work in the chapter on multipolar world order and the future of multilateralism. He argues that instead of political ideologies, cultural identities would now be in the focus of disputes. The rise of the concept of the civilizational state, however, is another proof of the resurgence of cultural affirmations and identity politics in an increasingly diverse world. We would like to draw attention to the danger of simplistic projections and claims related to identity and the instrumentalization of identity struggles by political leaders. In a complex world, many people are proud of their multiple identities, in professional and social life. In times of crisis and suppression, however, people tend to join simplistic identity movements in their struggle to (re)gain dignity and social protection by peers.

Chapter 14

Migration

Migrant and *migration* are umbrella terms that are not ultimately defined under international law. Migrants are persons who have moved away from their place of usual residence, whether within a country or across an international border, temporarily or permanently, and for a variety of reasons. The term *migration* includes different legal categories.[1] In political debates, distinctions are typically made between people who are solely or primarily motivated by economic opportunities and those who are seeking international protection.

In his recently published book *Move*, Parag Khanna presented a bold analysis on the future of migration. He argued that humanity will (have to) redistribute itself on Planet Earth in the next few decades. COVID-19 will not halt the long-term trend of migration. Due to climate change, many areas on Planet Earth will become almost uninhabitable. Demographic imbalances and shifting job opportunities will also influence migration trends.[2]

The migration trend meets all criteria of the Pentagon Model. Migration is extensively researched. The International Organization for Migration (IOM) has a Migration Research Division which guides and informs migration policy and practice. The Migration Research Hub, a platform by a network of 45 migration studies institutes and scholars, supports the systematic accumulation of knowledge in migration studies. It aims to be the go-to resource for finding knowledge on migration, from the latest literature to the most appropriate topical experts.[3] There are several academic journals focusing on migration, including the *Nordic Journal of Migration Research*, that publish theoretical and empirical analyses of migratory processes.

Migration has also received highest level political attention. In Europe, the major migration influx which was related to the prolonged war in Syria and other conflicts made headlines in 2015 and

2016. In summer and fall 2021, Europe witnessed another migrant crisis on the border between Belarus and Poland. Belarus was accused by Poland and the European Union of pushing migrants toward its borders to undermine security in response to sanctions imposed by the EU. The controversial debates on migration will continue. The renowned migration expert Professor Naika Foroutan of Humboldt University Berlin pointed to the huge opportunities of the migration influx for Germany. Germany could assume a new role as global leader in migration policies if it makes good use of the motivation of incoming refugees to make meaningful contributions to economic and social life in their host country.[4]

The International Business Forum stresses that migration, if well managed, can fill labor shortages in critical industries and offer benefits to employees, employers, and professions.[5] The race for talent attractiveness has fueled the migration of highly qualified professionals. For instance, a study by Remco Zweetslot of the Think Tank Center for Strategic International Studies points out that the United States could risk losing the "tech-talent competition" due to restrictive migration policies: "Talent is critical to innovation, and America's deep pool of skilled scientists and engineers is a key component of its technological primacy. But today, for the first time in decades, U.S. leadership is under serious threat."[6]

Migration is receiving wide media-coverage which contributed to spark populist sentiments against refugees. However, it has also encouraged many welcome initiatives. For example, on June 20, 2020, World Refugee Day, major sea rescue and civil society organizations involved in promoting health care and human rights for migrants launched the campaign "From the Sea to the City", which brings together mayors, city representatives, civil society initiatives, social movements, unions, organizations, and institutions from all over Europe to support migrants. Thus, migration meets all the criteria of the Pentagon Model for a global megatrend.

14.1 Rising Numbers of Migrants

Experts usually distinguish between push and pull factors for migration. Push factors typically include persecution (religious, political, persecution based on gender), poverty, hunger, environmental disasters, and climate change. Pull factors typically include labor demand (recruitment), higher wages, better business opportunities, family reunion, liberal immigration, and visa regimes.[7]

The International Organization for Migration (IOM) publishes a series of migration data. It also provides services and support to governments and migrants across the world. The latest available IOM data (2020) refers to 258 million international migrants, defined by people residing in a country other than their country of birth. This represented 3.4 percent of the world's total population.[8]

According to the United Nations High Commissioner for Refugees the number of forcibly displaced persons amounted to 79.5 million people in 2019. Many people have fled to other countries because of violence or natural disasters. Many more are on the run within their own country. According to the Global Report on Internal Displacement 2021, published by the Internal Displacement Monitoring Centre (IDMC), there are 55 million people living in internal displacement as of the end of 2020.[9] In 2019, 1.5 billion people crossed borders — a historic high — and 270 million people were considered to be living abroad. COVID-19 restrictions led to a serious decline, but the effect will remain temporary, according to Parag Khanna, the author of *Move*.

There are numerous push and pull factors influencing actual migration and immigration figures which are hard to predict. We believe that some of the factors working in favor of migration — such as demographic changes, climate change, and shortages of labor — tend to be underestimated, but we also admit that political regimes and their policies toward migration also matter. The Trump presidency, for example, cut legal immigration significantly.[10]

Global Perspectives on Megatrends

Figure 14.1: Total Number of International Migrants at Mid-Year 2020

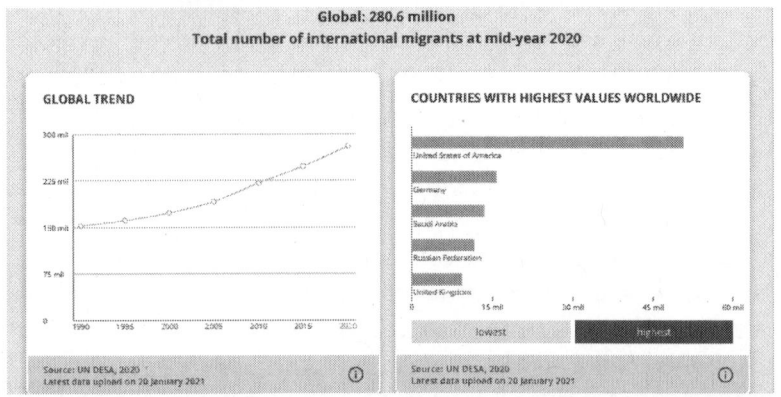

Source: UN DESA (2021)

Figure 14.2: Origins and Destinations of International Migrants in 2019 (in percent)

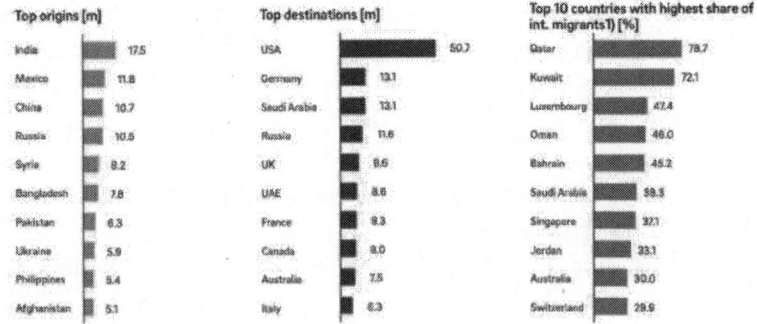

Sources: UN Population Division, IOM, Roland Berger (2021)

As shown by the graphs above, the number of international migrants has steadily increased in most parts of the world, reaching more than 280 million in the year 2020. The United States, Germany, and Saudi Arabia top the list of international migrants's destinations.[11]

14.2 Migration as Subject of Political Controversies

Migration has become a sensitive political issue in many countries and regions. It is intertwined with human rights, development, and geopolitical issues at different levels and, thus, subject to major political controversies. The arrival of large numbers of refugees fleeing war and terrorism in Syria, Afghanistan, and Iraq on Europe's shores in 2015 sparked huge political debates, solidarity actions, and protest movements. A Special Eurobarometer on "Integration of immigrants in the European Union" presented findings that 38 percent of Europeans think that immigration from outside the EU is more of a problem than an opportunity". However, the number varies across European countries. In Hungary, the percentage was the highest (63 percent) and in Sweden the lowest (19 percent) of all EU member states.[12]

The EU's relations with Turkey are subject to continuous quarreling on migration issues, despite the significant financial and humanitarian support the EU provides to Turkey for managing the settlement of refugees outside the borders of EU member states. Close to four million refugees have entered Turkey since the beginning of the civil war in Syria in 2011. This strong refugee presence has resulted in heightened social tensions in Turkey. Turkey's President Erdoğan repeatedly threatened that Turkey would "open the gates" and let the refugees enter the EU. On 28 February 2020, Turkey opened its borders with Greece and, from the perspective of the EU, was "setting the scene for a new refugee crisis."[13]

Funding support to migrants seeking international protection has increased. However, UNHCR is still chronically short of financial resources to manage crisis situations. It relies on voluntary contributions from governments, UN and pooled funding mechanisms, intergovernmental institutions, and the private sector.

In Germany, where the former chancellor Angela Merkel made a bold statement ("Yes, we can do it"), we have witnessed parallel developments of support and resistance. Many German citizens welcomed refugees and started all kinds of initiatives to assist them. In the central Schöneberg district in the city of Berlin,

Berthold Kuhn was involved in starting the nonprofit organization Schöneberg Hilft! This initiative provides practical support to refugees but also engages with the local administration and city government in talks about meaningful policies and measures to promote the integration of new arrivals. At the same time, anti-refugee sentiments have significantly increased in Germany. The nationalist political party Alternative for Germany (AFD) was able to establish itself in the German Parliament and in most parliaments in the states on the basis of their radical rhetoric against migrants, especially against refugees from Muslim countries.

14.3 The Future of Migration and Migration Management

There are two global compacts focusing on migration which were both prepared under the auspices of the United Nations: The Global Compact for Migration and the Global Compact on Refugees. The Global Compact for Migration (UN Resolution of January 11, 2019) is the more comprehensive document of the two, covering all dimensions of international migration. It is a "non-binding document that respects states' sovereign right to determine who enters and stays in their territory and demonstrates commitment to international cooperation on migration."[14] It comprises ten guiding principles, 23 main objectives, and a series of recommended actions for better managing migration at local, national, regional, and global levels, including collecting regular data, minimizing adverse drivers, and coordinating border management.[15] Targets and indicators related to migration are covered by SDG 10 (Reduced Inequalities) of the United Nations 2030 Agenda for Sustainable Development, especially indicator 10.7.2.

Migration remains a strong trend, though one that is hard to predict. Following Parag Khanna's arguments, people's desire to move to places that are safer than their own home and offer better income opportunities will always persist and even increase. Many governments support this trend by facilitating migration through the issuance of visas, specially targeted at those who fill labor shortage gaps and are willing to invest or pay considerable amounts of taxes in return for expected benefits for themselves in term of good education or medical infrastructure. Therefore, demographic trends, especially aging societies, put pressure on states to liberalize immigration regimes while nationalist sentiments often pull in the other direction.

Wars, political conflicts, and natural disasters will always lead to mass migration from dangerous places. Climate change is likely to accelerate this migration trend as livelihoods become threatened in more parts of the world. Parag Khanna estimated that per degree of temperature rise, we shall see about a billion people migrating to safer climate zones in the long run: we could see four billion people on the move.[16] However, such predictions are difficult to make. Immigration regimes of states will remain an important factor for the development of migration trends, as Prof. Theo Rauch, a Berlin-based development cooperation and migration expert, points out.[17]

Moreover, Khanna points to the "ultimate irony of Europe". Historically, it greatly benefited from migration. Now, it needs migration more than ever before because Europe, as a climate resilient region, has a shrinking population. His analysis of Europe's climate resilience may be too general or too simple, but we agree with him that Europe's problem is not migration but assimilation. He forecasts that in the decade ahead, the number of young and skilled "Asian-Europeans" may balloon as South Asians and East Asians augment and even substitute for the existing diasporas of Arabs and Africans.[18]

There is another dimension to the irony of the EU's response to foreigners, found in its response to refugee crises. In the wake of the Russian invasion of Ukraine in early 2022, the EU seemingly ignored any past established practices and opened its borders almost indiscriminately to all Ukrainian refugees (reports of racism at the border were rampant at the time). Pundits from both the US and Europe were explaining how this is only natural, as Ukrainians are "white" believing in the same religion as them, highlighting the hypocrisy at the heart of this tragedy. The language used is enlightening, as Europeans tend to view immigrants and refugees as two separate groups,[19] while the framing of the crisis as a "Ukrainian refugee crisis" in contrast to the 2015 "European migrant crisis", saw the people of Europe unequivocally support the influx of refugees.

Regarding refugees, many migration activists but also renowned researchers such as Klaus Bachmann, Professor at the SWPS University in Warsaw, agree that deterrents will not be very effective, especially if political debates continue to paralyze the harmonization of refugee and immigration policies and practices. Migrants and human traffickers will take more risks and find new routes. Many borders, especially island borders in Greece and Croatia, could not be protected.[20] A few days after Bachmann critically analyzed the effectiveness of migration policies in Europe, at least 27 migrants died while trying to cross the English Channel from France to Britain end of November 2021. Tragedies such as those experienced in the Mediterranean Sea and the English Channel will continue to claim lives until root causes of migration are more adequately analyzed and addressed and opportunities and limitations much better communicated to potential migrants. Family reunions and job opportunities play a critical role in understanding migration motives. Roberto Suro, Professor for Public Policy at the University of Southern California and Fellow of the American Academy in Berlin, explains that effective deterrence would require well-informed migrants who act in a rational way, which is not the case due to urgent threats or necessities of survival.[21]

In China, inward migration is unlikely to rise even though the country faces serious demographic challenges. Border control, visa policies, and immigration policies have become even more restrictive in the context of post-Covid worries. China recorded a very low number of foreigners in the latest census report published in 2021. The report counted 845,697 foreigners in the whole country. This equals only 0.06 percent of the population. With its proportion of foreigners, the supposedly globalized People's Republic of China ranks lowest of almost all other major nations in terms of inward migration.[22]

Migration

COVID-19 reduced migration. However, there are signs that many states already prepare for the future battle for talents. The number of countries granting digital nomad visas has significantly increased.

We talked with Prof. Anna Triandafyllidou from Ryerson University, Canada, on migration trends and factors influencing it.

Interview with Anna Triandafyllidou, Professor, Canada Excellence Research Chair on Migration and Integration at Ryerson University

Q: How do you expect migration trends to evolve? Will there be differences between regions?
Anna Triandafyllidou: For one, there is a pre-and-post pandemic world in migration. Since 2007 there has been an emerging global governance regime which is however nonbinding. There has been new impetus since the 2015 refugee emergency across the Mediterranean and in the EU, or the one Rohingya people experienced, as well as the one in Venezuela. The EU countries began to be more involved, and the realization that these are global issues led to the elaboration and signature of the Global Compact for Migration in 2018.

The overall international migration numbers are, in fact, quite stable, and we have seen a modest rise of 0.8 percent since 1990–2000, during which time, 2.7 percent of people were foreign born, now up to 3.5 percent. The question is if the trends we were observing will continue after the pandemic, given the halt in global mobility that the pandemic has caused.

The motivations to migrate remain though strong (for instance, Venezuelans having to leave and seek protection and a better life in Colombia or Peru, or highly skilled Indian workers coming to Canada). Something that might change is the idea that temporary or circular migration schemes are sustainable; for example, see the breakdown of the food processing system during the pandemic when migrant workers could not come to harvest or work in farms and food processing plans. See also the emergency repatriation of Filipino or Indian workers from the UAE or Singapore and the gaps

that have remained in these countries as the industries pick up again (construction, tourism, and also domestic/care work). So, the question is, can your economy be based on temporary migration?
Another issue is that the global race for talent is still happening, while China and India are implementing policies to attract these talents. And of course, one part that is not talked about enough is South-South migration. In West Africa for instance, 80 percent of migration takes place within the region, as the borders are more permeable, but the EU is trying to change this, as part of its strategy of externalizing border control. Weaker countries may agree to it but larger countries where regional trade and regional migration is important, like Nigeria for instance, may not agree because the hardening of borders has important negative side effects for regional economies.

Q: What will be the impact of environmental disaster and climate change on migration?

Anna Triandafyllidou: There are both direct and indirect ways that have to do with disaster events or slow environmental change. For example, floods in Bangladesh or drought in Africa affect regional movements, but it is not quite clear how these changes relate to each other. There are people leaving the countryside in Morocco because of drought, going to urban centers and then migrating internationally to, say, Belgium. While one cause of this movement is environmental degradation, neither the authorities nor the people involved may be aware of the importance of this factor.

On the other hand, nomadic groups, for example in Kenya, Somalia, and Tibet, have had to change trajectories or have people stay in one place. We are also currently examining the relationship of environmental change and ethnic conflict in South Africa, South Asia, and Central America. Some examples that are more traceable are the fact that groups in Myanmar or Bangladesh find themselves stateless partly due to environmental factors, or that Haitians have to migrate after floods and hurricanes. But the question is, will those affected by such catastrophes, like in the Caribbean, stay or will they leave?

Migration

Q: How would you evaluate the relevance and implementation of the different parts of the UN Global Compact on Refugees?

Anna Triandafyllidou: It is better to have it, its imperfections notwithstanding. It is absolutely necessary to bring countries together around the negotiating table, but of course a lot of what comes out the other end is not binding, or is in favor of western countries, which want to keep for instance refugees in their regions, in neighboring countries.

Q: How do you see digital technologies influencing migration and the management of migration?

Anna Triandafyllidou: I find it quite worrying to be honest. What I see is that we are in new territory regarding law, while for example Trump's wall was never a wall of bricks, rather one of new technologies like infrared cameras and so forth. Another huge problem with using AI is that there is this black box, where we do not really understand how it comes to the conclusions it does. So what happens if the AI concludes you are a threat, even if you are not, how do you appeal this? And then there is this expectation that governments have, that AI can solve all problems. However, there is a clear trade-off between data and efficiency, say, while there is also the idea that AI is not biased. But of course, if the initial data contains bias, then this will be reflected in the end process as well. So the question of digital technologies is quite complicated.

With the purpose to also cover the specific perspective and challenges of the European Union, we conducted an interview with Anna Knoll of the European Centre for Development Policy Management (ECDPM), an independent foundation that monitors and supports the EU's international and development co-operation policies, especially with countries in the African, Caribbean and Pacific (ACP) region. Anna Knoll leads ECDPM's portfolio on migration as Head of the Migration Program.

Global Perspectives on Megatrends

Interview with Anna Knoll, Team Leader at the ECDPM

Q: The European pact on migration and asylum puts renewed emphasis on the EU's partnerships with third countries. It is the subject of political controversies. How do you see the implementation of this pact and its future?

Anna Knoll: There are two sides to it, an internal and an external one. One of the great contentious areas is that of the Common EU Asylum System and EU member states have reached a political deadlock, which is why some view the Pact as dead all-together. Still, it is quite comprehensive and not everything is as contentious. EU officials have used the metaphor of a house with three floors to describe the Pact: partnerships with foreign states as the base floor, border management as the second floor, and the third floor being solidarity and asylum responsibility. There is convergence of ideas and almost universal agreement among EU member states about the need for stronger external partnerships, the base floor. There is also clearly a strong wish for stricter border control, the second floor, but the details are contentious. The most sensitive and difficult floor is to reach the top one and this concerns especially balancing responsibility and solidarity.

There is also the practical issue of the Pact being complex and on the internal dimension consisting of hundreds of pages of policy proposals with legal implications. Policymakers need time to understand and process it and this complexity will also pose challenges for implementation and monitoring. And while the negotiations are ongoing, countries like Poland and Denmark are engaging in asylum practices which contradict the proposals of the Pact as well as the current legal system.

This brings me back to the internal and external dimensions: While the EU is stuck regarding the former, it is implementing the latter quite effectively. Since 2015, the EU has reinforced its partnerships with third countries to halt and control migration flows. This has been an essential objective for the EU, as its internal asylum policies are simply not working and a potential crisis like the one in 2015 would be a catastrophe for the Union politically. Such external agreements and partnerships by themselves are not wrong, but there are valid concerns, primarily in regard to human rights abuses against migrants, especially in cases when partner countries have a poor human rights record. Improving transparency and accountability of external action on migration would be one way to go. This includes risks assessments, monitoring mechanism and redress systems as well as safeguards. Yet, since some EU member states seem to regard themselves as walking a thin line on the edge of legality and have been accused of engaging in violations of migrants's rights, they share little interest in third party monitoring. Secondly, the EU agenda influences other countries and regions, and its investment in migration governance in Africa does not always support the ideas of free movement and migration as opportunity. Finally, the promises of the EU to create and improve legal routes have not been followed through sufficiently with concrete and impactful actions for the moment.

Q: What elements are central to the sustainability of partnerships on migration with third countries?

Anna Knoll: The first is trust and credibility. This is an important element in any partnership. But will other countries trust the EU and enter agreements with the bloc if the EU internal house is not in order? Can the EU be a credible partner if internally there is no agreement on solidarity? The second point is that they need to be mutually beneficial in order to last. Or in other words, they need to take the priorities of both partners into account. In the past years the EU has approached partnerships rather unilaterally, offering money and projects in exchange for a wish list of migration governance activities, rather than starting a conversation. I also think that the EU's insistence on returns and migration conditionality in cooperation programming and now also visa policy or trade, risks undermining the EU's overall aim to build sustainable and lasting partnerships among equals. A third element is that they should, in my view, be aspirational from a sustainable development perspective. This means, they need to be comprehensive, explicitly take development aspects into account and serve migrants, their families as well as the host and origin societies by going beyond a state-centric approach.

Q: Europe remains a popular destiny for migration. Which countries and regions will be in the focus in the next years?

Anna Knoll: It of course depends on the type of migration we are talking about. On humanitarian issues, Afghanistan and Libya remain two of the most important countries the EU is looking to engage with. Then co-managing irregular migration and ensuring sustainable reintegration is also a top priority and here the focus is on countries of origin and transit in the direct and extended neighborhood of the EU, with a particular focus on Africa. The spotlight will also be on countries that bear the brunt of displacement and humanitarian situations, such as Lebanon and Jordan, with Turkey also playing a big role. Northern Africa and countries like Tunisia, Egypt, Libya, Algeria, and Morocco will also be on the forefront of cooperation to reduce irregular migration.

Another aspect is labor migration. Here economic considerations are strongly at play, and that is whether labor market needs match the skills profile of origin countries. More recently, the EU is trying to offer legal pathways to forge partnerships that in exchange help reduce regular migration or improve return and reintegration. North African countries are candidates, while smaller scale projects also have been carried out with Nigeria, Senegal, and Moldova. EU member states have also very specific countries where they receive labour migrants from. For Germany, India and the Philippines have been interesting; for Spain, it is Morocco; while from Poland, it is migrant workers from Ukraine.

Q: Will Europe be able to compete with other regions in the search for talents and professions in demand?

Anna Knoll: The EU has been frank about how it is losing the global race for talent and is trailing behind the likes of the U.S., Canada, and Australia. The reluctance of member states to have more harmonization in migration policy for fear of losing their own attractiveness has also meant that the EU overall has fallen back overall. The EU is currently in the process of introducing more flexibility and attractiveness in its Blue Card Scheme, although many of the initial ideas have been watered down. Whether the planned reforms help the EU to catch up on the global talent race and attract more skilled people will have to be seen. On the other hand, there is the question of whether the EU's stance as being tough on illegal migration influences potential attractiveness for migrant workers overall. There are also some missed opportunities to look at skills already in the EU; for example, through change of status to skilled asylum seekers.

Q: How do you see the role of international and development cooperation of the EU and EU member states in reintegration support, in the context of sustainable development?

Anna Knoll: International and development cooperation actors can address several factors at the individual, community, or structural level—for instance, providing financial or psychosocial support, supporting community-based projects or capacity building for local and national government structures. These may matter for sustainable development and can influence the sustainability of the reintegration process. Yet, development actors have also been pushed into roles that follow migration-related priorities, and this has raised skepticism about their engagement in this area and what purpose it serves.

Possible roles that development actors can assume are working with or within existing systems to support national and community development and help strengthen local systems and capacities; mitigating negative impacts emerging from larger scale returns with a focus on resilience, security, and development; accompanying return programs with development reintegration assistance; and incentivizing individuals to consider voluntary return.

Within these roles, they need to navigate various issues and dilemmas when designing and engaging in reintegration programs in partner countries, such as the fact that development programs may normally not prioritize settings where neither the region, nor the individuals are those "worst-off" in the first place. In my view it is better for development actors to approach reintegration from a structural and community level perspective with a view to strengthen state, business and civil society institutional capacities and infrastructure rather than focusing on individuals only.

Last, but not least, we also wanted to address the megatrend of migration in an interview with a leading researcher from the Global South. Professor Mehari Taddele Maru is a part-time professor at the Migration Policy Centre (MPC) of the European University Institute (EUI), where he is also a member of the Centre's advisory board.

Interview with Mehari Taddele Maru, Part-time Professor, Migration Policy Centre, EUI and Coordinator of the Young African Leaders Program

Q: How do you see push and pull factors for migration developing in the next decade? Do you see numbers rising or declining? What do you think of the argument of Parag Khanna in his book *Move* that humanity will (have to) redistribute itself on Planet Earth in the next few decades due to climate change, demographic factors, and job opportunities?

Mehari Maru: I think it is obvious in the numbers we have been seeing. Regular migration has increased on average by six million per year worldwide until COVID-19 and related restrictions acted as a great disruptor, but the trend will continue if not at higher speeds. Nevertheless, it might take a few years for this to occur. In some places, such as Africa or Asia, this trend might double with the development of agreements such as the free movement in Africa and the large populations.

Some regions will experience this trend more than others, while we cannot be sure if the distribution will be based on rational factors. That is dependent on many factors that are not easy to control, given the rise of identity politics and cultural traits. Some societies in the North especially feel that with increasing migration, there could be more backlash and it is already happening in well-established democracies in the EU and the U.S. unlike ever before. Identity politics is indeed undermining democracies and the rule of law.

Q: Brain drain is a major challenge for many African countries. How do African states address this issue? What could they do to retain talents?
Mehari Maru: It is a long-standing problem, as talent follows investment and money, as well as a normative framework that allow talents to flourish and provide them with opportunity. Brain drain will continue, and as such, Africa and the Global South must produce more than what is needed on a national level in terms of skilled persons so that even if there is brain drain, countries will sustain a sufficient number of skilled people. More effort is needed, as more attraction from the other side is present. You obviously cannot stop it as a human rights issue as well, because skilled professionals cannot be stopped from seeking better opportunities

Q: How do you see the impact of COVID-19 on reduced inflows from remittances? How seriously are African countries affected? Will the flow of remittances fully recover?
Mehari Maru: The reduction of flows might be difficult to quantify. There will be a noticeable change in the informal sector because it was done by people traveling. Overall, there will be a reduction because employment, income and expenses have all been affected. Employment has decreased, income as well, but we are also seeing fears of inflation, as the economy goes back to normal, so there will be more demand for income, and more migrants might be demanded in certain sectors and remittances might increase again.

Q: How would you evaluate the relevance and implementation of the different parts of the UN Global Compact on Refugees?
Mehari Maru: From an African perspective, there is significant progress. For the first time we have a normative framework, especially for migration, as the Global North has for a long time refused to come up with anything like this. Nevertheless, some important countries in the EU, as well as the U.S., are not part of it. What is important is that normative frameworks have the potential to change into hard ones in the long term, when enough countries practice them. Establishing such a framework is therefore an important step.

Still, the Global Compact on Migration lacks an emphasis on human rights of migrants, an issue that is simply not as pronounced as it should be. Generally, it is an improvement in migration governance or rather reflection on migration governance... but I wanted to see more.

As for refugees, I see it as a reinstatement of existing systems, and an abandonment of shared responsibility in the international community. The fact that it focuses mostly on local integration rather than resettlement and sharing burdens means nearby countries where there is displacement will be the ones sharing the largest burden in giving necessary protection/assistance, and that is simply unfair. Refugees are a responsibility of everyone wherever they are. The Global Compact did not do good enough. It is strongly biased toward local integration, including costs being shared unequally and unfavorably.

Burden sharing should have been well calculated, and resettlement should have been considered. It is unfair for Uganda to host 1.2 million while Austria is complaining about 40.000 migrants.

Q: How do you evaluate the partnerships on migration of the EU with third countries?

Mehari Maru: It is highly debated. I see an element of fatigue and only few effective deliveries. All sectors of partnership are subservient to migration issues. Humanitarian aid, diplomacy, trade, visa, tourism, are all subservient to the migration agenda. I do not understand why the EU is putting all its eggs in one basket. In my opinion it could have been better balanced in that regard and the result is but the hardening of borders in Africa, the expansion of European border control in Africa and FRONTEX meddling in the South as well, all of which impacts on the free movement in Africa which is necessary for integration. This completely undermines what the EU has been doing thus far. The model for free movement that the EU has poured money into in Africa, while also hardening the borders, is clearly undermining its own program.

Q: Let us go back to push and pull factors once more. What about countries, which are adamant about protecting their borders and

arguments that such attempts are futile, because people will take greater risks anyway?
Mehari Maru: I largely agree, but migration will continue. The push and pull framework has to be considered alongside many other accelerating factors: transportation, technology, Covid-related demand in some sectors. In general, an increase in displacement may increase secondary movement because of disasters. If the move occurs from the Global South to the Global North, there will be backlash — that much is certain.

Like for other megatrends, our aim was to provide an overview of the migration trend in general but also adopt a differentiated perspective on salient questions related to migration and migration governance. Driven by climate change, political conflicts and aging societies, the migration trend will remain a strong trend and a global phenomenon but play out differently across countries, regions, and different political systems. Global population and migration dynamics are usually underestimated by political leaders because such developments escape domestic policy planning. Many countries will realize that adopting smart migration policies and addressing brain drain could bring great benefits.

Chapter 15

Visions for the World in 2030 and Beyond

In this final chapter we summarize how the megatrends covered in the preceding twelve chapters will play out in the near future with a focus on the next 10–15 years. We refrain from offering distinct utopian or dystopian scenarios or black and white thinking.

Scenarios are probably the most emblematic foresight or future studies method.[1] However, we decided to address emerging trends and issues in a slightly different, more nuanced, and differentiated way. We have therefore opted for the megatrend approach. We strongly emphasize and elaborate on the connections between different megatrends, and we realize the limits of foresight research. With this book, we wanted to stress that megatrend analysis requires a comprehensive and critical analysis of opportunities and risks related to trends. This involves diverse expert opinions rather than the mere focus on promising business opportunities that we see in foresight studies, or the megatrend analyses of some strategy consulting firms or experts on future studies. We also refrained from indulging in populist or ideologically charged agendas which tend to fall short of understanding the complexity of topics. The Pentagon Model of megatrend analysis developed by Berthold Kuhn that we introduced in the first chapter provided us with good guidance to prioritize trends.

We begin this chapter with a summary analysis of each megatrend and latterly present a discussion about the future with three experts well versed in future studies.

We are optimistic about humanity's ability and capacity to live up to forthcoming challenges. However, we also foresee serious threats, especially related to climate change and growing inequalities. All countries will have to deal with unforeseen disasters and political upheavals, but we do not see a third world war or a major military confrontation between China and the U.S. on the horizon. The stakes are too high for investors and the business community, and they will apply sufficient pressure on political leaders to seek peaceful means of conflict resolution. Global connectivity will increase due to further breakthroughs in information and communication technologies. Groundbreaking discoveries in human biology will attract much attention and shape ethical and philosophical discourses. The modification of an individual's genetic heritage will advance and spark controversies. We shall see continued debates as to whether, how, and to what extent transhumanist goals are posing threats to human ethics.[2] Conspiracy theories will abound and spark social and political conflicts. We shall see healthier lifestyles and a reduction of chronic diseases in some parts of the world but also experience smaller and bigger disasters and shock waves triggered by different kinds of crisis situations, related to climate-change, new pandemics, and political confrontations.

A comprehensive and critical analysis of future trends in different fields can help us to anticipate challenges and prepare ourselves for positive and negative developments.

15.1 Outlook on Megatrends

Climate Action and Sustainability: A broadening and deepening of this trend in the next decade goes without saying. Awareness of climate change will continue to grow and spread quickly in almost all countries and regions, accelerated by urbanization and smart city concepts. Emissions trading will expand and become a major incentive for companies to cut emissions. The pressure on political leaders to arrive at far-reaching global agreements under the auspices of the United Nations will grow, but negotiations between states at climate summits will remain difficult, mainly because of the diversity of structural challenges in countries and regions, and issues related to claims for financial compensation for losses attributed to climate change in the most vulnerable countries. The next couple of years will be characterized by the last-remaining efforts from organizations, politicians, individuals, and interest groups to push back against progress. But such attempts will soon falter in the face of the inevitability of unprecedented harmonization and cooperation in goal-setting and accelerated transition efforts.

Visions for the World in 2030 and Beyond

Inequality: Inequality will be exacerbated in the context of asset inflation and greenflation and will hit many middle-class people, in rich countries and emerging economies alike. This will spark strikes and protest movements which will result in stark suppression, even in some liberal democracies. We shall see increasing attention paid by G20 countries to the issues of market regulation and taxation in an effort to increase tax revenues and regain the capacity to finance growing welfare states in the context of aging societies. A new era of strong government will emerge, but this time it will be focused on working together, as well as shaping markets to bring about societally desirable outcomes. North–South relations will become even more tense. Developing countries affected by climate change will become more assertive when it comes to compensation for the extraction of natural resources and losses from climate change. The inequality issue will become a major political challenge for authoritarian regimes as well as liberal democracies and will not be confined to poorer countries. The fight against hunger and poverty reduction will remain top issues of international and development cooperation.

Digitalization will impact business models and lifestyles significantly. From health care to e-governance, every sector will face a reckoning due to the disruption that digitalization brings along. The fast growth of data volumes and the significance of big data analyses will march on. Government regulations will proliferate, and tech companies will face ever more scrutiny over their handling of data and their manner of operating. Cryptocurrencies will continue to fluctuate in the context of regulatory and political interventions, but blockchain technology will make further breakthroughs and become more energy efficient.

Demographic trends will remain diverse. Aging societies will be the dominant trend in richer countries while population growth will flatten in some developing countries. We shall continue to see low birth rates and high life expectancy in rich countries, which lead to shrinking populations and aging societies. We shall see growing populations in poorer regions, even though some will remain affected by the outbound migration of younger people, the degradation of natural resources, and deadly local conflicts.

Urbanization and Smart Cities: We shall continue to see a strong and persistent relationship between urbanization and economic growth. Chinese technology firms will remain key drivers of smart cities with remarkable advancements. More investment in mobility will make suburbs grow. Political attention will be paid to better urban-rural integration. The greening of the building and construction sector will advance, and we shall see a growing use of renewable and reusable materials.

Health and Nutrition will attract more political attention and investment. New technologies, especially mRNA vaccinations, will be applied to combat more diseases. We shall see further breakthroughs in medical research and a proliferation of ethical committees dealing with moral issues. Access to quality health care will become more politicized. The rise of superbugs (microorganisms such as bacteria, fungi, viruses, and parasites), which mutate to possess genes that protect them against antimicrobial drugs, will present a grave danger to all countries, as these microorganisms know no borders. The food trend is developing an enormous dynamic, especially in affluent societies. The number of people following a vegetarian or vegan diet will further increase. Both the health and food sectors will be characterized by radical transformation and innovation, incorporating digital technologies, and promoting sustainability.

The Green Economy will become a strong reference point for an ever-growing number of stakeholders. Multinational companies will ride the trend, and sustainability experts and political leaders and will present green economics as a viable alternative to growth-focused economic strategies. Fundamental opposition to green growth, however, will continue to shape discourses, especially in social sciences and among activists, and a compromise will have to be reached.

Visions for the World in 2030 and Beyond

Sustainable Finance: The process of mainstreaming sustainable finance will gain further traction in the context of the implementation of the 2030 Agenda for Sustainable Development, the Paris Agenda, and accelerated efforts of energy transition in an attempt to reduce dependency from Russia. We shall see increasing regulatory efforts to make capital markets work for sustainability transformations of industries, and we expect them to succeed. Sustainable finance will also make substantial contributions to stabilizing financial markets, though we shall see fluctuations and further differentiation of indicators across sectors. Greenwashing will remain an issue, but activists and consumer organizations are more likely to see through and raise awareness on such practices.

Democracy and Governance: Democratic trends will play out differently across the spectrum of liberal democratic political systems, ranging from increasing efforts to consult experts from different professional backgrounds at national levels to a push for greater public participation in planning at the level of city governance. Outside Asia, there are growing signs that populism and the retreat of democracy might have peaked. We shall see an upsurge in public participation, facilitated through the use of information and communication technologies. However, political marginalization of different kinds of communities will also remain a key feature of many societies, especially for authoritarian regimes with a high proportion of migrants in their population. Digitalization will heavily impact election campaigns at different levels and new political marketing opportunities and risks of simplification and manipulation of content will come along with it.

Multipolar World Order and the Future of Multilateralism: Geopolitics will continue to develop toward a multipolar world order with Asia becoming a new center of gravity in world politics. China's rise will continue for a few years but not go unchallenged, especially by its neighbors. If the Communist Party of China (CCP) is not able to rejuvenate itself in the medium term, it risks political sclerosis that will seriously threaten economic performance and stability. Russia and China will forge closer relations. Ukraine has already relapsed into confrontation and division in light of the Russian invasion. The North Atlantic Treaty Organization (NATO) will experience a strong revival and the U.S. will re-engage in foreign affairs, especially in Europe and Asia. The EU stood largely united in its solidarity with Ukraine but decoupling from Russia will take its toll. Energy prices will rise, but efforts to speed up energy reforms will pay off in the long run. The UN will successfully continue to broaden and deepen its climate action and sustainability agendas. The G20 meetings will gain further profile, too. Thus, multilateralism is not in decline, but in transformation in the context of an emerging multipolar world order.

Civilizational Developments: Diversity, individualization and loneliness, gender shifts, and identity politics will remain important sub-trends in the social sphere, especially in Western countries. However, these trends will play out quite differently across countries and will cause political tensions and cultural clashes, especially in the United States and Europe. If not well managed, they could create further crisis scenarios in the Western world and weaken the soft power of liberal democracies. Authoritarian states will also face major challenges, risk abrupt crises, and even collapse if important social trends are ignored and rights are suppressed

Migration will be looked at in more differentiated ways in many countries, including in Asia, mainly due to aging societies, labor shortages, and competition over talent. Many states will be inclined to apply even more differentiated immigration and visa policies, including special visas for certain professions. The war in Ukraine, environmental disasters and climate change will produce more migrants. Pull factors such as labor demand, higher wages, better business opportunities, and family reunions will also contribute to migration trends. Countries which cannot easily protect their borders (for example, Greece and Croatia) or those close to conflict regions will continue to face challenges. The tension between advocacy for human rights from actors like the European Union, and the reality of practices at their borders, will be amplified and new frameworks will need to be established to ensure the safety of those on the move.

15.2 Vision Talk: Three Experts Share their Future Perspectives

We would like to round up the book by bridging from issue-oriented and trend-focused expert analysis to a broader perspective on megatrends. As the discussion demonstrates, the interconnection between megatrends is complex but not opaque. Thus, we can still find grounds for confidence in approaching the future with optimism.

Our three interview partners have dealt with future studies in different capacities and contexts. Rosa Alegria is a renowned futurist who has provided strategic foresight analysis to many companies in Brazil and in the Americas. Umar Sheraz has conducted extensive research on emerging issues and future trends. He has delivered lectures related to intellectual property rights, technology transfer, and strategic foresight at the renowned COMSTECH University in Islamabad. Dr. Andreas Rickert, founder and chief executive of the well-networked German nonprofit organization PHINEO, edited the book *Zukunftsrepublik* (Future Republic).

Interview with Rosa Alegria (Futurista), Umar Sheraz (COMSTECH University, Islamabad) and Andreas Rickert (PHINEO)

Q: Please introduce your work on emerging issues and trends to our readers in a few words.

Rosa Alegria: I am a professional futurista. My background includes a Bachelor of Arts in Literature and a master's degree in Future Studies. I am the founder and CEO of Perspektiva, my consulting company for strategic foresight, and I also act as CEO of the Millennium Project in Brazil. I am the director of Teach the Future

Brasil, a member of the Teach the Future global core team, and also involved in supporting start-ups.

Umar Sheraz: I am a futurist who used to work on innovation policy and am currently stationed in Islamabad. I was the blog editor of the *Journal of Future Studies* and have worked with the OECD and many Muslim countries. I used to look at indicators on how to improve innovation and technology and then the Arab Spring happened, which made me realize that we need more than just technological innovations to understand societal change.

Andreas Rickert: My background is quite diverse: I have a doctorate in molecular biology, and have worked at the World Bank, McKinsey, and the Bertelsmann Foundation. I am the founder and CEO of PHINEO, a think-and-do tank for strategic philanthropy impact investing. Our goal is to motivate people and provide them with the resources to create impact, which has two dimensions. For one, we look at issues from a helicopter perspective and ask questions such as "who is working toward solutions?" while the other perspective has to do with consulting donors and investors, so there is both a top-down and a bottom-up aspect to this work. My mission is to achieve impact by motivating people to do something good, by mobilizing resources for impact, and by providing tools to achieve impact. Besides PHINEO, I am also the co-CEO of Nixdorf Kapital, an impact investing funds platform. I am active as an impact business angel and serve on various boards. At the beginning of the year, I published the book *Zukunftsrepublik*, a compendium of 80 concrete ideas for a better world.

Q: How does your work connect to future studies, scenario development, or to the megatrends and emerging issues covered in this book?

Rosa Alegria: I personally research many topics with a current focus on education, so there is not something specific I would pick out. Still, I do advocate for teaching foresight in high schools, which I feel is missing. Why is it so relevant? Teaching the future is as important as teaching history, because with faster changes and changes in the job market, young people need to prepare for the future and to live with uncertainties. The courses I offer to professors and students broaden horizons and help to strengthen the imagination for the creation of personal, urban, governmental projects and, above all, new professions, those that do not yet exist.

Umar Sheraz: I also have a lot to say about education, but more recently I have focused more on ecosystems and climate change and now realize the scale of the problem and the challenges ahead. For me, methodology is key to creating awareness and understanding challenges ahead. For example, I came across the climate change game, which is a 44-card game that provides a more sensitized perspective on the issue. I also think that we should engage a lot with the younger generation in the process of reflecting on future trends. I still often engage the youth in Afghanistan, support them, and help out through storytelling.

Andreas Rickert: One thing that is clear to me is that all topics in this book are interconnected. One example is the connection between sustainable finance and climate change, as well as the Sustainable Development Goals, which, if we want to achieve, we must mobilize the capital markets to invest the trillions needed.

Q: From your perspective, which issues will be on top of the agenda of international cooperation in the next decade and beyond, related to your area of work and expertise? Who are the important players in agenda-setting?

Rosa Alegria: It is difficult to point to one of all these large issues facing us today, but climate change, water, the widening social gap, the threat of polarization, and potential conflicts are all things that concern me, while the players in each issue may be equally difficult to pinpoint. Ignoring climate change is fatal, of course, but there are also other issues like the fact that synthetic biology might turn out to be even more dangerous that AI, as well as a potentially increasing unemployment rate.

Umar Sheraz: One key aspect for me is that of intergenerational fairness, and how what we do today affects future generations. It does not necessarily have to do just with climate change and the state of the planet, but also things like pension policies in an age of an aging society facing the younger generation. Another big source of conflict is of course a polarized world; one in which a hegemon is declining in the U.S., while another is rising in China, and how third countries like India will respond to these changes. Of course, this changing world order offers opportunities for cooperation as well so let us hope it is indeed for the better.

Andreas Rickert: First of all, I agree with you Mr. Sheraz, let us hope that the latter is the case. We cannot build a sustainable world as individual nations; no nation has the power to go it alone. The question remains "who is working toward creating solutions?" To me this seems to be multinational organizations that need the help of strong governments working at both national and international levels, while the private sector contributes to growth through innovation and civil society is able to provide a normative perspective and create an inclusive approach.

Q: How do you see the role of the United Nations, and other international organizations and think tanks in shaping discourses and advancing global cooperation in the areas related to your work and expertise? Which are key challenges for global cooperation from your perspective?

Rosa Alegria: I just want to go back to something Mr. Sheraz said briefly and point out that this is the first time in human history that six generations have coexisted, which presents tremendous challenges, but also opportunities to come together as one. In regard to the UN, I see a need for more foresight specialists and advisors in the institution. We have in fact written a letter to António Guterres in the past and expect the creation of an office of global threats in the next year or so, which will define common global threats and work together to solve them.

Umar Sheraz: I personally looked at the UN with hope, but ever since the pandemic it feels to me like a case of the curse of Cassandra. All of these accurate predictions merely add to the frustration, as we cannot do anything about them. I also think that more regional consolidation is taking away power from the UN, with regional organizations having more influence, while I do have a lot of concerns around diversity within the institution itself. That being said, it is a great platform when it functions as a promoter of common universal goals.

Andreas Rickert: I do agree, but also disagree to some extent with Mr. Sheraz, but I do strongly believe that we need the UN as a unifying force to have one clear global vision and we need to believe in it, but then of course we also need strong implementation.

Q: Big data plays a key role in research on emerging issues and on megatrends. How do you rate the relevance, opportunities, and limitations of big data research?

Rosa Alegria: While I am no expert in the topic, I do consider the power of big data a great addition to our research and as providing us with new methodologies. In the foresight approach, it enriches our understanding, but I also see some clear limits, as human intuition must be part of the equation in making final decisions.

Umar Sheraz: A lot of human decision-making is based on emotion, and I think that big data can help us in making more informed decisions. At the same time, looking at current implementation, I see us heading down a path where we accept the invasion of our privacy as completely normal, and I am quite worried in that regard.

Andreas Rickert: All technology, every innovation, has no value by itself and cannot be said to be good or bad, until we decide how we put it to use. We thus need governments and international organizations to provide frameworks for how we move forward and put such technology to use, as this kind of data cannot be used for one's own sake and the process must be democratic.

Q: Spirituality has been a powerful driving force for humanity in many parts of the world. Will progress in research and technology lead to a retreat of spirituality? What are your personal thoughts on the relationship between science, technology, and spirituality?

Rosa Alegria: I believe that spirituality and technology can coexist, but if we look at the exponential and inevitable curve of technological progress, it has destroyed a number of aspects of our everyday lives, and of course destroyed nature itself for the sake of economic growth. To me it seems like consciousness is the final frontier and we should not lose touch with life, forgetting how to be human in the process and turning into machines. The human essence should prevail and if we integrate science, technology, and spirituality into our lives in a good way, there is a great opportunity to create such a global consciousness and build a sustainable future.

Umar Sheraz: For one, I would like to point out that spirituality may be much more personal in comparison to religion and requires a look inwards, which does not necessarily push a certain agenda. A look at Afghanistan and the rise of the Taliban reveals what such an aggressive religious agenda can look like. Indeed, I believe that spirituality can instead play an important role in shaping how societies define their direction.

Andreas Rickert: I would like to add one more thing, that being that a fairer and more equal world cannot simply be built on technological grounds and that we instead need a global ethical framework, which makes us responsible for each other. Regardless of spirituality, religion or nationality, humanity must agree on some common global human values.

Q: How does your work influence your lifestyle? What makes you personally optimistic or pessimistic about the future?

Rosa Alegria: I am always an optimist, even though other futurists may decide to engage in a more dystopian analysis of the future. A lot of people understandably fear uncertainty, but I see it as an opportunity to exercise human freedom and creativity. There is a need to look at futures, in plural form, where nothing is determined and there is a plurality of solutions, because without hope there is no future.

Umar Sheraz: There is this game I play with the youth in Afghanistan, where I ask them if the future is dark or bright and whether or not they believe themselves to have human agency and be able to influence the future. Though a lot of them may indeed see the future as dark, they then also believe that they can influence the future simply because it is necessary to do so. Even when we think of these dystopias, we have to be able to believe that we can avert them.

Andreas Rickert: I always think of myself as a realist optimist, not naive, as I can clearly see the immense challenges in front of us. At the same time, I can also see solutions through innovation, and technology, and it is the people that I see that have the power to do something positive that make me optimistic for the future.

Global megatrends are much more than business or investment opportunities. They will influence societies and cultures across the world. Even very educated people are puzzled by the complexity of these changes. We wanted to provide a comprehensive yet concise overview of the most important trends and their interconnections, alongside insightful analysis of how megatrends are shaped by international organizations, think tanks and influential political and social leaders in different parts of the world. Many of the megatrends are receiving increasing attention from the business community, political leaders, and people eager to understand and influence the future of humanity. We wanted to bridge perspectives and emphasize that a diversity of approaches is required to address multiple risks and explore opportunities to improve the quality of life on planet Earth. We are glad to see that the United Nations, with its 2030 Agenda for Sustainable Development, and many other international organizations and activists are engaged in making debates on future challenges for humanity more inclusive. More expertise, data, analysis, and the commitment of people with diverse backgrounds and orientations are needed to make the world a better place.

Endnotes

Chapter 1: What is a Megatrend?

1. Naisbitt, John (1982). *Megatrends. Ten New Directions Transforming Our Lives.* New York: Warner Books.
2. Aburdene, Patricia (2007). *Megatrends 2010. The Rise of Conscious Capitalism.* Hampton Roads Publishing.
3. European Environmental Agency (EEA) (2021). Drivers of Change: Challenges and Opportunities for Sustainability in Europe. https://www.eea.europa.eu/themes/sustainability-transitions/drivers-of-change
4. Asian Development Bank (April, 2020). Future Thinking in Asia and the Pacific. Why Foresight Matters for Policy Makers. https://www.adb.org/sites/default/files/publication/579491/futures-thinking-asia-pacific-policy-makers.pdf
5. Bertelsmann Foundation (2019). The Bigger Picture: How Globalization, Digitalization and Demographic Change Challenge the World, Gütersloh.
6. Pwc United Kingdom (n.d.) Megatrends. https://www.pwc.co.uk/issues/megatrends.html, accessed, accessed on 10 February, 2022.
7. EEA (2022). Drivers of Change: Challenges and Opportunities for Sustainability in Europe, last modified January 14, 2022. https://www.eea.europa.eu/themes/sustainability-transitions/drivers-of-change
8. United Nations (2015). The United Nations 2030 Agenda for Sustainable Development. https://www.un.org/sustainabledevelopment/development-agenda/ (regularly updated).
9. GIZ (2017). Trends and the Future of Development Cooperation. https://reporting.giz.de/2017/our-strategic-direction/strategy-and-outlook/trends-and-the-future-of-development-cooperation/index.html
10. Innovation is the "creative destruction" that develops the economy while the entrepreneur performs the function of the change creator, see: Śledzik, Karol (2013). Schumpeter's View on Innovation and Entrepreneurship. *SSRN Electronic Journal.* https://www.researchgate.net/publication/256060978_Schumpeter's_View_on_Innovation_and_Entrepreneurship
11. World Economic Forum (WEF) (2020). Global Risks Report 2020, https://www.weforum.org/reports/the-global-risks-report-2020
12. WEF (2021). Global Risks Report 2021. https://www.weforum.org/reports/the-global-risks-report-2021
13. WEF (2022). Global Risks Report 2022. What You Need to Know, https://www.weforum.org/agenda/2022/01/global-risks-report-climate-change-covid19/
14. Rifkin, Jeremy (2020). *The Green New Deal.* New York. St. Martin's Griffin.

Chapter 2: Who Shapes the Future?

1. World Economic Forum (2022). Global Risks Report 2022. What You Need to Know. https://www.weforum.org/agenda/2022/01/global-risks-report-climate-change-covid19/. Climate action failure, extreme weather events, and biodiversity loss and ecosystem collapse were considered the top three of the top ten global risks by severity over the next ten years in the annual Global Risks Perception Survey (GRPS).

2   Joyce, Kathrin. (May 18, 2020). The Long, Strange History of Bill Gates Population Control Conspiracy Theories. Huffington Post. https://www.huffpost.com/entry/bill-gates-coronavirus-vaccine-conspiracy_n_5eb9ab7ac5b69358ef8a9803
3   Startup Genome (2021). https://startupgenome.com/about-us, accessed August 3, 2021.
4   IPCC (2021). Sixth Assessment Report. https://www.ipcc.ch/assessment-report/ar6/
5   Smith, Noah. (2021). Why has Climate Economics Failed us? https://noahpinion.substack.com/p/why-has-climate-economics-failed, accessed August 1, 2021.
6   World Inequality Database. (n.d.). https://wid.world/, accessed August 10, 2021.
7   Piketty, Thomas. (2015). The Economics of Inequality. Harvard University Press; Piketty, Thomas (2013/2014). Capital in the Twenty-First Century. Harvard University Press. (French: Le Capital au XXIe siècle), both translated by Arthur Goldhammer.
8   Center for China and Globalization (CCG) (2021, November 4). CCG View. Newsletter.
9   United Nations Development Programme (2014). Thinking the Unthinkable From Thought to Policy – The Role of Think Tanks in Shaping Government Strategy. Retrieved from https://shop.un.org/zh/node/25520
10 University of Pennsylvania (2021). The Think Tanks and Civil Society Program (TTCPS). Global Go To Think Tanks Index Report (GGTI) (authored by James McGann). Retrieved from https://repository.upenn.edu/cgi/viewcontent.cgi?article=1019&context=think_tanks
11 Carnegie Endowment for Peace (2019). Defending Civic Space. Is the International Community Stuck? https://carnegieendowment.org/2019/10/22/defending-civic-space-is-international-community-stuck-pub-80110
12 SITRA (no date). Megatrends. What is this About? https://www.sitra.fi/en/topics/megatrends/#what-is-this-about, accessed December 13, 2021.
13 SITRA (no date) https://www.sitra.fi/en/topics/megatrends/#what-is-this-about, accessed January 7, 2022.
14 Megatrends Watch (2021). About us. http://www.megatrendswatch.com/about-mwi.html, accessed October 20, 2021
15 The Future Society (United States), https://thefuturesociety.org/; Resources for the Future (RFF) (United States); Future of Life Institute (United States); Geopolitical Futures (United States); Centre for the Future Intelligence, University of Cambridge (United Kingdom); Future of Humanity Institute (United Kingdom); Forum for the Future (United Kingdom); Institute for Future Engineering (IFENG); FKA Institute for Future Technology (Japan); Institute for Future Initiatives, University of Tokyo (Japan); ZOE Institute for Future-Fit Economies (Germany); Zukunftsinstitut (Germany); Future Innovative Thailand Institute (Thailand); Future Center for Advanced Researches and Studies (United Arab Emirates).
16 Zukunftsinstitut (n.d.). Über uns. https://www.zukunftsinstitut.de/ueber-uns/, accessed January 13, 2022.

Endnotes

17 McKinsey (April 01, 2015) The Four Global Forces Breaking all the Trends, https://www.mckinsey.com/business-functions/strategy-and-corporate-finance/our-insights/the-four-global-forces-breaking-all-the-trends

18 PwC (2016). Five Megatrends and Their Implications for Global Defense and Security. https://www.pwc.com/gx/en/archive/archive-government-public-services/publications/five-megatrends.html

19 Deloitte (n.d.). Cleared for Take-Off. Five Megatrends That Will Change Financial Services, https://www2.deloitte.com/kh/en/pages/financial-services/articles/five-megatrends-change-financial-services.html, accessed 13.12.2021

20 Roland Berger (2021). Trend Compendium 2050. Megatrends Shaping The Coming Decades. Retrieved from https://www.rolandberger.com/en/Insights/Global-Topics/Trend-Compendium/

Chapter 3: Climate Action and Sustainability

1 United Nations (n.d.). Climate Action. Tackling Climate Change. https://www.un.org/sustainabledevelopment/climate-action/, accessed on 10 February, 2022.

2 Callaghan, Max. W., Minx, Jan. C. and Forster, Piers. M. (2020). A Topography of Climate Change Research. *Nature Climate Change*, 10, 118–123. https://doi.org/10.1038/s41558-019-0684-5.

3 Carbon Neutral Cities (n.d.). Mobilizing Transformative Climate Action in Cities, https://carbonneutralcities.org/, accessed February 10, 2022.

4 Buckley, Tim. (February 27, 2019). Over 100 Global Financial Institutions Are Exiting Coal, With More to Come. (IEEFA) Institute for Energy Economics and Financial Analysis. http://ieefa.org/wp-content/uploads/2019/02/IEEFA-Report_100-and-counting_Coal-Exit_Feb-2019.pdf

5 Sustainable Finance Committee of the German Government (2021). Shifting the Trillions. https://sustainable-finance-beirat.de/wp-content/uploads/2021/02/210224_SFB_-Abschlussbericht-2021.pdf

6 Robeco (November 01, 2018). Three Megatrends Shaping the World. https://www.robeco.com/de/aktuelle-analysen/2018/11/three-megatrends-shaping-the-world.html

7 Pianta, Silvia, and Sisco, Matthew R. (2020). A Hot Topic in Hot Times: How Media Coverage of Climate Change is Affected by Temperature Abnormalities. *Environmental Research Letters*, 15, (11). https://iopscience.iop.org/article/10.1088/1748-9326/abb732

8 Ortiz, Diego Arguedas. (January 15, 2021). How Science Fiction Helps Readers Understand Climate Change. BBC. https://www.bbc.com/culture/article/20190110-how-science-fiction-helps-readers-understand-climate-change

9 IPCC (2014). AR5 Synthesis Report. Climate Change, p. 135.

10 Global Monitoring Laboratory (2021). The NOAA Annual Greenhouse Gas Index (AGGI). Retrieved from https://gml.noaa.gov/aggi/aggi.html

11 Lin, Mei Mayuri and Hidayat, Rafki. (August 13, 2018). Jakarta, the Fastest-Sinking City in the World. BBC. https://www.bbc.com/news/world-asia-44636934

12 Eise, Jessica, and White, Natalie (August 22, 2018). Coffee Farmers Struggle to Adapt to Colombia's Changing Climate. The Conversation. https://theconvers

ation.com/coffee-farmers-struggle-to-adapt-to-colombias-changing-climate-97916
13 Carbon Brief (2020). Nine 'Tipping Points' that Could be Triggered by Climate Change. https://www.carbonbrief.org/explainer-nine-tipping-points-that-could-be-triggered-by-climate-change
14 IPCC (n.d.). Global Warming of 1.5 °C. https://www.ipcc.ch/sr15/, accessed November 10, 2021.
15 Leyl, Sharanjit. (February 15, 2021). Mark Carney: Climate Crisis Deaths will be Worse than Covid. BBC. https://www.bbc.com/news/business-55944570
16 Timo Busch and Lena Judick provide an overview of climate-skeptic think tanks in Germany and the United States, see: Busch, T., and Judick, L. (2021). Climate change – that is not Real! A Comparative Analysis of Climate-sceptic Think Tanks in the USA and Germany. *Climatic Change*, 164(18). https://doi.org/10.1007/s10584-021-02962-z
17 Sing, Harjeet et al. (2020). Costs of Climate Inaction. Displacement and Distress Migration. Report for Brot für die Welt, CANSA, ActionAid. https://actionaid.org/sites/default/files/publications/ActionAid%20CANSA%20-%20South%20Asia%20Climate%20Migration%20report%20-%20Dec%202020.pdf
18 The ND-Gain, the Climate Change Vulnerability Index by the University of Notre Dame, measures the vulnerability of states and regions to the changing climate. It distinguishes between exposure to climate change and sensitivity of livelihoods to such change and considers different lifestyles and economic activities of communities. (Notre Dame Global Adaptation Initiative (2021). https://gain.nd.edu/, accessed November 10, 2021.
19 European Commission (2021). Biodiversity and Climate Change. Retrieved from https://ec.europa.eu/environment/nature/climatechange/index_en.htm#:~:text=Biodiversity%20and%20Climate%20Change
20 IPCC (n.d.). The Intergovernmental Panel on Climate Change. ipcc.ch, accessed November 23, 2021.
21 IPCC (2022). Climate Change 2022: Impacts, Adaptation and Vulnerability. https://www.ipcc.ch/report/ar6/wg2/
22 United Nations (n.d.) What is the Paris Agreement? https://unfccc.int/process-and-meetings/the-paris-agreement/the-paris-agreement , accessed November 27, 2021
23 The Economist (2021, January 02–08). Working Together to Reduce carbon Emissions. Vale, Partners and Clients – full-page advertisement published on page 3 of *The Economist*.
24 United Nations (n.d.) Transforming our World: the 2030 Agenda for Sustainable Development, https://sdgs.un.org/2030agenda, accessed January 12, 2022.
25 Kuhn, Berthold M. (2016). Sustainable Development Discourses in the P.R. China. *Journal of Sustainable Development*, 9(6), 158–167.
26 IUCN, UNEP, and WWF. (1980). World Conservation Strategy: Living Resource Conservation for Sustainable Development. IUCN: Gland, Switzerland. https://doi.org/10.2305/IUCN.CH.1980.9.en
27 United Nations, World Commission on Environment and Development (WCED). (1987). Our Common Future. New York

Endnotes

28 BMZ (2016). Partner für den Wandel. Religionen und Nachhaltige Entwicklung. Edition BMZ.
29 For a discussion of the formula see Shao, David (2021). The Kaya Identity: Carbon Dioxide Emissions and The Economy. https://www.youthareawesome.com/kaya-identity/. See also *The Economist* (2021, October 30). Flows and Fuel, p. 18.
30 Birnbaum, Michael (September 8, 2021). The World's Biggest Plant to Capture Carbon Dioxide from the Air just Opened in Iceland. *Washington Post.* https://www.washingtonpost.com/climate-solutions/2021/09/08/co2-capture-plan-iceland-climeworks/
31 World Economic Forum (2019). How Technology is Leading us to New Climate Change Solutions. https://www.weforum.org/agenda/2018/08/how-technology-is-driving-new-environmental-solutions
32 *Climate Policy Info Hub* (n.d.). The Global Rise of Emissions Trading. https://climatepolicyinfohub.eu/global-rise-emissions-trading , accessed 10 December 2021
33 The European Union Emissions Trading System Reduced CO_2 Emissions Despite Low Prices. (April 21, 2020). *Proceedings of the Natural Academy of Sciences of the United States of America* (PNAS), 117 (16) 8804–8812. https://www.pnas.org/content/117/16/8804
34 This opinion was also voiced in an interview with Olivia Heinke and Peter Renner, the CEOs of the Foundation of the Alliance for Development and Climate Action. Stiftung Allianz für Entwicklung und Klima (n.d.). https://allianz-entwicklung-klima.de/meldungen/allianz-fuer-entwicklung-und-klima-wird-stiftung/
35 Shue, Henry (January, 1993). Subsistence Emissions and Luxury Emissions. Law & Policy, 15(1), 39–60. https://onlinelibrary.wiley.com/doi/10.1111/j.1467-9930.1993.tb00093.x
36 International Energy Agency (2021). Total Primary Energy Demand in China in the Announced Pledges Scenario (APS), 1980–2060, IEA, Paris https://www.iea.org/data-and-statistics/charts/total-primary-energy-demand-in-china-in-the-announced-pledges-scenario-aps-1980-2060
37 International Energy Agency (IEA) (2021). An Energy Sector Roadmap to Carbon Neutrality in China. https://www.iea.org/reports/an-energy-sector-roadmap-to-carbon-neutrality-in-china
38 Elsevier (2020). The Power of Data to Advance the SDGs Mapping Research for the Sustainable Development Goals. https://www.elsevier.com/__data/assets/pdf_file/0004/1058179/Elsevier-SDG-Report-2020.pdf
39 Climate Change Performance Index (CCPI) (n.d.) https://ccpi.org/, website of the CCPI, accessed January 12, 2022.
40 Climate Change Performance Index (n.d.). Results. https://ccpi.org/wp-content/uploads/CCPI-2022-Results_2021-11-10_A4.pdf accessed 02 January 2022
41 Our World in Data (2020). Annual CO_2 Emissions (per capita). https://ourworldindata.org/grapher/co-emissions-per-capita?tab=table
42 Fridays for Future (n.d.). What We Do. Who We Are. https://fridaysforfuture.org/what-we-do/who-we-are/, accessed August 3, 2021
43 European Commission (2021). Circular Cities and Regions Initiative. https://ec.europa.eu/info/research-and-innovation/research-area/environm

ent/circular-economy/circular-cities-and-regions-initiative_en, accessed February 2, 2021.
44 C40 (2020). Climate Change Begins in the City. https://www.c40.org/ending-climate-change-begins-in-the-city
45 The Economist (November 11, 2021). To Prevent Floods, China is Building "Sponge Cities" Soaking it up. https://www.economist.com/china/2021/11/18/to-prevent-floods-china-is-building-sponge-cities.
46 Berlin City Government (n.d.). Digital Monitoring of BEK (2030): diBEK https://dibek.berlin.de/?lang=en, accessed July 10, 2021.
47 Volksentscheid Berlin Autofrei (n.d.) Wir haben es geschafft! (We made it!), https://volksentscheid-berlin-autofrei.de/, accessed December 15, 2021
48 University of Cambridge Institute for Sustainable Leadership (2015). Unhedgeable Risk. How Climate Change Sentiments Impacts Investment. Cambridge.
49 Deutsche Welle (2019). Climate Solutions: Technologies to Slow Climate Change. https://www.dw.com/en/climate-solutions-technologies-to-slow-climate-change/a-51660909
50 Favolini, Alessia. (2018). Mass Tourism—Problems and Solutions to an IncreasinglyWwidespread Phenomenon. *Lybra Tec* https://medium.com/lybra-tech/mass-tourism-problems-and-solutions-to-an-increasingly-widespread-phenomenon-a3570477d83f
51 United Nations (n.d.). Sustainable Tourism. https://sustainabledevelopment.un.org/topics/sustainabletourism, accessed October 26, 2021.
52 Scott, Daniel, and Gössling, Stefan (2021). Destination Net-zero: What Does the International Energy Agency Roadmap Mean for Tourism? *Journal of Sustainable Tourism*. DOI: 10.1080/09669582.2021.1962890
53 United Nations Environment Programme (2019). The German Islet Putting Wind into the Sails of Climate Action and Clean Seas, https://www.unep.org/news-and-stories/story/german-islet-putting-wind-sails-climate-action-and-clean-seas.

Chapter 4: Digitalization

1 Gerhards, Jürgen and Zürn, Michael (2020) … and the Winner Is China; SCRIPTS Berlin, Cluster of Excellence, 22/2021, https://www.scripts-berlin.eu/blog/blog-22-And-the-winner-is____-China/index.html.
2 Statista (2021) Amount of Data Created, Consumed, and Stored 2010-2025, Statista, https://www.statista.com/statistics/871513/worldwide-data-created/
3 Wang, Xiaowei (2020). Blockchain Chicken Farm, New York.
4 *The Economist* (January 02, 2021). Digitizing Japan's Government, 37-38.
5 Sieren, Frank (January 02, 2021) Drohnen. Von Farming bis Militär. *Table China Professional News*.
6 KPMG. (August 10, 2021). Record-Breaking VC Investment in Fintech in First Half of 2021. https://home.kpmg/xx/en/home/media/press-releases/2021/08/record-breaking-vc-investment-in-fintech-in-first-half-of-2021.html
7 Desjardins, Jess/Visual Capitalist (September 7, 2016) Infographic: The 27 Fintech Unicorns, and Where They Were Born (visualcapitalist.com)

Endnotes

8   Lebow, Sara (2021) Proximity Mobile Pay Is on the Rise Worldwide, *Insider Intelligence,* https://www.emarketer.com/content/proximity-mobile-pay-on-rise-worldwide
9   Saarinen, Jeppe (August 30, 2018). Mobile Payments in China: Why Foreign Businesses Should Adopt a Strategy. *China Briefing News.* https://www.china-briefing.com/news/mobile-payments-china-foreign-businesses-china-adopt-strategy/
10 Belen, Martin (January 04, 2021). Boom, Bust and Beyond: What Does the Future Hold for Cryptocurrencies?, EU Start-ups. https://www.eu-startups.com/2021/01/boom-bust-and-beyond-what-does-the-future-hold-for-cryptocurrencies/
11 *The Economist* This Week, (December 30, 2020)
12 *The Economist* (January 02, 2021). The Great Mall of China.
13 *Forbes,* (June 20, 2020) Facebook Copies China's WeChat Once Again. Who Would Have Guessed This? (forbes.com)
14 Stanoevska-Slabeva, Katarina, Lenz-Kesekamp, Vera, and Suter, Viktor (2017). Platforms and the Sharing Economy: An Analysis EU H2020 Research Project Ps2Share: Participation, Privacy, and Power in the Sharing Economy, 2017. SSRN Electronic Journal. https://doi.org/10.2139/ssrn.3102184
15 BBC/Chris Fox (December 20, 2019) Uber Promises Changes to Avoid Germany Ban – BBC News
16 Settle in Berlin.com (2020) The Impact of the Airbnb Ban in Berlin - 6 Months after | Settle in Berlin (settle-in-berlin.com)
17 IBM (2020) Artificial Intelligence. What is Artificial Intelligence (AI)? | IBM
18 What is Artificial Intelligence and how is it Used? | News | European Parliament (europa.eu)
19 *The Economist* (16 January, 2021) The New Era of Innovation-Why a Dawn of Technological Optimism is Breaking. https://www.economist.com/leaders/2021/01/16/why-a-dawn-of-technological-optimism-is-breaking
20 Zuboff, Shoshana (2019). *The Age of Surveillance Capitalism: the Fight for a Human Future at the New Frontier of Power.* Profile Books.
21 Hari, Johann (2022). Stolen Focus: Why You Can't Pay Attention. *Bloomsbury UK.*
22 York, Jillian. C. (2021). Silicon Values. *Adfo Books.*
23 Elliott, Vittoria, Christopher, Nilesh, Deck, Andrew, and Schwartz, Leo. (October 26, 2021). The Facebook Papers Reveal Staggering Failures in the Global South. *Rest of World.* https://restofworld.org/2021/facebook-papers-reveal-staggering-failures-in-global-south/
24 Reuters (April 23, 2019). Facebook's Flood of Languages Leave it Struggling to Monitor Content. *Reuters.* https://www.reuters.com/article/us-facebook-languages-insight-idUSKCN1RZ0DW
25 Chang, Lennon YC and Grabosky, Peter 2017. The Governance of Cyberspace, in: Peter Drahos (eds.) *Regulatory Theory: Foundations and Applications,* Chapter: 31, Publisher: ANY Press
26 Feick, Jürgen, and Werle, Raymund (2010). Regulation of Cyberspace. In R. Baldwin, M. Cave and M. Lodge (Hrsg.), The Oxford handbook of regulation (S. 523–547). Oxford: *Oxford University Press.*
27 Ericson, Richard (2007) Crime in an Insecure World. Cambridge: Polity.

28 Masja Zandbergen, Albers (November 1, 2018). Three Megatrends Shaping the World. Asset Management in Reinform | Robeco.com. https://www.robeco.com/de/aktuelle-analysen/2018/11/three-megatrends-shaping-the-world.html
29 European Commission (2021) https://ec.europa.eu/digital-single-market/en/digital-services-act-package, accessed 27 January 2021.
30 Technology Can Help Us Save the Planet. But More Than Anything, We Must Learn to Value Nature | World Economic Forum (weforum.org)
31 Hilty, Lorenz and Bieser, Jan (2017) Opportunities and Risks of Digitalization for Climate Protection in Switzerland, https://www.ifi.uzh.ch/dam/jcr:06677 6d8-d2b0-4c7c-b75d-6b7283cb5791/Study_Digitalization_Climate_Protection_Oct2017.pdf
32 Econsense and Accenture. (2017). How Companies Can Improve Their Impact on the Sustainable Development Goals (SDGs) and Harness the Power of Digitalization. https://econsense.de/app/uploads/2018/06/econsense_Companies-for-Change_Handbook_2017_3MB.pdf
33 Nuffield Trust/Imison C, Castle-Clarke S, Watson R and Edwards N (2016) Delivering the Benefits of Digital Health Care. Research summary. *Nuffield Trust*. delivering-the-benefits-of-digital-technology-summary-web-final.pdf (nuffield trust.org.uk)
34 Unwin, Tim (2018) ICTs and the Failure of the SDGs and Unwin, Tim 20 February 2020. Digital Technologies are Part of the Climate Change Problem; https://www.ictworks.org/digital-technologies-climate-change-problem/#.X_6xueh-KiUk

Chapter 5: Inequality

1 Avenir Suisse. (2019). An International Think Tank Report on Inequality and Quality. https://www.avenir-suisse.ch/en/publication/inequality/
2 Oxfam International. (January 20, 2020) World's Billionaires Have More Wealth than 4.6 Billion People. *Oxfam International*. https://www.oxfam.org/en/press-releases/worlds-billionaires-have-more-wealth-46-billion-people
3 United Nations. (n.d.). Inequality – Bridging the Divide. https://www.un.org/en/un75/inequality-bridging-divide accessed 02 December 2021
4 Lugo, Maria Ana, Raiser, Martin, and Yemstov, Ruslan (September 24, 2021). What's Next for Poverty Reduction Policies in China? *Brookings*. https://www.brookings.edu/blog/future-development/2021/09/24/whats-next-for-poverty-reduction-policies-in-china/
5 *BBC News*. (February 25, 2021). China's Xi Declares Victory in Ending Extreme Poverty. https://www.bbc.com/news/world-asia-china-56194622
6 Kopf, Dan (April 11, 2019). Thomas Piketty's New Research Shows Rising Inequality in China. *Quartz*. https://qz.com/1591961/thomas-pikettys-new-research-shows-rising-inequality-in-china/
7 Piketty, Thomas, Yang, Li, and Zucman, Gabriel (August 16, 2021) Income Inequality is Growing Fast in China and Making it Look More Like the US. *LSE Business Review*. https://blogs.lse.ac.uk/businessreview/2019/04/01/income-inequality-is-growing-fast-in-china-and-making-it-look-more-like-the-us/

Endnotes

8 Piketty, Thomas and Goldhammer, Arthur (2017). Capital in the Twenty-First Century (Reprint ed.). *Belknap Press*: An Imprint of Harvard University Press.
9 Wilkinson, G. Richard, and Pickett, Kate (2009). *The Spirit Level: Why Equality is Better for Everyone* (2nd ed.). Penguin Books.
10 Wilkinson, G. Richard, and Pickett, Kate (2020). *The Inner Level: How More Equal Societies Reduce Stress, Restore Sanity and Improve Everyone's Well-Being* (Reprint ed.). Penguin Books.
11 Capgemini. (June 29, 2021). World wealth report 2021: North America Breaks 5-Year Trend and Overtakes APAC in High-Net-Worth Population and Wealth. *Capgemini*. https://www.capgemini.com/news/world-wealth-report-2021-north-america-breaks-5-year-trend-and-overtakes-apac-in-high-net-worth-population-and-wealth/
12 Makarov, Igor and Schoar, Antoinette (2021). Blockchain Analysis of the Bitcoin Market. *SSRN Electronic Journal*. https://doi.org/10.2139/ssrn.3949206
13 Mazzucato, Mariana (2021). *Mission Economy: A Moonshot Guide to Changing Capitalism*. Harper Business.
14 Chancel, Lucas, Piketty, Thomas, Saez, Emmanuel, Zucman, Gabriel et al. World Inequality Report 2022, *World Inequality Lab*
15 Scheidel, Walter (2018). *The Great Leveler: Violence and the History of Inequality from the Stone Age to the Twenty-First Century* (The Princeton Economic History of the Western World, 69) (Reprint ed.). Princeton University Press.
16 Piketty, Thomas, and Goldhammer, Arthur (2020). *Capital and Ideology*. Belknap Press: An Imprint of Harvard University Press.
17 Chancel, Lucas, Piketty, Thomas, Saez, Emmanuel, Zucman, Gabriel et al. (2022) World Inequality Report 2022, *World Inequality Lab*.
18 Horobin, William (July 29, 2021). Tax Me If You Can. *Bloomberg*. https://www.bloomberg.com/news/newsletters/2021-07-29/what-s-happening-in-the-world-economy-global-tax-race-to-the-bottom
19 Milton, Friedman (September 13, 1970). A Friedman Doctrine—The Social Responsibility of Business Is to Increase its Profits. *The New York Times*. https://www.nytimes.com/1970/09/13/archives/a-friedman-doctrine-the-social-responsibility-of-business-is-to.html
20 World Bank Group. (January 8, 2020). January 2020 Global Economic Prospects: Slow Growth, Policy Challenges. World Bank. https://www.worldbank.org/en/news/feature/2020/01/08/january-2020-global-economic-prospects-slow-growth-policy-challenges
21 Hope, David, and Limberg, Julian (2022). The Economic Consequences of Major Tax Cuts for the Rich. *Socio-Economic Review*. https://doi.org/10.1093/ser/mwab061
22 Piketty, Thomas, Saez, Emmanuel, and Stantcheva, Stefanie (2014). Optimal Taxation of Top Labor Incomes: A Tale of Three Elasticities. *American Economic Journal: Economic Policy*, 6(1), 230–271. https://doi.org/10.1257/pol.6.1.230
23 Gechert, Sebastian, and Heimberger, Philipp (June 9, 2021). Do Corporate Tax Cuts Boost Economic Growth? wiiw. https://wiiw.ac.at/do-corporate-tax-cuts-boost-economic-growth-p-5821.html
24 Gale, William G., and Samwick, Andrew A. (2014). Effects of Income Tax Changes on Economic Growth. *SSRN Electronic Journal*. https://doi.org/10.2139/ssrn.2494468

25 Kim, Lisa (October 7, 2021). Ireland Agrees to Raise Corporate Tax Rate to a Minimum of 15 Percent, in Effort to Craft Global Pact to Rein in Tax Havens. *Forbes*. https://www.forbes.com/sites/lisakim/2021/10/07/ireland-agrees-to-raise-corporate-tax-rate-to-a-minimum-of-15-in-effort-to-craft-global-pact-to-rein-in-tax-havens/
26 Smith-Meyer, Bjarke, Lorenzo, Aaron, and Scott, Mark (December 22, 2021). EU Pushes on With Global Minimum Tax Rate Despite US Stalemate. *Politico*. https://www.politico.eu/article/eu-pushes-on-with-global-minimum-tax-rate-despite-us-stalemate/
27 Cobham, Alex, Garcia-Bernardo, Javier, Palansky, Miroslav, and Bou Mansour, Mark (November 20, 2020). The State of Tax Justice 2020. *Tax Justice Network*. https://taxjustice.net/reports/the-state-of-tax-justice-2020/
28 Fitzgibbon, Will, and Hudson, Michael (April 3, 2021). Five Years Later, Panama Papers Still Having a Big Impact. *ICIJ*. https://www.icij.org/investigations/panama-papers/five-years-later-panama-papers-still-having-a-big-impact
29 ICIJ. (December 20, 2021). Pandora Papers. https://www.icij.org/investigations/pandora-papers/
30 ICIJ. (October 3, 2021). Offshore havens and hidden riches of world leaders and billionaires exposed in unprecedented leak. *ICIJ*. https://www.icij.org/investigations/pandora-papers/global-investigation-tax-havens-offshore/
31 Eisinger, Jesse, Ernsthausen, Jeff, and Kiel, Paul (June 8, 2021). The Secret IRS Files: Trove of Never-Before-Seen Records Reveal How the Wealthiest Avoid Income Tax. *ProPublica*. https://www.propublica.org/article/the-secret-irs-files-trove-of-never-before-seen-records-reveal-how-the-wealthiest-avoid-income-tax
32 Gilbert, Ben (June 13, 2021) How Billionaires Like Jeff Bezos and Elon Musk Avoid Paying Federal Income Tax While Increasing Their Net Worth by Billions. *Business Insider*. https://www.businessinsider.com/how-billionaires-avoid-paying-federal-income-tax-2021-6?international=true&r=US&IR=T
33 To be sure, this is not to demonize "the rich". In this chapter we do not seek to make a normative assessment as to the morality of such realities, but rather present evidence in support of the urgent need to tackle inequality, which inevitably means that the wealthiest must become much less wealthy. A discussion on how, or whether this is even feasible will come in the next sections.
34 Revuelta, Julio (2021). The Effects of the Economic Adjustment Programmes for Greece: A Quasi-Experimental Approach. *Sustainability*, 13(9), 4970. https://doi.org/10.3390/su13094970
35 Tyrovolas, Stefanos et al. (2018). The Burden of Disease in Greece, Health Loss, Risk Factors, and Health Financing, 2000–16: an Analysis of the Global Burden of Disease Study 2016. *The Lancet Public Health*, 3(8), e395–e406. https://doi.org/10.1016/s2468-2667(18)30130-0
36 World Inequality Database. (2020). Global Inequality Data - 2020 update. World Inequality Database. https://wid.world/news-article/2020-regional-updates/
37 Kirsten, Johann and Sihlobo, Wandile (August 3, 2021). How a Land Reform Agency Could Break South Africa's Land Redistribution Deadlock. *The Conversation*. https://theconversation.com/how-a-land-reform-agency-could-break-south-africas-land-redistribution-deadlock-165480

Endnotes

38 Alvaredo, Facundo, Cogneau, Denis and Piketty, Thomas (2021) Income Inequality under Colonial Rule. Evidence from French Algeria, Cameroon, Tunisia, and Vietnam and Comparisons with British Colonies 1920–1960. *Journal of Development Economics*, 152, 102680. https://doi.org/10.1016/j.jdeveco.2021.102680
39 Wealth Inequality Database. (2021). Tunisia. Wealth Inequality Database. https://wid.world/country/tunisia/
40 Acemoglu, Daron, & Robinson, A. James (2012). Why Nations Fail. Crown.
41 Belcher, Erica (March 24, 2017). Inequality in Mexico and How to Address It. LSE Government Blog. https://blogs.lse.ac.uk/government/2017/03/24/inequality-in-mexico-and-how-to-address-it/
42 Banerjee, V. Abhijit and Duflo, Esther (2021). *Good Economics for Hard Times*. New York: PublicAffairs.
43 Autor, David, Dorn, David, Katz, Lawrence F., Patterson, Christina and Van Reenen, John (2020). The Fall of the Labor Share and the Rise of Superstar Firms. *The Quarterly Journal of Economics*, 135(2), 645–709. https://doi.org/10.1093/qje/qjaa004
44 Wiltshire, C. Justin (2021) Walmart Supercenters and Monopsony Power: How a Large, Low-Wage Employer Impacts Local Labor Markets [Doctoral dissertation, University of California, Davis]. Squarespace. https://static1.squarespace.com/static/5e0fdcef27e0945c43fab131/t/618639fa292dc404223f562a/1636186621526/JustinCWiltshire_JMP.pdf
45 Kleven, Henrik Jacobsen (2014). How Can Scandinavians Tax so Much? *Journal of Economic Perspectives*, 28(4), 77–98. https://doi.org/10.1257/jep.28.4.77
46 Pomerleau, Kyle (June 10, 2015). How Scandinavian Countries Pay for Their Government Spending. *Tax Foundation*. https://taxfoundation.org/how-scandinavian-countries-pay-their-government-spending/
47 Gornick, Janet C. and Smeeding, Timothy M. (2018). Redistributional Policy in-Rich Countries: Institutions and Impacts in Nonelderly Households. *Annual Review of Sociology*, 44(1), 441–468. https://doi.org/10.1146/annurev-soc-073117-041114
48 Gornick, Janet C. and Smeeding, Timothy M. (2018). Redistributional Policy in-Rich Countries: Institutions and Impacts in Nonelderly Households. *Annual Review of Sociology*, 44(1), 441–468. https://doi.org/10.1146/annurev-soc-073117-041114
49 Eaton, George (October 18, 2021). How Redistributive was New Labor? *New Statesman*. https://www.newstatesman.com/politics/labour/2021/10/how-redistributive-was-new-labour
50 Donado, Alejandro and Wälde, Klaus (2012). How Trade Unions Increase Welfare. The Economic Journal, 122(563), 990–1009. https://doi.org/10.1111/j.1468-0297.2012.02513.x
51 Akee, Randall, Copeland, William, Holbein, John B. and Simeonova, Emilia (2020). Human Capital and Voting Behavior Across Generations: Evidence from an Income Intervention. *American Political Science Review*, 114(2). https://doi.org/10.1017/S000305541900090X
52 Schoene, Matthew and Allaway, Isabel (2019). Income Inequality and European Protest Activity. *Michigan Sociological Review*, 33, 76–97. https://www.jstor.org/stable/26868252

53 Solt, Frederick (2015). Economic Inequality and Nonviolent Protest. *Social Science Quarterly*, 96(5), 1314–1327. https://doi.org/10.1111/ssqu.12198
54 Scheve, Kenneth and Stasavage, David (2016). *Taxing the Rich: A History of Fiscal Fairness in the United States and Europe*. Princeton University Press, p. 10, Figure 1.1.
55 Chancel, Lucas, Piketty, Thomas, Saez, Emmanuel, Zucman, Gabriel et al. (2022) World Inequality Report 2022, World Inequality Lab
56 Chancel, Lucas, Piketty, Thomas, Saez, Emmanuel, Zucman, Gabriel et al. World Inequality Report 2022, *World Inequality Lab*
57 *The Economist*. (November 19, 2020). Why Money is Changing Hands Much Less Frequently. https://www.economist.com/finance-and-economics/2020/11/21/why-money-is-changing-hands-much-less-frequently
58 Bruenig, Matt (November 30, 2017). A Simple Fix for Our Massive Inequality Problem. *The New York Times*. https://www.nytimes.com/2017/11/30/opinion/inequality-social-wealth-fund.html
59 Atkinson, B. Anthony (2018). Inequality: What Can Be Done? (Reprint ed.). *Harvard University Press*.
60 Berman, Yonatan and Milanovic, Branko (2020). Homoploutia: Top Labor and Capital Incomes in the United States, 1950−2020 (LIS Working Paper no. 806) Luxembourg Income Study (*LIS*), asbl. http://www.lisdatacenter.org/wps/liswps/806.pdf.
61 Esping-Andersen, Gøsta (1990). The Three Worlds of Welfare Capitalism. *Princeton University Press*.
62 In Chapter 8, we shall further discuss the overlap of inequality and urban planning, by examining food deserts.
63 King, Noel (April 7, 2021). A Brief History of How Racism Shaped Interstate Highways. *NPR*. https://choice.npr.org/index.html?origin=https://www.npr.org/2021/04/07/984784455/a-brief-history-of-how-racism-shaped-interstate-highways?t=1641037036886
64 Advani, Arun, Smith, Sarah, Waltmann, Ben and Xu, Xiaowei (October 4, 2021). Gender Differences in Subject Choice Leads to Gender Pay Gap Immediately After Graduation. *Institute for Fiscal Studies*. https://ifs.org.uk/publications/15657
65 Conference on Diversity and Inclusion in Economics, Finance, and Central Banking. (November 9, 2021). Board of Governors of the Federal Reserve System. https://www.federalreserve.gov/conferences/conference-on-diversity-and-inclusion-in-economics-finance-and-central-banking.htm
66 Gruver, Jackson (November 30, 2021). Racial Wage Gap for Men−Payscale. Payscale−Salary Comparison, Salary Survey, Search Wages. https://www.payscale.com/research-and-insights/racial-wage-gap-for-men/
67 Shih, Margaret, Pittinsky, Todd L. and Ambady, Nalini (1999). Stereotype Susceptibility: Identity Salience and Shifts in Quantitative Performance. Psychological Science, 10(1), 80–83. https://doi.org/10.1111/1467-9280.00111
68 Blair, Irene V., Judd, Charles M. and Chapleau, Kristine M. (2004). The Influence of Afrocentric Facial Features in Criminal Sentencing. Psychological Science, 15(10), 674–679. https://doi.org/10.1111/j.0956-7976.2004.00739.x
69 Farber, Henry S., Herbst, Daniel, Kuziemko, Ilyana and Naidu, Suresh (2021). Unions and Inequality Over the Twentieth Century: New Evidence from

Endnotes

Survey Data. *The Quarterly Journal of Economics*, 136(3), 1325–1385. https://doi.org/10.1093/qje/qjab012

70 The White House. (September 8, 2021). Remarks by President Biden in Honor of Labor Unions. The White House. https://www.whitehouse.gov/briefing-room/speeches-remarks/2021/09/08/remarks-by-president-biden-in-honor-of-labor-unions/

71 Farber, Henry. S., Herbst, Daniel, Kuziemko, Ilyana, and Naidu, Suresh (2021). Unions and Inequality over the Twentieth Century: New Evidence from Survey Data. *The Quarterly Journal of Economics*, 136(3), 1325–1385. https://doi.org/10.1093/qje/qjab012

72 Sullivan, Daniel and von Wachter, Till (2009). Job Displacement and Mortality: An Analysis Using Administrative Data. *Quarterly Journal of Economics*, 124(3), 1265–1306. https://doi.org/10.1162/qjec.2009.124.3.1265

73 Autor, David H., Dorn, David and Hanson, Gordon H. (2016). The China Shock: Learning from Labor-Market Adjustment to Large Changes in Trade. *Annual Review of Economics*, 8(1), 205–240. https://doi.org/10.1146/annurev-economics-080315-015041

74 Paul, Mark, Darity, William, Jr and Hamilton, Darrick (March 9, 2018). The Federal Job Guarantee – A Policy to Achieve Permanent Full Employment. *Center on Budget and Policy Priorities*. https://www.cbpp.org/research/full-employment/the-federal-job-guarantee-a-policy-to-achieve-permanent-full-employment

75 Dube, Arindrajit (March 22, 2021). Using Wage Boards to Raise Pay. Economics for inclusive prosperity. https://econfip.org/policy-briefs/using-wage-boards-to-raise-pay/

76 The Economist. (October 21, 2021). A Real-Time Revolution Will Up-End the Practice of Macroeconomics. https://www.economist.com/leaders/2021/10/23/a-real-time-revolution-will-up-end-the-practice-of-macroeconomics

77 Stepek, John (September 30, 2021). Rising Bond Yields are Unnerving Markets and it Could Get Worse Before it Gets Better. MoneyWeek. https://moneyweek.com/investments/bonds/government-bonds/603925/rising-bond-yields-are-unnerving-markets

78 Rudd, Jeremy B. (2021). Why Do We Think That Inflation Expectations Matter for Inflation? (And Should We?). Finance and Economics Discussion Series, 2021-062. Board of Governors of the Federal Reserve System. https://doi.org/10.17016/FEDS.2021.062

79 Irwin, Neil (October 15, 2021). How Does the Economy Work? A New Fed Paper Suggests Nobody Really Knows. *The New York Times*. https://www.nytimes.com/2021/10/01/upshot/inflation-economy-analysis.html

80 Smialek, Jeanna (October 11, 2021). David Card, Joshua Angrist and Guido Imbens Win Nobel in Economics 2021. *The New York Times*: https://www.nytimes.com/2021/10/11/business/nobel-economics-prize-david-card-joshua-angrist-guido-imbens.html

81 Wren-Lewis, Simon (April, 2019). Views on the Minimum Wage Show Economics to be an Inexact Science. BlogSpot. https://mainlymacro.blogspot.com/2019/04/views-on-minimum-wage-show-economics-to.html?utm_source=feedburner&utm_medium=feed&utm_campaign=Feed:+MainlyMacro+(mainly+macro)

82 Florida, Richard (April 26, 2019). In Praise of a Higher Minimum Wage. *Bloomberg*. https://www.bloomberg.com/news/articles/2019-04-26/economists-are-learning-to-love-the-minimum-wage

83 Martinez Hickey, Sebastian, Cooper, David (August 24, 2021). Cutting Unemployment Insurance Benefits did not Boost Job Growth: July State Jobs Data Show a Widespread Recovery. *Economic Policy Institute*. https://www.epi.org/blog/cutting-unemployment-insurance-benefits-did-not-boost-job-growth-july-state-jobs-data-show-a-widespread-recovery/

84 Government of New Zealand. (May 20, 2021). Wellbeing Budget 2021: Securing Our Recovery. treasury.govt.nz. https://www.treasury.govt.nz/publications/wellbeing-budget/wellbeing-budget-2021-securing-our-recovery-html

85 Bivens, Josh (December 12, 2017). Inequality is Slowing U.S. Economic Growth: Faster Wage Growth for Low- and Middle-Wage Workers is the Solution. *Economic Policy Institute*. https://www.epi.org/publication/secular-stagnation/

86 Auclert, Adrien and Rognlie, Matthew (2018). Inequality and Aggregate Demand (NBER Working paper no. 24280). *NBER*. https://doi.org/10.3386/w24280

87 Ostry, Jonathan, Berg, Andrew and Tsangarides, Charalambos (2014). Redistribution, Inequality, and Growth. Staff Discussion Notes, 14(02), 1. https://doi.org/10.5089/9781484352076.006

88 Cingano, Federico (2014), Trends in Income Inequality and its Impact on Economic Growth, OECD Social, Employment and Migration Working Papers, No. 163, OECD Publishing. http://dx.doi.org/10.1787/5jxrjncwxv6j-en

89 Petersen, Thieß (2019). Einfluss der Einkommensungleichheit auf das Bruttoinlandsprodukt: Theoretische Überlegungen. Wirtschaftsdienst, 99, 267–271. https://doi.org/10.1007/s10273-019-2442-8

90 Kontrast.at (November 10, 2020). Finland Ends Homelessness and Provides Shelter for All in Need. *Scoop*. https://scoop.me/housing-first-finland-homelessness/

91 Watson, Bridgette (October 7, 2020). A B.C. Research Project Gave Homeless People $7,500 Each – the Results Were "Beautifully Surprising." CBC. https://www.cbc.ca/news/canada/british-columbia/new-leaf-project-results-1.5752714

92 Piketty, Thomas (2017). *Capital in the Twenty-First Century* (A. Goldhammer, Trans.). Belknap Press.

93 DIW Berlin. (2016). Wer trägt die Steuerlast in Deutschland? Verteilungswirkungen des deutschen Steuer- und Transfersystems: Forschungsprojekt, gefördert von der Hans-Böckler-Stiftung. *DIW Berlin*. https://www.diw.de/de/diw_01.c.542155.de/publikationen/politikberatung_kompakt/2016_0114/wer_traegt_die_steuerlast_in_deutschland__verteilungswirkung___forschungsprojekt__gefoerdert_von_der_hans-boeckler-stiftung.html

94 Felbermayr, Gabriel, Baumgarten, Daniel and Lehwald, Sybille (2015). Increasing Wage Inequality in Germany. *Global Economic Dynamics*. https://www.bertelsmann-stiftung.de/fileadmin/files/BSt/Publikationen/GrauePublikationen/Studie_NW_Increasing_Wage_Inequality_2015.pdf

95 Felbermayr, Gabriel, Baumgarten, Daniel and Lehwald, Sybille (2015). Increasing Wage Inequality in Germany. *Global Economic Dynamics*. https://www.bertelsmann-stiftung.de/fileadmin/files/BSt/Publikationen/GrauePublikationen/Studie_NW_Increasing_Wage_Inequality_2015.pdf

Endnotes

96 Beramendi, Pablo and Rueda, David (2007). Social Democracy Constrained: Indirect Taxation in Industrialized Democracies. *British Journal of Political Science*, 37(4), 619–641. https://doi.org/10.1017/s0007123407000348

97 Hakelberg, Lukas and Rixen, Thomas (2021). Is Neoliberalism still Spreading? The Impact of International Cooperation on Capital Taxation, *Review of International Political Economy*, 28:5, 1142-1168, DOI: 10.1080/09692290.2020.1752769

98 Frankovic, Kathy (July 26, 2021). The Public Supports the Child Tax Credit, but They View it as a Temporary Solution. *YouGovAmerica*. https://today.yougov.com/topics/politics/articles-reports/2021/07/26/public-supports-child-tax-credit

99 Ait Bihi Ouali, Laila (2020). Effects of Signaling Tax Evasion on Redistribution and Voting Preferences: Evidence from the Panama Papers. *PLoS ONE*, 15(3), e0229394. https://doi.org/10.1371/journal.pone.0229394

100 Perez-Truglia, Ricardo (2020). The Effects of Income Transparency on Well-Being: Evidence from a Natural Experiment. *American Economic Review*, 110(4), 1019–54. https://doi.org/10.1257/aer.20160256

101 Gimpelson, Vladimir and Treisman, Daniel (2015). Misperceiving Inequality. *SSRN Electronic Journal*. https://doi.org/10.2139/ssrn.2655048

102 Bellani, Luna, Bledow, Nona, Busemeyer, R. Marius and Schwerdt, Guido (2021). When Everyone Thinks They're Middle-Class: (Mis-)Perceptions of Inequality and Why They Matter for Social Policy. *Das Progressive Zentrum*. https://www.progressives-zentrum.org/wp-content/uploads/2021/05/210521_UKZ_Policy_Paper_06_Bledow-Bellani_EN_web_RZ.pdf

103 Hauser, Oliver P. and Norton, Michael I. (2017). (Mis)perceptions of Inequality. *Current Opinion in Psychology*, 18, 21–25. https://doi.org/10.1016/j.copsyc.2017.07.024

104 Bartels, M. Larry (2005). Homer gets a tax cut: Inequality and Public Policy in the American mind. *Perspectives on Politics*, 3(1), 15–31. https://www.jstor.org/stable/3688108

105 Hauser, Oliver P., Kraft-Todd, Gordon T., Rand, David G., Nowak, Martin A. and Norton, Michael I. (2019) Invisible inequality Leads to Punishing the Poor and Rewarding the Rich. *Behavioural Public Policy*, 5(3), 1–21. https://doi.org/10.1017/bpp.2019.4

106 Hoy, Christopher and Toth, Russell (2019). Aligning Preferences for Redistribution of Right and Left Wing Voters by Correcting Their Beliefs about Inequality: Evidence from a Randomized Survey Experiment in Australia. *SSRN Electronic Journal*. https://doi.org/10.2139/ssrn.3359391

107 Emmenegger, Patrick and Marx, Paul (2018). The Politics of Inequality as Organized Spectacle: Why the Swiss Do not Want to Tax the Rich. *New Political Economy*, 24(1), 103–124. https://doi.org/10.1080/13563467.2017.1420641

108 Stantcheva, Stefanie (2021). Perceptions and Preferences for Redistribution (NBER Working Paper No. 29370). *National Bureau of Economic Research*. https://doi.org/10.3386/w29370

109 Alesina, Alberto F. and Stantcheva, Stefanie (2020). Diversity, Immigration, and Redistribution. *SSRN Electronic Journal*. https://doi.org/10.2139/ssrn.3514360

Chapter 6: Demography

1. Malthus, Thomas (1798). *Essay on the Principle of Population.* London.
2. Marx, Karl (1867). *Das Kapital 1,* in the edition translated by Ben Fowkes (1976), the reference to Malthus is on the pages 782–802.
3. Rockey, Francisca / Euronews Green (2021). https://www.euronews.com/green/2021/03/21/the-dangers-of-eco-fascism-and-why-it-s-a-veneer-for-racist-beliefs
4. Megatrends Watch (2021). http://www.megatrendswatch.com/demographic-megatrends.html
5. The Economist (December 11, 2021). Why the Demographic Transition is Speeding up. https://www.economist.com/finance-and-economics/2021/12/11/why-the-demographic-transition-is-speeding-up
6. German Federal Statistical Office (2021). Press Release. https://www.destatis.de/EN/Press/2021/09/PE21_459_12411.html;jsessionid=E06201EC15F720 2FCEB51A3F9497737A.live712, accessed October 19, 2021.
7. The Economist (December 11, 2021). Why the Demographic Transition is Speeding up. https://www.economist.com/finance-and-economics/2021/12/11/why-the-demographic-transition-is-speeding-up
8. European Commission (2021). The Impacts of Democratic Change in Europe, https://ec.europa.eu/info/strategy/priorities-2019-2024/new-push-european-democracy/impact-demographic-change-europe_en
9. Blystad, Astrid et al. (2020). Reproductive Health and the Politics of Abortion. International Journal of Equity in Health 19, 39 (2020). https://doi.org/10.1186/s12939-020-1157-1
10. Pew Research Center (2021). Public Opinion on Abortion. https://www.pewforum.org/fact-sheet/public-opinion-on-abortion/, accessed 10.10.2021.
11. Club of Rome (1972). *The Limits of Growth.* Rome.
12. Bongaarts, John (2009). Human Population Growth and the Demographic Transition, Philos *Trans R Soc Lond B Biol Sci.* 2009 Oct 27; 364(1532): 2985–2990, doi: 10.1098/rstb.2009.0137
13. Berlin-Institut / Konrad Adenauer Foundation (2022). Glaube in Aktion. Wie religiöse Organisationen den demografischen Wandel in Westafrika voranbringen. https://www.kas.de/de/web/westafrika/publikationen/einzeltitel/-/content/la-foi-en-action
14. Population Reference Bureau (2021). Total Fertility Rate.
15. Population Reference Bureau (2021). The World's Population https://interactives.prb.org/2021-wpds/, accessedOctober 10, 2021
16. Davies, N.G., Klepac, P., Liu, Y. et al. Age-dependent Effects in the Transmission and Control of COVID-19 Epidemics. Nat Med 26, 1205–1211 (2020). https://doi.org/10.1038/s41591-020-0962-9
17. Wichterich, Christa/Heinrich Böll Foundation (2012). The Future We Want. A Feminist Perspective. Publication Series on Ecology, Vol. 21, Berlin. https://www.boell.de/sites/default/files/endf_the_future_we_want.pdf
18. Bertelsmann Foundation 2019. Megatrend Report 1. The Bigger Picture. https://www.bertelsmann-stiftung.de/de/publikationen/publikation/did/the-bigger-picture-1

Endnotes

19 Jarzebski, Marcin P., Elmqvist, Thomas, Gasparatos, Alexandros et al. (2021), Ageing and Population Shrinking: Implications for Sustainability in the Urban Century. npj Urban Sustain 1, 17 (2021). https://doi.org/10.1038/s42949-021-00023-z.

20 Bertelsmann Foundation (2019). Megatrends, https://www.bertelsmann-stiftung.de/de/publikationen/publikation/did/megatrends (e-book).

21 Tremmel, Jörg Chet (2008) An Ethical Assessment of the Legitimacy of Antinatalistic Birth Policies. In: Tremmel J. (ed.) Demographic Change and Intergenerational Justice. Springer, Berlin, Heidelberg. https://doi.org/10.1007/978-3-540-77084-8_8

22 Table China Professional Briefing (February 02, 2021). https://table.media/china/en/

23 National Statistics Bureau/Reuters (January 17, 2022). China's Birth Rate Drops to Record Low in 2021, https://www.reuters.com/world/china/birth-rate-mainland-china-2021-drops-record-low-2022-01-17/

24 PopulationPyramid.net (2021). List of Countries Ordered by their Population Size, https://www.populationpyramid.net/population-size-per-country/2050/

25 Eurostat (2020). Populations to Decline in Two-thirds of EU Regions. https://ec.europa.eu/eurostat/de/web/products-eurostat-news/-/ddn-20210430-2

26 Eurostat (2020). Ageing Europe - Statistics on Population Developments.

27 United Nations, Department of Economic and Social Affairs. Population Dynamics, World Population Prospects (data of 2019). https://population.un.org/wpp/Graphs/DemographicProfiles/Line/908

28 United Nations. Department of Economic and Social Affairs (2019). World Population Ageing 2019. https://www.un.org/en/development/desa/population/publications/pdf/ageing/WorldPopulationAgeing2019-Highlights.pdf

29 United Nations. Department of Economic and Social Affairs (2019). World Population Ageing 2019. https://www.un.org/en/development/desa/population/publications/pdf/ageing/WorldPopulationAgeing2019-Highlights.pdf

30 United Nations. Department of Economic and Social Affairs (2019). World Population Ageing 2019, pp. 11-12.

31 Chen, Cynthia; Maung, Kenwing and Rowe, John (2021). Gender Differences in Countries' Adaptation to Societal Ageing: an International Cross-sectional Comparison, The Lancet Healthy Longevity, Vol. 2, Issue 8, E460-E469, August 1, 2021

32 European Parliament (December, 2020). Japan's Ageing Society. https://www.europarl.europa.eu/RegData/etudes/BRIE/2020/659419/EPRS_BRI(2020)659419_EN.pdf

33 Srivastava, Shobhit and Muhammad, T. (2021). In Pursuit of Happiness: Changes in Living Arrangement and Subjective Well-Being among Older Adults in India. Population Journal of Population Ageing (2021). https://doi.org/10.1007/s12062-021-09327-5

34 Tai, Tsui-o and Tu, Hsien-Chih (2021). The Effect of Grandparental Care on Men's and Women's Parenting Practices in Taiwan. Journal of Population Ageing (2021). https://doi.org/10.1007/s12062-021-09324-8

35 Hardin, Garrett (1968). Tragedy of the Commons. Science 162/1968, pp. 1243-1248.

36 Club of Rome (2016). Reinventing Prosperity. https://www.clubofrome.org/publication/reinventing-prosperity-2016/

37 Cod, David J. (2019). The Dangerous Intersection of Demographics and Digitalization. Aart Jan De Geus gives his thoughts on how Sitra can help prepare Finland for the future. SITRA News, September 26, 2019. https://www.sitra.fi/en/articles/the-dangerous-intersection-of-demographics-and-digitalisation/
38 The Economist (August 2, 2012). Demography and Inequality. https://www.economist.com/feast-and-famine/2012/08/02/demography-and-inequality
39 The Economist (August 2, 2012). Demography and Inequality. https://www.economist.com/feast-and-famine/2012/08/02/demography-and-inequality
40 Japaridze, Irakli (2019). Envy, Inequality and Fertility. Review of Economics of the Household 17, pp. 923–945 (2019). https://doi.org/10.1007/s11150-018-9427-z

Chapter 7: Urbanization and Smart Cities

1 United Nations Habitat (2021). World Cities Report 2020: The Value of Sustainable Urbanization. https://unhabitat.org/World%20Cities%20Report%202020
2 Our World in Data / Ritchie, Hannah and Roser, Max. Urbanization (n.d.). https://ourworldindata.org/urbanization#urbanization-over-the-past-500-years, accessed February 1, 2022.
3 Our World in Data / Ritchie, Hannah and Roser, Max. Urbanization. https://ourworldindata.org/urbanization#urbanization-over-the-past-500-years
4 China Table (November 19, 2021). Professional Briefing. English edition, #215. https://table.media/china/en/
5 OECD (2020). Africa's Urbanisation Dynamics 2020. https://www.oecd-ilibrary.org/development/africa-s-urbanisation-dynamics-2020_b6bccb81-en;jsessionid=Dkc6WATizzQ48oN126TSoGHn.ip-10-240-5-37
6 Blackrock (2021). Megatrends. Rapid Urbanization. https://www.blackrock.com/ch/individual/en/themes/megatrends/urbanisation, accessed August 08, 2021
7 Habitat (n.d.) The New Urban Agenda. https://habitat3.org/the-new-urban-agenda/, accessed December 14, 2021.
8 Glaeser, Edward and Steinberg, Bryce Millett (2016). Transforming cities. Does urbanization promote democratic change?, National Bureau of Economic Research Working Paper 22860, https://www.nber.org/papers/w22860
9 The Line (n.d.) https://www.neom.com/whatistheline/, accessed December 14, 2021; Deutsche Welle (January 11, 2021). Saudi Arabia to Build a Zero Emissions City. https://www.dw.com/en/saudi-arabia-to-build-a-zero-emissions-city/a-56189240
10 *The Economist* (January 16, 2021), The Line in Saudi Arabia is an Urbanist's Dream, p. 26.
11 A Giant Car-Free City Is Being Built in Shenzhen, China — autoevolution. https://www.autoevolution.com/news/a-giant-car-free-city-is-being-built-in-shenzhen-china-144990.html, accessed January 21, 2022
12 Ellen MacArthur Foundation/ARUP (2019). Urban Buildings Systems Summary, Buildings_All_Mar19.pdf (ellenmacarthurfoundation.org)
13 Digi.City (2021). https://www.digi.city/smart-city-definitions, accessed September 09, 2021

Endnotes

14 Brügge, Fernando Alberto/Cities today (January 26, 2021). Smart Cities of the Future: Seven Things that Successful Cities Do. https://cities-today.com/industry/smart-cities-of-the-future-7-things-that-successful-cities-do/
15 Smart City Berlin (2021). https://smart-city-berlin.de/en/actors/about-the-network/, accessed 08.04.2021
16 Shenzhen Government (March 24, 2021). City Unveils GEP System for Sustained development. http://www.sz.gov.cn/en_szgov/news/latest/content/post_8645665.html, accessed 10.12.2021
17 Urban Hub (2021). People Sharing Cities. https://www.urban-hub.com/cities/
18 New York Times (November 8, 2021). Hidden Toll of the Northwest Heat. https://www.nytimes.com/interactive/2021/08/11/climate/deaths-pacific-northwest-heat-wave.html
19 Euronews (December 8, 2021). Greece wildfires 'worst ecological disaster' in decades, says PM Mitsotakis. https://www.euronews.com/green/2021/08/12/greece-wildfires-worst-ecological-disaster-in-decades-says-pm-mitsotakis
20 Westen, Phoebe and Watts, Jonathan/The Guardian (August 11, 2021). Highest Recorded Temperature of 48.8C in Europe Apparently Logged in Sicily. https://www.theguardian.com/world/2021/aug/11/sicily-logs-488c-temperature-possibly-highest-ever-recorded-for-europe
21 Michael G. Jacobides, Michael (2021). We need an environmental protection agency now. https://www.ekathimerini.com/opinion/1166211/we-need-an-environmental-protection-agency-now/
22 Pierer, Carl and Creutzig, Felix (2019), Star-shaped cities alleviate trade-off between climate change mitigation and adaptation, Environmental Research Letters. https://iopscience.iop.org/article/10.1088/1748-9326/ab2081
23 Hotz, Robert Lee/The Wall Street Journal (June 4, 2021). To Offset Climate Change, Scientists Tout City Trees and Ultra-White Paint. https://www.wsj.com/articles/to-offset-climate-change-scientists-tout-city-trees-and-ultra-white-paint-11622822424
24 Watson, Vanessa (2015). The Allure of 'Smart City' Rhetoric: India and Africa. Dialogues in Human Geography, 5(1), 36–3 https://doi.org/10.1177/2043820614565868
25 Saha, Sagatom (November 21, 2019). Chinese Companies Are Worse at Business Than You Think. *Foreign Policy.* https://foreignpolicy.com/2019/11/21/malaysia-china-forest-city-development-project/
26 Burdett, Ricky (2016). Inequality and Urban Growth. OECD Forum 2016. https://www.oecd.org/social/inequality-urban-growth.htm
27 Tacoli, Cecilia (2017). Migration and Inclusive Urbanization, UN Expert Group Meeting on Sustainable Cities, Human Mobility, and International Migration, Population Division Department of Economic and Social Affairs United Nations Secretariat New York, September, 7-8, 2017.
28 Hawkes, Corinna; Harris, Jody and Gillespie, Stuart (2017). Changing Diets: Urbanization and the Nutrition Transition, in: IFPRI. Global Food Policy Report https://ebrary.ifpri.org/digital/collection/p15738coll2/id/131089
29 Larsson, Naomi/The Guardian (January 17, 2019) Which is the World's Most Vegan City? https://www.theguardian.com/cities/2019/jan/17/which-is-the-worlds-most-vegan-city

30 Shenoy, Sanjana (December 2, 2021) Israel's Tel Aviv Becomes Vegan Capital Of The World. https://curlytales.com/israels-tel-aviv-becomes-vegan-capital-of-the-world/
31 World Green Building Council 2017. Global Status Report 2017. Global Status Report 2017 | World Green Building Council (worldgbc.org)
32 Lobet, Ingrid/Green Tech Media (January 05, 2021). Cutting Concrete's Carbon Footprint. https://www.greentechmedia.com/articles/read/cutting-concretes-carbon-footprint#.YAhWtd2tdLc.linkedin
33 World Green Building Council 2021. https://www.worldgbc.org/news-media/WorldGBC-embodied-carbon-report-published, accessed 26 January 2021.
34 Ellen MacArthur Foundation (2021). The Built Environment. https://web.archive.org/web/20201129112426/https://www.ellenmacarthurfoundation.org/our-work/activities/covid-19/the-built-environment
35 Chinnotopia (December 14, 2021). Future Designed by China. Webinar Series of Technische Universität Berlin. From Smog to Smart: Chinas Städte der Zukunft (Chinese Cities of the Future), www.chinnotopia.de

Chapter 8: Health and Nutrition

1 United Nations. THE 17 GOALS | Sustainable Development. Un.Org. https://sdgs.un.org/goals
2 Ortiz-Ospina, Esteban, Roser, Max (2016). Global Health. Our World in Data. https://ourworldindata.org/health-meta
3 Roser, Max, Ortiz-Ospina, Esteban, Ritchie, Hannah (2013). Life Expectancy. Our World in Data. https://ourworldindata.org/life-expectancy#twice-as-long-life-expectancy-around-the-world
4 WHO. (2020). World Health Statistics 2020 visual summary. World Health Organisation. https://www.who.int/data/gho/whs-2020-visual-summary
5 Zukunftsinstitut. (December 17, 2021). Megatrend Gesundheit. Zukunftsinstitut, 2021. https://www.zukunftsinstitut.de/dossier/megatrend-gesundheit/
6 GTAI. (2021). Healthcare Market. Germany Trade & Invest. https://www.gtai.de/gtai-en/invest/industries/life-sciences/healthcare-market-65626#:%7E:text=Healthcare%20spending%20in%20Germany%20exceeds,largest%20economic%20sectors%20in%20Germany.
7 Wippermann, Peter and Krüger, Jens (2020). *Werteindex 2020*. Deutscher Fachverlag.
8 World Health Organization. (April, 2019). WHO Global Strategy on Digital Health 2020–2024.
9 WHO. (June 24, 2020). An Update on the Fight Against Antimicrobial Resistance. World Health Organisation. https://www.who.int/news-room/feature-stories/detail/an-update-on-the-fight-against-antimicrobial-resistance
10 WHO. (January 29, 2018). High Levels of Antibiotic Resistance Found Worldwide, New Data Shows. World Health Organization. https://www.who.int/news/item/29-01-2018-high-levels-of-antibiotic-resistance-found-worldwide-new-data-shows
11 The Alexander Fleming Laboratory Museum, London, U.K. (1999). The Discovery and Development of Penicillin 1928–1945 [booklet]. American Chemical

Endnotes

Society. https://www.acs.org/content/dam/acsorg/education/whatischemistry/landmarks/flemingpenicillin/the-discovery-and-development-of-penicillin-commemorative-booklet.pdf

12 Kocher, Bob and Emanuel, Zeke (March 5, 2019). Will Robots Replace Doctors? *Brookings*. https://www.brookings.edu/blog/usc-brookings-schaeffer-on-health-policy/2019/03/05/will-robots-replace-doctors/

13 See for example: Hoffman, Kelly M., Trawalter, Sophie, Axt, Jordan R. and Oliver, M. Norman (2016). Racial Bias in Pain Assessment and Treatment Recommendations, and False Beliefs about Biological Differences Between Blacks and Whites. *Proceedings of the National Academy of Sciences*, 113(16), 4296–4301. https://doi.org/10.1073/pnas.1516047113

14 Choi-Schagrin, W. (August 14, 2021). In the West, a Connection Between COVID and Wildfires. *The New York Times*. https://www.nytimes.com/2021/08/13/climate/wildfires-smoke-covid.html?campaign_id=54&emc=edit_clim_20210818&instance_id=38209&nl=climate-fwd%3A&i_id=83007827&segment_id=66565&te=1&user_id=67e1fa5e9e1c2e5cdb1b62bca3aaeb35

15 The Equality Trust (n.d.). Health. The Equality Trust. https://www.equalitytrust.org.uk/health , accessed November 08, 2021

16 Dickerson, S. Sally and Kemeny, E. Margaret, (2004). Acute Stressors and Cortisol Responses: A Theoretical Integration and Synthesis of Laboratory Research. *Psychological Bulletin*, 130(3), 355–91.

17 Vohra, Karn, Vodonos, Alina, Schwartz, Joel, Marais, Eloise A., Sulprizio, Melissa P. and Mickley, Loretta J. (2021) Global Mortality from Outdoor Fine Particle Pollution Generated by Fossil Fuel Combustion: Results from GEOS-Chem. *Environmental Research*, 195, 110754. https://doi.org/10.1016/j.envres.2021.110754

18 Christensen, K., Doblhammer, G., Rau, R. and Vaupel, J. W. (2009). Ageing Populations: the Challenges Ahead. *The Lancet*, 374(9696), 1196–1208. https://doi.org/10.1016/s0140-6736(09)61460-4

19 Pega, Frank et al. (2021). Global, Regional, and National Burdens of Ischemic Heart Disease and Stroke Attributable to Exposure to Long Working Hours for 194 Countries, 2000–2016: A Systematic Analysis from the WHO/ILO Joint Estimates of the Work-related Burden of Disease and Injury. *Environment International*, 154, 106595. https://doi.org/10.1016/j.envint.2021.106595

20 Eurofound and the International Labour Office (2017), Working Anytime, Anywhere: The Effects on the World of Work, Publications Office of the European Union, Luxembourg, and the International Labour Office, Geneva. http://eurofound.link/ef1658

21 Pandey, Ashutosh (2021). Iceland Takes to Shorter Hours After Four-Day Week Trials. *DW*. https://www.dw.com/en/iceland-takes-to-shorter-hours-after-four-day-week-trials/a-58177060

22 Boston Medical Center. (n.d.). Weight Management. *Boston Medical Center*. https://www.bmc.org/nutrition-and-weight-management/weight-management, accessed November 21, 2021

23 World Population Review. (2021). Most Obese Countries 2021. *World Population Review*. https://worldpopulationreview.com/country-rankings/most-obese-countries

24　The Annie E. Casey Foundation. (May 26, 2021). Exploring America's Food Deserts. https://www.aecf.org/blog/exploring-americas-food-deserts
25　Bower, Kelly M., Thorpe, Roland J., Jr., Rohde, Charles and Gaskin, Darrell J. (2014). The Intersection of Neighborhood Racial Segregation, Poverty, and Urbanicity and its Impact on Food Store Availability in the United States. *Preventive Medicine*, 58, 33–39. https://doi.org/10.1016/j.ypmed.2013.10.010
26　Jürgens, Ulrich (2018), 'Real' Versus 'Mental' Food Deserts from the Consumer Perspective—Concepts and Quantitative Methods Applied to Rural Areas of Germany. – *DIE ERDE* 149 (1): 25-43. https://www.die-erde.org/index.php/die-erde/article/view/350
27　Su, Shiliang, Li, Zekun, Xu, Mengya, Cai, Zhongliang and Weng, Min (2017). A Geo-Big Data Approach to Intra-Urban Food Deserts: Transit-Varying Accessibility, Social Inequalities, and Implications for Urban Planning. *Habitat International*, 64, 22–40. https://doi.org/10.1016/j.habitatint.2017.04.007
28　Cherry, Kendra (March 19, 2020) A List of Psychological Disorders. Verywell Mind. https://www.verywellmind.com/a-list-of-psychological-disorders-2794776
29　Foulkes, Lucy (2021). *Losing our Minds: What Mental Illness Really Is – and What It Isn't*. Bodley Head.
30　WHO (2021) Confirmed COVID-19 Infections by Region, https://covid19.who.int/
31　The Economist. (January 16, 2021). *Why a Dawn of Technological Optimism is Breaking*. https://www.economist.com/leaders/2021/01/16/why-a-dawn-of-technological-optimism-is-breaking
32　Tozzi, John (August 3, 2021). *Breakthrough Infections, in Context*. Bloomberg. https://www.bloomberg.com/news/newsletters/2021-08-03/breakthrough-infections-in-context
33　Kates, Jennifer, Dawson, Lindsey, Anderson, Emma, Rouw, Anna, Michaud, Josh and Singer, Natalie (June 30, 2021) COVID-19 Vaccine Breakthrough Cases: Data from the States. KFF. https://www.kff.org/policy-watch/covid-19-vaccine-breakthrough-cases-data-from-the-states/
34　Scobie, Heather M., Johnson, Amelia G., Suthar, Amitabh B., et al. (April 4-July 17, 2021) Monitoring Incidence of COVID-19 Cases, Hospitalizations, and Deaths, by Vaccination Status—13 U.S. Jurisdictions, MMWR Morb Mortal Wkly Rep 2021;70:1284–1290. DOI: http://dx.doi.org/10.15585/mmwr.mm7037e1
35　Collins, Keith and Holder, Josh (December 15, 2021). What Data Shows About Vaccine Supply and Demand in the Most Vulnerable Places. The New York Times. https://www.nytimes.com/interactive/2021/12/09/world/vaccine-inequity-supply.html
36　Kay, Chris and Pandya, Dhwani (December 29, 2021). How Errors, Inaction Sent a Deadly Covid Variant Around the World. Bloomberg. https://www.bloomberg.com/news/features/2021-12-29/how-delta-variant-spread-in-india-deadly-errors-inaction-covid-crisis
37　Anand, Abhishek; Justin Sandefur; and Arvind Subramanian, 2021. "Three New Estimates of India's All-Cause Excess Mortality during the COVID-19 Pandemic." CGD Working Paper 589. Washington, DC: Center for Global Development. https://cgdev.org/publication/three-new-estimates-indias-all-cause-excess-mortality-during-covid-19-pandemic

Endnotes

38 Mueller, Benjamin and Robbins, Rebecca, (October 7, 2021). *Where Covax, the Vast Global Vaccine Program, Went Wrong*. The New York Times. https://www.nytimes.com/2021/08/02/world/europe/covax-covid-vaccine-problems-africa.html

39 WHO. (December 23, 2021). Achieving 70% COVID-19 Immunization Coverage by Mid-2022. https://www.who.int/news/item/23-12-2021-achieving-70-covid-19-immunization-coverage-by-mid-2022

40 Hotez, J. Peter and Bottazzi, Maria Elena (December 30, 2021). A COVID Vaccine for All. *Scientific American*. https://www.scientificamerican.com/article/a-covid-vaccine-for-all/

41 Clancy, Rebecca (August 2, 2021). Lewis Hamilton Fears He Has Long Covid. *The Times*. https://www.thetimes.co.uk/article/lewis-hamilton-fears-he-has-long-covid-7xj3vqs5k

42 Jones, Stephen (July 23, 2021) Long COVID Poses a Subtle Workplace Crisis as Sufferers Say They're Working Longer Hours and Feel More Stressed. *Insider*. https://www.businessinsider.com/long-covid-work-crisis-longer-hours-stress-2021-7?international=true&r=US&IR=T

43 Jaslow, Ryan (October 14, 2021). Parosmia: Causing Foods to Taste Like "Garbage" and Affecting Everyday Life. *FOCUS*. https://focus.masseyeandear.org/parosmia-causing-foods-to-taste-like-garbage-and-affecting-everyday-life/

44 See for example: Sabel, A. Bernhard et al. (2021). Non-Invasive Brain Microcurrent Stimulation Therapy of Long-COVID-19 Reduces Vascular Dysregulation and Improves Visual and Cognitive Impairment. *Restorative Neurology and Neuroscience*, 39(6), 393–408. https://doi.org/10.3233/rnn-211249

45 OECD. (2020). Trust in Government. *OECD*. https://www.oecd.org/gov/trust-in-government.htm

46 Khazan, Olga (December 6, 2021). What's Really Behind Global Vaccine Hesitancy. *The Atlantic*. https://www.theatlantic.com/politics/archive/2021/12/which-countries-have-most-anti-vaxxers/620901/

47 Our World in Data. (November 15, 2021). Willingness to Get Vaccinated Against COVID-19. Our World in Data. https://ourworldindata.org/grapher/covid-vaccine-willingness-and-people-vaccinated-bycoutry?coutry=CAN%7EDNK%7EFRA%7EDEU%7EITA%7ENOR%7EKOR%7EGBR%7EUSA

48 Barbero, Michele (July 27, 2021). Macron's Big Vaccination Gamble. *FP*. https://foreignpolicy.com/2021/07/27/france-macron-covid-vaccination-mandate-gamble/

49 Bhatia, Gurman, Dutta, Prasanta Kumar, Canipe, Chris and McClure, Jon (2021). COVID-19 vaccination tracker. *Reuters*. https://graphics.reuters.com/world-coronavirus-tracker-and-maps/vaccination-rollout-and-access/

50 Menzies, G. Ross and Menzies, E. Rachel. (October 20, 2021). Why do Some People Delay Getting Vaccinated or Pretend COVID Doesn't Exist? Paradoxically, Denial of Death. *The Conversation*. https://theconversation.com/why-do-some-people-delay-getting-vaccinated-or-pretend-covid-doesnt-exist-paradoxically-denial-of-death-168485

51 Robson, David (July 23, 2021). Why Some People Don't Want a COVID-19 Vaccine. *BBC Future*. https://www.bbc.com/future/article/20210720-the-complexities-of-vaccine-hesitancy

52 Rodó, Xavier, San-José, Adrià, Kirchgatter, Karin and López, Leonardo, (2021). Changing Climate and the COVID-19 Pandemic: More Than Just Heads or Tails. *Nature Medicine*, 27(4), 576–579. https://doi.org/10.1038/s41591-021-01303-y

53 Strusani, Davide, Houngbonon, V. Georges (2020). What COVID-19 Means For Digital Infrastructure In Emerging Markets. *International Finance Corporation*. https://www.ifc.org/wps/wcm/connect/8f9237d2-eceb-433f-a2d0-3009078 08722/EMCompass_Note_83-for+web.pdf?MOD=AJPERES&CVID=n7M5wS.

54 Panchal, Nirmita, Kamal, Rabah, Cox, Cynthia and Garfield, Rachel (February 10, 2021). The Implications of COVID-19 for Mental Health and Substance Use. *KFF*. https://www.kff.org/coronavirus-covid-19/issue-brief/the-implications-of-covid-19-for-mental-health-and-substance-use/

55 Bloomberg. (November 30, 2021). The Covid Resilience Ranking: The Best and Worst Places to Be as Covid Reopening Gathers Pace. *Bloomberg*. https://www.bloomberg.com/graphics/covid-resilience-ranking/

56 Lewars, Michael (May 4, 2021). Eight Reasons for Rising Healthcare Costs Globally. William Russell. https://www.william-russell.com/blog/reasons-rising-healthcare-costs-globally/

57 Sanger-Katz, Margot (December 11, 2020). It's not Just You: Picking a Health Insurance Plan is Really Hard. *The New York Times*. https://www.nytimes.com/2020/12/11/upshot/choosing-health-insurance-is-hard.html

58 Brot-Goldberg, Zarek, Layton, Timothy J., Vabson, Boris and Wang, Adelina Yanyue (2021). *The behavioral foundations of default effects: Theory and Evidence from Medicare part D* (SSRN Working Paper No. 2021-03). SSRN. https://doi.org/10.2139/ssrn.3763957

59 Braithwaite, Jeffrey et al. (December, 2018). The Future of Health Systems to 2030: a Roadmap for Global Progress and Sustainability. *International Journal for Quality in Health Care*, 30(10), 823–831. https://doi.org/10.1093/intqhc/mzy242

60 Global Burden of Disease Health Financing Collaborator Network (2019). Past, Present, and Future of Global Health Financing: a Review of Development Assistance, Government, Out-of-Pocket, And Other Private Spending on Health for 195 Countries, 1995–2050. *The Lancet*, 393(10187), 2233–2260. https://doi.org/10.1016/s0140-6736(19)30841-4

61 Solbach, Thomas, Kremer, Malte, Grünewald, Patrick, Ickerott, Daniel (2019). *Driving the Future of Health: How Biopharma Can Defend and Grow its Business in an Era of Digitally Enabled Healthcare*. Strategy&. https://www.strategyand.pwc.com/de/de/industrie-teams/gesundheitswesen/die-zukunft-der-gesundheit-vorantreiben/Driving-the-future-of-health.pdf

62 Solbach, Thomas, Kremer, Malte, Grünewald, Patrick, Ickerott, Daniel (2019). Driving the Future of Health: *How Biopharma can Defend and Grow its Business in an Era of Digitally Enabled Healthcare*. Strategy&. https://www.strategyand.pwc.com/de/de/industrie-teams/gesundheitswesen/die-zukunft-der-gesundheit-vorantreiben/Driving-the-future-of-health.pdf

63 Allen, Stephanie (June 25, 2021). *2021 Global Health Care Outlook*. https://www2.deloitte.com/global/en/pages/life-sciences-and-healthcare/articles/global-health-care-sector-outlook.html

Endnotes

64 Mu-Hyun, Cho (November 26, 2018). Samsung Applies AI to Medical Imaging. ZDNet. https://www.zdnet.com/article/samsung-applies-ai-to-medical-imaging/
65 See for example: Sungho Lee et al., All-day Mobile Healthcare Monitoring System Based on Heterogeneous Stretchable Sensors for Medical Emergency, IEEE Transactions on Industrial Electronics (2019). DOI: 10.1109/TIE.2019.2950842
66 Zuboff, Shoshana (2020). The Age of Surveillance Capitalism: The Fight for a Human Future at the New Frontier of Power (Reprint ed.). *PublicAffairs*.
67 The Economist. (January 29, 2020). Interest in Veganism is Surging. https://www.economist.com/graphic-detail/2020/01/29/interest-in-veganism-is-surging
68 Banis, Davide (December 31, 2018). Everything is Ready to Make 2019 the "Year Of The Vegan". Are You? *Forbes*. https://www.forbes.com/sites/davidebanis/2018/12/31/everything-is-ready-to-make-2019-the-year-of-the-vegan-are-you/
69 Ipsos. (2021). Vegan Trends in the U.S. *Ipsos*. https://www.ipsos-retailperformance.com/en/vegan-trends/
70 The Business Research Company. (May, 2021). Vegan Food Global Market Report 2021: COVID-19 Growth and Change to 2030. Research and Markets. https://www.researchandmarkets.com/reports/5321378/vegan-food-global-market-report-2021-covid-19?utm_source=CI&utm_medium=PressRelease&utm_code=pnt786&utm_campaign=1626310+-+Vegan+Food+Global+Market+Report+2021&utm_exec=jamu273prd
71 Meyer, Mandy (June 25, 2021). This Is How Many Vegans Are in the World Right Now (2021 update). *The VOU*. https://thevou.com/lifestyle/2019-the-world-of-vegan-but-how-many-vegans-are-in-the-world/
72 Good Food Institute. (2018). China Plant-based Meat Industry Report 2018.
73 Good Food Institute. (2020). 2020 Plant-Based State of the Industry Report.
74 Pew Research. (June 29, 2021). 10. Religion and Food. Pew Research Center's Religion and Public Life Project. https://www.pewforum.org/2021/06/29/religion-and-food/
75 Ritchie, Hannah (January 24, 2021). You Want to Reduce the Carbon Footprint of your Food? Focus on What you Eat, not Whether your Food is Local. Our World in Data. https://ourworldindata.org/food-choice-vs-eating-local
76 Steel, Carolyn (2021). Sitopia: How Food Can Save the World. *Vintage*.
77 Rockefeller Foundation. (November 13, 2020). Black Soldier Flies: Inexpensive and Sustainable Source for Animal Feed. *The Rockefeller Foundation*. https://www.rockefellerfoundation.org/case-study/black-soldier-flies-inexpensive-and-sustainable-source-for-animal-feed/
78 Food and Agriculture Organization of the United Nations. (2013). Edible Insects: Future Prospect for Food and Feed Security (Fao Forestry Paper). *FAO*.
79 Heinrich Böll Stiftung, Bund für Umwelt und Naturschutz Deutschland and Friends of the Earth Europe. (2021, September). Meat Atlas 2021. Heinrich Böll Stiftung. https://eu.boell.org/en/MeatAtlas
80 Fesenfeld, Lukas Paul (September 7, 2021). Active State: the Political Economy of Transforming the Meat System | *Heinrich Böll Stiftung* | Brussels office - European Union. Heinrich-Böll-Stiftung. https://eu.boell.org/en/2021/09/07/

active-state-political-economy-transforming-meat-system?dimension1=ecology
81. Impossible Foods. (December, 2020). Turn Back the Clock 2020 Impact Report. https://impossiblefoods.com/impact-report-2020
82. The Economist. (October 12, 2019). Plant-Based Meat Could Create a Radically Different Food Chain. https://www.economist.com/international/2019/10/12/plant-based-meat-could-create-a-radically-different-food-chain
83. Farrimond, Stuart (May 17, 2020). The Future of Food: What We'll Eat in 2028. *BBC Science Focus Magazine*. https://www.sciencefocus.com/future-technology/the-future-of-food-what-well-eat-in-2028/
84. Jacobsen, Bruno (January 23, 2018). Food Scanners - Will They Change Your Diet? *Future Proof*. https://www.futuresplatform.com/blog/food-scanners-will-they-change-your-diet-calorie-molecular
85. The Medical Futurist. (August 11, 2020). The Future of Food and Eating. *The Medical Futurist*. https://medicalfuturist.com/the-future-of-food-the-food-of-the-future/
86. *The Medical Futurist.* (August 7, 2018). Nutrigenomics: Could your Genes Choose the Right Cheese for You? *The Medical Futurist.* https://medicalfuturist.com/nutrigenomics/
87. Burgen, Stephen (February 23, 2021). "A Role Model": How Seville is Turning Leftover Oranges into Electricity. *The Guardian.* https://www.theguardian.com/environment/2021/feb/23/how-seville-is-turning-leftover-oranges-into-electricity
88. Friedrich, Michael (January 3, 2022). Milan's "Hubs" Are a Local Answer to the Global Food Waste Problem. *GOOD.* https://www.good.is/milan-food-hubs
89. Crippa, Monica et al. (2021). Food Systems Are Responsible for a Third of Global Anthropogenic GHG Emissions. *Nature Food*, 2(3), 198–209. https://doi.org/10.1038/s43016-021-00225-9
90. Alaimo, Katherine, Packnett, Elizabeth, Miles, Richard A. and Kruger, Daniel J. (2008). Fruit and Vegetable Intake Among Urban Community Gardeners. *Journal of Nutrition Education and Behavior*, 40(2), 94–101. https://doi.org/10.1016/j.jneb.2006.12.003
91. Orsini, Francesco (2020). Innovation and Sustainability in Urban Agriculture: the Path Forward. *Journal of Consumer Protection and Food Safety*, 15(3), 203–204. https://doi.org/10.1007/s00003-020-01293-y
92. Kozai, Toyoki, Hayashi, Eri and Amagai, Yumiko (2020). Plant Factories with Artificial Lighting (PFALs) Toward Sustainable Plant Production. *Acta Horticulturae*, 1273, 251–260. https://doi.org/10.17660/actahortic.2020.1273.34

Chapter 9: Green Economy

1. Planetary boundaries is a concept developed by a group of earth system and environmental scientists, including Johan Rockström and Will Steffen from the year 2009 onwards. It refers to nine boundaries that — if transgressed — could trigger a possibly catastrophic and perhaps unreversible process and destroy the safe operating space for humanity on Planet Earth. Boundaries include climate change, biodiversity loss, biogeochemical, ocean acidification, land use, freshwater, ozone depletion, atmospheric aerosols, and chemical pollution.

Endnotes

    Rockström, Johan, Steffen, Will, Noone, Kevin, et al. (2009). A Safe Operating Space for Humanity. *Nature* 461, 472–475.
2   Green Economy Coalition (2020). The 5 Principles of Green Economy. https://www.greeneconomycoalition.org/news-and-resources/the-5-principles-of-green-economy
3   Death, Carl (2015). Four Discourses of the Green Economy in the Global South, *Third World Quarterly*, Volume 36, 2015 - Issue 12: The Green Economy in the Global South: Experiences, Redistributions and Resistances, 2207-2224.
4   Global Green Growth Institute (2020). Green Grwoth Index 2020. https://greengrowthindex.gggi.org/wp-content/uploads/2021/03/2020-Green-Growth-Index.pdf
5   World Bank (2012). Inclusive Green Growth: The Pathway to Sustainable Development. Washington, DC. © World Bank. https://openknowledge.worldbank.org/handle/10986/6058 License: CC BY 3.0 IGO."
6   Corporate Knights (2021). 2021 Global 100 Ranking | Corporate Knights; Corporate Knights 2020. 2020 Global 100 | Corporate Knights.
7   EUREC Campus (2021). Green Garage/Climate Klick Accelerator. https://euref.de/entry/green-garage-climate-kic-accelerator/, accessed 15 July 2021.
8   UN ESCAP (2021). Environment and Development. Green Growth. https://www.unescap.org/our-work/environment-development/green-growth
9   Hickel, Jason and Kallis, Giorgos (2020). *Is Green Growth Possible?*, New Political Economy, 25:4, 469-486, DOI: 10.1080/13563467.2019.15989
10   OECD (2019). Taxing Energy Use. http://www.oecd.org/tax/taxing-energy-use-efde7a25-en.html
11   OECD (2011). Green Growth Strategy. http://www.oecd.org/greengrowth/
12   OECD (2011). Green Growth Strategy. http://www.oecd.org/greengrowth/
13   Agarwal, Mukesch (2020). Green Economy. *The International Journal of Analytical and Experimental Modal Analysis*, Volume XII, Issue IV, April/2020, p. 133.
14   One key reference is the book of Giorgos Kallis: Kallis, Giorgos (2018). *Degrowth*. New York: Columbia University Press. http://cup.columbia.edu/book/degrowth/9781911116806
15   Wichterich, Christa/ Heinrich Böll Foundation (2012). *The Future We Want. A Feminist Perspective*. Berlin.
16   Kliemann, Christiana/Zukunftsinstitut (2015). https://www.zukunftsinstitut.de/artikel/degrowth-eine-realistische-vision/
17   Lepenies, Philipp (2016). *The Power of a Single Number*. Columbia University Press.
18   Quote taken from the book presentation by Columbia University Press (n.d.). *The Power of a Single Number by Philipp Lepenies* (2016). http://cup.columbia.edu/book/the-power-of-a-single-number/9780231175104, accessed January 12, 2022.
19   Hickel, Jason (2020). *Less is More*. London: Windmill, p. 28.
20   Umweltbundesamt (2020). Indicator: National Welfare Index. https://www.umweltbundesamt.de/en/indicator-national-welfare-index#at-a-glance
21   World Happiness Report (2021) https://worldhappiness.report/ed/2020/ and Economist Intelligence Unit. Global Liveability Index, https://www.eiu.com/topic/liveability, accessed April 14, 2021.

22   Malm, Anders (2016). *Fossil Capital. The Rise of Steam Power and the Roots of Global Warming*. London and New York: Verso Books.
23   Klein, Naomi (2014). *This Changes Everything: Capitalism vs. the Climate*, New York: Simon & Schuster.
24   Elsenhans, Hartmut (2021). *Capitalism, Development and Empowerment of Labour. A Heterodox Political Economy*. London. Routledge.
25   Xue, Yujie/*South China Morning Post* (December 6, 2021). China's Five-year Green Development Plan for Industrial Sector Lacks Road Map, Analysts Warn. https://www.scmp.com/business/china-business/article/3158643/chinas-five-year-green-development-plan-industrial-sector
26   Global Green Growth Institute (GGGI) (2021). The Promise of Green Growth: A Pathway to Prosperity While Achieving National and Global Ambitions. Presentation Slides. March 25, 2021; see also the following endnote for reference of the comprehensive report of GGGI (2019). https://gggi.org/site/assets/uploads/2021/03/The-Promise-of-Green-Growth-Queens-Uni-final.pdf
27   Global Green Growth Institute (GGGI) (2019). Green Growth Index. Concept, Methods and Applications. Technical Report 5, p. 22.
28   GIZ (no date). Green Economy Transformation. https://www.giz.de/en/worldwide/78187.html, accessed 1 November 2021.
29   International Cooperative Alliance (ICA) – EU Partnership (2021). Cooperation for the Transition to a Green Economy. Brussels.

Chapter 10: Sustainable Finance

1   Friede, Gunnar, Busch, Timo, Bassen, Alexander (2015). ESG and Financial Performance: Aggregated Evidence from More than 2000 Empirical Studies. *Journal of Sustainable Finance & Investment*, Volume 5, Issue 4, p. 210-233, 2015, DOI: 10.1080/20430795.2015.1118917, https://ssrn.com/abstract=2699610
2   Stemshorn, Iason (January 27, 2021). Presentation on Green and Sustainable Finance in the Bachelor Course on "Global Megatrends and International Cooperation", taught by Berthold Kuhn in Fall/Winter 2020/2021 at the Department of Political and Social Sciences, Freie Universität Berlin.
3   Steffen, Bjarne (2021). A Comparative Analysis of Green Financial Policy Output in OECD Countries, *Environmental Research Letters*, July 2, 2021, https://iopscience.iop.org/article/10.1088/1748-9326/ac0c43
4   According to a statement of Damien de Saint Germain, Head of credit research and strategy at Crédit Agricole (January 20, 2021). https://www.environmentalleader.com/2021/01/sustainable-finance-expected-to-see-55-growth-in-2021-says-credit-agricole-group/
5   United Nations Climate Change (2021). New Financial Alliance for Net Zero Emissions Launches, External Press Release, April 21, 2021. https://unfccc.int/news/new-financial-alliance-for-net-zero-emissions-launches.
6   Investopedia (2021). Environmental, Social, and Governance Criteria (ESG). https://www.investopedia.com/terms/e/environmental-social-and-governance-esg-criteria.asp
7   European Union (2019). Regulation (EU) 2019/2088 of the European Parliament and of the Council of November 27, 2019 on sustainability-related disclosures

Endnotes

      in the financial services sector. (https://eur-lex.europa.eu/eli/reg/2019/2088/oj
8   Carbon Tracker (2017). Stranded Assets. https://carbontracker.org/terms/stranded-assets/, accessed 09.07.2021
9   Kuhn, Berthold M. (2020). Sustainable Finance in Germany: Mapping Discourses, Stakeholders, and Policy initiatives, *Journal of Sustainable Finance and Investment*, DOI: 10.1080/20430795.2020.1783151
10 Here we agree with an analysis of potential crash factors published in *The Economist*, see: *The Economist* (February 12, 2022). The Next Crisis. What Could Happen What would Happen if Financial Markets Crashed? https://www.economist.com/leaders/2022/02/12/what-would-happen-if-financial-markets-crashed
11 Aramonte, Sirio and Zabai, Anna (2021). Sustainable Finance: Trends, Valuations and Exposures, *BIS Quarterly*, September 20, 2021. https://www.bis.org/publ/qtrpdf/r_qt2109v.htm
12 Kuhn, Berthold M. and Tober, Claudia (2021) The Sustainable Finance Landscape in Germany, in: Ibrahim Gök (ed.) *Global Aspects of Sustainable Finance in Times of Crises*, Business Science Reference (Verlag), pp. 286-311.
13 Principles for Responsible Investment (no date). RRI Home. https://www.unpri.org/, accessed November 24, 2021.
14 Shelagh Whitley et. al / World Resource Institute, Rocky Mountain Institute andThird Generation Environmentalism (2018). Making Finance Consistent with Climate Goals, p.6. https://seors.unfccc.int/applications/seors/attachments/get_attachment?code=QAAXZVXARPBR36CWS00QM4OZ8LOLE5TT
15 MSCI ESG Research (December 7, 2020). 2021 ESG Trends to Watch. https://www.msci.com/www/blog-posts/2021-esg-trends-to-watch/02227813256
16 See: Mack; Sebastian (February 15, 2022). Turning Green into Gold - How to Make the European Green Bond Standard Fit for Purpose, Policy Brief of Jacques Delors Centre/Hertie School. https://www.delorscentre.eu/en/publications/detail/publication/green-bond-standard. "To establish the EuGBS as the new gold standard, the European Parliament and EU Council should improve it in three respects. They should (i) strengthen its environmental credentials, (ii) regulate the entire green bond market and not just the EuGBS niche, and (iii) ensure the enforceability of investor rights."
17 Sustainable Digital Finance Alliance (October 2018).Digital Technologies for Mobilizing Sustainable Finance, p. 2 https://greendigitalfinancealliance.org/wp-content/uploads/2019/11/Digital-Technologies-for-Mobiizing.pdf
18 EURACTIV (2021). The Green Brief. The Green Brief: Gas, Nuclear and the EU Taxonomy Saga, 27.10.2021, https://www.euractiv.com/section/energy-environment/news/the-green-brief-gas-nuclear-and-the-eu-taxonomy-saga/
19 WWF (October 22, 2019). EU Countries Split Over Green Investment Taxonomy. https://www.wwf.eu/?354717/EU-countries-split-over-green-investment-taxonomy
20 Flossbach von Storch is a German financial services institution specializing in asset management. Flossbach von Storch AG founded the Flossbach von Storch Research Institute as a think tank headed by Thomas Mayer, the former Chief Economist of Deutsche Bank. Bert Flossbach stated that "The new taxonomy, will divide companies into good (green) and bad (brown), and asset allocation

decisions will have to be made based on this framework. 'Thousands of companies have to be analysed and classified based on hundreds of often blurry criteria. What is still manageable in the analysis of a single windmill, borders on megalomania where global groups are concerned" (Kirakosian, Margaryta (April 19, 2019). EU's Sustainable Finance Action Plan: Bureaucracy or Breakthrough? https://citywireselector.com
21 Principles of Responsible Investment (PRI) (2020). Using the EU Taxonomy. https://www.unpri.org/sustainable-markets/eu-sustainable-finance-taxonomy, accessed April 10, 2020
22 Beckert, Nico/Table China 2021. Sustainable financial investments: China's vulnerability to greenwashing. *Table China Professional Briefing*. August 04, 2021.
23 Natixis (2021). Green-washing Allegations are Jolting the Financial Industry: Heightened Needs for Cautiousness, Integrity and Guidance https://gsh.cib.natixis.com/our-center-of-expertise/articles/green-washing-allegations-are-jolting-the-financial-industry-heightened-needs-for-cautiousness-integrity-and-guidance
24 Bloomberg Green (2021). Regulators Intensify ESG Scrutiny as Greenwashing Explodes, 01.09.2021, https://www.bloomberg.com/news/articles/2021-09-01/regulatory-scrutiny-of-esg-greenwashing-is-intensifying
25 Cuvelier, Lara and Pinson, Lucie/Reclaim Finance/ Urgewald (2021). One Year on. Blackrock is Still Addicted to Fossil Fuels, January 2021 https://reclaimfinance.org/site/wp content/uploads/2021/01/OneYearOnBlackRockStillAddictedToFossilFuels.pdf
26 Economist (November 6, 2021). The Uses and Abuses of Green Finance, p. 6
27 Technology companies such as AMD, Apple and Nvidia have shown strong upward trends in market capitalization over the past decades. Tesla is probably the most striking examples for outperforming in the stock market. Recycling companies such Waste Management Inc. or Tomra System are examples for relatively stable and long-term growth in market capitalization.

Chapter 11: Democracy and Governance Innovations

1 Roland Berger (2021). Trend Compendium 2050. Megatrends Shaping the Coming Decades. https://www.rolandberger.com/en/Insights/Global-Topics/Trend-Compendium/
2 History.Com (2021). Ancient Greek Democracy. https://www.history.com/topics/ancient-greece/ancient-greece-democracy, accessed 12. August 2021.
3 World Bank (2021). https://www.worldbank.org/en/topic/governance/overview, accessed 25.02.2021
4 The full text of the document of the State Council Information Office of the People's Republic of China in English is available at: *Xinhuanet* (December 4, 2021). China: Democracy That Works. http://www.news.cn/english/2021-12/04/c_1310351231.htm
5 Fukuyama, Francis (1992). *The End of History and the Last Man*. Free Press
6 Mezran, Karim and Pavia, Alissa (2021). Tunisia was the Only Democracy to Blossom from the Arab Spring. Now it's a Mess, *Atlantic Council*, 28. July 2021.
7 Throughput legitimacy is a criterion concerned with the quality of governance processes, focusing on "accountability of the policy-makers and the

Endnotes

transparency, inclusiveness and openness of governance processes" (Schmidt, Vivien A. (2013). Democracy and Legitimacy in the European Union Revisited: Input, Output and 'Throughput'. Political Studies, 6, 2–22).

8 Striebel, Michael, Kübler, Daniel, Marcinkowski, Frank (2018). The Importance of Input and Output Legitimacy in Democratic Governance: Evidence from a Population-based Survey Experiment in four West European Countries, *European Journal of Political Research*, https://ejpr.onlinelibrary.wiley.com/doi/10.1111/1475-6765.12293

9 Lentsch, Josef (2019). *Political Entrepreneurship: How to Build Successful Centrist Political Start-ups*, Springer Nature Switzerland.

10 Lentsch, Josef (2019). *Political Entrepreneurship: How to Build Successful Centrist Political Start-ups*, Springer Nature Switzerland, p. xi (Preface).

11 Schäfer, Achim and Zürn, Michael 2021. *Die demokratische Regression*. Berlin: Edition Suhrkamp.

12 European Council on Foreign Relations. The Crisis of American Power: How Europeans see Biden's America, https://ecfr.eu/publication/the-crisis-of-american-power-how-europeans-see-bidens-america/ and Table China *Professional Briefing (February 22, 2021)*..

13 Center for China and Globalization (CCG) (2021). Consultative Democracy is a Key Part of China's Approach to Democracy | *CCG View*, November 4, 2021.

14 *The Economist* (January 11, 2022). Invitation to a webinar for subscribers on the issue of "The New Interventionism: Business and the State." On January 23, 2022. Speakers were Jan Piotrowski (Business Editor), Don Weinland (China business and finance editor), and Sacha Nauta (Executive Editor).

15 The Nobel Price. Douglass C. North. Price Lecture 1993. https://www.nobelprize.org/prizes/economic-sciences/1993/north/lecture/

16 Kasparov, Garry and Halvorssen, Thor/*The Washington Post* (13. February 2017). Why the Rise of Authoritarianism is a Global Catastrophe. https://www.washingtonpost.com/news/democracy-post/wp/2017/02/13/why-the-rise-of-authoritarianism-is-a-global-catastrophe/

17 Dahl, Robert A., (1971): *Polyarchie. Participation and Opposition*. New Haven/London.

18 Freedom House. (2022). Expanding Freedom and Democracy. https://freedomhouse.org/

19 BTI (2020). Global Dashboard. https://www.bti-project.org/en/reports/global-dashboard.html?&cb=00000 accessed 12. August 2021.

20 BTI (2022). Global Findings. https://bti-project.org/en/reports/global-report, accessed February 23, 2022 and BTI Project News (February 23, 2022), www.bti-project.org

21 V-DEM (no date). Global Standards, Local Knowledge,m https://www.v-dem.net/en/, accessed on October 28, 2021.

22 Biswas, Soutik / BBC (March 16, 2021). 'Electoral Autocracy': The Downgrading of India's Democracy, https://www.bbc.com/news/world-asia-india-56393944

23 V-DEM Institute (2020). Democracy Report 2020. Autocratization Surges – Resistance Grows; Roland Berger (2021). Trend Compendium 2050. Megatrends shaping the coming decades. https://www.rolandberger.com/en/Insights/Global-Topics/Trend-Compendium/

24 V-DEM Institute (2021). Autocratization Turns Viral. Democracy Report 2021. Gothenburg. https://www.v-dem.net/media/filer_public/74/8c/748c68ad-f224-4cd7-87f9-8794add5c60f/dr_2021_updated.pdf
25 V-DEM (2021). Variable Graphs. Women political participation index. https://www.v-dem.net/en/analysis/VariableGraph/
26 Kuhn, Berthold (1998). *Participatory Development in Rural India*, New Delhi: Radiant Publishers, p. 271.
27 Chattopadhyay, Raghabendra and Duflo, Ester (2004). Women as Policy-makers. Evidence from a Randomized Policy Experiment in India, Econometrica, Vol. 72, No. 5 (September, 2004), pp. 1409-1443. https://economics.mit.edu/files/792).
28 European Institute for Gender Equality (2020). Statistical Brief: Gender Balance in Politics 2020. https://eige.europa.eu/publications/statistical-brief-gender-balance-politics-2020
29 IPU Parline. (2020). IPU comparative data on Structure of parliament. Parline: The IPU's Open Data Platform. https://data.ipu.org/women-ranking?month=10&year=2020
30 *Economist Intelligence Unit (EIU)* (2021). The Economist Intelligence Unit's Democracy Index. https://www.eiu.com/n/campaigns/democracy-index-2020/
31 EIU (2022). The Economist Intelligence Unit's Democracy Index. https://www.eiu.com/n/campaigns/democracy-index-2021/
32 World Justice Project (2021). Rule of Law Index 2021. https://worldjusticeproject.org/our-work/research-and-data/wjp-rule-law-index-2021
33 Kuhn, Berthold (2011). Nutzung und Wertschätzung von BTI und FHI in Wissenschaft und Praxis, in: *Zeitschrift für Politikwissenschaft (Journal of Political Science)*, 4/2011, pp. 577-602, https://www.zpol.nomos.de/archiv/2011/heft-4/
34 Pogrebinschi, Thamy (2021): Thirty Years of Democratic Innovations in Latin America, WZB Berlin Social Science Center, Berlin
35 United Nations. Department of Social and Economic Affairs/Le Blanc, David 2020. E-participation: a quick overview of recent qualitative trends. DESA Working Paper No. 163, January 2020. https://www.un.org/esa/desa/papers/2020/wp163_2020.pdf
36 Anstein, Sherry R. (1969). A Ladder of Citizen Participation *Journal of the American Planning Association*, Vol. 35, No. 4, July 1969, pp. 216-224.
37 United Nations, DESA 2018. Gearing E-government to Support Transformation towards Sustainable and Resilient Societies, E-Government Survey 2018, Department of Economic and Social Affairs, New York
38 Nanz, Patrizia and Fritsche, Miriam 2021. *Handbuch Bürgerbeteiligung*. Bundeszentrale für politische Bildung. Bonn.

Chapter 12: Multipolar World Order and the Future of Multilateralism

1 Khanna, Parag (2019). *The Future Is Asian: Commerce, Conflict and Culture in the 21st Century*. New York: Simon & Schuster.
2 Mahbubani, Kishore (2020). *Has China Won? The Chinese Challenge to American Primacy*. New York: Public Affairs.

Endnotes

3 *China.Table Professional Briefing* (October 18, 2021). Professional Briefing, https://table.media/china/en/
4 Munich Security Conference (2020). Westlessness – The Munich Security Conference 2020. https://securityconference.org/en/news/full/westlessness-the-munich-security-conference-2020/
5 Bloomberg New Economy Forum 2021. https://www.bloombergneweconomy.com/nef2021/, accessed December 21, 2021. The Economist (November 27, 2021). In the Flesh. In a Recoupling of Global Business Leaders, Decoupling is the Last Thing on Their Mind. Schumpeter Column, 64.
6 Mehmood, Zaeem Hassan (2September 3, 2019). Reassessing Realities of a Multi-Polar World Order. *Modern Diplomacy*. https://moderndiplomacy.eu/2019/09/03/reassessing-realities-of-a-multi-polar-world-order/
7 Barboda, David (August 16, 2020). Parag Khanna on China-centric Bias. The Wire China. https://www.thewirechina.com/2020/08/16/parag-khanna-on-being-blinded-by-a-china-centric-bias/
8 Freedom Lab (August 12, 2020). The Evolutionary Impact of the Crisis. https://freedomlab.org/category/hegemonic-shift/
9 Dasym (January 23, 2020). Towards a Multipolar World Order. https://www.dasym.com/towards-a-multipolar-world-order/
10 Krastev, Ivan and Leonard, Mark/European Council on Foreign Relations (ECFR) (2021). The Crisis of American Power. How Europeans see Biden's America, ECFR. https://ecfr.eu/publication/the-crisis-of-american-power-how-europeans-see-bidens-america/
11 E-International Relations (November 25, 2021). Interview – Ties Dams. https://www.e-ir.info/2021/11/25/interview-ties-dams/
12 Mayer, Maximilian and Kavalski, Emilian (October 21, 2021). Have We Reached Peak China? Beijing's Growing Influence on the Global Stage Masks an Overlooked Insecurity. *Politico*. https://www.politico.eu/article/have-we-reached-peak-china/
13 Maddison, Angus / OECD (2013). The World Economy: Historical Statistics. Development Centre Studies. Paris: OECD Publishing. https://doi.org/10.1787/9789264104143-en.
14 Edelman (2022). Edelman Trust Barometer 2022. https://www.edelman.com/trust/2022-trust-barometer
15 In Germany, the results of the Edelman Trust Barometer 2022 were quoted and discussed by China expert Wolfgang Hirn in his newsletter *CHINAHIRN* on February 10, 2022.
16 *The Harvard Gazette* (July 09, 2020). Taking China's Pulse, https://news.harvard.edu/gazette/story/2020/07/long-term-survey-reveals-chinese-government-satisfaction/
17 Fratzscher, Marcel (February 09, 2022). China könnte der Auslöser sein. Die nächste Weltfinanzkrise wird immer wahrscheinlicher. *Der Tagesspiegel (Berlin)*, https://www.tagesspiegel.de/politik/china-koennte-der-ausloeser-sein-die-naechste-weltfinanzkrise-wird-immer-wahrscheinlicher/28049446.html
18 Roach, Stephen (August 5, 2021). China's Private Initiative Deficit. *China.Table Professsional Briefing*, https://table.media/china/

19 Reuters. (March 5, 2014). China to 'declare war' on pollution, premier says. https://www.reuters.com/article/us-china-parliament-pollution-idUSBREA2405W20140305
20 Holbig, Heike (May 25, 2021). How China Is Reshaping Global Economic Governance. Presentation at the GIGA Forum by Prof. Heike Holbig of Goethe University Frankfurt, May 25, 2021 (online webinar).
21 The China Africa Project (August 6, 2021). https://chinaafricaproject.com/
22 Quirk, Patrick W. (February 19, 2021). The Democracy Summit must be paired with a democracy strategy. Brookings. https://www.brookings.edu/blog/order-from-chaos/2021/02/19/the-democracy-summit-must-be-paired-with-a-democracy-strategy/
23 *China.Table Professional Briefing* (December 2, 2021). Professional Briefing.
24 Cheng, Evelyn/China News Broadcasting Corporation (CNBC) (2021, October 12). China trade surplus with the U.S. rises to monthly record in September. CNBC. https://www.cnbc.com/2021/10/13/china-trade-data-imports-grow-17point6percent-in-september-miss-expectations.html
25 *China.Table Professional Briefing* (February 5, 2021).
26 Münkler, Herfried (October, 2021). Eine Weltordnung ohne Hüter: Afghanistan als globale Zäsur. *Blätter*. https://www.blaetter.de/ausgabe/2021/oktober/eine-weltordnung-ohne-hueter-afghanistan-als-globale-zaesur
27 *The Economist* (January 15, 2022), Standemonium, pp. 11-12.
28 Higgott, Richard (2020). Three Scenarios for World Order after COVID-19: Can Multilateral Cooperation be Saved? Dialogue of Civilizations Research Institute, Berlin. https://doc-research.org/2020/06/three-scenarios/, accessed October 12, 2021
29 Pratt, Simon Frankel and Levin, Jamie (2021, April 29). Vaccines will Shape the New Geopolitical Order. *Foreign Policy*. https://foreignpolicy.com/2021/04/29/vaccine-geopolitics-diplomacy-israel-russia-china/.
30 *China-Africa News* (April 30, 2021). https://chinaafricaproject.com/
31 European Parliament (2020). The Geopolitical Implications of the COVID-19 pandemic. https://www.europarl.europa.eu/RegData/etudes/STUD/2020/603511/EXPO_STU(2020)603511_EN.pdf
32 Tooze, Adam (June 2, 2020). The Death of Globalization Has Been Announced Many Times. But this is a Perfect Storm, *The Guardian*. https://www.theguardian.com/commentisfree/2020/jun/02/end-globalisation-covid-19-made-it-real
33 UN Today (September 27, 2021). The Future of Multilateralism after COVID-19. https://untoday.org/the-future-of-multilateralism-after-covid-19/
34 Global Solutions. The World Policy Forum (2021). The Future of Multilateralism. https://www.global-solutions-initiative.org/press-news/the-future-of-multilateralism
35 *China.Table Professional Briefing* (October 27, 2021).
36 Coker, Christopher (2018). *The Rise of the Civilizational State*. Cambridge: Polity Press.
37 Huntington, Samuel (1996). *The Clash of Civilizations and the Remaking of World Order*. New York: Simon and Schuster.
38 Huntington, Samuel (1993). Clash of Civilizations? *Foreign Affairs*. https://www.foreignaffairs.com/articles/united-states/1993-06-01/clash-civi

Endnotes

lizations; Huntington, The Clash of Civilizations and Remaking of the World Order.

39 Huntington, Samuel (1993). Clash of Civilizations? *Foreign Affairs*. https://www.foreignaffairs.com/articles/united-states/1993-06-01/clash-civilizations
40 Kennedy, Michael (2013). *Critical Review: The Clash of Civilizations (Samuel P. Huntington)*. Grin Verlag. https://www.grin.com/document/268261
41 Pabst, Adrian (May 8, 2019). China, Russia and the Return of the Civilisational State. *New Statesman*. https://www.newstatesman.com/2019/05/china-russia-and-return-civilisational-state
42 Kharas, Himi (Brookings Institution), Snower, Dennis J. (Global Solutions Initiative), Strauss, Sebastian (2020). The Future of Multilateralism: Towards A Responsible Globalization That Empowers Citizens and Leaves No One Behind. G20 Insights. https://www.g20-insights.org/policy_briefs/multilateralism-responsible-globalization-citizens-no-one-behind/
43 You can find Parag Khanna's biography at https://www.paragkhanna.com/short-bio/
44 The Thucydides Trap is a term coined by Graham Allison (see Introduction chapter). The term refers to the likelihood of violent encounters between a rising power and an incumbent hegemon. Nicholas Ross Smith, adjunct fellow at the University of Canterbury, New Zealand, has presented arguments why Thucydides Trap or Cold War analogies are deeply unhelpful in understanding the rise of China and the current confrontations between China and the U.S. „The differences between our era and the Peloponnesian war era are astronomical. Although the political, ideological and systemic differences alone are enough to invalidate any practical use of the analogy, the technological differences are undoubtedly the greatest hurdle to making any meaningful comparison… Technology is, traditionally, an often-overlooked aspect of international relations. But technological advancements have continually changed the nature of diplomacy, trade and war." (Smith, Nicholas R. (December 10, 2021). US and China at War? Why Thucydides Trap or Cold War Analogies are Deeply Unhelpful. *South China Morning Post*, https://www.scmp.com/comment/opinion/article/3158816/us-and-china-war-why-thucydides-trap-or-cold-war-analogies-are
45 Kuhn, Berthold (September 27, 2019). The United Nations Climate Action Summit 2019: Well-timed Initiative Confirms New Engagement Strategy of UN. Dialogue of Civilizations Research Institute. https://doc-research.org/2019/09/united-nations-climate-action-summit-2019/
46 Kuhn, Berthold (2005/2009). Entwicklungspolitik zwischen Markt und Staat. Möglichkeiten und Grenzen zivilgesellschaftlicher Organisationen. Frankfurt a.M. and New York: Campus-Verlag, translated into Chinese by Prof. Sui Xueli and published in 2009 by Renmin University Press, Beijing.
47 Helbe, Matthias (November, 2006), On the Influence of World Religion on International Trade. *Journal of Public and International Affairs*, Princeton University. https://jpia.princeton.edu/sites/jpia/files/2006-11.pdf
48 Reiter, Yitzhak (2010). Religion as a Barrier to Compromise in the Israeli-Palestinian Conflict, Chapter 6 in Bar-Siman-Tov, Yaacov/Konrad Adenauer Stiftung/The Jerusalem Institute for Israel Studies. *Barriers to Peace in the Israeli-Palestinian Conflict*, pp. 228-263. https://www.kas.de/c/document_library/get_file?uuid=4cb0072a-4282-bf4f-a40d-1e2186ac72af&groupId=252038

49 The arguments on the emergence of an aristocratic or feudal world order were inspired by talks with Dr. Pepe Jacopo, German Council on Foreign Relations and Kim Vender, University of Edinburgh, in January 2022 in Berlin.

Chapter 13: Civilizational Developments: Diversity, Individualization and Loneliness, Gender Shift, and Identity Politics

1   Huntington, Samuel (1993). Clash of Civilizations? *Foreign Affairs*. https://www.foreignaffairs.com/articles/united-states/1993-06-01/clash-civilizations
2   Zukunftsinstitut (2021). Die Megatrends. https://www.zukunftsinstitut.de/, accessed 10.10.2021.
3   Pew Research Center (2021). About Pew Research Center, https://www.pewresearch.org/about/, accessed October 15, 2021
4   For example, Kantar Consulting focuses on new consumer and retail trends. https://www.kantar.com/marketplace/solutions, accessed October 10, 2021
5   Refinitiv (2021). Diversity & Inclusion—Trends and Investment Strategies. https://lipperalpha.refinitiv.com/2018/09/diversity-inclusion-trends-and-investment-strategies/
6   Kuhn, Berthold (2005/2009). *Entwicklungspolitik zwischen Markt und Staat. Möglichkeiten und Grenzen zivilgesellschaftlicher Organisationen*. Frankfurt a.M. and New York: Campus-Verlag, translated into Chinese by Prof. Su Xueli and published in 2009 by Renmin Publishers, Beijing.
7   European Parliament (2020). Japan's Ageing Society, Briefing. https://www.europarl.europa.eu/RegData/etudes/BRIE/2020/659419/EPRS_BRI(2020)659419_EN.pdf
8   Khanna, Parag (2021). *Move. The Forces Uprooting us*. https://www.paragkhanna.com/book/move/ and Khanna Parag (2021). *Move. Das Zeitalter der Migration*. Hamburg: Rowohlt.
9   Our World in Data (n.d.) Number of Marriages in Each Year per 1,000 people in the Population, accessed January 13, 2022.
10 Bundesministerium für Familie, Frauen, Senioren und Jugend (BMFFSJ) (October 1, 2020). Einsamkeit im Alter vorbeugen. https://www.bmfsfj.de/bmfsfj/aktuelles/alle-meldungen/einsamkeit-im-alter-vorbeugen-160856
11 FreedomLab (2019). Individualism in the 21st century. https://freedomlab.org/tag/modernization/
12 Kaufmann, Mark (2020). The Carbon Footprint Shame. *Mashable*. https://mashable.com/feature/carbon-footprint-pr-campaign-sham?europe=true
13 World Economic Forum (WEF) (2021). These Countries Have the Highest Percentage of Female Managers. https://www.weforum.org/agenda/2021/02/women-gender-roles-manager-global/, with reference to data of the International Labor Organization (ILO) (2021).
14 The European Institute for Gender Equality ((EIGE) (n.d.) collects, analyzes, processes and disseminates data and information on gender equality issues. EIGE is an autonomous body that operates within the framework of European Union policies and initiatives. The European Parliament and the Council of the

Endnotes

European Union defined the grounds for the Institute's objectives and tasks in its Founding Regulation, accessed January 13, 2022.
15 EIGE (n.d.) https://eige.europa.eu/publications/gender-equality-index-2021-health, accessed January 13, 2021.
16 EIGE (2021). Gender Equality Index 2021 Highlights, see EIGE (2021) Gender Equality Index 2021. https://eige.europa.eu/gender-equality-index/2021
17 EQUALS-EU.org (2021). Gender Equality Index 2021. Fragile Gains, Big Losses. https://equals-eu.org/gender-equality-index-2021-fragile-gains-big-losses/
18 Kelber, Cornelia (2020). Gender Shift: Zukunft der Geschlechter [Online]. Zukunftsinstitut. https://www.zukunftsinstitut.de/artikel/gender-shift-zukunft-der-geschlechterrollen/
19 The Economist (April 24, 2021). Transgender Treatments. Blocked, p. 33.
20 Naipaul, Vidiadhar Surajprasad (1990). *India. A Million Mutinies*. Chapter "Little Wars". London: William Heinemann Ltd.
21 Bramen, Carrie Tirado (2002/2010). Why the Academic Left Hates Identity Politics, *Textual Practice* 16(1):1-11, March 2002. DOI: 10.1080/09502360110103676, Published online: November 5, 2010.
22 Fukuyama, Francis (2018). *Identity: Contemporary Identity Politics and the Struggle for Recognition*. London: Profile Books.
23 Fukuyama, Francis (2018). *Identity: Contemporary Identity Politics and the Struggle for Recognition*. London: Profile Books, p. 219.
24 Mandle, Joan (no date). How Political is the Personal?: Identity Politics, Feminism and Social Change. https://userpages.umbc.edu/~korenman/wmst/identity_pol.html, accessed October 20, 2021.
25 Chua, Ami/*The Guardian* (March 1, 2018). How America's Identity Politics Went from Inclusion to Exclusion. https://www.theguardian.com/society/2018/mar/01/how-americas-identity-politics-went-from-inclusion-to-division
26 *Neue Zürcher Zeitung (NZZ)* (November 24, 2020). Aayan Hirsi Ali über Freiheit, Religion und Identitätspolitik (in German). https://www.nzz.ch/feuilleton/ayaan-hirsi-ali-ueber-freiheit-religion-und-identitaetspolitik-ld.1587611
27 Wagenknecht, Sahra (2021). *Die Selbstgerechten*, Frankfurt. Campus Publishers.
28 Coker, Christopher (2018). *The Rise of the Civilizational State*. Cambridge: Polity Press.

Chapter 14: Migration

1 International Organization for Migration (IOM) 2021. https://www.iom.int/who-is-a-migrant
2 Khanna, Parag (2021). *Move. The Forces Uprooting us*. https://www.paragkhanna.com/book/move/
3 Migration Research Hub (2021). About CrossMigration. https://migrationresearch.com/about
4 Fourutan, Naika (2021). Warum Deutschland mehr Migration braucht, *Der Spiegel* (December 12, 2021). https://www.spiegel.de/politik/deutschland/einwanderung-warum-deutschland-mehr-migration-braucht-a-6aff98de-cb19-4763-ba8b-cb1ab793d64a.

5   International Business Forum (2010). Business and Migration. From Risk to Opportunity. http://gbsn.org/wp-content/uploads/2016/04/BusinessAndMigration.pdf
6   Zweetslot, Remco/Center for Strategic and International Studies (2021). Winning the Tec Talent Competition. https://www.csis.org/analysis/winning-tech-talent-competition
7   See for example: Demokratiezentrum Wien (n.d.), accessed January 12, 2022. http://www.demokratiezentrum.org/fileadmin/media/pdf/wissen_push_pull_faktoren.pdf
8   International Organization for Migration (IOM) 2021. https//www.iom.int/
9   UNHC (2020). https://www.unhcr.org/globaltrends2019/
10 President Trump Reduced Legal Immigration. He Did Not Reduce Illegal Immigration. (2021, January 21). Cato Institute. https://www.cato.org/blog/president-trump-reduced-legal-immigration-he-did-not-reduce-illegal-immigration
11 Migration Data Portal (2021) with reference to UN Department of Economic and Social Affairs (DESA). https://www.migrationdataportal.org/international-data?i=stock_abs_&t=2020, accessed October 26, 2021.
12 Eyes on Europe (2020). Explaining the Main Drivers of Anti-immigration Attitudes in Europe. Reference is paid to the 2017 Special Eurobarometer 469. https://www.eyes-on-europe.eu/explaining-the-main-drivers-of-anti-immigration-attitudes-in-europe/
13 European Parliament (2020). EU-Turkey relations in light of the Syrian conflict and Refugee Crisis. https://www.europarl.europa.eu/RegData/etudes/BRIE/2020/649327/EPRS_BRI(2020)649327_EN.pdf
14 International Organisation for Migration (IOM) (n.d.) Global Compact for Migration, https://www.iom.int/global-compact-migration, accessed January 12, 2022.
15 International Organisation for Migration (IOM) (2019). Global Compact for Safe, Orderly and Regular Migration (A/RES/73/195), https://www.iom.int/resources/global-compact-safe-orderly-and-regular-migration/res/73/195
16 Khanna, Parag (2021). *Move. The Forces Uprooting us*. https://www.paragkhanna.com/book/move/
17 Berthold Kuhn discussed migration trends with Prof. Theo Rauch on November 9, 2021, and at other occasions. Prof. Rauch has extensive research and consulting experience in Africa and teaches at the Department of Geography of Freie Universität Berlin. He regularly contributes to migration debates in Germany.
18 Khanna, Parag (2021). *Move. The Forces Uprooting us*. https://www.paragkhanna.com/book/move/
19 Abdelaaty, Lamis, & Steele, G. Liza (2020). Explaining Attitudes Toward Refugees and Immigrants in Europe. Political Studies, 70(1), 110–130. https://doi.org/10.1177/0032321720950217
20 Bachmann, Klaus (November 20, 2021). Stacheldraht ist keine Lösung. *Berliner Zeitung*, p. 11-13.
21 Suro, Roberto (November 1, 2019). Warum Abschreckung nicht funktioniert. *Der Tagesspiegel*.

Endnotes

22 Ehrling, Johnny (2021). Foreigners in China: a Fleeting Minority. *China.Table Professional Briefing* # 165, September 10, 2021. https://table.media/china/en/

Chapter 15: Visions for the World in 2030 and Beyond

1 European Foresight Platform (EFP) (n.d.). Scenario Method. http://www.foresight-platform.eu/community/forlearn/how-to-do-foresight/methods/scenario/, accessed February 14, 2021.

2 Luc Ferry, philosopher and former French Education Minister, published a groundbreaking book on the transhumanist revolution which reflects on the impact of technomedicine and the uberification of the economy on the further trajectory of humanity. Ferry, Luc (2016). *La Révolution Transhumaniste*, Paris: Plon.

ibidem.eu